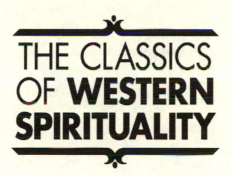

THE CLASSICS
OF **WESTERN**
**SPIRITUALITY**

# THE CLASSICS OF WESTERN SPIRITUALITY
## A Library of the Great Spiritual Masters

President and Publisher
Lawrence Boadt, C.S.P.

## EDITORIAL BOARD

# John of Avila

*Audi, filia*—Listen, O Daughter

TRANSLATED AND INTRODUCED BY
**JOAN FRANCES GORMLEY**

FOREWORD BY
FRANCISCO JAVIER MARTÍNEZ FERNÁNDEZ

PAULIST PRESS
NEW YORK • MAHWAH

**Cover Art:** *The Blessed John of Avila* by Pierre Hubert Subleyras (1600–1749). A French artist best known for his religious paintings, Subleyras settled permanently in Rome after winning the Prix du Rome in 1727. *The Blessed John of Avila* hangs in the Louvre Museum in Paris. Used by permission of Enrich Lessing/Art Resource, New York.

*Cover and caseside design by A. Michael Velthaus*
*Book design by Lynn Else*

Library of Congress Cataloging-in-Publication Data

John, of Avila, Saint, 1499?-1569.
   [Audi, filia. English]
   Audi, filia / John of Avila ; introduction, translation, and notes by Joan Frances Gormley ; foreword by Francisco Javier Martínez Fernández.
      p. cm. (The Classics of Western Spirituality)
   Includes bibliographical references (p.   ) and index.
   ISBN 0-8091-4200-7 (pbk. : alk. paper)
   ISBN 0-8091-0562-4 (cloth : alk. paper)
   1. Spirituality—Catholic Church. 2. Spiritual life—Catholic Church. 3. John, of Avila, Saint, 1499?-1569. I. Gormley, Joan Frances. II. Title. III. Series.
   BX2350.65.J62 2006
   248.4'82—dc22

2005028077

Published by Paulist Press
997 Macarthur Boulevard
Mahwah, New Jersey 07430

www.paulistpress.com

Printed and bound in the
United States of America

# Contents

Translator of This Volume

JOAN FRANCES GORMLEY is Professor of Scripture and
Homiletics at Mount Saint Mary's Seminary in Emmitsburg,
Maryland. A native of Philadelphia, Sister Joan holds a Master's
Degree in Classics from Harvard University and a PhD in New
Testament Studies from Fordham University. She did postgraduate
work at the Ecole biblique in Jerusalem. Before coming to Mt. St.
Mary's Seminary, she taught classics and theology at Trinity College in
Washington, D.C.


Author of the Foreword

FRANCISCO JAVIER MARTÍNEZ FERNÁNDEZ, formerly
Bishop of Cordoba, the diocese of John of Avila, is now the Archbishop
of Granada. Archbishop Martínez holds a Licentiate in Biblical
Theology from the Pontifical University of Comillas and a PhD in
Semitic Languages from the Catholic University of America. He also
studied at the Ecole biblique in Jerusalem. He has been a member of
the faculties of the Seminaries of Toledo and Madrid.

# FOREWORD

It is a great joy to present this English translation of Saint John of Avila's classic guide to the Christian life, the *Audi, filia*. For most readers of this volume, this particular saint and his works have long been among those proverbial best kept secrets of the church's history, in this case, from the golden age of Christian sanctity in sixteenth-century Spain. It can only benefit us to discover this diocesan priest of immense zeal and burning love for Christ and his church. In the *Audi, filia* we have the most complete expression of his teaching and spiritual direction.

Christian experience shows that saints have a way of remaining contemporary, even if elements of their lives and works become outdated. This is certainly true of John of Avila. He lived at a crucial moment in the church's life, when the new humanism of the Renaissance was broadening the horizons of knowledge, and daring explorations were expanding the horizons of the physical world. In the midst of all this progress the church was threatened by divisions and corruption. John of Avila was well aware of advances changing the world and of the church's need to be revitalized in order to proclaim Christ effectively in a new context. He wrote the *Audi, filia* as a call to holiness directed to the "modern" Christians of the sixteenth century. He does not present a formula or a program to solve the problems facing the church of his day, but the person of Jesus Christ. He called his contemporaries to hear and heed God's Word, to look upon the face of Christ and enter into conversation with him, to make him their center by living in the communion of the church. In the new world under construction, Christ remained the only guarantee of personal and social peace and of eternal salvation.

Translations of the *Audi, filia* into other languages and situations are a sign of the enduring value of the Master's work. Versions quickly appeared in French, Italian, and German. The French version influenced Francis de Sales, Vincent de Paul, and Cardinal Bérulle and the members of his priestly school. Most striking, in my view, is the English translation of 1620, almost fifty years after publication of the definitive edition of the *Audi, filia* in Spanish. Once again, the church was facing a crisis, this time in England. Not only was the unity of the church broken, but Catholics were beset by persecutions and penalties of various kinds, including confiscation of property, fines, imprisonment, and even death. Many had already suffered martyrdom. The translator offers "all English Catholics" the *Audi, filia* in their own tongue. He affirms that he can find no better book for their instruction and consolation "in these difficult times," and so offers it in the hope that they may continue as true children of the Holy Catholic Church.

There is no doubt that the church of today is once again living through "difficult times." Avila's teaching on redemption in Christ reminds us of the treasure we possess and of our responsibility to live the life Christ gives us as fully as possible in the communion of the church. Only then can we offer him to the men and women of our time as their true life and hope for salvation.

+Francisco Javier Martínez Fernández
Archbishop of Granada

# PREFACE

"I was a sower" *(Messor eram)*. These words, placed on the lips of Saint John of Avila in his epitaph, eloquently summarize the life and ministry of this sixteenth-century diocesan priest, author of the treatise on the spiritual life *Audi, filia*. The epitaph recalls Jesus' use of the image of the sower in gospel parables to describe aspects of his own and his disciples' mission. He is the Sower who casts the seed of God's word widely in good soil and bad, waiting for an abundant harvest (Mark 4:1–20). He encounters hostility and opposition from another sower, an enemy who sows weeds among the wheat in an attempt to destroy the harvest (Matt 13:24–30). Jesus tells his disciples that the sower might not have the satisfaction of gathering the fruit of his labors since, at times, "one sows and another reaps" (John 4:36–38). The sower may even have to become the seed that falls into the ground and dies in order to bear fruit (John 12:24).

The parallels between the priestly ministry of John of Avila and that of the divine Sower are striking. As a sower, Father Avila cast the seed widely through the cities and towns of Andalusia in southern Spain through several decades of the sixteenth century. A diocesan priest, he labored as a preacher, confessor, spiritual director, catechist, evangelizer, educator, and theologian. He worked for conversion and reform among all classes of society and the church: men and women; rich and poor; nobles and peasants; professors and mine workers; religious and laity; sinners and saints. He encountered many forms of opposition, including resentment of his Jewish ancestry, suspicion of his humanistic education, envy of his success in preaching, and misunderstanding of his life of poverty. In many of his endeavors it appears that he sowed the seed but did not reap the harvest. A striking example of this is the fading away of his group of priest-disciples with the arrival and expansion of the Society of Jesus in Spain. Finally, Avila, as the seed that falls into the ground and dies, passed through long years of physical suffering when his apostolic activities were severely curtailed, and during which he saw all of his writings, including the first published edition of the *Audi, filia*, censured by the Inquisition and placed on the list of forbidden books.

In spite of appearances of a meager harvest, John of Avila was a major figure in the ecclesial reform and spiritual renewal that finally came to pass in the sixteenth century. In the period before the Council of Trent, when the church suffered greatly from neglect of the pastoral office, Father Avila devoted himself tirelessly to the "care of souls" to the point that he embodied the reforms he would write about in memorials he sent to the council. His spiritual masterpiece, the *Audi, filia*, is really a written expression of his pastoral ministry. In many ways the book reflects the time in which it was written, but it also transcends it to provide direction for a faithful and mature Christian life in any age. Father Avila was well aware of the permanent validity and wide usefulness of the work he had prepared to help one person in his flock. For that reason he labored in the last years of his life to make the book accessible to a wider audience. Through his work, and with the help of his disciples, the definitive edition of the book was printed in 1574–75, a few years after his death.

The English translation of the *Audi, filia* in this volume is based on the definitive Spanish text published in 2000 by Biblioteca de Autores Cristianos in volume 1 of the latest critical edition of the works of John of Avila. I am grateful to the *Fundación Nuevo Inicio* of the Archdiocese of Granada in Spain for their financial support in securing the rights to use the material in this landmark edition of Master Avila's works. I am especially grateful to Francisco Javier Martínez Fernández, Archbishop of Granada, for all the encouragement and help he has given me in the preparation of this volume. As Bishop of Cordoba, he suggested the project and then opened the resources of the diocesan library to me and helped me in a thousand ways. Thanks are also due to Donatella Mansi, former diocesan librarian in Cordoba, who guided me through the library's resources and also to the home of Saint John of Avila in Montilla. Our guide in Montilla, Father Antonio Maldonado Correa, SJ, placed Master Avila into the context of the house where he spent his final years. He also provided me with the biography of Father Avila by Luís de Granada and that of Sancha Carrillo, for whom the *Audi, filia* was first written. Thanks are due also to Father Francisco Martín Hernández, professor emeritus of the Pontifical University of Salamanca, who, with Father Luís Sala Ballust, prepared the edition of John Avila's complete works in 1970–71 and has been working on the new critical edition that began to be published in 2000–2001. Father Martín helped me especially with presentation of the vicissitudes of the

# PREFACE

*Audi, filia* in its journey from its original brief form through to publication of the definitive edition. I am also grateful to Bishop Kevin Rhoades, now Bishop of Harrisburg, Pennsylvania. When he was Rector of Mt. St. Mary's Seminary, Bishop Rhoades encouraged this project, which touches upon the mission of the seminary, the formation of diocesan priests. Last but not least, I am greatly indebted to Dr. Charles Merrill, professor of foreign languages at Mt. St. Mary's Seminary, who reviewed the entire translation and made many valuable suggestions.

The reader is asked to read John's words in the inclusive manner he intended them, even though the language used at the time appears exclusive to modern eyes.

# ABBREVIATIONS

*ACI*           *El Maestro Avila: Actas del Congreso Internacional.* Madrid: Conferencia Episcopal Española, 2000.

*AF*           *Audi, filia:* Listen, O Daughter

BAC        Biblioteca de Autores Cristianos

CEE        Conferencia Episcopal Española

*OC* I/*OC* II    San Juan de Avila. *Obras Completas: Nueva edición crítica.* Vols. 1–2. Edited by L. Sala Balust and Francisco Martín Hernández. Madrid: BAC, 2000–2001.

*OC [1970]*  San Juan de Avila. *Obras Completas.* Vols. 1–6. Edited by L. Sala Balust and Francisco Martín Hernández. Madrid: BAC, 1970.

*PG*           *Patrologia Graeca*

*PL*           *Patrologia Latina*

# INTRODUCTION TO
# JOHN OF AVILA

## *His Life and Works*

John of Avila was born on the feast of the Epiphany in 1499 and died on May 10, 1569.[1] The seven decades of his life coincided with an extraordinary period in the history of Spain and the world. Less than a decade before his birth, on January 2, 1492, the Catholic monarchs Ferdinand and Isabella reclaimed Granada, the last Muslim stronghold in Spain, thus completing the reconquest of Spain after more than seven hundred years of Islamic occupation. In October of the same year Christopher Columbus, sailing under the flag of the two monarchs, discovered the New World. These two events in 1492 had enormous repercussions for the future of the whole world and for civilization. For the church in Spain, they were especially significant because they opened up two vast mission fields: one at home, where ignorance of the faith was widespread among Christians and potential converts; the other abroad, among the inhabitants of the newly discovered world on the other side of the ocean. Facing unprecedented opportunities for taking the gospel to the ends of the earth and for renewing Christian life at home, the church in Europe and in Spain was sorely in need of reform at all levels of the hierarchy and among the laity. Failure to accomplish this long–recognized task would lead to the Protestant Reformation within twenty years of Avila's birth, and he would live to witness the Counter–Reformation and its most significant event, the Council of Trent.

To understand John of Avila, it is necessary to realize that he was a participant in a vigorous movement of Catholic Reformation under way long before the Protestant Reformation erupted and long before the Council of Trent was convoked to address the serious dogmatic and pastoral issues of the times. There is a temptation to isolate the Council of Trent, regarding it as a sudden turning point in history that healed the ills of the church quickly and easily and ushered in the movement of

1

reorientation and renewal known as the Counter–Reformation. This oversimplification is completely understandable if we limit our view to the results of the council, with its unexpectedly lucid formulations of the Catholic dogma of justification and the appropriate remedies it mandated to strengthen the church's apostolic ministry. But while it is true that the events of a single day or year or even a single century may appear to end one era and begin another, in fact, transformations are generally in the making long before they happen.[2] This is true for the successful measures for reform finally adopted at Trent; they were by no means brought about overnight, but, on the contrary, were long in the making by the efforts of "reformers" such as John of Avila, whose first contribution was conversion of life, their own and those they touched in their life and ministry. Hubert Jedin has clearly shown that the good soil for the reforms at Trent and the church's response to Protestantism in the so–called Counter–Reformation were the life of the church continuing even in the midst of corruption. There were many faithful people actively seeking to restore the church's vitality through fervent lives in accord with the church's liturgy, dogma, and discipline. Jedin uses the term *Catholic Reformation* to denote the sum total of efforts on the part of those individuals and groups, who did not passively surrender in the face of abuses and corruption, but rose up, both before and after the Protestant Reformation, to rebuild the church from within. In so doing, these Catholic reformers, John of Avila among them, provided the impetus and foundation for the reform of the papacy, the episcopacy, the priesthood, and the whole body of the faithful.[3]

In the pages that follow, John of Avila takes center stage as one of the foremost figures in the spectacular drama of spiritual renewal and reform played out in the sixteenth–century Spanish church. Since this Spanish saint is little known in the English–speaking world, we will spend some time presenting an overview of his seventy years: his Jewish background, his humanistic education, his difficulties with the Inquisition, his labors in founding educational institutions, his gathering of priest–disciples, his relationship with the early Jesuits, and his illness and death. Next, we will survey his works: sermons and spiritual conferences; letters of spiritual direction to disciples and friends; memoranda of reform for the Council of Trent and diocesan synods charged with implementing the council's decrees; commentaries on Sacred Scripture and several minor works. Finally, we will consider Father Avila's masterpiece, the *Audi, filia,* tracing the stages of its composition and providing a comprehensive overview of the work in its definitive form. Throughout, we will see John of Avila as a diocesan priest whose principal contribution to the reform of the church was his tireless pastoral activity of working for the conversion, sanctification, education, and consolation of those in his care. Indeed, the *Audi, filia*, his classical work on the spiritual life, is best seen as the fruit of his priestly ministry.

# Introduction to the Life of John of Avila

## *Sources for His Life*

There are three major sources for the life of Saint John of Avila, two biographies and the records of the processes of beatification.[4] Fray Luís of Granada wrote the earliest biography about fifteen years after the Master's death at the request of some of his disciples. In a letter from Lisbon (April 15, 1585) the friar expressed reluctance to undertake the project because of advanced age and his scant knowledge of Avila's early life and ministry. He could only write, he said, if others would fill in the blanks. Various disciples contributed their reminiscences, enabling Granada to complete the biography in June 1587. The Dominican was not entirely satisfied with his work and apologized for being unable to reach the level of the man that Avila had been. When they saw the work, Avila's disciples were disappointed that the account was so brief and lacking in chronological references. They lamented the lack of reference to Father Avila's studies, to the school of priestly disciples that he had gathered, and to his work as a reformer. Contemporary readers might add their own lament upon noting that the biography is organized in terms of Father Avila's virtues. So laudatory and congratulatory is this first biography that the person and personality of the Master do not stand out as clearly as they might if readers were able to see him in the determining events and decisions of his life. But as inadequate as this first biography was in the eyes of its author and of Father Avila's disciples, and as incomplete as it is likely to appear to the modern reader, it was destined to become a precious treasure, being the source nearest to eyewitness testimony to Father Avila's life and ministry.[5] With all of its strengths and weaknesses, the work was also destined to become a necessary source for subsequent biographers.

A second source for material on John of Avila's life was the process of beatification held in 1624–25 in the cities where the priest had lived and worked. Some biographical information came to light, but little of substance was added to Father Granada's account. The twenty–seven eyewitnesses who survived were speaking from a distance of more than five decades and appeared at times to offer idealized versions of Father Avila. Much of the testimony came from secondary sources, such as disciples of Avila's disciples. Another source used in the beatification process was the records of the Inquisition at Seville, which had investigated Avila in 1531–33. These, together with records of the University of Baeza, where Avila had inaugurated a program of higher studies around 1544, also yielded some information, but not enough to fill in the gaps in the record of Avila's early life.

The third source for the life of John of Avila is the biography by Luís Muñoz, *Life and Virtues of Master John of Avila*, published in Madrid in 1635. Muñoz admitted that he had used as his two principal sources the biography by Luís of Granada and the informational processes for the cause of beatification. Insofar as Muñoz's biography is based on these two sources, it offers nothing new. However, the work does make one important and unique contribution to knowledge of Father Avila's ministry. Muñoz includes biographical material on twenty–two of the priests who belonged to the group of disciples that had gathered around John of Avila. He expresses the fear that if he does not include this material, the record of the Master with his school of disciples will disappear from history.

The paucity of personal material on John of Avila, especially the lack of information about his early life in the family and in his studies, hampers attempts at biography. Another difficulty is that the authors of the earliest accounts of the life of John of Avila and the witnesses at the beatification process revered him as a saint; thus, they emphasized the marks of his sanctity manifest in a series of virtues. Such strongly hagiographical interest fails to highlight Avila's personal development in grace and in the Christian life and tends to present him instead as a paragon of virtue from the beginning to the end of his life. This may have been one of the reasons that Father Avila's disciples complained that the person of the Master did not come through clearly enough in the biography by Fray Luís of Granada.

## Avila's Family and Jewish Background

John of Avila was born on the feast of the Epiphany in 1499 in Extremadura in the ecclesiastical province of Toledo, the only child of his parents, Alfonso of Avila and Catherine Xixon.[6] According to Father Granada, Avila's parents were people of excellent reputation and among the most honored and wealthy of the town.[7] A silversmith at the beatification process reported that his father had done business with the father of John of Avila, who owned a silver mine in Sierra

Morena. It was also said that, at the time of his ordination, Father Avila, whose parents had died, sold his estate and his patrimony for more than five thousand ducats, a substantial amount of money at the time, and gave the money to the poor. Throughout his ministry, evangelical poverty was a cornerstone of Father Avila's way of life and an essential element in the life of his disciples.[8]

Though information about Father Avila's family life is scarce, consisting of little more than a few anecdotes that may or may not have their basis in fact, there is one certain fact that had enormous consequences for him throughout his life. His father was of Jewish ancestry, and his mother may also have been Jewish. Consequently, John of Avila "had race" (tenía raza), to use the expression current at the time to distinguish "new Christians" or converts from "old Christians." Luís of Granada describes Avila's parents as devout Christians. However, as converts (conversos), they were considered "new Christians" even several generations after the family entered the church. In Spain during the fifteenth and sixteenth centuries, many "old Christians" of pure Spanish blood harbored suspicion and hostility toward Jewish and Muslim converts. Many times in his life John of Avila bore the brunt of such animosity.

The question of relations between old and new Christians is much more complex than is obvious at first glance.[9] From the late fourteenth century on, many converts from Judaism became fervent Catholics and held high ecclesiastical and political positions. But there were others who allowed themselves to be baptized while continuing to live as Jews and encouraging others to do the same. When the Inquisition was authorized in Spain in 1478, one of its major tasks was to inquire into the status of Jewish converts and to take measures to ensure that they did not work against the Christian faith. The expulsion of the Jews in 1492 was an element in the project of the Catholic monarchs to unify the Spanish kingdoms in one faith. Measures taken before had been only partially successful, so Ferdinand and Isabel decided, apparently with the strong encouragement of some inquisitors, to take an extreme measure to defend the Christian faith. Thus, on March 31, 1492, they decreed that all unconverted Jews had to leave their realms by July 31 of the same year. Many Jews accepted baptism in order to remain in Spain; many others left and then later returned to Spain and were baptized, having found a bitter lot outside Spain. Ironically, the expulsion that was meant to solve the problem of unity ended up complicating it. Now, instead of a population that included mostly committed Jewish converts, there were many Jewish converts who had accepted baptism under duress.[10] It is unsurprising that their knowledge of the Catholic faith and attachment to it were often weak or nonexistent and that, in many cases, they continued to practice their Jewish faith and customs. It did not help that instead of finding a welcome within the Christian community, converts from Judaism found themselves subject to discrimination.

Avila was born less than a decade after the expulsion of the Jews from Spain. Moreover, he was born in a part of Spain, Ciudad Real, where during the latter part of the fifteenth century there had been riots against Jewish converts and where the Inquisition, since its establishment, had been examining Jewish converts. For his part, Father Avila firmly opposed any form of discrimination against anyone because of race or lineage. With penitents and those he directed, he insisted on the dignity of Jewish and Muslim converts.[11] In the *Audi, filia*, commenting on the injunction in Psalm 45 to "forget your father's house," Avila condemns vanity about noble lineage as self-deceit. He argues that souls are not inherited but created by God, while to boast of one's earthly inheritance is to glory in the flesh, which withers like the grass of the field. "The esteem in which God holds you is not because of your lineage but because you are a Christian. It is not because you were born in a canopied room, but because you were born again in holy baptism. The first birth is with dishonor; the second, with honor. The first is to lowly station; the second, to nobility" (chap. 99).[12] Upon discovering that the newly founded Society of Jesus was concerned about racial background, Avila expressed profound disappointment. As we review the life of Master Avila, we will see that he and his disciples, many of them "converts" like himself, had firsthand experience of this particular kind of racial discrimination that, though understandable in light of the historical context, nonetheless caused many innocent converts to suffer and obscured the light of Christ on the face of the church.

## *University Education and Ordination to the Priesthood*

When John of Avila had completed his elementary studies, his father sent him to the University of Salamanca to study liberal arts and law. The boy was a student there from 1513 until 1517, when he withdrew without receiving a degree. The prestige of the University of Salamanca, especially in the area of law, could well have been an important factor in the choice of the school for Avila's studies of canon and civil law. Another possibility is that the University of Salamanca accepted converts from Judaism as students. In any case, it would have been difficult to choose a school with a better reputation than the University of Salamanca. From its founding in 1227 by Alfonso IX, king of Leon, the university had emphasized the study of church and civil law. Over the years it had added chairs of theology, medicine, Arabic, and music, and in the sixteenth century was at the apex of its glory, one of the most famous in Europe and ranked with Paris, Bologna, and Oxford among the top four universities. Popes and kings consulted its theologians. Christopher Columbus submitted to its scholars his proposals for a voyage to the Indies. After the discovery of the New World, the University of Salamanca, especially through the work of Francisco de Vitoria (1483–1546), became a center for the study of moral questions concerning colonization and evangelization of the New World. It thus became in a certain sense the first university with a School of International Law.[13]

Avila did not receive a degree after his four years of study, but the reason for his not doing so is obscure. One possibility is that laws or royal decrees against granting degrees to converts began to be applied in Salamanca while Avila was in the course of his studies. It is known that provisions of the Inquisition in 1509 prevented new converts from Judaism from receiving degrees from the University of Salamanca, but there is no evidence that they were put into effect. A second possibility is that a profound religious experience prompted John of Avila to give up his studies. This is the view taken by Father Granada, who attributes Avila's premature departure from Salamanca and return to his parents' house not to his status as a converted Jew, but to his desire to respond to God calling him with a very special and particular call. Of course, another possibility is that both factors came into play. In any case, during his break from formal study Avila lived a solitary life of prayer and penance in a secluded part of his parents' home. He received the sacraments frequently and cultivated the ardent devotion to the Eucharist that would characterize him throughout his life. It appears that he also attempted entrance into religious life during that time, though it is not known whether or not he made profession of vows.

After three years of austerity and penance, the young Avila was advised by a visiting Franciscan priest to resume his studies. For this purpose he matriculated at the University of Alcalá, where he studied philosophy and theology from 1520 to 1526. It appears that Avila earned his bachelor's degree during his years at Alcalá and then left without completing requirements for the licentiate degree.

Avila's years at the University of Alcalá had a profound and permanent influence on his life and thought and brought him into direct contact with the rich intellectual dimension of the Catholic Reform Movement.[14] The institution, founded in 1499 (the year of Avila's birth) by Francisco Ximénez de Cisneros, Archbishop of Toledo and primate of Spain, was meant to be an instrument for the reform of the Spanish clergy. To Cardinal Cisneros, reform required not only a more intense and mature life of prayer, asceticism, and charity, but it also meant that priests and bishops had to have the best possible education for their pastoral mission. The institution he founded was truly a renaissance university, open to the currents of Christian humanism circulating in Italy and Northern Europe and dedicated to a return to intellectual and literary sources, both classical and ecclesiastical. The university required study of the original languages in which the scriptures had been written so that students would have direct access to the Bible and to the writings of the fathers of the church. One of the university's greatest achievements was the Polyglot Bible in Hebrew, Greek, and Latin, printed in six volumes by the university's press from 1514 to 1517 and published in 1522. The dedication of the work to Pope Leo X, written by Cardinal Cisneros, reveals the high caliber of scholarly work and the careful study of the scriptures pursued at the University of Alcalá. He speaks of employing the most outstanding scholars of the languages and meticulously comparing the readings of the best manuscripts so as to arrive at correct and authentic readings:

> And so that every student of Holy Scripture might have at hand the original texts themselves and be able to quench his thirst at the very fountainhead of the water that flows unto life everlasting and not have to content himself with rivulets alone, we ordered the original languages of Holy Scripture with their translations adjoined to be printed and dedicated to your Holiness.[15]

Besides profiting from the rigorous study of the scriptures and the fathers that were part of every student's curriculum at Alcalá, John of Avila also came under the influence of Erasmus of Rotterdam (1469–1536), one of the most celebrated scholars of the day. The university was the center in Spain for the study of this great humanist, who blended in himself a love of the ancient classics and the biblical and patristic writings. He possessed a flair for satire, which he used unsparingly in his trenchant criticisms of ecclesiastical corruption. Though Erasmus did not accept the chair that Cardinal Cisneros offered him at Alcalá, he nonetheless exercised magisterial authority there through his writings. Indeed, the Complutensian Press of the University of Alcalá published a Latin edition of the *Enchiridion militis christiani*

*(Handbook of a Christian Knight)* of Erasmus in 1525, and another in the vernacular the following year. Thus began a period of almost half a century when the teacher from the Netherlands was a dominant force in Spanish thought in every area of life, including that of Christian spirituality. Erasmus was considered the master of Christian humanism, the craftsman of an interior spirituality, the prophet of a new Christian peace, and the herald of authentic reform. His works were enormously popular, not just among scholars and students, but everywhere: "In the court, in convents, in cathedrals, in schools, even in inns along the roads, readers and enthusiasts of Erasmus were swarming."[16] His biting satires on the corruption of the clergy rang true for people who could see examples before their very eyes of the scandals Erasmus described. In addition to satires aimed at reform, he advocated a simple Christian life characterized by an interior relationship with Christ and nourished by meditative prayer and reading of the Bible and the fathers of the church. He interpreted the body of Christ with emphasis on the brotherhood of all, regardless of class, and the consequent requirement of showing charity toward all others. It is a fact that in Spain the teachings of Erasmus appealed to many "new Christians," converts from Judaism who were treated as second–class citizens and discriminated against by the "old Christians" who boasted of "pure blood." John of Avila was one of those enthusiastic about Erasmus during his years at Alcalá, and later he suggested that some of his disciples consult Erasmus, though with caution.[17]

Without doubt, Father Avila was influenced by Erasmus and shared many of his interests and emphases. However, the two were actually poles apart in their approach to Christ, the spiritual life, and reform of the church, though this dissimilarity was not always clear to Avila's opponents. The teacher from Rotterdam saw Christ as the embodiment of virtues and consequently mainly as an ethical model. His call for a simple interior life and private reading of the Bible included a downplaying of the sacramental and ecclesial life. His written calls for reform were not clearly mirrored in his own life as a priest. As one author puts it, it is likely that Erasmus had never experienced a Damascus, which is to say, a personal and life–changing encounter with Christ. Father Avila, on the other hand, preached and practiced a way of life centered in a personal relationship with Christ, especially in Christ's passion. His instructions on prayer are accompanied by emphasis on sharing in the sacramental life of the church and on submitting to the church's authority. Finally, his life as a priest is the most powerful proclamation of his call for the reform of the church, head and members.

## *Ordination and Early Ministry in Seville*

In the spring of 1526 John of Avila was ordained to the priesthood and soon after arrived in Seville to await departure for the Indies in January of 1527 with Julián Garcés (1452–1542), the first Bishop of Mexico. While waiting to set sail, the newly ordained priest engaged in catechesis and preaching. He so impressed Father Fernando Contreras, a diocesan priest in Seville, that the latter urged the Archbishop of Seville to keep Avila in Spain, where an enormous mission field needed to be worked in the aftermath of the conquest of the Muslims. The archbishop agreed, and John Avila began the missionary work in southern Spain that would earn him the title Apostle of Andalusia.

This early period of Avila's priestly ministry provided him with a kind of pastoral formation to supplement his academic work. During this time he came under the influence of Father Fernando de Contreras, a zealous priest whose cause for beatification has been introduced. He had been chaplain of the College of San Ildefonso at the University of Alcalá until the death of Cardinal Cisneros in 1517 and then returned to his native Archdiocese of Seville, where he was widely known for teaching the faith to children, for whom he founded a school in 1526. The process for his beatification describes his manner of caring for the poor children he was educating in grammar and the arts and catechizing in Christian doctrine. After mornings of learning he would lead them into the nearby fields for play, singing, and catechism. A musician, he not only taught the children to sing and wrote Christmas carols and other songs for them, but he also put doctrine to music for easy learning. It appears that Avila adopted the methods of Father Contreras in his work with children. For him and for his disciples, it remained a privileged field of work even when they were involved in higher education at the college and university level.[18]

According to Father Granada, Avila lived during these initial years in Seville in a small house with another priest, probably Father Contreras, and disciples began to gather around him. These were priests engaged in preaching, teaching, and evangelizing, or men desiring to become priests. They wanted to share Father Avila's approach to priestly vocation and apostolic ministry and for this purpose joined together in a loosely structured fraternal life. These early disciples came from Seville and neighboring towns and villages. By the time sickness forced his retirement more than twenty years later, there were about one hundred priests who regarded Master Avila as their director. Records of the Inquisition tell something of Father Avila's ministry during this time when he worked in Seville and the surrounding areas, including Ecija, a prosperous commercial city not far from Cordoba. He resided in the homes of some noblemen there, gave commentaries on the Letter to the Hebrews to his disciples, and sent some of them to study in universities. He taught catechism to children and mental prayer to adults and was a popular preacher and confessor. He lived evangelical poverty and would not accept stipends or alms for himself but only for the poor. As disciples continued to gather around him, he instructed them and members of the laity in the Bible. In the spring of 1527 he first met Sancha Carrillo, the younger sister of one of his priest–disciples. It would be at this woman's request that Father Avila would begin to write the *Audi, filia*.

## *John of Avila and the Inquisition*

In 1531, John of Avila was denounced to the Inquisition in Seville for suspicious doctrine, arrested, and put in prison in the summer of 1532; after a year's incarceration, he was absolved and released in July 1533. In a certain sense, he was a prime candidate for investigation by the Inquisition. First of all, he was from a family of converted Jews and, therefore, automatically under suspicion. Moreover, he had studied at the University of Alcalá, which welcomed the new humanism and had a special fascination with Erasmus and his works. Father Avila taught mental prayer even to laypeople of various levels of society and thus opened them to the dangers of involvement with the pseudo–spirituality and mysticism of the "enlightened ones" *(alumbrados)*. It is not surprising, then, that statements he had made in various settings were returned to him as charges. For example, he was accused of saying in confession that those burned by the Inquisition were martyrs and of asking penitents about their treatment of new Christians. It was charged that in a sermon he had said: "What I say is true and if it is not true, God is not true." In the course of the process other accusations were made: that he had said that the rich could not be saved; that Christ was present in the Eucharist as a man with his face covered; that it was better to give alms than to leave money for chaplaincies. He was also charged with saying that mental prayer was superior to vocal prayer, and of turning out the lights in order to foster contemplation in a group.

The records of the Inquisition show that in December of 1532 Avila was given twenty–two points to address orally and in writing. He

answered all of these charges carefully and in detail, distinguishing true
from false. He had not said that those condemned for heresy were martyrs but that if they were repentant and died in grace, their painful
death was equivalent to a kind of martyrdom. He said this to encourage the condemned to patience and to forgiveness of those who judged
them. He had questioned some penitents about their treatment of new
Christians because he was aware that some did not consider these converts their neighbors and would insult them by calling them "dogs."
He denied that he had said that the rich cannot be saved, but he
acknowledged saying what the gospel says, namely, that it is difficult
for the rich to enter heaven and that it will be especially difficult for the
rich who have no care for others. He admitted to emphasizing prayer
and saying that mental prayer was better than vocal, though he also
said that the latter should not be devalued. He spoke of Christ's face
being as though veiled in the Eucharist in order to distinguish the
sacramental vision from the face–to–face vision of heaven. His purpose
in extinguishing external sources of light was so that the prayer groups
he organized could listen without distraction to God's word.

The Inquisition accepted Avila's answers and declared him innocent on July 5, 1533. They did require him, however, under pain of
excommunication, to correct and clarify some things he had said that
had caused scandal. According to Father Granada, the Inquisition
specified that Avila should do this on a feast day in the Church of the
Savior in Seville. He also recounts how Father Avila's disciples treated
the event as a kind of victory celebration, breaking out into applause
and sounding trumpets when Avila ascended into the pulpit.[19]

Avila used his year in prison to study scripture, especially the letters of Paul. He also translated the *Imitation of Christ* into Spanish and,
according to two witnesses at the beatification process, began working
on the *Audi, filia*. Besides allowing time for study, the sojourn in prison
was also an opportunity for spiritual growth and new insight. Years
later Father Avila confided to Father Granada how grateful he was for
his time in prison and for the persecutions leading up to it. He said that
he had received a precious favor of a very special understanding of the
mystery of redemption in Christ and of the great reasons we have for
loving God and rejoicing in the midst of our sufferings. In a few days
in prison he had learned more about living the mystery of Christ than
he had in all his years of study. A witness at the beatification process
said that when his disciples asked him how he arrived at his understanding of Saint Paul, he suggested that his understanding came from
seeing himself in danger of the death sentence on the testimony of

three witnesses. A letter apparently written to his disciples from prison reveals his dispositions in the face of his trial and his counsels to his followers.[20] He blesses and gives thanks to God for the honor of suffering dishonor as Christ had for the salvation of the world. He urges his disciples to see that they are walking on the narrow way that leads to life, the very way walked by the Son of God. He exhorts them to continue as disciples of Christ, who gave the kiss of peace to the traitor and prayed for forgiveness of his enemies. With these sentiments Avila resumed his priestly ministry, at first in Seville and then in Cordoba and other parts of the south of Spain.

## Middle Period: Preaching; Education; Gathering of Disciples (1535–46)

Around the end of 1534 or the beginning of 1535, Father John Avila was incardinated in the Diocese of Cordoba, where he received a small benefice. This city became his base for directing his disciples and for moving about Andalusia, preaching in various neighboring cities and establishing schools and colleges. It is thought that during this period Avila received the title of Master in Sacred Theology, probably in Granada around 1538. The title Master, an academic title, became the customary way of designating Avila as he grew in renown as a preacher, spiritual director, educator, and head of a school of active diocesan priests.

From his earliest days in Seville, Avila was a renowned preacher. Granada says that when Avila preached it was as though burning arrows came from his own flaming heart and set fire to the hearts of his listeners. The story is told of an instance when a priest arrived to publish the various papal bulls and decrees and told Avila, who was scheduled to preach, that he would have to postpone his sermon. When Father Avila yielded the pulpit to the visitor and left the church, the people followed him and listened to his sermon outside. In Cordoba a Dominican heard Father Avila preach and left the church saying that he had heard Saint Paul interpreting Saint Paul. The Master's sermons were the occasion for many conversions, the most famous being those of Francis Borgia, later the general of the Jesuits, and John of God, both of whom were later canonized. Avila's aim in preaching was always the conversion and sanctification of his hearers, and for this reason his priestly ministry extended beyond the pulpit to confession and spiritual direction. At the University of Baeza he insisted on preaching as an integral element in the curriculum for students for the priesthood. The secret of preaching, he taught, was much study and more prayer, especially before the crucifix. His disciples became known for their preaching in his style, and others, such as Anthony Mary Claret, took him for a model in preaching.

A substantial part of Master Avila's time and energy during the middle years of his ministry was taken up with the task of education at all levels: schools of doctrine for children, who learned to read and write while studying the faith; schools for general studies, which taught the humanities, theology, and science; universities, especially that of Baeza, which could grant advanced degrees and which included a program for education of the clergy. The Master shared the view of many in sixteenth–century Spain that education was an essential means for bringing about changes such as the reform of the clergy, the assimilation of new Christians, and the betterment of the lot of the poor.

It has already been noted that from the beginning of his priesthood Father Avila attracted disciples. Many of these were laypeople, either married or living a consecrated life under his direction. The most numerous and distinctive of Avila's disciples were those who were already priests or desirous of ordination, who followed the Master's directions for an evangelical way of life and ministry and who, at least for a while, saw themselves as a group with the possibility of becoming a more structured community. Father Avila's biographer, Luís Muñoz, includes sketches of the lives of twenty–two of these disciples. They worked in universities as well as among workers and the poor: miners, fishermen, farmers. They had a number of things in common as priests: they preached the mystery of Christ and reform of the church; they taught Christian doctrine, especially to children; as far as possible, they avoided ecclesiastical offices or dignities. Many of them, like Master Avila, were new Christians of Jewish descent.

It appears that the group of his disciples was beginning to take shape as a community during the time Avila spent in Granada in 1538 and 1539. There are indications that he had in mind "a congregation of working and holy priests" with a spirituality centered on the mystery of Christ and his cross, the Eucharist, and the mystical body at its center. Two letters with similar content written in 1538 outline the way of life to which Avila directed priests who asked his counsel: how to pray and what to read; the daily schedule of rising, sleeping, study, and eating; dispositions for offering Mass, going to confession or hearing confessions; preparation for preaching.[21] Though the life Father Avila traces out for his priest–disciples is in many respects austere and ascetic, its orientation is always to the priest's apostolic endeavors. During the years 1546 to 1555, Avila lived with about twenty disciples in Cordoba, making it seem that a formal foundation was imminent.[22] However, two factors converged to alter any plans the Master had for beginning a congregation of apostolic priests. One was the arrival of the Jesuits and his acquaintance with them; the other was the deterioration of his health.

## John of Avila and the Jesuits

While Master Avila and his disciples were engaged in various pastoral and educational works and developing a certain identity as a group of priests, Ignatius of Loyola and his companions were engaged in a similar project. The Society was formally established in 1540 by the decree of Paul III in accord with the way of life Ignatius and his companions had presented for approbation. In that document they stated that their work was principally for

> the advancement of souls in Christian life and doctrine, and for the propagation of the faith by public preaching and the ministry of God's Word by spiritual exercises and works of charity, more particularly by grounding in Christianity boys and unlettered persons, and by hearing the confessions of the faithful, aiming in all things at their spiritual consolation.

All the members were to have solemn vows of poverty, chastity, and obedience, and those who were priests would be bound to pray the divine office, but in private, so as to be free day and night to go anywhere to engage in the works of charity to which their vocation called them. [23]

Similarities in purpose and way of life between the Jesuits and the followers of Master Avila were soon recognized by members of both groups. Ignatius desired that Jesuits in Spain who had contact with Father Avila would speak with him about joining the Society. In the early part of 1551, Avila began to experience poor health, a condition that lasted till the end of his life. It was then that Avila began actively encouraging his disciples who so desired, and were accepted, to join the Jesuits. In all, about thirty of Father Avila's disciples went to the Society. Up until the time of the death of Ignatius in 1556, there was also discussion of the Master following his disciples, like Jacob following his sons down to Egypt.[24] But, in the end, though he esteemed and supported the Jesuits, he decided not to enter the Society, fearing that his deteriorating health would burden the new community.[25]

During this latter period of Father Avila's life, the priestly school that had gathered around him began to fade as a movement. A core of disciples, especially those who, like him, were new Christians, remained under his direction, some of them continuing to teach at the University of Baeza. As time went on, those disciples who had not gone to the Jesuits found their way into other religious communities or to the missions. Some, who were said to lack the Master's balance and prudence, joined the ranks of the heterodox *alumbrados*. Reflecting on the demise of so much of his life's work, Master Avila compared himself to John the Baptist, who rejoiced when the one greater than he came even though it meant his own diminishment (John 3:29–30). In a letter to Father Nadal, assistant to Ignatius Loyola, Father Avila described his experience as like that of a child who tries mightily, but unsuccessfully, to roll a stone uphill, only to see another come and succeed with ease where he had failed.[26]

Father Avila spent the last years of his life in semi–retirement in Montilla in the Diocese of Cordoba. When his health allowed him, he continued to engage in the ministry by preaching, hearing confessions, and giving spiritual direction and spiritual conferences to priests and to the Jesuit novices. He also wrote many letters to people in various states of life. John of Avila died on May 10, 1569, and, in accord with his wishes, was buried in the Jesuit church in Montilla. He was beatified on September 15, 1894, and canonized on May 31, 1970. On July 2, 1946, Pope Pius XII declared him patron of diocesan priests in Spain.

# Survey of Avila's Writing

The written works of John of Avila reflect his vocation as preacher, teacher, and spiritual director. The critical edition of 1970 presents his complete works in six volumes: the two redactions he made of the *Audi, filia;* eighty–two sermons and spiritual conferences; a few biblical commentaries; 257 letters, mostly of spiritual direction; several treatises on reform and other minor treatises. Though the Master studied theology, the scriptures, and the fathers, he had no desire to be a systematic scholar in these or any other areas. For himself and for his disciples, he desired a life of study that would inform their exercise of the priesthood and would nourish those they served in their ministry. It is to be expected, then, that the corpus of Avila's writings should consist largely of sermons and letters addressed to individuals or groups whose faces he recognized and whose lives and struggles he knew intimately. Even his memoranda, treatises, and commentaries on the scripture have a certain dialogic and interactive quality, written as they were to help specific people that he knew and worked with. The same is true of his masterpiece, *Audi, filia*, which was first addressed to a particular woman he was directing and only later addressed in revised and expanded form to a broader audience of disciples and readers at large, who desired its publication so that they could have the spiritual wisdom of the Master near at hand for their personal use.

## Sermons

The sermons of Father Avila provide a direct witness to the content and character of a privileged part of his priestly activity throughout the course of his ministry. During Avila's sermons some of his disciples took notes and then transcribed them afterward, at times with Avila's help and correction. After the Master's death Father Juan Díaz, a disciple and relative of Father Avila, prepared many of his writings, including the collection of his sermons, for publication. Consequently, we can hear the Master extending God's invitation to conversion, acceptance of pardon, and transformation of life by living in Christ. It is characteristic of Father Avila that he not only invites his hearers to enter into the gospel scene, but he also opens their eyes, ears, and hearts to the interior dispositions of Christ, especially in the incarnation and passion, and now in the Eucharist and the church. The sermons show how Master Avila engages his hearers through a lively dialogue form in which he raises questions and proposes answers, presents the frail humanity of his hearers in concrete terms and examples, and seeks to persuade them to accept redemption in Christ. The sermons are obviously well prepared and rich in their use of scripture, often interpreted allegorically; they emphasize Avila's favorite theme of God's mercy in Christ continued in the church, the mystical body of Christ. According to Father Granada, Avila told him that he always mounted the pulpit with a hunger to touch some soul or souls for Christ.[27]

## Letters

A second important part of the Master's writings consists of personal letters. Like the sermons, the more than 250 extant letters reflect the Master's teachings and activities over a long period of time, in this case the three decades from 1538 until his death in 1569. Moreover, they reveal Avila in one of the most characteristic and fruitful parts of his ministry of spiritual direction of people of every stripe and condition: men and women, little and great, rich and poor, laity and consecrated. The collection includes letters to prelates who consulted him, such as Pedro Guerrero, Archbishop of Granada, and John of Ribera and Thomas of Villanova, both archbishops of Valencia, later canonized. He wrote to founders of religious orders, such as Ignatius of Loyola and John of God. He wrote to Teresa of Avila, the great Carmelite reformer.

As with the sermons, the letters reveal the Master directly engaged with his flock, addressing them in a lively and engaging manner and showing the way to conversion of life. The crucial difference, of course, is that in a sermon, the preacher speaks to individuals as part of a group, while, in a letter, he addresses a particular individual in all his or her uniqueness. The collection of Avila's letters, the most popular part of his writings after the *Audi, filia*, permits us to look over the shoulder of the recipient of the letter, as it were, and to read the Master's counsel for dealing with concrete problems and situations that his correspondent has revealed to him. Avila's approach is to look at the problem in its concrete reality, sometimes with a touch of humor but always with sympathy and respect for the person he deals with. He tries to illuminate the problem with words from scripture and almost always includes an invitation to look at Christ in his passion and to carry the cross with him.

According to his secretary, Father Juan de Villarás, the day's mail would arrive while they were eating. Avila's custom was to read it immediately after they were finished and, unless he needed further reflection, he would dictate answers immediately. He would speak from the abundance of his heart and send the first draft without erasing or editing. Father Granada admired the Master's ability to address the needs of so many different people, to warn against the enemy, and to recognize the signs of grace; to uncover the vanity of the world and to exhort to confidence in God and in the blood of Christ. He concludes that anyone with sense who reads the letters will recognize that "the finger of God is here.[28]

## *Memorials and Treatises*

In addition to letters and sermons directed to the conversion of the faithful one by one, or congregation by congregation, Master Avila authored several short works or treatises on subjects having to do with reform or the spiritual life. He wrote two systematic documents on the subject of reform of the clergy for his friends in the hierarchy who were participating in the Council of Trent. In 1551 he wrote the "Memorial" or "Memorandum" entitled "Reform of the Ecclesiastical State." The Archbishop of Granada, a friend of Avila's from their days at the University of Alcalá, had invited Avila to attend a session of the council of Trent as an expert (peritus). Because of failing health the Master was unable to accept, but he wrote this document for Guerrero's use. In 1561 Avila wrote a second "Memorial" for the same council with the title "Causes and Remedies of Heresies." In this document he advocated reform at every level, including the papacy and the episcopacy, as essential to the reform of the church. He wrote in a similar way for synods and provincial councils held in Spain to implement conciliar decrees.

One important consideration to take into account when studying these documents is that they were written without the expectation of their publication beyond the ecclesiastical circle for which they were written as guides. Avila, therefore, is free to paint in graphic colors the picture of the church in Spain and Europe and its need for reform. He minces no words as he points out the widespread corruption and neglect at every level of the church's life, but especially among the clergy and bishops, some of whom respond not to God's call but to "the call of money and an easy life." Only when there is repentance and reform can those in the ecclesiastical state act as shepherds for their people and as examples of the evangelical life they are charged with fostering in others. For the bishops gathered in the council, Avila advocates not only conversion of heart but action for reform in line with the many laws and statements they have already issued. Among the most important steps he advocates is the establishment of schools, or "seminaries," for the education of the clergy.[29]

Just how effective and influential Avila's contributions were in the Council of Trent is difficult to measure. It is known that Archbishop Guerrero, a leading figure in the deliberations at Trent, often consulted "his papers" and admitted that Master Avila was their source. Comparison of the decrees of Trent for reform of the clergy support the view that Avila's "Memoranda" did exercise some influence on the council, especially with regard to reform of the clergy, the establishment of seminaries, and seminary programs. Avila was probably more demanding than the council in his vision of preparation for the priesthood, but, at the same time, it adopted many of the ideas he proposed for the universal church, ideas he had already tested years before the council in his own attempts at education and formation of priests, above all at the University of Baeza.[30]

## Short Treatises and Biblical Commentaries

Two short treatises of the Master also deserve mention. The "Treatise on the Priesthood" was written about 1563, apparently in preparation for some conferences on the priesthood he was planning to give. The Master calls for renewal of the priesthood and then gives practical suggestions for parish priests, preachers, and confessors.[31] A second work, "Treatise on the Love of God," a brief study of the mystery of Christ as priest, has been called a "pearl of Spanish literature on ascetical theology."[32] It was first published in 1596 by Father Juan Díaz, a relative of the Master, who placed it at the head of a collection of treatises on the Blessed Sacrament. In it, the dynamic of Christ's priesthood is rooted in his intimate relationship with the Father and externalized in his spousal love for the church. Father Avila expresses this in terms of the loving gaze of Christ directed toward his Father and toward his bride, the church. This christological idea is found also in *Audi, filia* (chaps. 112–13).

Like his other writings, Master Avila's commentaries on Sacred Scripture are pastoral rather than scholarly in tone. Having studied at the University of Alcalá, he was influenced by the renaissance of biblical studies in the new humanism as encouraged by Cardinal Cisneros and, of course, by the popular Erasmus of Rotterdam, and he encouraged his disciples to read the Bible and to memorize at least parts of it. In all his writings he makes generous use of both Old and New Testaments, borrowing from them words, images, examples, and stories, and interpreting freely in an allegorical sense to fit the context or situation he addresses. In the "Memorials" he wrote for the Council of Trent he stressed the need of advanced study of the Bible by all who would preach it in the priestly ministry. According to Father Granada, Master Avila knew by heart the letters of Saint Paul, his chosen patron and model. A witness at the process of beatification testified that Father Avila "understood the Letters of St. Paul as the glorious St. John Chrysostom understood them."[33]

There is discussion about whether Avila is actually the author of the biblical commentaries or "lessons" *(lecciones)* ascribed to him, but the evidence is strong that he wrote the commentaries on Saint Paul's Letter to the Galatians and on the First Letter of Saint John. It is likely that, as with his sermons, several of his disciples took notes on the lessons as they were being delivered and afterward brought together a text to be checked by Father Avila. These lessons are at a popular level and constitute a kind of biblical catechesis in which the preacher touches on important topics of the Catholic faith such as the Trinity, Christ, the church, grace, and the sacraments, together with instruction on the ascetical and moral life.

## Introduction to the *Audi, filia*

Among the spiritual treatises of Saint John of Avila, the most precious is the *Audi, filia*, one of the most important spiritual books to come from the extraordinarily rich sixteenth century in Spain. It is really the book of John of Avila's lifetime, since he began writing it in his younger years in Seville and was occupied in correcting and polishing it when he died in Montilla in 1569. Without doubt it is the work of the Master that has been printed most often both within and outside Spain. Originally written for a young woman whom Avila was guiding in the way of sanctity, its revised and expanded version provides a way of life for any Christians who desire to walk unencumbered along the way of Christ, living by his life as it is made available in the church. Before examining the structure and content of Master Avila's masterpiece, we must take a brief look at the long and tortuous history of composition and redaction that culminated in the definitive edition (1574). Indeed, the trials and tribulations of Avila's life as a sower of the seed of God's word are reflected in the complicated history of *Audi, filia*.

Testimony given at the beatification process supports the conclusion that the *Audi, filia* was written at different times and then unified around verses 11–12 of Psalm 45. Witnesses at the process affirmed that it was during his imprisonment (1532–33) that the Master began to put on paper "his ideas on the mystery of our justification and incorporation in Christ," and that, by God's favor, he had light during his imprisonment for writing *Audi, filia*.[34] After his release from prison, Avila enlarged on his notes. According to his disciple and secretary, Father Juan de Villarás, who shared house and table with Avila for sixteen years at Montilla, the Master began writing the book at the request of Sancha Carrillo, a young woman he was directing in the spiritual life. She had asked her director for some written advice to serve as a rule of life that she could read for her consolation and benefit. In response, the Master wrote four to six pages and sent them to her. She then asked for more, and he wrote another eight to ten pages, and so the process went. It appears that a first version of the work, probably consisting of chapters 97–100 and 103–13 of the definitive edition, was completed before Sancha Carrillo's death in 1537, and that this became the core of the later expanded versions. Handwritten copies of this brief work were already circulating among friends of Sancha Carrillo and John of Avila before 1539, when Father Luís Granada refers in a letter to the Master's treatment of prayer in a book about to be printed. For some reason, publication did not take place, perhaps because of Avila's many trips and projects during the following years.

In 1545, Father Avila once again set out to revise his work, and the next year he wrote the dedication to the Count of Palma, Luís de Puertocarrero, who had often encouraged him to publish the book. In the dedication Avila tells of seeing a copy of his treatise with so many errors that it seemed necessary to publish a corrected edition. His intention was to expand on what he had written before so that all would understand. He then makes explicit his reasons for writing: "The purpose of the book is to give some Christian instructions and rules for beginners in God's service so that, through his grace, they may know how to put their desires into effect." Avila desires that the rules he gives should be safe rather than lofty, to avoid inciting pride; he will give some advice on defense against enemies and then exercises in self–knowledge and knowing Jesus Christ.[35]

Although the *Audi, filia* was dedicated and revised around 1545–48, it was still far from publication, though handwritten copies were in circulation. John of Avila probably deferred the printing of his revised work until he had time to see the decrees on justification from the Council of Trent. But though the Master did not judge the time opportune for publication of his treatise, an admirer who possessed a handwritten copy of the work as it had been dedicated and revised in 1548 had it published by the publishing house of Juan Brocar in Alcalá de Henares in 1556 under the cumbersome title *Christian Counsels and Rules for Those Who Desire to Serve God, Advancing in the Spiritual Way. Composed by Master Avila on that Verse of David: Audi, filia, et vide et inclina aurem tuam.* Luís Guttierez, the admirer who arranged the publication, wrote in his preface to the devout reader that, in publishing this book, "presuming the consent of its author," he serves God and helps his neighbor by printing something so spiritual and excellent. The motive for this "pirate edition" of the *Audi, filia* was noble, but it came as an unwelcome shock to Master Avila. He had just taken up the book again to revise it, knowing that some points in the earlier version needed refining lest they be associated with theological and spiritual currents that the Inquisition was laboring to keep out of Spain.[36]

Indeed, the timing for the publication of the *Audi, filia* could not have been less opportune. The Inquisition in Valladolid and Seville was on the verge of investigating groups suspected of Lutheran tendencies, and the inquisitors were on the lookout for spiritual and theological books, especially in the vernacular, that they considered dangerous for the Christian people. As the proceedings unfolded, Avila's name came up many times, either because some of those investigated had portions of his writings, or because one or another of his disciples had some contact with those investigated. In 1559 the *Catalogue of Forbidden Books* was published. The list included the name of Juan de Avila, identified as the author of a treatise beginning with the words "Counsels and Christian Rules." Moreover, the prohibition extended to Avila's other works: "any and all sermons, letters, treatises, or anything written by hand that speaks of Sacred Scripture or of the Sacraments of Holy Mother Church and Christian religion, which the heretics in their craftiness use to communicate their errors."[37] One of Avila's disciples, Father Alonso Molina, records that as soon as the news of the prohibition of his writings reached Father Avila, he immediately burned, to the great sorrow of his disciples, the many notebooks he had written by hand at the universities of Alcalá and Salamanca, without even looking at them.[38]

It was natural that Master Avila would suspend his work, and that before continuing with the correction of the *Audi, filia* he would want to find out the extent of the prohibition and what in his writings had been found worthy of censure. Allowing time for these tasks, Avila's new revision had to have been complete at the latest by the end of 1564, since by 1565 copies of the book were once again in circulation. Father Avila presented the revision to the Bishop of Cordoba, Cristóbal Rojas Sandoval, who gave his approval on June 7, 1565. The prologue of the 1564 edition, which remains the prologue in the definitive edition, indicates the Master's desire that this corrected and expanded text should replace all earlier versions of the work, especially the "pirate edition" of 1556. Greater precision is obvious in his revised expression of the doctrine of justification. Father Avila was at pains to address the principal inadequacy highlighted by the Inquisition, namely, that he so emphasized confidence in God's mercy that he appeared to leave little or no room for the believer's transformation by and cooperation in grace.[39] Also, in this final revision the Master added a long apologetic treatise on faith (chaps. 32–44) and new material on the passion (chaps. 76–81).

When the Inquisition learned of the new manuscript and its approval by the Bishop of Cordoba, it assigned theologians to review the book. These theologians sent their highly positive opinion to the highest tribunal with some notes for Master Avila to take into account before sending his book to be printed. After his death on May 10, 1569, two of his disciples, Juan Villarás, his secretary, and Juan Díaz, a relative, undertook the publication of the Master's works, beginning with the *Audi, filia*. The approbation of Bartholomé Isla, SJ, dated November 26, 1573, includes the note that "even though the book had been printed before under another title and with the name of the same author, in fact, the author did not know about it and if he had known about such a printing, he would not have given his consent because he had not then finished revising it." The book appeared the following year (1574) in Toledo with the cumbersome title *A Spiritual Book that Deals with the Evil Languages of the World, the Flesh, and the Demon and Remedies Against Them; Faith and Self-Knowledge; Penance, Prayer, Meditation on the Passion of Our Lord Jesus Christ; Love of Neighbor.* The edition could not have been very numerous because copies of it are extremely rare. Shortly after, Juan Díaz signed a contract with the printer Pedro Cossin, who in the same year (1574) published an edition of fifteen hundred copies in Madrid. The following year the treatise was printed again in Salamanca in the publishing house of Matthias Gast under the original title, *Audi, filia*. With this edition the title and text of John Avila's major work were definitively fixed. All editions before the 1574 edition continued to be prohibited and listed on the Index and Catalogue of the Inquisition.[40]

## *Comparison of the Two Editions*

It is instructive to consider some of the more significant differences between the editions of 1556 and 1574 in order to observe how the Master clarified Catholic teaching, especially with regard to faith and justification.[41] However, before considering the differences between the two editions, it should be noted that the text published in 1556 has passed almost in its entirety into the definitive edition of 1574, even if Father Avila has interrupted the flow of the first edition by adding quotations from one or another of the fathers to support some of his statements. But there are very few instances in the final edition of suppression of material from the first edition. This means that the spiritual doctrine that Master Avila expounded and the way of perfection he advocated in the first edition of the *Audi, filia* were essentially safe, sound, and in accord with tradition. The guidance for walking along the path of perfection includes the traditional elements: vocal prayer; fasting, watching, and almsgiving; veneration of the saints and use of sacred images; reading of spiritual books; obedience to superiors; prayer for the souls in purgatory. Moreover, he already warned in the 1556 edition against the excesses of the so–called enlightened (*alumbrados*) and the errors of the Protestants.

What, then, were the objections that the Inquisition posed to the 1556 edition of Father Avila's work and which governed many of the changes he made in the definitive edition? In other words, what struck the inquisitors as so dangerous to Christian faith? Generally speaking, there were two types of corrections to be made. The first was responses to general observations of the Inquisition calling for clarification or expansion of some statements. These could be handled without much difficulty in the revision. But the second type of modification of the text of the *Audi, filia* was more important because it touched upon the question of justification and faith, so current and crucial in the mid–sixteenth century, given the Protestant teachings and the formulations of the Council of Trent. Some of Father Avila's statements on these issues suggested to the critics assigned to study the work an interpretation of Paul more or less influenced by Erasmus or Luther. As such, these statements were liable to misinterpretation and therefore needed revision in light of the formulations of Trent. Luís of Granada tells us that Father Avila was deeply aware of the mystery of Christ's blood and the riches and benefits we receive from him. In his preaching and teaching the Master extolled the benefits and merits of Christ's saving works and the mercy of God that far exceeds the malice of any sin. To such a degree did he emphasize these aspects of the mystery of salvation that some questioned whether he took sufficient account of humanity's cooperation in the order of salvation or was moving in the direction of the Lutheran view of grace and justification.

Other aspects of the question of justification also needed clarification. For example, in the first edition of *Audi, filia*, some statements seemed to indicate that justifying grace was not inherent to the soul but merely a kind of external covering that left the person untransformed. At times, there was some imprecision about the role the author gives to faith as "the principle of the spiritual life" and "our salvation," which could be confusing to the reader given the Lutheran slogan that faith alone is needed for salvation. He also had to avoid blurring the distinction between faith and confidence, which also could suggest the teaching of Luther.

A few examples of modifications Avila made will serve to illustrate the care with which he revised the second edition of his work so that its conformity to Catholic teaching would be beyond question. Most obviously, he had studied and incorporated the teaching on justification that had been formulated and promulgated by the Council of Trent between his writing of the first and second redactions of *Audi, filia*. The first illustration comes from a passage in which Avila is giving counsel on dealing with despair because of previous sins. In the first edition, he says:

> If the devil should try to disturb us by aggravating the sins we have committed, let us consider that he is neither the offended party nor the judge who will pronounce the sentence. God was the one we offended when we sinned, and he is the one who must judge both human beings and devils. Therefore, we should not be disturbed that the accuser accuses. Instead we should be comforted that the one who is the offended party and the judge, pardons and absolves us. (chap. 18)

As far as it goes, the statement is valid and certainly "comforting" to the sinner. However, it could mislead the reader to think that salvation is the work of God's grace alone without any contribution from the one who is pardoned. The revised edition clarifies that, while God, "the offended party and the judge," grants pardon freely, the sinner must cooperate by using the means available in the church for receiving the pardon offered by God in Christ and through the church. Thus God pardons and absolves us *through our penance and through his priests and sacraments*. The added phrases are brief, to be sure, but round out the statement so that the cooperation of the sinner is given its rightful place in the dynamic of salvation.

Continuing in the same passage, Avila quotes Saint Paul, asking who can condemn one whom God has justified (Rom 8:31–33). In the first edition of *Audi, filia*, Father Avila says that our sins ought not to frighten us because God has laid the penalty for them on Christ, and "therefore pardon may come to the one deserving of punishment." Once again, the Master gives sound Christian teaching, but he omits reference to the role of the sinner in accepting and acting on the pardon granted in Christ. In his revision Avila clarifies that such pardon comes to the sinner if *such a one is disposed to receive it*. Similarly, Avila clarifies another general statement of the accomplishment of salvation.

At first he had said that "already the justice due for all the sins of the world was accomplished upon the cross and fell upon the innocent Lamb, Jesus Christ our Lord. Thus every guilty person who desires to approach him may be pardoned." In itself, the statement is true, but it is incomplete because it fails to mention the action required of the penitent. Thus, in the revised edition Avila adds the specific requirement of the need for repentance and penance: "Every guilty person who desires to approach him, *and to rejoice in his redemption through penance*, may be pardoned."

When Avila was beginning his priestly ministry, the Protestant Reformation was in its infancy, and few recognized it as the departure from the faith of the church that it would eventually reveal itself to be. The clarifying formulations of the Council of Trent on the issues of justification and faith and works were still many years in the future, and even faithful adherents of the church's teaching were uncertain about the differences between heresy and orthodoxy. It is understandable that an author writing a treatise on the spiritual life in the early part of the sixteenth century could unwittingly neglect to clarify points that in other times and circumstances could be taken for granted.

## The Structure of the Audi, filia

We may divide the work into six parts that conform to the elements in Psalm 45:11–12, as these verses are unevenly, and with some modification, divided by Master Avila: "Listen, daughter [1], and see [3]; incline your ear [2]. Forget your people [4] and your father's house [5], and the King will desire your beauty [6]." From the outset, the reader becomes aware that, although the work starts out with a quotation from scripture, it is by no means a commentary on these verses from scripture. Rather, the two verses from Psalm 45 provide a framework for the Master to present his own treatment of the spiritual life. In so doing, he appears to be following Saint Jerome, who uses the same verses in his famous letter to Eustochium, exhorting her to evangelical chastity.[42]

## Part One: *"Listen, O Daughter!"* (chaps. 1–44)

The first long section of the *Audi, filia* is concerned with the injunction addressed to the soul by God through the Psalmist: "Listen, daughter." Following Saint Paul, who said that faith comes "by hearing" (Rom 10:17), the Master regards the spiritual life of the Christian as beginning with the listening or hearing that opens the door to faith.

Receptivity to God's word through hearing or listening is made possible through the sacrament of baptism, which includes the ritual of the opening of the ears. However, given the fact of the fall of Adam and Eve, the baptized Christian must tune out the cacophony of diverse languages that can drown out the voice of God. The host of evil languages can be reduced to three: that of the world, which is all lies and causes the one who listens to it to turn from the truth in its quest for honor (chaps. 2–4); that of the flesh, which speaks enticingly of pleasures when tempting and adopts an accusatory tone to torment the guilty sinner (chaps. 5–16); that of the devil, whose malicious cunning can exalt his listeners to the heights of pride or cast them into the abyss of despair, but whose words are always of evil and bitter things (chaps. 17–30). After showing how to silence these evil languages with their deadly messages, the author turns to the language of divine revelation, which the baptized soul is capable of hearing since it has ears opened in faith. This section, greatly expanded in the definitive edition, is really a small treatise on faith and the motives for believing (chaps. 31–44).

## Part Two: *"Incline Your Ear!"* (chaps. 45–55)

In Psalm 45:11–12, the command to hear is immediately followed by the command to see, and then by the injunction to incline the ear: "Listen, daughter, and see; incline your ear." But since the command to "incline the ear" continues the theme of hearing, Avila transposes the second and third commands in order to complete his discussion of "hearing" before taking up the topic of "seeing." He interprets the command to "incline the ear" to mean that the believer should listen with obedient submission to God's word as interpreted and taught in the church, and to close the ears to mere human opinions, such as those of Luther, that deceive many (chaps. 45–49). In a second step he warns against the dangers of extraordinary revelations, visions, and sentiments experienced by some devout people (chaps. 50–55). It is clear that Master Avila has in mind the excesses of the "enlightened ones" *(alumbrados)* who consider themselves in perfect union with God. He poses many examples from the past to show the foolishness and deception of ascetics and mystics who believed they were the recipients of supernatural revelation and thus in no need of direction or counsel from others. Swollen with pride, such people become their own demons. The remedy for such pride and deception is humble and obedient listening to God's word as interpreted in the church.

# INTRODUCTION

## Part Three: *"See!"* (chaps. 56–96)

In this third section the Master reflects on the role of "seeing" or "looking" or "contemplating" in the spiritual life of recollection and interior prayer (chap. 56). Taken in itself, this section in the definitive edition really amounts to a small treatise on the life of prayer. One begins by looking at oneself in order to gain self-knowledge and humility (chaps. 57–67); one then looks at Christ especially in his passion, and approaches God through Christ (chaps. 68–93); finally, one looks at the neighbor with love born of self-knowledge and love of Christ (chaps. 94–96). The general structure is the same in the editions of 1556 and 1574, but there have been significant changes in the final edition. Most notably, the section on looking at Christ has been revised and expanded, and many new chapters added. Especially significant is the addition of chapters 88–93, which have the flavor of the Council of Trent and probably represent the last chapters written by Father Avila before his death. In them, he clarifies his teaching on justification in accord with the decrees of the Council of Trent.

## Parts Four to Six (chaps. 97–113)

The original unpublished version of the work as Sancha Carrillo possessed it before her death in 1537 includes all of chapters 97–113 with the exception of two chapters that were added later (chaps. 101–102). This was the book that Master Avila had written for her and that she called "my treasure."[43] The edition revised around 1545 and published in 1556, as well as the final revision printed in 1574–75, incorporates this original material without change.

## Part Four: *"Forget Your People!"* (chaps. 97–99).

Master Avila interprets the injunction to forget one's people in several ways. First, he interprets it in terms of the two cities described by Augustine in *The City of God*, where each person is faced with the choice between the earthly city and the heavenly city. God summons the soul to leave the world of sin as he called Israel out of Egypt to enter the Promised Land and later called his people to return from exile in Babylonia. He summons the sinner to return home as the prodigal son returned from the land where he was not even given the food of pigs. Avila then interprets the command in terms of forgetting one's family, not meaning that they should not be loved, but that they should be loved in Christ so that they do not become obstacles to one's journey to God. Finally, the Master interprets the passage in terms of vanity about lineage and family origins: "The only place for vanity about lineage is in the thoughts of those who do not hold heavenly things more important than earthly things" (chap. 99).

## Part Five: *"Forget Your Father's House!"* (chaps. 100–102)

Once again, the Master uses allegory to interpret this scriptural command. He identifies the "father" as the devil who dwells within the wicked as in his own house because they have decided to be children of the devil by imitating him:

> If we reflect carefully on this "house of the devil" we find that it is the evil self–will of the wicked. There the devil sits like a king on his throne, and from there, he gives orders to everyone. Therefore, "to forget your father's house" is nothing other than to forget and forsake one's own will in which, at some time, we have given lodging to this evil father; it is to embrace the divine will with all one's heart, saying: "Not my will, Lord, but yours be done." (Luke 22:42)

The two chapters added in the final revision (chaps. 101–2) give directions for denying self–will and doing God's will. It is interesting to note that Father Avila regards the intense prayer of petition, not as a means of getting one's own will, but as a way of doing God's will: "Such prayer is a means, and a very good one, for doing the will of God, who commands us to depart from evil and do good."

## Part Six: *"The King Will Desire Your Beauty!"* (chaps. 103–13)

Permeating all the chapters in this last part of the *Audi, filia* is wonder and thanksgiving at the fact that God is attracted by the beauty of the soul. That beauty, with its four characteristics of fullness, proportion, light, and grandeur, is absent from the soul in sin and restored by the blood of Christ.

> If the beautiful Word of God had not come to beautify us, the ugliness of sin would have endured forever. But when the Lamb without stain came, he had the power, knowledge, and will to wash away our stains. He destroyed our ugliness and gave us his beauty. (chap. 108)

# INTRODUCTION

Christ's beauty was hidden on the day he suffered to make us beautiful. Many failed to see his glory when Pilate displayed him with the words, "Behold, the Man." However, those with faith looked on "that most blessed face as in a shining mirror" and, seeing his beauty, desired to be "crucified in heart" along with him and to share his beauty (cf. chap. 69). Repeatedly, Master Avila encourages the soul to "look at this man" in faith, fully aware of the reciprocity of the contemplation: "Look then at Christ so that Christ may look at you" (chap. 112). In another place Avila speaks of the reciprocity in the terms of Psalm 45:11–12. He observes that God, who tells us to hear and see him and to incline the ear to him, does the same with us: "he hears us, sees us, and inclines his ear to us" (chap. 82). This last section and the entire work culminate in the final vision of Christ in glory:

> Let Christ appear to you like the sun, and the souls redeemed by him, white as snow. I am speaking of those souls who confess and abhor with sorrow their own deformity, and beg to be made beautiful, just, and rich with grace and with the gifts they receive through Christ, that they are able to enamor the very eyes of God. Thus, to him may be sung with great truth and joy: "The king will desire your beauty" (Ps 45:12). (chap. 113)

31

# *Audi, filia*

# LISTEN, O DAUGHTER

# AUTHOR'S PROLOGUE

It is twenty–seven years, Christian reader, since I wrote for a young religious woman,[44] now dead for many years, a treatise on the verse of Psalm 44 [45], which begins: "Listen, daughter, and see."[45] Although many friends had many times asserted that, if I corrected and ordered the treatise for printing, it would be of spiritual benefit to its readers, I had not done it. It seemed to me that, for anyone who wanted to benefit from reading in Spanish, there were many good books, and this one was not necessary. For one who did not want to read in Spanish, this book would be as superfluous as the rest. Also contributing to my hesitation was my continuous infirmity during almost eight years, which caused me exertion enough. So I did not have the treatise printed, and I scarcely even remembered it until last year. Then, already swayed by the requests of friends, I was beginning little by little to correct it and add to it so that it might be printed, even though I knew that it would be at great cost to my health. At the end of a few days, I learned that a treatise had been printed under this same verse of the psalm, and entitled with my name, in Alcalá de Henares, in the publishing house of Juan de Brocar, in 1556.[46] I thought it strange that anyone would dare to print a book for the first time without the correction of the author. It seemed even stranger that anyone had given as author of a book someone whom he had not questioned as to whether he was the author. I tried with greater care to engage in what I had begun, so that once this treatise had been printed, the other would be discredited. But my infirmities, which afterward had increased with some things added, have been the reason why the book has not been completed sooner. Now that it is going forth, receive it with charity, and do not consider the other as mine, nor give any credit to it. I say this not only about this treatise, but also if you should see other things printed in my name, right up to today. For I have not arranged anything for printing except this present treatise and a "Declaration of the Ten Commandments" for children learning catechism to sing. I also caution you that you not take as mine, writings by hand that might come to you under my name, unless you recognize my handwriting or signature. Even in this case, one must watch out, because some have attempted forgery. Also, I thought it good to warn you that this treatise was written for the young religious woman that I mentioned above. She and those like her have more need to encourage their hearts with confidence than to frighten them with severity. So this book is directed more to the first than to the second. But if the disposition of your soul demands more the severity of justice than the gentleness of mercy, take from here what you find suitable for you and leave the rest for those who need it. This whole book, together with the author, continues subject to the correction of our Mother, the Holy Roman Church.

# BRIEF SUMMARY BY THE AUTHOR

So that you may have a brief summary of what is treated in this book, you should know that from the second to the fifth chapter, it deals with the evil language of the world. From the fifth chapter till chapter sixteen, it deals with the language of the flesh. From the sixteenth to the thirtieth chapters, it deals with the deceptions of the demon. In each part of these, some remedies against these evil languages are set forth. From chapter thirty to chapter forty–two, it treats of some reasons proving that the Catholic faith is true. From chapter forty–three to chapter forty–nine, it treats of the same Catholic faith, infused by God's mercy, and sometimes taken away as punishment for sins. Chapters fifty to fifty–six treat of some deceptions with regard to spiritual feelings and some remedies for them. From there till chapter seventy–eight, it treats of self–knowledge. From there to chapter eighty–five, it treats of prayer and meditation, penance, and the passion of our Lord Jesus Christ. From there till chapter ninety–four, it deals with how God hears us and sees us with mercy and love, through the merits of our Lord Jesus Christ.

Chapters ninety–four to ninety–seven deal with love of neighbor. From there to chapter one hundred and three, it deals with how we have to leave our people and our own will and despise the lineage of the flesh. From there until the end of the treatise, it deals with how the beauty of the soul, lost through sin, is recovered by the merits of Jesus Christ our Lord and through penance. Through his mercy, may he please to give you his grace so that you may read it for your profit and his glory.

# PART ONE

# "Listen, O Daughter!"

(CHAPS. 1–44)

# INTRODUCTION:
## CLARITY OF GOD'S WORD
## VERSUS CONFUSION OF
## EVIL LANGUAGES (CHAP. 1)

**CHAPTER 1**

*Listen, O Daughter, and see; incline your ear, and forget your people and your father's house. And the King will desire your beauty* (Ps 45:11–12).

Devout Spouse of Jesus Christ, the prophet David speaks these words; or rather God speaks through him to the Christian Church, advising her of what she ought to do so that the great king Jesus Christ may be drawn to love her.[47] For it is from his love that all goods come to her. Since, by God's mercy, your soul belongs to this church, I have thought it good to declare these words to you. First, I have invoked the power of the Holy Spirit so that he may direct my pen that I may not speak badly, and that he might prepare your heart, so that you may not hear without fruit. Rather, may my writing and your hearing be to the perpetual honor of God and the accomplishment of his holy will.

With good reason, the first thing we are told to do in the words of this psalm is to "hear." Since the beginning of the spiritual life is faith, which, as Saint Paul says, enters the soul "through hearing," it is right that we be admonished first concerning what we must do first (cf. Rom 10:17). For it is of little advantage that the voice of divine truth should sound from outside, if within there are not ears desirous of hearing it. Nor is it enough that, when we were baptized, the priest put his finger into our ears, saying, "let them be opened," if we keep them shut to the word of God and thus fulfill in ourselves what the prophet David said about idols: "They have eyes and see not. They have ears and hear not" (Ps 115:5–6).

But since some speak so badly that to hear them is to hear Sirens that kill those listening to them, it is well for us to see whom to hear and whom not to hear. For this, it is to be noted that when they were created, Adam and Eve spoke only one language. That language lasted

41

in the world until human pride, desirous of building the tower of confusion, was punished. Then, instead of one language by which all could understand one another, there came about a host of languages through which people could not understand one another (cf. Gen 11:9). We learn from this that, until they rose up against their Creator and broke his commandment with impudent pride, our first parents spoke only one spiritual language in their souls. Because of this, they had perfect concord with one another, within themselves, and with God. They lived in the quiet state of innocence, with their passions obeying reason and reason obeying God. They were at peace with God, within themselves, and with each other. But when, through foolhardy disobedience, they rose up against the Lord of the heavens, they were punished, and we in them. Instead of one excellent language by which they could understand each other exceedingly well, there sprung up innumerable very evil languages, full of such confusion and darkness that people could not agree with one another. Nor could one man be in harmony within himself, and even less with God.

These languages have no order among them, for they are disorder itself. However, in order to speak of them, we may reduce them to the order and number of three: the languages of the world, of the flesh, and of the devil. As Saint Bernard says, the function of the first is to speak of vain things, that of the second to speak of pleasures, and that of the third to speak of evil and bitter things.[48]

# A. EVIL LANGUAGES (CHAPS. 2–30)

## 1. Language of the World (chaps. 2–4)

### CHAPTER 2

We must not listen to the language of the world because it is all lies, exceedingly harmful for those who believe them. They cause us to turn away from the truth that really is, to follow the lie that exists only in appearance and by convention. So deceived, a person casts God and his holy will behind his back and orders his life by the blind guide of what pleases the world. Thus is engendered a heart desirous of honor and of being esteemed by others. The person becomes like those proud ancient Romans of whom Saint Augustine said that "for love of worldly honor they desired to live and did not hesitate to die."[49] Such people prize their honor so much that they can in no way bear even the slightest word against it, or anything that tastes or smells like contempt, even if it comes from far away. On the contrary, there are such subtleties and trifles in all this that it is a wonder that anyone escapes stumbling on something and offending the sensitive man of the world, often without meaning to do so. But these people, so quick to feel contempt, are hard and slow when it comes to overlooking and pardoning it. Even if they wanted to, what a troop of false friends and relatives will rise up, citing the laws and customs of the world! Thus, the conclusion is drawn that it is better to lose fortune, health, house, wife, and children, and even all this seems little to such people. They say that it is better to lose the life of body and soul and all that is of earth and heaven, and that even God himself and his law must be counted as little and placed underfoot, so that this utterly vain honor might not be lost but be esteemed above all things, even over God himself.

O vain honor, condemned by Christ on the cross at the cost of his great dishonor! Who gave you "a place in that temple of God" (cf. 2 Thess 2:4), which the heart of the Christian is, with such great esteem that, like the Antichrist, you want to be esteemed more than the most high God? Who made you a competitor with God so that you would even have the advantage in some hearts of being accounted more precious than he, thus renewing that grave insult done to him when they preferred Barabbas (cf. John 18:40)? Your tyranny in the hearts of your subjects is great indeed, and with great readiness and ease they serve you, however costly it might be. Aaron asked for the golden earrings worn by the wives and children of those who wanted an idol. He thought that they would cease from their evil demand for an idol rather than see those they loved without their adornments. But that did not happen. No sooner were the adornments asked for than they were given (cf. Exod 32:2–3). People did not then, nor do they now, take account of what they need for house or children, as long as they have an idol of honor to which they can offer sacrifice. Often it happens that some of those who serve you realize how empty and without substance you are, and what a waste it is to follow you. If they wanted, they could free themselves from your heavy yoke just by breaking with you. Yet so great is their weakness and misery that they choose to burst asunder in acting against God's honor, rather than to rest in honoring him and fleeing from you.

"You shall serve strange gods day and night" (Jer 16:13). God hurls this forth as a curse against those who serve false gods, and it is fulfilled very clearly in those who adore honor. Speaking of the principal people

43

of Jerusalem, who believed in Christ but did not dare to be known as his followers because of human respect, Saint John said with great reproach that "they loved the honor of men more than the honor of God" (John 12:43). With good reason the same can be said truly of those who love honor. So as not to be despised by human beings, they despise God and are ashamed to follow his laws lest they be ashamed before men.

But let them do as they wish. Let them honor their honor until they can do no more. Yet firm and fixed is the sentence pronounced against them by Jesus Christ, the sovereign judge, who says: "Whoever shall be ashamed of me and of my words, of him the Son of the Virgin shall be ashamed, when he shall come in his majesty, and that of his Father, and of the holy angels" (Luke 9:26). Then shall all the angels and saints sing out: "You are just, O Lord: and your judgments are just" (Ps 118:37). If this lowly worm is ashamed to follow you, O Lord, the King of Majesty, you who are honor and greatness itself, you should be ashamed that one so vile and so evil should remain in your company and that of those who belong to you. Oh, with what great force will the honor of Babylonia be hurled into the deepest hell (cf. Rev 18:21), to be in the company of the torments of the proud Lucifer, since these people want to be his companions in the fault of pride! Let no one mock, or take for an insignificant sin, the love of the honor of the world, for the Lord, who searches hearts, said to the Pharisees: "How can you believe in me, since you seek to be honored by one another and do not seek the honor which comes from God alone?" (John 5:44). Since this evil affection is powerful enough to make people give up believing in Jesus Christ, what evil can it not do? Who will not make the sign of the cross against it? Because of this, Saint Augustine said that no one knows his strength for overcoming the love of vainglory, except the one who has waged war against it.[50]

## CHAPTER 3

It should be a great help to us against this evil that the very light of nature condemns it, teaching us to do works worthy of honor but not for the sake of honor. We must deserve it but not place great value on it. The noble heart should despise neither being esteemed nor being without esteem. Nothing should be considered great except virtue.

But, if in spite of all this, the Christian does not have the heart to despise this vanity, let him raise his eyes to the Lord on a cross and see him so laden with dishonor that it can compete with the grievousness of the torments he endured. For a reason the Lord chose death in extreme dishonor. He realized how powerful a tyrant the love of honor is in the hearts of many. Such people would not hesitate to expose themselves to death, but they would flee from the type of death that brings dishonor with it. In order to teach us not to fear either the one or the other, he chose death on a cross, in which grave torments were joined with extreme dishonor.

If you have eyes to see, look upon Christ esteemed as the lowest of men and debased with awful dishonors. Some were brought on by the very death of the cross, the most disgraceful of all deaths. With other dishonors they offended our Lord in particular ways, since all kinds of people took part in despising, injuring, and blaspheming him with dishonors unknown before (cf. Luke 22:65). You appreciate then how completely he fulfills what he had said when he was preaching: "I do not seek my own honor" (John 8:50). You must act in the same way. If you directed the ears of your soul to hear attentively that sad edict against innocence itself, proclaiming through the streets of Jerusalem that Jesus Christ our Lord was a malefactor, then you would be embarrassed to see yourself honored or desiring to be honored. You will say with a heartfelt sigh: O Lord, are you proclaimed as wicked and I praised as good? What greater grief is there? Not only will you lose the desire for worldly honor, but you will desire to be despised in conformity with the Lord, for as scripture says, "to follow him is great honor" (Sir 23:27). Then you will say with Saint Paul: "God forbid that I should glory, save in the cross of Jesus Christ our Lord" (Gal 6:14). You will desire to fulfill what the same apostle says: "Let us go to Christ outside the camp, and let us imitate him in his dishonor" (Heb 13:13).[51]

If the passion of vainglory is a powerful thing, the medicine of Christ's example and grace is much more powerful. These so conquer and uproot vainglory that the heart finds it abhorrent that a Christian should see the Lord of Majesty abasing himself to such contempt, while the Christian, a lowly worm, is puffed up with love of honor. Therefore, the Lord invites and encourages us with his example saying: "Have confidence, I have overcome the world" (John 16:33). It is as if he had said: "Before I came here, it was difficult to contend with the deceitful world, casting aside what flourishes there and embracing what it casts aside. But it has employed all its forces against me, even inventing new kinds of torments and insults. All of these, I endured without turning my face away. Not only did the world show itself to be weak in encountering one who could suffer more, but it is overcome for your benefit. By the example which I gave you and the strength I gained for you, you can easily conquer, overcome, and trample it underfoot."

The Christian should see that, since the world dishonored the blessed Son of God, eternal truth and highest good, it makes no sense to esteem or believe it in anything. Since the world was deceived in not recognizing such a brilliant light and in not honoring the one who is the truest and most perfect honor, Christians should condemn what the world approves and prize and love what the world hates and despises. With great care they should flee from being prized by that world which despised their Lord. For them, it is a great sign of Christ's love to be despised by the world with and for him.

Just as those who belong to the world do not have ears to listen to the truth and the teaching of God, but rather they despise it, so anyone who belongs to the company of Christ has no ears to listen to or believe the lies of the world. For at one time it flatters and at another time persecutes; at one time it promises and at another time threatens; at one time it terrifies and at another appears gentle. But in everything it deceives and intends to deceive. With such eyes we must look upon it. For it is certain that we have caught the world in such great lies and false promises that, if anyone should have told us even half as many, we would not trust that person again in anything. Even if such a one were to speak the truth, we would find it hard to believe. What the world can do is neither good nor bad, for it cannot give or take away the grace of God. Even where it seems to have power, it can do nothing since, without the will of the Lord, it cannot even reach to a hair of our head (cf. Luke 21:18). If the world wants to tell us otherwise about itself, let us not believe it. Who then will not dare to struggle against an enemy that can do nothing at all?

## CHAPTER 4

To better comprehend all this, you must realize that it is one thing to love honor and human esteem for themselves and to rest in them, which is evil, and it is another thing to love these things for some good end, which is not evil. Clearly, those who hold authority or position for the good of others may desire the honor and esteem needed to discharge their office for the greater good. For, if people hold the one who commands in little esteem, they will also take little account of his command, even if it is good. Not only persons in authority, but Christians in general, should practice what is written: "Take care of a good name" (Sir 41:12). This does not mean to rest in it, but that a Christian has to be such that, whoever hears or sees his life, may glorify God, as we usually do at the sight of a rose or a tree with fruit and shade. This is what the holy gospel commands: that our light might so shine before men that, seeing our good works, they may give glory to the heavenly Father (Matt 5:16) from whom all good proceeds.

To honor God and help his neighbors, Saint Paul recounted the great and secret favors that our Lord had done for him (cf. 2 Cor 12:1–12). In so doing, he did not regard himself as violating the scriptural passage that says: "Let another praise you, and not your own mouth" (Prov 27:2). Paul recounted his own praises without attributing anything to himself and, indeed, as if he were not speaking of them. Thus he fulfilled what he had said to the people in Corinth, that those who have wives should be as if they had none, and those who weep as though they did not weep (1 Cor 7: 29–30), and other similar things. By this he intends to say that those whose hearts are not attached to temporal things can use them profitably, whether they are prosperous or adverse, happy or sad. They pass through the temporal as through something vain that passes quickly. Certainly when Saint Paul reported these things about himself, he told them with a heart that not only despised honor but loved being despised and dishonored for the sake of Jesus Christ, whose cross he regarded as the supreme honor (cf. Gal 6:14). Hearts such as his can be trusted to receive honor and to tell things that will lead them to receive it, for they will never do these things unless it is very necessary for some good end.

It requires a lot of virtue to possess something as if one did not have it. So too, it is extremely difficult to keep the honor others give us from cleaving to our hearts. Very few succeed in doing this. As Saint Chrysostom says, "To be in the midst of honors with the heart unaffected is like being among beautiful women without ever looking at them with unchaste eye."[52] Experience has shown us that honors and exalted positions have seldom made the wicked good, but that very frequently they have made the good wicked. To bear the weight of honor and the occasions that come with it requires great strength and virtue. As Saint Jerome says, "The highest mountains are assaulted by the strongest winds."[53] Greater virtue is required for commanding than for obeying. Not without reason, and good reason, did our sovereign Master and Lord, who knows all things, flee from being chosen as king (cf. John 6:15). Now, there was no danger for him in any state, however high, and so it is clear that this doctrine was given to help us in our weakness. We, therefore, ought to flee

47

from what is dangerous, since he who was completely secure from danger fled from it.

It is great audacity and contrary to the example of Christ to accept a position of honor when it is offered. What will it be, then, to desire such a position and seek to procure it? No one can express how great an evil it is to pay money for a place of honor. It would be very strange indeed if a person able to travel safely on level ground chose the dangers of a voyage by sea, not with fair weather, but with constant storms. As Saint Gregory says, "What is the power of high position but a storm for the soul?"[54] After the labors and dangers in a high place, follows that terrible threat spoken by God, though few heed or understand it: "A most severe judgment shall be for them that command" (Wis 6:5). What shall this be when even God's ordinary judgment is such that the most advanced in virtue tremble and say: "Enter not into judgment with your servant, O Lord" (Ps 143:2)? Yet some people are so bold that, they not only choose to enter into judgment, but they enter into one that is exceedingly strict and severe. They see the case of King Saul, to whom God offered the kingdom without Saul's prizing it or paying much attention to it. In fact, he even went into hiding so as not to receive it and was found only because God pointed him out. In spite of all this, the height of his office and its circumstances affected him badly. Though preceded by God's election (cf. 1 Sam 10:21–22) and his own flight, his life turned out so wicked and his death so wretched, that it ought to put fear and fair warning in those who enter into positions of honor, even when they are called and enter by the right door. All the more is this so for those who do not enter by so good a way.

Certainly it is cause for wonder that some people are so ungenerous in the Lord's service that even if they are told to do something very good, they go about considering and reconsidering whether it obliges under pain of mortal sin, and this in order to avoid doing it. They claim that they are weak and do not want to involve themselves in matters of great perfection but prefer to remain on the plain and beaten path. These people are cowardly about seeking for themselves that perfect virtue that, with the grace of the Lord, would be easy to attain. On the other hand, they are extremely bold in putting themselves into positions of dignity, authority, and honor, where tried–and–true virtue is required both to use them well and to avoid personal harm. They convince themselves that they have such virtue and will render a good account of their exalted position, without endangering their conscience as many others have. The desire for honor, authority, and personal advantage so completely blinds people, that it causes those who dare not do what is easy and safe to undertake what is full of dangers and difficulty. Those who do not trust God to help them in good works regarding themselves, boldly assure themselves that God will lead them by the hand in things that pertain to governing others. But God can answer with complete justice that, since they placed themselves in this danger, they can help themselves in passing through it. For of such people, God says: "They have reigned, but not by me: they have been princes, and I did not know it" (Hos 8:4). This means "I did not approve it nor did it seem good to me." Whoever considers how God (the same God who had placed him in the kingdom) rejected Saul will find good reason to undeceive himself. No one will assure him that he is not as weak as Saul. Only his pride and desire to command will do that. However good was his entry into a position of honor, it will not be better than that of Saul.

Saint Augustine rightly said that a high station is necessary for ruling the people, and that when a man possesses it, he must administer it properly, but that when he does not possess it, it is wrong to desire it. Of himself, he said that he desired and endeavored to be saved in a low station so as not to endanger himself in a high one.[55] This is especially to be done when the position concerns the direction of souls, a work of such difficulty that it is called the art of arts. We should flee these dangers as far as possible, imitating the example, already mentioned, that the Lord gave us when he fled from accepting a kingdom, and the example of many holy and wise persons who have fled such honors with all their heart. To enter well into these positions, it is necessary to have either a revelation from the Lord, or obedience to one who has the authority to command, or the counsel of a person who understands well the obligation of the office and its dangers. Such a one should keep the judgment of God before his eyes and all temporal considerations behind his back. If these conditions are not found, it will at least be necessary that there be strong reasons for thinking that God will be served by this. These reasons have to be sufficiently weighty that the man himself may trust in them as he enters into such great danger. Even with all of this, one must fear. It is fitting to be vigilant and to beg the Lord that, since he kept the entrance free from evil, he will likewise watch over its outcome, lest it end in eternal condemnation. We have seen many who lived contentedly in these offices die wishing that they had not had them. They are full of fears about what, at the beginning, caused them no fear. The truth of temporal things appears more clearly as people distance themselves from them, and the more they approach the judgment of God in whom all truth abides.

# 2. Language of the Flesh (chaps. 5–16)

**CHAPTER 5**

The flesh speaks of delights and pleasures, at times clearly, and at other times, under the heading of necessity. The war waged against us by this enemy, besides being very troubling, is more dangerous, because it fights with pleasures, the strongest weapons of all. Thus, many who have not been overcome by riches, honors, or cruel torments, have been overcome by pleasure. It is no wonder that this happens, for the war is so hidden and treacherous that much caution is needed to defend oneself. Who would believe that under cover of soft and sweet pleasures, death, eternal death, comes hidden? Death is the most bitter of all things, while delight is sweetness itself. False pleasure is a golden cup with poison inside that intoxicates those who look only at external appearance. It is the treachery of Joab (cf. 2 Sam 20:9–10), who killed Amasu as he was embracing him; it is the treachery of Judas, who, with a false kiss of peace, handed his blessed Master over to death (cf. Luke 22:47). So, when one drinks from the pleasure of mortal sin, Christ dies in the soul, and when he is dead, the soul dies, because its life comes from him. This is what Saint Paul says: "If you live according to the flesh, you shall die" (Rom 8:13). In another place he says that "the widow that lives in pleasures is dead while she is living" (1 Tim 5:6). She lives in the life of her body but is dead in that of her soul. The more closely the flesh is joined to us, the more it is proper to fear it, for the Lord says that "a man's enemies are those of his own house" (Matt 10:36). Not only does the flesh belong to our house, but it is one of its two walls.

For this and other reasons, Saint Augustine said that "the struggle of our flesh is continual and the victory very difficult."[56] Anyone who wants to emerge victorious must go armed with many strong weapons. The precious jewel of chastity is not given to all, but to those who, through the labor of many earnest prayers and holy deeds, obtain it from our Lord. He desired to be wrapped in a clean linen sheet, passed through many scrubbings to become white. This teaches that the man who wants to arrive at or to preserve chastity, and thus to have Christ lodge within himself as in a new sepulcher, must be content to earn this purity at great cost and labor. So rich is this virtue that whatever the cost, it is a bargain.

Those who have offended our Lord a great deal must perform many more difficult works of penance and satisfaction than those who have offended less. All of us who live in the flesh must fear it, watch over it, hold it in check, and rule it with prudent moderation. But those who are especially assaulted need particular remedies and labors. Therefore, those who feel this necessity within themselves must first of all deal severely with their flesh by cutting down on food and sleep, by using a hard bed and the hair shirt, and by other helpful means of this kind. As Saint Jerome says, "Through fasting are the plagues of the flesh healed."[57] Saint Hilary addressed his own flesh: "I will tame you and make sure that you do not kick any more, but that, hungry and weary, you will think more about eating than about lust."[58] Saint Jerome advises the virgin Eustochium that, even though she was raised with many delicacies, she should be serious about abstinence and corporal penances. He assures her that without this medicine she will not be able to possess chastity.[59] If weakness of the flesh or damage to health follows from such treatment, Saint Jerome says in another place that "it is better that the stomach should suffer rather than the soul, that you command the body rather than serve it, that the legs tremble from weakness rather than that chastity should waver."[60] (It is also true that elsewhere he says that fasts should not be so excessive as to weaken the stomach. In still another place he corrects some whom he learned had run the risk of losing their judgment through excessive fasting and vigils.)

In all these things, it is impossible to lay down a general rule that fits everyone. Some means help some and not others, and what harms the health of one person may not harm another. Also it is one thing when the war is so fierce that a person is in danger of losing chastity, in which case it is fitting to inconvenience the body so that the soul may live. But it is another thing to struggle with a moderate temptation in which a person does not fear such great danger and does not have to put forth such great effort to have the victory. Taking the most fitting means in these cases is the responsibility of the one who prudently guides the person being tempted, but both must pray humbly to our Lord that he will give his light in all this. Saint Paul, a "vessel of election" (cf. Acts 9:15) did not trust his flesh. He says that he chastises it and brings it into subjection lest, while he preaches to others about living virtuous lives, he might himself become wicked (1 Cor 9:27) by falling into some sin. How can we, who have less virtue and greater causes for fear than Saint Paul, think that we can be chaste without disciplining the body? It is very hard to preserve humility in the midst of honors, temperance in the midst of abundance, and chastity in the midst of pleasures. Anyone who sought to quench the fire burning up his house by throwing dry wood on it would be worthy of scorn. Much more worthy of scorn are those who, on the one hand, desire chastity, and on the other hand, satiate their flesh with delicacies and pleasures and give themselves to idleness. These things not only do not quench the fire that is already burning, but they suffice to rekindle it where it has been practically quenched. The prophet Ezekiel testifies that the reason why the unfortunate city of Sodom arrived at the height of such an abominable sin was "the fullness and abundance of bread and the idleness which it had" (Ezek 16:49). Who will dare to live in pleasures and idleness, or even to look on them from afar? For the things that were able to produce the greater sin in them can more easily produce lesser sins in us. Let those who love chastity also love temperance and discipline of the flesh. If they seek to have the one without the other, they will not succeed but will end up with neither. What God has joined together, no one should desire to separate (cf. Matt 19:6). Nor will anyone be able to do so, even if he so desires.

## CHAPTER 6

The remedy of afflicting the flesh that we have spoken about usually helps when temptations spring from the flesh, as happens with young people and those in good health who are used to the pleasures of the flesh. In these cases it is helpful to apply the remedy to the flesh since that is the root of the infirmity.

In other cases the temptation may come from the devil. One sign by which to recognize this is that the struggle is more with thoughts and foul images than with impure feelings in the body. If there are such feelings, the temptation did not begin in them. Rather, the temptation that began in thoughts leads to feelings in the flesh. As the flesh is sometimes very weak and almost dead, evil thoughts can be very lively in it. This happened to Saint Jerome, according to his own account.[61] Another sign that such temptations come from the devil is that they come suddenly, when the person least wants them, and when there is least motive for them. Such temptations do not respect times of prayer or of Mass, or sacred places, where a person, however wicked, usually is reverent and abstains from such thoughts. At times, these thoughts are so many and so terrible that the person never heard, knew, or thought of the kinds of things that come to his imagination. By the strength with which they come and by the things he hears within himself, the person experiences that they do not spring from himself, but that another says and does them. When you have these and other signs, hold it as certain that the devil is persecuting the flesh. But what you suffer in the flesh does not spring from there. This war is more dangerous than that against the flesh, in that the one who wages it wishes such evil upon us. He is an enemy who never wearies of the fight, whether we are awake or sleeping, and at all times and places.

The remedy for this evil is to find some good occupation that requires attention and effort, by which one may forget such foul images. With this intention, Saint Jerome, by his own account, undertook the study of the Hebrew language, with much labor though not without fruit. He says: "Let the devil always find you well employed."[62] So advantageous is this for those living in monasteries that Jerome gives the following advice:

> See that every day you perform whatever is in your charge and submit yourself to whomever you would not. Go to bed so weary that, even as you are walking along, you are falling asleep. Oblige yourself to get up before you have satisfied your desire for sleep. Recite your psalm when it is your turn; serve your brethren and wash the feet of strangers; when you are wronged, be quiet. Fear the abbot of the monastery as though he were a lord and love him as a Father. Believe that everything that he commands is good for you. Do not judge your superiors since your office is to obey and fulfill what is commanded, according to the words of Moses: "Hear, O Israel," and hold your peace (cf. Dt 6:3). If you are occupied in such matters, there will be no place for evil thoughts, and as you pass from one occupation to another, keep in mind only what you are obligated to do in the present.[63]

This is what Saint Jerome says, and in conformity with it, it was the custom in the monasteries to exercise their young men more in good occupations than in solitude and lengthy prayer, because of the danger that might, and at times did, come upon them, because of their flesh and its as yet unmortified passions.

But even this rule has its exceptions, because people have different dispositions and receive their particular gifts from God. Consequently, there may be just cause for allowing a young man to have a long period of time for prayer while shortening that of someone who is older. I said that young men should not be occupied in long prayer. By "long prayer" I mean that in which almost all their time is spent as if they had no other office. But not to permit him to have some periods of prayer would be a very great error because of the goods he would lose. Also, for a person to perform any occupation well, it is necessary for him to gain spirit and strength in prayer. Otherwise, those who are busy at their work often complain and go about grumbling. Without the tenderness of devotion, they are like a heavily loaded cart with squeaky wheels.

Let beginners be warned that the devil particularly tries to trouble them with impure images at the time of prayer. He does this to make them leave prayer and that he may take a rest. Though the devil tires us out a lot with his temptation, we tire him much more, and our devout prayers even set him on fire. Therefore, he tries to prevent us from making them or from making them well. But we must, as it were, stubbornly, do everything possible not to stop our exercise of prayer, for even the persecution that he wages against us demonstrates how advantageous it is. If the war presses down on us while we are praying mentally, and we sense that we are in danger from impure images, we must do everything possible to pray vocally. We can beat our breast, mortify our flesh, extend our arms in the form of a cross, raise our hands and eyes to heaven, asking the Lord for help. In this way we end by spending well the time designated for prayer. We might also do something to distract ourselves, especially speaking with a wise person who may encourage us. However, this last has to be a last resort, lest our weakness become used to trying to conquer by flight, and lest our enemy cause us to leave the battlefield and to lose our strength for fighting. In the end, when it is good for us, our Lord, full of pity and full of power, will command our adversary to keep quiet and not to prevent the secret and friendly conversation we were accustomed to have with the Lord.

## CHAPTER 7

These skirmishes in the war of chastity usually happen when the Lord permits his warriors to be tested to determine if they truly love him and the chastity for which they struggle. Once he has found them faithful, he sends his omnipotent favor and forbids our adversary to hinder our peace and secret conversation with him. Man then rejoices at the work accomplished; he is aware of it, and it is more meritorious.

It is also necessary, and very much so, for preserving chastity, to avoid familiar conversation of women with men, however good or close in relation these men might be. The ugly and unexpected falls that have happened in this world ought to be for us a perpetual warning of our weakness, and the lessons we learn from others' punishment should disabuse us of any false security. Our pride would promise us that we, weak as we are, will pass through without injury, where those who were so strong, wise, and, what is more, such great saints, were very seriously wounded. Who will trust in blood relationship, reading of the error of Ammon with his sister Tamar (2 Sam 13:11–14), and many other very ugly things and worse, which have happened to persons blinded by this bestial passion of the flesh? Who will trust in his own holiness or anyone else's, seeing David, "a man according to God's own heart" (1 Sam 13:14), so blindly fallen into many ugly sins, only for looking at a woman (2 Sam 11:2–4)? Who will not tremble at his own weakness, hearing of the sanctity and wisdom of King Solomon when he was young, and the horrible falls against chastity that corrupted his heart in old age, so that he even set up a throng of idols and adored them as the women he loved did and desired (1 Kgs 11:1–8). Let no one be deceived in this, or trust in chastity past or present, even though he feels his soul to be very strong and hard as a stone against this vice. The experienced Jerome spoke a great truth: "Lust masters souls of iron."[64] Saint Augustine did not want to live in the same house with his sister, saying: "The women who converse with my sister are not my sisters."[65] Through this path of modest reserve all the saints have traveled, and we ought to follow them if we do not wish to stray.

Therefore, my daughter in Christ, do not be careless in this. Rather, hear and fulfill what Saint Bernard says: "Virgins who are truly virgins fear in all things, even in those that are safe."[66] Those who do not act this way are soon seen to be as miserably fallen as at first they were miserably deceived by false security. Even though pardon of sin is obtained through penance, the crown of lost virginity is not attained. It is a horrible thing, says Saint Jerome, if a young woman who was awaiting a crown should have to ask pardon for having lost it.[67] It would be as if the king had a much–loved daughter whom he kept for a marriage in conformity with her dignity. When the time for it came, the daughter told him that she asked pardon for not being ready for the marriage because she had disgracefully lost her virginity. The remedies of penitence, says Saint Jerome, are remedies for misfortunes, and there is no greater misfortune or misery than to commit mortal sin, for the remedy of which penitence is needed.[68] Therefore, you should work with all vigilance to be faithful to the one who has chosen you and to keep what you have promised him, because you know by experience what is written: "Know and see what a bitter thing it is to have left the Lord your God, and that his fear has not been with you" (Jer 2:19). But rejoice at fecundity, and at the name of the chaste spouse, and at the crown that is prepared for such.

## CHAPTER 8

Be aware that the devout do not at first understand their falls as what they are, and for that very reason, such falls are more to be feared. At first, the devout think that they experience benefit in their souls when they engage in conversation. Trusting in this, they accustom themselves to frequent the conversation more often as something safe. Thus is engendered in their hearts a love that captivates them and makes them experience sorrow when they do not see each other and rest when they do see and talk with each other. The next stage is that one attempts to make the other understand the love between them. They enjoy talking about this and about other things for some time, though not as spiritually as at the beginning. Little by little, they experience the conversation that at first had benefited their souls as holding them captive. Each remembers the other many times, and they have the care and desire of seeing each other and of sending loving presents and affectionate messages or letters. These and other similar marks of tenderness, holy love does not have, as Saint Jerome tells us.[69] Step by step, they usually come to realize, much to their cost, that the beginning and middle of the relationship that they had considered of God and free of evil inclination were nothing but the false deceptions of the clever devil. At first, he reassured them so that afterward he might catch them in his hidden trap. So, after they have fallen, they learn that "a man and a woman are nothing if not fire and flax." The demon labors to bring them together, and, once they are together, he blows on them by a thousand ways, intending to set them on fire with the fire of the flesh, and afterward, to lead them to the flames of hell.

Therefore, daughter, flee familiarity with any man, and guard until the end of your life the practice you have adopted of never being alone with any man except your confessor. And be with him only while you are confessing. Even then, tell briefly what is necessary without mixing other conversations, fearing the account you are to give to the strict judge of what you say and hear in the conversation. All the more are you to avoid this in confession, which is for the purpose of taking away sins, not committing other new ones. The medicine is not supposed to make you sick. The spouse of Christ, especially if young, ought not to choose her confessor lightly but should look around for someone mature of good and proven life and reputation. In this way your conscience will be secure before God, and your reputation will be transparent and without stain before men. You should understand that you need both of these things to fulfill the high state of virginity. When you find such a confessor, give thanks to our Lord. Obey and love him as a gift that the Lord has given you.

But, be very careful. Although this love, being spiritual, may be good, it can be excessive and thus place at risk the one who has it. Spiritual love easily becomes carnal love. If you do not restrain yourself, your heart will be as occupied as those of married women with their husbands and children. You already see what disrespect this would be, given the loyalty that you owe to our Lord, whom you took as spouse. As Saint Augustine says, "Jesus Christ is to occupy in your heart all the space that a husband would have occupied, if you had married."[70] Do not then place your spiritual father into the most intimate part of your heart, but keep him near your heart, as a friend of the bridegroom, who is not the spouse. Remember him in order to put his teaching into practice, without dwelling any more on him. Consider him a gift that God has given to help you to be united completely with your heavenly spouse, without interfering in the union. Also, you have to be ready to be patient when you are deprived of him, if God ordains it, for in him alone your hope and support are placed. We read in Saint Jerome that the love and familiarity between him and Saint Paula was within these rules.[71] However, many things, licit and safe for those with sanctity and mature age, are not so for those lacking one or the other or both. Thus you are to conduct yourself with the spiritual father that you choose, and he should be such as I have said.

But if you do not find such a one, it is much better for you to confess and receive communion two or three times a year. You can take account with God and with your good books in your cell, so as not to expose your reputation to risk by confessing many times. Saint Augustine says that "a good reputation with our neighbors is necessary for all of us."[72] How much more necessary will it be for the virgin belonging to Christ? The reputation of these women is very delicate, according to Saint Ambrose.[73] So much is this so that to have a confessor who is lacking in any of the qualities mentioned places a spot on the good name of these women. Because it is a cloth so precious and pure, the stain appears very ugly and is in no way to be tolerated. Some virgins are content with saying, "There is no evil at all; my conscience is clear." They put little stock in their good name. If they resort to saying that some disgrace of this type was imputed to the most holy Virgin Mary, one should answer that her most blessed Son desired that she should be considered married. He preferred that people should take him as Joseph's son, though he was not, than that anyone would say anything evil about his most holy Mother, on the grounds that she had a son without being married. Therefore, let those who do not strive to avoid these scandals look for someone in whom to find protection. From their most holy Mother and from the holy women they can learn purity within and a good reputation and good example without, as well as modesty and prudence in their conversation.

Even if none of these things follows from too much conversation, still one ought to flee it because, with the thoughts that it brings, it deprives the soul of the liberty to fly freely in thought to God. It takes away the purity proper to the secret place of the heart, that place where Christ desires to dwell alone. When there is within the heart the thought of a man, it seems that the heart is not so alone and cut off from every creature as is fitting in the chamber of so majestic a spouse, nor does it possess chastity that is perfectly pure.

Understand that what has been said applies when there is excess in familiarity, or scandal arising from it. When neither of these things is present, you are not to converse in a worried or frightened manner with anyone, since often from this, the same temptation comes. You are to deal with others in holy and prudent simplicity, being neither careless nor malicious.

## CHAPTER 9

In an earlier chapter I told you what a strong weapon prayer is for struggling against the vice of impurity, even when the prayer is not very long. Now you must understand that if the prayer is devout, lengthy, and full of delight in divine sweetness, as is given to some, not only is it a weapon in the fight, but it beheads this beastly vice. When the soul is alone wrestling with God, using the arms of its devout thoughts and affections, it obtains from him in a very special way, like another Jacob (cf. Gen 32:25–30), that God should bless him with a multitude of graces and with a deep tenderness. And the soul remains wounded "in the sinew of his thigh," which means in the sensual appetite, which mortifies itself in such a way that from then on it limps. But it remains alive and strong in its spiritual affections, signified by the other thigh, which remains sound. Just as carnal pleasure makes one lose the taste for and strength of the spirit, so when the spirit has been tasted, the flesh becomes insipid. Sometimes the sweetness that the soul tastes when God visits is so great that the flesh cannot endure it and ends up weak and in a state of collapse, as it would be after having passed through some long physical illness. At other times, with the strengthening that the spirit feels, the flesh is helped and gathers new energy, experiencing in this exile something of what will happen in heaven. Then, since the soul is blessed in her God and full of unspeakable joys, there shall return to the body strength and delight, together with other very precious gifts that the Lord will give.

O sovereign Lord, how inexcusable you have made the fault of those who, for the sake of finding delights in creatures, forsake and offend you! The joys within you are so worthy of esteem that, if all created joys were joined together, they would truly be bitter gall in comparison with your joys. Rightly is this so, for the joy or delight taken from a thing is like the fruit that thing gives of itself. As is the tree, so is the fruit. Therefore, the joy drawn from creatures is brief, vain, tainted, and mingled with sorrow, because the tree from which it is taken has the same qualities. But what deficiency or shortage can touch the joy within you, Lord, since you are eternal, gentle, most simple, most beautiful, and you are unchanging and perfectly infinite good? A partridge tastes like a partridge, and a creature tastes like a creature. Whoever knows who you are, Lord, will know how to say how you taste. Beyond all understanding is your being, and so too is "your sweetness, which you have kept hidden for those that fear you" (Ps 30:20), and for those who renounce from the heart the taste of creatures in order to rejoice in you. You are infinite goodness; you are infinite delight. Because of this, the angels and the blessed in heaven rejoice in you with the strength that you give them, which is not small. If countless more joined with the blessed to rejoice in you with even greater strength, the ocean of your sweetness is so boundless that even with them swimming and walking in it, intoxicated and full of sweetness, there would remain infinitely more to enjoy. If you, omnipotent Lord, did not rejoice in yourself with the infinite strength that you have, the delight within you would remain complaining, as it were, because there would be no one to enjoy all that there is to enjoy.

Wisest Lord, as our Creator you know that we are inclined to rest and delight, and that a soul cannot be long without looking for consolation, either good or bad. You invite us through holy delights in you, lest we get lost by looking for evil delights in creatures. It is your voice, Lord, that says: "Come to me, all you that are weary and burdened, and I will refresh you" (Matt 11:28). You commanded that it be proclaimed in your name: "All you that thirst, come to the waters" (Isa 55:1). You showed us that "there are delights at your right hand that last even to the end" (cf. Ps 16:11), and that "from the river of your delight," without measure or fee, "you will give your own to drink" in your kingdom (Ps 36:9). Sometimes you give your friends a taste of this here when you say to them: "Eat and drink and be inebriated, my beloved friends" (Song 5:1). All this, Lord, is with the desire of attracting to yourself by delight those you know are such good friends of delight. Let no one, then, Lord, find fault with you by saying that you lack goodness to be loved or delight to be enjoyed, and let no one search for pleasing or delightful conversation outside of you. For the reward that you are to give your own is to say to them: "Enter into the joy of your Lord" (cf. Matt 25:23). From what you eat and drink, they will eat and drink, and with the same joy that you rejoice, they will rejoice, because you have invited them to "eat at your table in the kingdom of your Father" (cf. Luke 22:30).

What will you say to these things, carnal man? You are so deceived that your deception reaches to the point of enjoying the foul delights of the flesh. Base and evil men, and even the beasts of the fields, enjoy these in the greatest abundance. They enjoy them more than the sovereign tenderness in God, in which the saints and angels rejoice, as does God himself, the Creator of them all. It is a thing of beasts that you value and love, and your passions are beasts. You place the most high God beneath the feet of your most vile beasts as often as you offend him with your carnal pleasures.

Flee, daughter, from anything as evil as this. Climb the mountain of prayer (cf. Song 8:14). Beg the Lord to give you some delight in him, so that, your soul having been animated by his sweetness, you may despise the muddy pleasures of the flesh. You will then have profound compassion for people who go along lost in the lowly valleys of a bestial life. In dread you will say: "O people, how much you are losing! And for what? You are losing the dearest God for the vilest flesh! And what punishment is merited by such a false weight but eternal torment?" And certainly, it will be given to them.

**CHAPTER 10**

The advice that you have heard as remedy for this infirmity has to do with things that you ordinarily must practice, even outside the time of temptation. Now listen to what you must do when it attacks you and deals the first blow. Immediately make the sign of the cross on your forehead and heart, invoking with devotion the holy name of Jesus Christ. Say: "I will not sell God so cheap! O Lord, you are worth more, and I love you more."

If the temptation does not leave you with this, descend by thought to hell. See how terribly that lively fire burns and makes the wretches who burned here with the fire of lust, cry out and howl and blaspheme as the sentence of God is carried out on them: "Give her as much torment and sorrow as she glorified herself in delights" (Rev 18:7). Feel terror in the face of such grave punishment, even though completely just, and that a moment's delight is punished by eternal torments. Say within yourself what Saint Gregory says: "Momentary is that which delights and eternal that which torments."[74]

If this does not benefit you, ascend by thought to heaven. Represent to yourself the purity of chastity in that blessed city, and how "no beast will be able to enter there" (cf. Isa 35:9), which means no bestial man. Remain there a while, until you experience some spiritual strength, whereby here you may abhor what there God abhors.

Also, it helps to think of the body in the tomb, and to look very carefully at how repulsive and in what state the bodies of men and women are there. After this, it also helps to have recourse to Jesus Christ on the cross, especially when he is tied to the column and beaten, bathed in blood from head to foot. Say to him with loving sighs: "Your virginal and divine body, Lord, is so tormented and full of grievous pains. Can I, who am worthy of every punishment, desire delights for my body? Since you pay with such cruel blows for the delights that men enjoy against your will, I do not want to have enjoyment that is so costly to you, Lord."

Likewise, it may help you to represent before you in an instant the most pure Virgin Mary. Consider the purity of her heart and the integrity of her body. Immediately abhor the indecency that came upon you, as darkness that vanishes in the presence of light. But, if you know how to shut tightly the door of your understanding, as is usually done in the intimate recollection of prayer, as we shall say below, you will easily find help closer at hand than in the other remedies. Many times it happens that when we open the door for a good thought, the evil one slips in. But closing the door to both, we turn our backs on our enemies and do not open the door until they have left. Thus they are left in scorn.

Other things that may help are to extend the arms in the form of a cross, to kneel down, and to strike one's breast. What helps more, or as much as all others together, is to receive, with fitting preparation, the holy body of Jesus Christ our Lord, who was formed by the Holy Spirit and is very far from all impurity. It is a wonderful remedy for the ills that come to us from our flesh, conceived in sin. If we knew how to ponder well the gift we receive, by which Jesus Christ enters into us, we would consider ourselves as precious reliquaries. We would flee from all sordidness for the honor of the one who entered into us. With what heart is one able to harm his body when it has been honored by being joined with the most holy body of God made man? What greater obligation could be thrust upon me? What greater motive could be given me for living purely than to see with my eyes, touch with my hands, receive with my mouth, place in my breast, the most pure body of our Lord Jesus Christ? He gives me an ineffable honor so that I may not return to baseness but may attach myself to him and dedicate myself to him through his coming to me. How or with what body will I offend the Lord, since into my body the author of purity has entered? I have eaten him and eaten with him at one table. Am I going to be a traitor now or at any point in my life? It is right that we thus esteem this gift, so that we, in our weakness, may receive the crown. But if we receive or treat him badly, the contrary effect follows. Such a man experiences himself more possessed by impurity than he was before he had received communion.

If with all these considerations and remedies, the bestial flesh is not quieted, you must treat it as a beast, burdening it with salutary afflictions, since it does not understand such right reasons. Some experience a remedy in pinching themselves hard, recalling the excessive pain that the nails caused our Lord Jesus Christ. Others discipline themselves, remembering how our Lord was struck. Others extend their arms in the form of a cross or lift their eyes to heaven or strike their faces, or do other things like these that cause pain in the flesh that, in this moment, does not understand any other language. We read that past saints acted in this way. One stripped and rolled naked in thorny bushes and, by hurting the body to the point of blood, ended its war against the soul. Another, during winter, placed himself in a lake with very cold water and stayed there until his body was half dead. But his soul was free of all danger. Another placed his fingers into a fire and, by burning some of them, extinguished the fire tormenting his soul. One martyr, bound hand and foot, with the pain of cutting off his tongue with his own teeth, emerged the conqueror in this battle. Some of these things are not to be imitated, because they were done by a particular instinct from the Holy Spirit and not according to the normal standard. However, we ought to learn from them that, in time of war, when the life of the soul is at stake, we ought not to be quiet or lazy, waiting for our enemies to strike blows against us. Rather, we should recoil before sin "as before a serpent" (Sir 21:2), as scripture says. Each one must take the remedy that is most appropriate for him and as his prudent confessor directs him.

**CHAPTER 11**

No cost or labor spent to guard chastity should seem too much to anyone that knows how to esteem its price and merit, as well as its reward. Since our Lord has made you understand the value of this jewel and has given you the grace to choose and promise it, I do not need so much to tell you about its excellence as to give you some advice so that you may not lose it. I will show you some causes, other than those already mentioned, why some do lose it, so that recognizing these, you may avoid them, so as to not lose chastity and yourself with it.

Some lose it because they have strong natural inclinations against it. So as not to be bothered and not to engage in such a hard and cruel war against themselves, they, with shameful purpose, surrender hand-cuffed to their enemies. They do not understand that the Christian's intention must be to die or to conquer, with the grace of him who helps those who fight for his honor.

There are others who, although not seriously tempted, have a natural baseness and meanness of heart that inclines them to base things. Since this is something vile and base and is close at hand, they quickly meet up with it and give themselves to it as to something proportionate to their base and corrupt hearts that do not elevate them to undertake any sort of human life directed by reason. Taught by reason alone, one man said that in carnal delights, there is nothing worthy of a magnanimous heart. Another said that the life of carnal delights is the life of beasts. This is so because, not only the light of heaven, but even that of natural reason, condemns those who yield themselves to this baseness. They are people who do not live as human beings, whose life is meant to be in harmony with reason, but like beasts, whose life is ruled by appetite. Seen rightly, it would be possible with justice to take from such as these the name of men, for, while they have human form, they live the life of beasts and are the dishonor of men. It would be no little monstrosity and would cause no little wonder to those who saw it, that a beast should bridle and lead a man wherever it wanted, ruling the one that ought to rule it.

Many, both low and high, are ruled by the bridle of their bestial appetites. I do not know if there are so many that no one notices, or—as I think more likely—few have light to see how wretched is a soul, dead because of carnal pleasures, beneath a body that is especially beautiful and young. How many souls of these and others are burning in this infernal fire, without anyone to shed tears of compassion or to pray from the heart, "To you, Lord, will I cry, because fire has devoured the beautiful things of the wilderness!" (Joel 1:19). Certainly, if there had been widows in Naim, weeping bitterly over their sons whose souls were dead, Christ would have used his mercy to revive them, just as he used it to raise the body of the son of the other widow, of whom the gospel makes mention (cf. Luke 7:11–15). The one in the church who has the office of praying and interceding for the people with the affection of a mother must not fall asleep lest God punish both the one who has this obligation of praying and his people. "I sought among them for a man that would set himself as a wall and would set himself against me so that I would not destroy the earth, but I found no one. And I poured out over them my anger, and in the fire of my wrath, I consumed them" (Ezek 22:30–31).

Take care then not to have a heart so small and base that these vile things please you and you content yourself with them. Remember what Saint Bernard says, that if you consider the body and what issues from it, it is more loathsome than anything else you have seen. Heartily despise it together with all its delights, finery, and splendor. Consider it as already in the tomb, changed into a handful of earth. When you see some man or woman, do not pay too much attention to the face or the body, or, if you do look at it, let it be without satisfaction. Instead, direct your inner eyes to the soul that is shut up and hidden in the body. In it, there is no difference between man and woman. Praise that soul as a creature of God, for one single soul is more precious than all bodies already created and to be created.

Having separated yourself thus from the lowliness of bodies, search for greater goods and undertake noble endeavors, no less than to make God welcome in your body and in your soul, by profound purity of heart. Look at yourself with these eyes, for Saint Paul says, "Do you not know that you are temples of God and that the Spirit of God dwells in you?" (1 Cor 3:16). And in another place he says, "Do you not know that your members are temples of the Holy Spirit who dwells in you, the one whom God has given you, and that you are not your own? You have been bought at a high price. Glorify God in your body" (1 Cor 6:19–20). Consider, then, that when you received holy baptism, you were made a temple of God, and your soul was consecrated to him by his grace. So, too, your body was consecrated by being touched with holy water. The Holy Spirit, as master of the house, makes use of the soul and the body, moving the one and the other toward good works. For this reason, it is said that "our members are the temple of the Holy Spirit." God honors us greatly by desiring to dwell within us and ennobling us with the truth and the name of temple. He casts upon us the great obligation that we be "pure," since "purity is fitting for the house of God" (cf. Ps 93:5). Consider that, as Saint Paul puts it, you were bought "at a high price," the life of God–made–man who handed himself over for you. Then you will see how reasonable it is that you "honor God" and bear him "in your body," serving him with it, and not doing anything in it that may be for the dishonor of God and your own harm. This is because it is a true and just sentence that "whoever profanes the temple of God, God will destroy him" (1 Cor 3:16). It is also true that there should be nothing in his temple except what is for his honor and glory. Remember what Saint Augustine said: "After I understood that God had redeemed me and bought me with his precious blood, I decided that I would never sell myself again."[75] And you might add, "How much less will I sell myself for the baseness of the flesh."

You have begun a work for which a great deal of courage is needed: you desire to possess incorruption in corruptible flesh; you desire to have as your way of virtue what the angels have by nature; you desire to aspire to a special crown in heaven as a companion of the virgins who "sing the new song and accompany the Lamb wherever he goes" (Rev 14:4). Consider well the title that you now have as spouse of Christ. Consider also the good that you hope for in heaven when your spouse places you there in his wedding chamber. Then you will so love the purity of virginity that you will gladly lose your life for it, as many holy virgins have done who, to avoid losing virginity, suffered martyrdom with greatness of heart. You also must endeavor to have a great heart, for it is very necessary for persevering in the high state in which God has placed you.

**CHAPTER 12**

There have been others who have lost the jewel of chastity when God punished them by his just judgment. As Saint Paul says, "He gave them up to the indecent desires of their hearts" (Rom 1:24) as into the hands of cruel executioners, thus punishing their sins by other sins. He did not incite them to sin, for it is very far from the Supreme Good to cause anyone to sin. But he does take his help from a man because of his sins. This is the work of a just judge, and if he is just, he is also good. Thus scripture says, "A deep well is the wicked woman and a narrow well is the wife of another" (Prov 23:27). "He that the Lord is angry with will fall into it" (Prov 22:14). Let no one be unafraid of offending God in the area of chastity if he offends him in other things. For God is wont to let a man fall into what he was not wont to fall into and did not want to fall into, as punishment for falling into other things he should have avoided.

This is true with regard to all sins, since God is angered by them all and is wont to punish them. But, as Saint Augustine says, God is especially "wont to punish secret pride with manifest lust."[76] An example of this is Nebuchadnezzar. In punishment for his pride, he lost his kingdom and "he was cast out from conversation with men, and a beast's heart was given to him, and he dwelt among the beasts" (cf. Dan 4:13, 22, 29, 30). It was not that he had lost his human nature, but that, even to himself, he seemed not to be human. He was like this until God gave him the knowledge and humility to recognize and confess that "majesty and dominion belong to God and that he gives them to whomever he wishes" (cf. Dan 4:14). Surely, it happens in this way. God casts out from among his own the one who attributes the building of chastity to his own strength. Once he has departed from the company that was like to the angels, he dwells among the beasts. He has a heart so bestial that it is as if it had never loved God, or known what chastity is, or known that there are realities such as hell or glory or reason or shame. So much is this the case that they themselves are appalled at what they do. It seems to them that they have not human judgment or strength but are like beasts, completely given over to this beastly vice. This continues until the Lord in his mercy has compassion on such misery. He lets the one that has thus fallen know that he fell through pride, and that he is to rise up and recover by means of humility. Then he confesses that the dominion of chastity, by which he was reigning over his body, is a gift of God that he gives through his grace, and takes away because of men's sins.

The evil of pride is difficult to recognize and therefore much to be feared. At times, a man has it so buried in the secret chamber of his heart that he himself does not perceive it. Saint Peter and many others witness to this (cf. John 13:36–38; Mark 14:29–31). While they were self–satisfied and self–confident, they thought that they were trusting in God. In his infinite wisdom he sees their infirmity and, by his mercy and justice together, cures and heals them. He makes them understand, even to their cost—since they see themselves so miserably fallen—that they were mistakenly satisfied and mistakenly confident in themselves. Though the fall is costly, it is not as dangerous as the secret evil of pride in which they were living before. For if they do not recognize pride, they do not seek a remedy, and so, they are lost. But understanding their wickedness through their fall, and having humbled themselves before God's mercy, they obtain his remedy for both ills. Because of this, Saint Augustine said that "God punishes secret pride with manifest lust."[77] The second evil is manifest to the one who commits it, and, through it, he comes to know the other secret evil that he had.

You should know that these people are sometimes proud only within themselves and sometimes through disdain for their neighbor, because they see them as having little virtue, especially with regard to chastity. But, Lord, how displeasing to you were the thanks the

Pharisee gave you when he said: "I am not wicked like other men, nor am I an adulterer or a thief, as is that tax collector there!" (Luke 18:11). You do not leave him, Lord, without punishment. You do punish him, and very severely. To punish his sin, you allow the one standing to fall, and to satisfy for the insult against him, you raise the fallen. There is a sentence of yours that you observe very well: "Do not condemn and you will not be condemned" (Luke 6:37). "With the same measure that you measure, you will be measured," and "Whoever exalts himself shall be humbled" (Matt 7:2; 23:12). You commanded that it be published as coming from you to those who despise their neighbors: "Woe to you who despise, for you shall be despised" (cf. Isa 33:1). How many people I have seen punished according to this sentence! They never understood how much God abhors this sin until they found themselves fallen into that which they had judged in others, and even into worse things. "In three things," said an old man of long ago, "I judged my neighbor, and into each of the three, I have fallen."

Let one who is chaste thank God for his favor and live in fear and trembling lest he fall. Let him help the fallen to rise, taking compassion on him and not despising him. Let him realize that he and the fallen one are of the same clay and that, just as the other falls, so too does he, insofar as the matter rests with him. As Saint Augustine puts it, "There is no sin that one man commits, that another man would not also commit, if the Maker of man were not guiding him."[78] Let one who is chaste benefit from another's ill–fortune by humbling himself when he sees the other fall. Let him benefit from the good of another by rejoicing at the good of the neighbor. Let him not be like the poisonous serpent that draws evil out of everything: pride out of the falls of others and envy out of their prosperity. Such people do not escape God's punishment. He will let them fall into the same things as others have, and he will not give them the good things they envied.

## CHAPTER 13

Among the miserable failures in chastity known in history, we ought not to forget that of the king and prophet David. The fall was so miserable, and the one who fell was so highly esteemed, that it gives the listener a great lesson, namely, that there is no one who may cease to fear his own frailty. Saint Basil says that David fell because of the slight complacency that he had in himself once the hand of God visited him with an abundance of consolation.[79] He dared to say, "I said in my abundance, I shall never be moved" from this state (cf. Ps 30:6). But how differently the thing turned out! How he understood afterward what he did not understand before! "In the day of good things, we ought to remember the evils into which we can fall" (cf. Sir 11:25). We should accept divine consolation with the balance of humility, accompanied by the holy fear of God, so as not to have to experience what David then said: "You hid your face from me and I was troubled" (Ps 30:7).

Holy scripture shows us another cause of his fall, saying that "at the time when the kings of Israel would go to war" against the infidels, "King David stayed at home and, taking a walk along a terrace (cf. 2 Sam 11:1–2), he saw" that which became the cause of his adultery and the murder, not of one, but of many men. All of this would have been avoided if he had gone to wage the wars of God as other kings were accustomed to do, and as he himself had done in other years.

Perhaps you are strolling about when the servants of God are recollected and at leisure when they are laboring in good works. Perhaps you cast your eyes about without restraint, when others are weeping bitterly with theirs, for themselves and for others. Perhaps when they are rising at night to pray, you remain asleep and snoring. Perhaps, for any whim at all, you abandon the good spiritual practices you used to have, that, by their strength and ardor, kept you standing. How then do you expect to keep chastity when you are so careless and without arms to defend it, and when there are so many strong, vigilant, and well–armed enemies who fight against it? Do not deceive yourself. If your desire to be chaste is not accompanied by works in defense of your chastity, your desire will be in vain. What happened to David will happen to you, for you are no more privileged or strong or holy than he was.

To conclude this material on the causes by which the precious jewel of chastity is usually lost, you should know why God permitted the flesh to rise up against reason in our first parents, whose heirs we are. Because they rose up against God by disobeying his command, he punished them by that in which they sinned. So it was that, since they did not obey their superior, their inferior did not obey them. Thus, the rebellion of the flesh, a slave and a subject, against its superior, reason, is the punishment of the disobedience of reason against God, its superior. Consequently, guard yourself carefully against disobeying your superiors lest God permit your inferior, the flesh, to rise up against you, as he permitted that Adad should arise against King Solomon, his lord (cf. 1 Kgs 11:14 ff.). Then the rebellious flesh would flog and harass you, and because of your weakness, cast you down into the depth of mortal sin.

If you have understood well in the interior of your heart the things that you have read with your bodily eyes, you will see how right it is to watch out for yourself and what is within you. Because you cannot know yourself, you should beg our Lord for the light to search the most secret corners of your heart. Let there be nothing in you, known or unknown, by which you run the risk of losing, by some secret judgment of God, the jewel of chastity, which is so important that it should be guarded with divine protection.

## CHAPTER 14

All that has been said and more that could be said concern the usual means to attain this precious purity. But many times it happens as with the building of a house. After bringing stone and wood and everything needed, we do not get around to actually building the house. In the same way it happens that, in spite of using all remedies, we do not attain the chastity desired. To the contrary, there are many who, after lively desires and great labors, see themselves miserably fallen or violently tormented by the flesh. They say with great sorrow: "We have labored all the night and have taken nothing" (Luke 5:5). It seems to them that what the Sage says is fulfilled in them: "The more I sought it, the more it fled from me" (Eccl 7:23–24). This often happens because of a secret self–confidence that these proud laborers have in themselves. They think of chastity as the fruit of their own efforts rather than as a gift given by God. Since they do not know from whom the gift must be asked, they rightly remain deprived of it. It would be greater harm for them to possess it, when they are proud and ungrateful to the Giver, than to be without it, weeping, humbled, and pardoned by penance. It is no little wisdom to know whose gift chastity is, and a person has covered a good part of the way toward obtaining it when he realizes that it does not come from human strength but from our Lord's gift. This is what the holy gospel teaches us when it says: "Not all are capable of this word, but they to whom it is given by God" (Matt 19:11). Even though the remedies already mentioned to obtain this virtue are helpful and should be used, it has to be on condition that we do not put our trust in them. Rather, let us devoutly pray to God as David did, and advised us to do, saying, "I have lifted up my eyes to the mountains, whence help shall come to me. My help is from the Lord, who made heaven and earth" (Ps 121:1–2).

The glorious Jerome is a good witness to all this. He recounts how temptations of the flesh placed him in affliction so great that nothing freed him, neither strict fasts, nor sleeping on the ground, nor long vigil, nor that his body was half dead. Then, like a man deprived of all help and unable to find a remedy in any remedy, he threw himself at the feet of Jesus Christ our Lord, bathed them with his tears, and dried them with the hair of his devout thoughts. Sometimes he cried out to Christ night and day. But finally, he was heard, and God gave him the desire of his heart, as well as such great serenity and spiritual consolation that it seemed to him that he was among the choirs of angels.[80] In this way God helps those who call on him with their whole heart and who remain faithful in the war until he sends them help.

Not only must we call upon God to favor us, but we must also call upon his saints. These are signified by the "mountains" of which David speaks here (Ps 121:1). Especially, more than any others, we must invoke the most pure Virgin Mary, asking her persistently by acts of veneration and by prayers to obtain this grace for us. She will gladly receive our acts of veneration and hear our prayers because she is a true lover of what we are imploring. I have especially seen great favors coming from this blessed Lady upon persons troubled by temptations of the flesh. They have been helped by praying some prayer in memory of the purity whereby she was conceived without sin and of that virginal chastity by which she conceived the Son of God. Take this blessed Lady then for your special advocate, so that, through her prayers, she may obtain and preserve your purity. Consider that some women of this world are such friends of purity that they support with all their strength anyone who wants to leave behind the baseness of vice and to walk along the path of pure chastity. How much more must we expect this most pure Virgin of virgins to turn her eyes and ears to the services and prayers of those who desire to preserve the chastity that she so dearly loves?

Be sure that you do not lack the desire for this great good. Do not fail in confidence in Christ or in persistent prayer and other actions that we have mentioned. For his saints will not fail to love, care, and pray for us, and there will be no lack of heavenly mercy in granting this gift that God alone gives. He desires that anyone who receives it should recognize it as his gift and glorify him, as indeed is his due.

## CHAPTER 15

It is necessary to consider attentively that God does not give this gift equally to all, but differently according to his holy will. To some he gives more and to others less. To some he gives chastity of soul. This consists in a firm and deliberate purpose not to fall into the opposite vice for anything whatsoever. Yet together with this good intention, such a one may have in his soul foul imaginings and painful temptations in the sensitive part of his soul. Though they do not cause the reasonable part to consent to evil, they do afflict the person and make him defend himself against their pestering. This is like Moses and his people. When he was atop the mountain in God's company, the people were at its foot adoring idols (cf. Exod 32:7–9). Whoever is in this state ought to thank our Lord for the good he has given to his soul and to endure patiently the poor obedience that his sensitive part gives him. If Eve alone had eaten from the forbidden tree, and Adam, her husband, had not consented and eaten, the original sin would not have been committed (cf. Gen 3:6). Just so, while that firm purpose of not consenting to any evil is alive in the highest part of the soul, the sensitive part, no matter how much it may eat, cannot commit mortal sin. This is because her husband does not consent with her but is displeased and reprimands her. In this, you see that you must be on guard so as not to allow images or movements to stay within you but to drive them away. For if anyone sees the danger in which he is, with that hellish fire within him and the serpent in his bosom, and does not cast them out, his negligence is a mortal sin, since he saw the danger and loved it by not casting it out. This is all the more so if he has experienced at other times that, from this, he is wont to consent to the evil action or delight. But as long as you keep a lively purpose of not consenting to the evil action or delight, but of resisting, even if weakly, when you see the danger in which you are, you are to think that the Lord has not allowed you to fall into mortal sin. Because in this it is difficult to give a certain judgment without information from the one suffering, it is important to speak about it with a wise confessor and to accept his advice. If, with all this, it upsets you to suffer such a continuous war within yourself, consider that by the trouble of temptation, past sins are purged, and a man is animated to serve God better, since he sees how much he needs him. Also, as foolish as we are, we recognize our weakness when we find ourselves in such great danger and on the horns of the bull. If God should remove his hand from us even a little, we would fall into the terrifying abyss of mortal sin. Until you acknowledge and confess this weakness, temptations of the flesh will not cease in you. They are like torture and blows that will make you confess that no good dwells within you unless it is given you from above. If you are a faithful servant of God, the more your flesh attacks you, so much the more will you strive with all your soul to guard your chastity. Then the temptations will be like blows that help to root you more completely in purity, and you will see the wonders of God. Just as his greater goodness appears on the

71

occasion of our wickedness, so in our weakness, his strength works in the soul. Thus, the spirit refuses the invitation of the flesh and affirms itself anew in the love of chastity as often as the flesh invites it to lose it. By means of such a troublesome and vile obstacle, God works the opposite, which is precious and praiseworthy. It is chastity.

Keep in mind that a good war is better than a bad peace. It is better to labor not to consent, and thus give pleasure to the Lord, than to take for ourselves a little animal pleasure that, once passed, leaves double affliction and causes us to displease the one we ought to love and please. Call upon him with humility and confidence, for he will not fail to succor one who fights for his honor. In the end, he will make you come out of this struggle with gain, and he will count this labor as if it were martyrdom. Just as the martyrs preferred to die rather than deny the faith, so you should prefer to suffer what you suffer, as long as you do not break his holy will. He will make you a companion of the martyrs in glory since you were their companion here in trouble. Meanwhile, be consoled that you have within you a proof that you love God, since for love of him, you do not do that for which your flesh longs.

## CHAPTER 16

To others, our Lord gives this blessing of chastity more abundantly. Not only does he give their souls this hatred for such delights, but they possess such moderation and peace in their flesh that they enjoy great peace and scarcely know what a troublesome temptation is. This usually happens in two ways. Some possess peace and purity by their natural constitution, while others possess it through election and the grace of God.

Those who possess chastity by their natural constitution ought not to be too conceited at the peace they have, nor should they look down on anyone they see tempted. The virtue of chastity is not measured by having this peace but by having the firm purpose in the soul of not offending the Lord by this sin. If a person, while tempted in the flesh, has this good purpose more firmly in his soul than the other who lacks these struggles, he will be more chaste in his combat than the other will be in his peace. But neither should those with this natural constitution be discouraged and say, "I do or gain little in being chaste." Rather, they ought to take advantage of their good inclination and, with their spirit, choose, for the sake of pleasing God, that chastity to which their inclination invites them. In this way they will serve God with the higher part of their soul by their virtuous choice, and in their sensitive part, by their obedience and good inclination.

There are others who are chaste, not by natural inclination, but by the grace of our Lord. These experience in their souls a deep hatred for this vileness, and in their sensitive part, such obedience that they do not drag themselves to what reason commands, but obey readily and with delight. In both parts they experience profound peace. Some philosophers described this excellent condition. They said that there were some men so excellent and with spirits so purified that not only did they do the good without war from the passions, but that the passions were so vanquished that they almost forgot about them. Not only did the passions not conquer these men, they did not even engage them in battle. Philosophers talked about this virtue without possessing it because without grace there is no true virtue. But good Christians possess it, those to whom God wills to grant this perfect gift. They have not won it by effort, but God has granted it to them through his strong and celestial Holy Spirit, given through Jesus Christ our Lord. They are in the likeness of the same Lord, who kept the integrity of virginity in corruptible flesh.

This heavenly Spirit infuses perfect chastity in those that he wants. He so does this that the superior part of the soul is perfectly subject to God in obedience and receives from him mighty strength and brilliant light. So perfectly is it united with him and so ruled by his will that, as the Apostle says, "He who is joined to the Lord, is one spirit with him" (1 Cor 6:17). Furthermore, such is the efficacy of God, who infuses strength and puts a disposition in the sensitive part of the soul, that he causes the person to leave behind bestiality and its natural ferocity and to obey reason with delight and complete subjection to it. Although the parts are diverse in nature, with one being spiritual and the other sensual, yet the sensitive part adheres so closely to reason and accepts its restraint so well that it goes its way subject and docile. The sensitive part is not reason, but it walks reasonably, not hindering but helping the spirit, as a faithful wife helps her husband. The souls of some people are so miserably given to the flesh that its appetite is the only compass directing them. Though they are of a spiritual nature, they yield to a miserable subjection to their bodies. So transformed are they into their flesh that they become nothing but flesh. In their will and in their thinking, they appear to be nothing more than a lump of flesh, just as the sensuality of the others is so joined with reason that it seems more like reason than even the souls of the others do.

All this appears difficult to believe, but, in the end, it is God's work and gift through Jesus Christ, his only Son, especially in the time of the Christian Church. Of this time it was prophesied that "the wolf and the lamb, the bear and the lion, would eat together" (Isa 11:6). This means that the irrational inclinations of the sensitive part, that like wild animals wanted to mistreat and swallow up the soul, are pacified by the gift of Jesus Christ. Having abandoned their own war, they live in peace. As Job says, "The beasts of the earth shall live in peace with you, and you shall have friendship with the stones of the region" (Job 5:22–23). Then is fulfilled what is written in the psalm that says, "You, O man, had one soul with me, and you were my guide and my familiar friend; you ate sweet foods with me, and we walked together in the house of God" (Ps 55:14–15). The interior man addresses these words to the exterior, holding him so subject that he says that they have only one soul, and so conformed to his will that he says that they ate sweet foods together and walked together in the house of God. This means that they are such friends that, if the interior man nourishes himself on chastity or prayer or fasts or keeping vigil, or if he performs other holy exercises and finds great sweetness in them, the exterior man also performs these works and savors them as a sweet delicacy.

But do not think because of this that anyone in this exile arrives at the possession of such an abundance of peace that he does not at times experience movements against reason in this or in other things. Except to Christ our Redeemer and to his holy Mother, this privilege has not been granted to anyone. But you have to understand that, even though these motions occur in persons to whom God has given this gift of chastity, they are not of such a kind or number that they cause a lot of trouble. Without being put into the difficulty of great struggle and without being deprived of true peace, those who receive the gift of chastity easily overcome these motions. If the inhabitants of a city are in peace, and we see there two boys quarreling and then making up, we will not say that because of this short fight there is no peace in the city. Since the philosophers acknowledged this state without knowing the strength of the Holy Spirit, it ought not to be difficult for Christians to confess and desire it for the glory of the redemption and power of Christ, for whom nothing is impossible. Of his coming, it was prophesied that there was going to be an "abundance of peace" (cf. Ps 72:3, 7). Isaiah says that the peace is to be "like a river" (Isa 66:12), and Saint Paul says that "it surpasses all understanding" (Phil 4:7).

Well then, when the flesh is thus obedient and quieted, then we shall indeed be far from listening to its language and free from falling under the terrible curse that God cast upon Adam, our father "because he listened to his wife" (Gen 3:17). Instead, we make her serve and obey us, and we teach her, like a bird in its cage, to speak our language.

And she learns it and obeys us with alacrity. From long obedience to reason, she becomes so well practiced that, if she asks for anything, it is not for delights, but for necessity. Then we can well hear her, as God commanded Abraham that "he should pay attention to Sara, his wife" (cf. Gen 21:12), who was already very old, and her flesh was so weakened and worn that she no longer had the periods that younger women have (cf. Gen 18:11).

However, we should not trust the flesh so completely that its word alone is sufficient for us. Instead, we must examine it with prudence of spirit, since it may not be dead, as we thought, but deceptively playing dead. In that case, the more trustworthy we considered it, the more dangerously does it bring us down.

# 3. Language of the Devil (chaps. 17–30)

## CHAPTER 17

The languages of the devil are as innumerable as the types of his malice. For just as Christ is the fountain of all the graces communicated to the souls of those who submit themselves obediently to him, so the devil is the father of sins and darkness. By inciting and persuading his wretched sheep, he induces them to wickedness and lies, so that they might perish eternally. Since his deceits are so many that only the Spirit of the Lord can discover them, we will say only a few words and leave the rest to Christ, the true teacher of our souls.

The devil is called by many names in order to express the evils within him. From among these names, we will speak of two, *dragon* and *lion*. He is called a dragon, says Saint Augustine, because he secretly lays traps; he is called a lion because he openly pursues.[81] The trap that the devil lays to deceive is this. He exalts us with vanity and lies, and afterward knocks us down in a truly miserable fall. He puffs us up with thoughts that incline us to high self–esteem in something, and thus makes us fall into pride. He knows through experience that this evil was enough to change him from an angel into a demon. So he works with all his might to make us like him in pride so that we may be like him in his torments. He knows very well how displeasing pride is to God, and that, by itself, it is enough to render useless everything else that a person may possess, however good it may appear. The devil works very hard to sow this bad seed in the soul. Many times he even speaks the truth and gives good advice and devout feelings, solely for the purpose of inducing us to pride. He counts it as a small loss that someone does something good, as long as he is able to win that person completely by the sin of pride and the other sins that follow in its train. Just as a king usually comes accompanied by many people, so pride comes accompanied by many other sins. Scripture says: "Pride is the beginning of all sin, and whoever has it shall be filled with maledictions" (cf. Sir 10:15). This means that he will be full both of sins and of punishments.

We read of a solitary to whom the devil appeared for a long time in the form of an angel of God and gave many revelations. Every night, the devil illuminated the hermit's cell as though with the brightness of a candle or a lamp. After all this, he persuaded the hermit that he should kill his own son so that he would be equal in merits to the patriarch Abraham (cf. Gen 22:1ff.). Having been deceived, the solitary would have been ready to do this if the son had not suspected it and fled.

To another also the devil appeared in the form of an angel and, over a long period of time, told him much that was true in order to win his trust. Afterward, when the devil told him a great lie against the faith, the man, having been deceived, believed it.

We read of yet another who had lived fifty years in the most singular abstinence and in stricter solitude than any of the others in that desert. The devil, in the form of an angel, made this man think that he should throw himself into a very deep well in order to prove by his own experience that neither this action nor any other could harm one who had served God as much as he had. The man believed all of this and carried it out. After he was, with great labor, taken out of the well half dead, the holy fathers of the desert warned him that he should repent of his action because it had been an illusion from the devil. But he would neither believe them nor do what they suggested. What is worse is that the deception had taken such deep root in his heart that, even though he saw himself dying because of the fall (for he died three days later), he still believed that it had been a revelation of an angel of God.

Oh, how helpful it is for those advanced in virtue to live in holy fear of themselves, as people who, although they may conjecture that they stand in God's favor, have no certainty of this. They do not know if they are worthy of love or of hate in the present, and even less do they know what will become of them in the remainder of their lives! Especially they must take care not to believe a great deal in themselves, remembering that profound saying of Saint Augustine: "Pride deserves to be deceived."[82]

If I were to recount deceptions that people have suffered in the present as I have told you about the past, I would not be able to write them in a small book, and you would not be able to read them without great weariness. On the one hand, as far as we can judge, God pours into many hearts the rain of his particular mercies, through which they produce good fruit, even externally. They also enjoy interior communication with our Lord, so familiar that it can hardly be believed. On the other hand, we also have experience of how the devil, by God's permission, is particularly diligent at these times. His purpose is to deceive those who are proud and attached to their own opinion as though it were the will of God. He does this by false sentiments, false speeches, both interior and exterior, and false light for the understanding. God allows all this to exercise in various ways those who serve him with humility and prudence. Therefore, in the times when it appears that Satan has been set loose, as Saint John says (Rev 20:7), God's servants ought to be doubly careful not to believe things too easily. They ought to have profound humility and holy fear so that God may not permit them to be deceived. They should promptly take account of what they feel and yield in these things to their prelates and superiors, who are able to instruct them in the truth.

The prophet says that "under the tongue of the wicked is the venom of vipers" (Ps 140:4). How much more will this be so with the language of the devil, the most wicked of all the wicked? If he should try to exalt us, let us humble ourselves by considering the wicked things we do and have done. These have been very great. If the Lord were not near us in his great mercy, and if he had not come into our path—as he did with Saint Paul—as we were walking along with hearts disposed to leave him, we would be growing in wickedness as in age, to the point where the torments of hell would be slight punishment. O Abyss of mercy! What moved you to call out to our hearts from heaven and to say, "Why do you persecute me" (cf. Acts 9:4) by your wicked life? With these words you knock us down from our pride and fill us with a salutary fear and trembling so that, with sorrow for having offended you and with the desire to please you, we say, "Lord, what do you want me to do?" (cf. Acts 9:4). What you want, Lord, is that we expect the remedy for our afflictions from you, through the medicine of your word and the sacraments, dispensed by your ministers in your church. For this, you command us to go to them, as Saint Paul went to your servant Ananias (cf. Acts 9:10–11). Thus we know that our destruction came from ourselves and our remedy came from you (cf. Hos 13:9). We confess that your infinite goodness made you call to yourself those who had turned their backs on you and to remember those who had forgotten you. You showed favor to those who deserved torments, and you took for sons and daughters those who had been wicked slaves. Though royal, you dwelt in those who formerly had been so corrupt and, as it were, "a filthy stable." The evils that we then committed were our own, and if we are otherwise now, it is only through God and in God. As the Apostle says: "Before you were darkness, but now you are light in the Lord" (Eph 5:8).

To be secure in the blessed state in which God has placed us through his mercy, it is helpful to remember the miserable state in which we placed ourselves through our own weakness. We should consider it entirely true that, if God withdrew his mighty and merciful hand from us, we would do the same now as we did before. If we considered the many dangers to which we are subject because of our weakness, we would not dare to rejoice completely in the grace we have at present through fear of the sins we may commit in the future. We would know how sound the counsel of scripture is: "Blessed is the one who is always fearful" (Prov 28:14). And again: "Work out your salvation with fear and trembling" (Phil 2:12). And yet again: "Let him that stands, take heed lest he fall" (1 Cor 10:12). Sorrow is the cost of pardon for sin already committed; fear is the cost of preservation from sin that may yet be committed. This is well represented in the fear of Esau that Jacob had when he came from Mesopotamia, even though God had told him to come (cf. Gen 32:8–13).

Great was the joy of the Israelites and devout were the songs they addressed to God when he worked the great miracle by which they passed through the sea without getting wet (cf. Exod 15:1ff.). Since in such great danger they had run no risk, they thought that nothing could cause them to fall or prevent them from reaching the land promised by God. But their experience was otherwise. After that great favor came temptations and trials, and those who had been devout and joyful after crossing the sea turned out to be weak and impatient in the midst of trial and struggle. The only ones who attain the crown promised by God are those who remain faithful in the tests that he sends them. Since the Israelites were not faithful, they did not arrive at the crown. Rather, instead of the life that had been promised, they were punished with death in the desert. Who then, whether looking at the past or at the future, will be so off target as to lift up their heads in pride? For they see how miserably they have fallen in the past and how great are the fears to which they are subject for the future. If they know and recognize the truth that all good comes from God, they will see that possessing God's gifts should not exalt those who have them but should humble them more as people who owe greater gratitude and service. Those who consider, as the gospel says (Luke 12:48), that an increase of favors brings with it an increase in the account to be given for them, see the goods they have as a weighty responsibility causing them to sigh and to be more careful and humble than before.

Since our inconstancy is so great and this secret pride reaches to our very bones, no human strength suffices to cleanse us completely of this sin. We must implore this gift from God, begging him persistently not to permit us to fall into the great treachery of robbing him of the honor due him for all good things. Diseases of the body are cured by fasting, those of the soul by prayer. Therefore, anyone who suffers this disease of the soul should pray before God with all possible diligence and perseverance. One should beg God to open one's eyes so that they may recognize who God is and who the self is, and so that one may not attribute to God anything evil or attribute to the self anything good. Thus we will be far from hearing the false language of the prideful devil who would like to beguile us through self–esteem. But listen to God's truth that says that a creature's true honor and worth do not lie within itself but in receiving grace and in being valued and loved by its Creator (cf. 2 Cor 10:18). Since I will be saying more on this subject later, when I speak about self–knowledge, I will not say more about it now.

## CHAPTER 18

Another cunning trick of the devil is the opposite of that described above. Instead of exalting the heart, he humiliates and discourages it to the point of driving it to despair. He recalls past sins, aggravating them as much as possible, so that the person, terrified and falling dismayed under such a heavy burden, is reduced to despair. So the devil acted with Judas. When he was at the point of committing his sin, the devil removed its gravity from his sight; afterward, he brought to his mind the gravity of his crime in having sold his Master at so low a price and unto such a death. Thus, the devil blinded his eyes with the greatness of his sin and, having caught him in the snare, led him to hell (cf. Matt 27:3–5). So, he blinds some people by their good works. He places them before them and hides their sins from their sight, thus deceiving them with pride. He blinds others by hiding from them the memory of God's mercy and the good works they have performed by his grace. By then bringing their sins to mind, he pulls them down through despair.

The remedy for the first temptation would be that, when the devil would want to exalt us in vanity to the sky, we should cling fast to the earth, considering not our peacock feathers, but our feet covered with the mud of the sins we have committed—or would commit if it were

79

not for God's grace. For the other deceit of the devil, the remedy is to turn our eyes away from our sins and to fix them on God's mercy and on the good things that we have done by his grace. For in the time when our sins fight against us through despair, it is good to recall the good things that we have done or that we do. This is in accord with the example we have in Job (cf. Job 13:18) and in the king Hezekiah (cf. 2 Kgs 20:3). The purpose here is not to put confidence in our good works insofar as they are ours, for this would be to flee from one trap and fall into another. Rather, the purpose is to hope in the mercy of God, who has favored us so that, by his grace, we might do good. He will reward what we do, including even the cup of water that we have given for love of him. Since he has placed us in the path of his service, he will not abandon us in the middle of it, for his works are perfect (cf. Deut 32:4), as he himself is. He has done more in drawing us out of our enmity against him than in preserving us in his friendship. Saint Paul teaches this when he says: "If when we were enemies, we were made friends with God through the death of his Son, much more, now that we have been made friends, shall we be saved in his life" (Rom 5:10).

It is certain that, since his death was powerful enough to raise the dead, his life will be able to preserve life in those who live. If he loved us when we did not love him, he will not be without love for us when we do love him. Thus we dare to say with Saint Paul: "I am confident that he who began this good work in us will complete it, even to the day of Jesus Christ" (Phil 1:6).

If the devil should try to disturb us by aggravating the sins we have committed, let us consider that he is neither the offended party nor the judge who will pronounce the sentence. God was the one we offended when we sinned, and he is the one who must judge both human beings and devils. Therefore, we should not be disturbed that the accuser accuses. Instead, we should be comforted that the one who is the offended party, and the judge, pardons and absolves us through our penance and through his priests and sacraments. This is what Saint Paul says: "If God is for us, who shall be against us? He did not spare his own Son but delivered him up for us all. How then is it possible that, having given us his Son, he would not give us all things together with him? Who shall be able to accuse God's chosen ones? It is God who justifies. Who then shall condemn?" (cf. Rom 8:31–33). All this Saint Paul says. Reflecting on it should strengthen our hearts to hope for what we need since we have such tokens from the past.

Let not our sins frighten us, for the Eternal Father has laid the penalty for them upon his only–begotten Son. Therefore, pardon may come to the one deserving the punishment if such a one is disposed to receive it. Since God pardons us, what good is it for the devil to cry out demanding justice? Already the justice due for all the sins of the world was accomplished upon the cross. It fell upon the innocent Lamb, Jesus Christ our Lord. Thus every guilty person who desires to approach him and to rejoice in his redemption through penance may be pardoned. What justice would it be to punish the penitent's sins again in hell, when they have already been sufficiently punished in Jesus Christ? I speak of punishment in hell because I am talking about a penitent who has been baptized and who has now, through the sacrament of penance, received pardon and the grace that had been lost. For such, the eternal punishment of hell is changed into temporal punishment, to be satisfied in this life by good works, or in purgatory by suffering the pains of the other world. But let no one think that all the punishment is not taken away because of any deficiency in the redemption of the Lord, whose power is present and works in the sacraments. For, as David says, his redemption "is plentiful" (Ps 130:7). Rather, it is through the fault of the penitent, for not bringing to the sacrament the disposition to receive more. For the penitent may bear such sorrow and shame as to rise from the feet of the confessor pardoned of all guilt and punishment, as with the reception of holy baptism, which removes all of this from anyone who is even moderately disposed to receive it. Let everyone know that the oil which our great Elisha (cf. 2 Kgs 4:1–7), Jesus Christ our Lord, gave us when he gave us his passion, works in his most precious sacraments so that, with it, we may be able to pay all our debts, living here the life of grace and afterward, that of glory. But we, like the other widow in the story of Elisha, must bring the vessels of our good dispositions, according to which each one will receive the effect of Christ's sacred passion, which in itself is completely sufficient and even superabundant.

**CHAPTER 19**

God has good reason to complain, and his heralds have good reason to reprove those ungrateful for this gift, which deserves that thanks be given to God night and day. This is because, as Saint John says: "God so loved the world that he gave his only-begotten Son so that everyone who believes in him" and loves him "may not perish, but may have eternal life" (John 3:16). In this gift all others are enclosed, as the lesser in the greater and the effects in the cause. It is clear that he who provided the sacrifice for sins granted pardon as far as it lies in him. He who gave the Lord also gave lordship. Finally, he who gave his Son—

and such a Son, given to us and born for us—will not deny us anything that we need. Whoever does not have what is needed should complain of himself, because he has no reason to complain about God. To make us understand this, Saint Paul did not say, "He that gave the Son *will give* us all things together with him." Rather, he said, "He *has given* us all things with him" (cf. Rom 8:32). Everything has already been given on the part of God: pardon, grace, and heaven. O men, why do you waste such a good? Why are you ungrateful to the one who so loves you and for such a gift? Why do you neglect preparing yourselves to receive it? Consider a man who goes about starving, naked, and miserable. If someone bequeathed him great wealth so that he could pay his debts, leave his bad fortune, and live in peace, he would be blameworthy if he ended up not enjoying it because he did not want to travel three or four leagues to probate the will. The accomplished redemption is so abundant that the fact that God pardons the offenses that man commits against him is a gift beyond all human calculation. The passion and death of Jesus Christ our Lord exceeds man's debt in value much more than the highest heaven exceeds the lowest depths of the earth. As Saint Augustine says, "Man, by his sins, should have been beaten, imprisoned, mocked, and killed. Does it not seem to you that these debts are well paid by the scourges, torments, and death of a man, who not only is just, but who is God and man?"[83]

It is an ineffable gift that God adopts the sons of men, little worms of the earth, as his sons. But so that we may not doubt this gift, Saint John speaks of another greater gift: "The Word of God was made flesh" (John 1:14). It is as if he says, do not stop believing that men are born of God by spiritual adoption, but take as token of this marvel, another greater one, namely, that the Son of God has become man and the son of a woman.

It is also marvelous that a poor little earthly man is enjoying God in heaven, accompanied by the angels with ineffable honor. But much more marvelous was it that God should have been tormented and scorned on a cross and should die between two thieves (cf. Matt 27:38). Divine justice was so satisfied by all that the Lord suffered, and above all, because it was God who suffered, that it pardons our past and blesses us so that our sterility produces the fruits of a good life, worthy of heaven. This was prefigured in the son given to Sara when she was already old and sterile (cf. Gen 21:2). The tender calf prepared (cf. Gen 18:7) in the house of Abraham—that is, Jesus Christ, crucified among the people that proceeded from Abraham—pleased God so much that he became calm instead of wrathful and replaced a curse with a blessing. This was because he had received something that pleased him more than all the sins of the world could displease him.

Why then do you despair, O man, if you have God–become–man, whose merit is infinite, as remedy and payment? Dying, he put our sins to death, much more effectively than Samson's death caused the Philistines to die (cf. Judg 16:30). Even if you had committed as many sins as the demon himself, that lead you to despair, you must recover your courage in Christ, "the Lamb of God who takes away the sins of the world" (John 1:29). It was prophesied of him that "he would cast all our sins into the bottom of the sea" (Mic 7:19) and that "the saint of saints was to be anointed, and that sin would be finished, and there would be everlasting justice" (Dan 9:24). Well then, if sins are to be drowned, taken away, and dead, why is it that enemies, so weak and already conquered, conquer you and make you despair?

**CHAPTER 20**

But I already hear, O man, what your weakness answers to what I have said. What good is it for you that Christ has died for your sins if pardon is not applied to you? And even if Christ has died for all men, many are in hell, not because the redemption is insufficient, since that is abundant (cf. Ps 130:7), but because man is not prepared to receive it. From this comes your desperation.

To this I say that, though you speak the truth, you do not make good use of it. Saint Bernard says that for one to have the testimony of a good conscience, which gives him the happiness of a good hope, it is not sufficient to believe in a general way that his sins are pardoned through the death of Christ. Rather, it is necessary that such a man trust and hold it as reasonably probable that pardon is applied to him in particular, if he has the dispositions that the church teaches. Even if he believes the first, he can fall into despair. But he cannot if he has the second because, while he hopes, he cannot despair.[84] But you must see how right this is. You see the heart of the celestial Father open to give his Son, as he did give him. You also see that this payment has been made and that the divine Lamb has already died so that you may eat of him and not die. Therefore, you must cast from you all faint-heartedness and laziness and try to profit from the redemption, trusting in God that he will help you in it. In order that you may be pardoned, it is not necessary that Christ should suffer or die again, or should suffer a little or a lot. Since this is so, why do you think that, since he has paid the price for his banquet, the guests should not come to eat? Certainly, it is not so, "nor is it his will that the sinner die, but rather that he be converted and live" (Ezek 33:11). So that it may be so, he died on the cross.

No matter how weak you are, do not think that what you need to do in order to enjoy his redemption is impossible or so difficult that you have to despair of obtaining it. It is enough for you to direct a heartfelt sigh to God, with sorrow for having offended such a Father and with the intention of amendment. Make known your sins to a priest who can absolve you. For your greater consolation, even your ears of flesh will hear the sentence of your trial in what is said to you: "I absolve you from all your sins in the name of the Father and of the Son and of the Holy Spirit."

Even if it seems to you that your sorrow is not as perfect as it ought to be, and for this reason you lose heart, do not be discouraged. So great are the Lord's desires that you be saved that he supplies what we lack with the privilege he gave to his sacrament of making one who is without sorrow to be contrite. If it seems to you that you are not even capable of doing this little bit, I tell you not to presume to do it on your own, but call upon the heavenly Father. Ask him, through Jesus Christ, his Son, to help you to be sorry for your past life, to propose amendment for the future, to confess well, and finally, for whatever else may be necessary. He is such that there is no reason to expect from his hands anything other than every kind of tenderness and help. Since he is the one who gives pardon, he inspires the disposition for it.

If, with all this, you do not feel consolation, even though you have heard the sentence of your absolution, do not be discouraged or abandon what you have begun. If in one confession you do not experience consolation, in another or in others you will. There will be fulfilled in you what David the penitent said: "To my hearing, you will give joy and gladness, and my humbled bones will rejoice" (Ps 51:10). Certainly, it happens that the words of sacramental absolution may not give the man such certainty of pardon that he may have security or evidence of it. But they do provide such rest and consolation that the powers of his soul, humiliated and broken by sin, rejoice.

Let no one cease seeking pardon. If he persists in his request, the Father of mercies will go out to meet his prodigal son and will clothe him in the heavenly garment of grace and will rejoice to see that, through penance, he has recovered his son who had been lost through sin (cf. Luke 15:20–24). Let no one find it incredible that God applies to sinners such tender and gentle laws, drawn forth from his most true goodness and love, while with his Son, whom he loved as much as he loves himself and who is who he is, he applied such rigorous laws. Even though he was paying for the sins of others, God did not dispense him from satisfying his justice for even one sin. Therefore, it is similar to the case of a fierce lion. If it is well satisfied and content, it does not harm the animals that it would swallow if it were hungry. So the divine justice, with the satisfaction that it has in Jesus Christ, the divine Lamb, does not harm those that it sees approaching him to be incorporated into his body. Neither does he prevent his mercy from working in them according to his custom. Thus, it comes about that God, instead of being an angry judge, is a kind Father toward us.

## CHAPTER 21

Whoever commits a sin drinks a dangerous poison. Sin's face is so ugly and terrible that it horrifies anyone who really encounters it. It is entirely capable of causing death to anyone who pauses to consider seriously what he has done, against whom he has done it, the promises of good he has lost, and the evil threats hanging over his head. Seeing these things, David, brave though he was, exclaimed, "My heart has forsaken me" (Ps 40:13). But, as I have said, God does not leave this evil without remedy. So that the person who needs this remedy may take it, I shall explain the grandeur of God's mercy that he applies to sinners who beg pardon.

As I have said, the demon will act according to his ways and will frighten you with the number and magnitude of your sins. Do not answer him but turn to God and say, "For your name's sake, Lord, you will pardon my iniquity, for it is great" (Ps 25:11). If God grants that you understand the mystery of these words, you will certainly be far from despairing, no matter how much you have sinned. Have you ever seen or heard of a judge's tribunal where a man is accused of many grave sins so that he may be condemned and punished, as he deserves? Then he himself confesses his guilt, agreeing with the accusation. Using confession as a means to gain absolution, he confesses the very things that his accuser was exaggerating and relying on for his condemnation. The guilty one says to the judge: "Sir, I admit and confess that I have sinned much, but pardon me for the honor of your name." And he obtains it when it is a case of God and himself.

The Lord God is just and merciful. When he looks upon our faults in his justice, they provoke him to wrath, and the more sins we have, the greater is the punishment to which we provoke him. But when he looks upon our sins in mercy, they do not move him to wrath but to compassion, and he does not regard them as an offense against him but as an evil for us. Since no evil that can come upon us causes such great damage as sin, none is so properly matter for mercy as guilt, considering it as I have said. The more we have sinned, so much the more have we done evil. So much the more also is the heart that possesses and wants to use mercy, provoked to use it. Such is the heart of the Lord, who is "merciful and shows mercy" (cf. Exod 34:6; Ps 103:8).

Consider now that those who have sinned much act in one of two ways. Some, like Cain, in despair of finding a remedy (cf. Gen 4:13–16), turn their backs on God. As Saint Paul says, they "give themselves up…to all uncleanness" and sin (Eph 4:19). Their hearts become daily more hardened to all good. When they fall into the depth of sins, they think nothing of it, but glory in their malice. The less they weep over themselves, the more they deserve to be wept over. What happens to them is what scripture says, "Upon the hard heart, evil will come in its last days" (Sir 3:26, 29). Woe to the one who has to taste this evil! How much better for him if he had not been born! There are others that, when they have committed many sins, return to themselves with God's help, wounding their hearts with sorrow and full of confusion and shame. They humble themselves before God's mercy with humility and lamentation, as much greater as their sins have been more and greater. Since God "has his heart set on the contrite and humbled heart" (Ps 51:19) and "gives his grace to the humble" (Prov 3:34), he gives more grace to those who are more humble. The occasion for this is that they confess and weep over the many sins they have committed. But they do not despair. Rather, they assert that, since their misery and injury are very great, his mercy may be plentiful and very great with them.

As David said, "Have mercy on me, Lord, according to your great mercy" (Ps 51:3). Since, as was said, God looks upon the contrite and humbled sinner with eyes of mercy, he gives greater pardon and greater mercy here than he does where there are neither such great sins nor such deep humility. He thus fulfills the words of Saint Paul that "where sin abounded, grace superabounded" (Rom 5:20). The greater fall of man redounds in greater praise of God for bestowing greater pardon and more grace.

Who then, understanding this, will be without hope because of his many sins? For he sees that the Lord's generosity and mercy are more manifest and more glorified when he pardons more and that God takes it as the honor of his name to pardon and to pardon a lot. Instead, realizing that it is just that the Lord and his name be glorified, we shall say, not with desperation but with full confidence, "For your name's sake, Lord, pardon my sins, for they are many" (Ps 25:11). The glory that

God draws from this does not arise from our sins, which, in them-selves, are scorn and contempt toward God. But the glory proceeds from omnipotent divine goodness that draws good from evil and makes his enemies serve him by giving occasion for them to praise him as friends.

Remember that when the people of God came out of Egypt, they were in great difficulty, expecting death at the hands of their enemies who were pursuing them. Moses addressed them: "Do not be afraid because the Egyptians shall perish, and you will never see them again" (Exod 14:13). When the sea had swallowed up the Egyptians and then cast them out on the shore, the Israelites stopped to look at them. Though they were looking at them, they were looking at them dead and were so fearless in looking upon them that it was as if they had never seen them again. They took the occasion to glorify the one who had slain their enemies saying, "Let us sing to the Lord because he has been gloriously magnified; horse and rider he has drowned in the sea" (Exod 15:1). All this is a figure of that affliction into which our sins place us, representing themselves to us as powerful enemies that desire to kill and devour us. But the word of God, full of all good hope, infuses courage in us. It tells us that we ought not to despair nor turn back to the vices of Egypt, but that we should continue with the good intention with which we began along the way of God. Thus let us remain standing, strengthened by his help, so that we may come to see his wonders. These consist in the fact that our sins remain drowned in the sea of his mercy and in the crimson blood of Jesus Christ his Son. Also drowned is the demon that came mounted like a horseman upon our sins. Thus, neither he nor they can harm us. Instead, even if it causes sorrow to remember our sins, as it should, they give us an occa-sion for giving thanks and glory to the Lord our God. In pardoning our sins he has acted as our loving Father, most wise in drawing good things from our evils and truly slaying the sin that was causing us death. What remains alive in us, the memory of having committed sin, serves to make his elect profit more than before and exalt more the honor of God.

## CHAPTER 22

God's great masterpiece of drawing from the poison its own anti-dote and drawing from sin its own destruction springs from and is sim-ilar to another powerful work that the Most High accomplished, not a work that is smaller but one that is greater and the greatest. It is the work of his incarnation and passion. In it, God did not desire to struggle against his enemies with the arms of his great majesty but to take up the arms of our lowliness and clothe himself in human flesh. Although he was free from all sin, "he was like to sinful flesh" (Rom 8:3), for he was subject to the sufferings and death that sin placed in the world. With the suffering and the death that he freely took upon himself, he overcame and destroyed our sins. Having destroyed them, he destroyed the sufferings and death that gained entrance because of them. It is as though someone set fire to the trunk of a tree by using the very branches of the tree. Thus, both the trunk and the branches would burn. How magnified, Lord, is your glory! How right it is that we should sing and praise you more than the other David. He went out into the field against Goliath who was afflicting God's people without there being anyone who was able to vanquish him, or anyone who would even dare to fight with him in a duel (cf. 1 Sam 17). But you, Lord, our king and our honor, hiding the arms of omnipotence and divine life that you have as God, fought against him. Taking in your hands the staff of your cross, and bearing in your body the five stones that are the five wounds, you overcame and killed him. Though there were five stones, one alone was enough for victory, because even if you suffered less than you did, you would have merited enough to redeem us. But you, Lord, wanted your redemption to be plentiful (cf. Ps 130:7) and overflowing so that thus the weak would be strengthened and the lukewarm inflamed, seeing the boundless love with which you suffered and destroyed our sins. These were prefigured by Goliath, whom David killed, not with the sword that he was carrying, but with the giant's own sword. For this reason the victory was more glorious and the enemy more dishonored. The Lord would have gained great honor if he had struggled against our sins and against death and had destroyed them, using the arms of his divine life and omnipotence. But he gained still more by overcoming them without drawing his sword. Rather, he took hold of the very sword of sin and its effect, sufferings and death, and "he condemned sin in the flesh." He offered his flesh so that punishment might be imposed on it and it would be treated as though it were the flesh of a sinner, whereas it was the flesh of the just man and of God. He did this so that, in this way, as Saint Paul says, "the justification of the law might be fulfilled in us who do not walk according to the flesh but according to the spirit" (Rom 8:4).

Because the justification of the law is fulfilled in us by our walking according to the spirit, it is clear that the works that fulfill the law are those that the law requires and with which it is satisfied. Evidently, he spoke falsely who said that "all the works that a just man does are sin."

Christ conquered sin perfectly, meriting pardon for the sins we had committed and strength not to go on committing them. So he freed our soul from the law of sin, since it is no longer our master. And he freed us from harm in our sufferings by giving us grace to endure them. Thus, by them we pay the debt we owe in purgatory and win crowns in heaven. He also delivered us "from the law of death" (cf. Rom 8:2). Thus, although we have to pass through it, we shall not remain in it. Instead, like someone who goes to bed and afterward awakes, the Lord will revive us to live a life that never dies again, a life so blessed because "he shall reform the body of our lowliness" and will make it "like his own body in glory" (Phil 3:21). Then, happy and safe from everything, despising our enemies and in triumph over them, we shall say: "Where is your victory, O death? Where is your poisonous sting, O death?" (1 Cor 15:55). The sting is sin, through which death has its power to wound, as the bee with its sting, since "through sin, death entered into the world" (Rom 5:12). Both the one and the other enemies that were wont to dominate and wound men are left drowned in the blessed blood of Jesus Christ and dead through his precious death. In their stead there succeeds that eternal justice by which the soul is justified here, and hereafter, the face–to–face vision of God in heaven and a blessed life in body and soul forever.

What shall we say to these things, daughter, other than what Saint Paul teaches us when he says, "Thanks be to God who has given us the victory through Jesus Christ?" (1 Cor 15:57). Adore him and speak to him with a loving and grateful heart: "Let all the earth adore you and sing to you; let it sing a hymn to your name" (Ps 66:4). Say this many times a day, especially when his most sacred body is elevated at the altar by the hands of the priest.

## CHAPTER 23

Despair and discouragement of heart are dangerous shots fired by our enemy. Recalling the great damage they have caused to the consciences of many, I desire to add something more about the remedy for these evils, in case it might be of some benefit.

It happens that some persons go about weighed down by a multitude of grave sins but without knowing even what despair is and without even a little fear crossing their minds. Instead, they go about secure with a false confidence and a foolish presumption, offending God without fear of punishment. If the mercy of God enlightens their souls, they begin to see rightly the gravity of their evils, and they ask God for mercy with the desire of amendment. They receive the benefit and consolation of the sacraments. With this, they should be encouraged with regard to the past and for all that might present itself along the path of God. However, they experience signs of excessive fear just as before they experienced false security. They do not understand that those who offend God without repentance have reason to fear and tremble, even if the whole world is in their favor, since they have provoked against themselves the wrath of the Omnipotent, whom no one can resist; but those who humble themselves before God, receive his holy sacraments, and desire to do his will, must have, as they say, the courage of a lion, because with these tokens, they are commanded to trust that God is with them. As they consider him an enemy to those who are evil—and since they have been such, they fear him—so there is good reason for them to consider him a friend of the good. Because of the good will that he has given them, they can be confident that he is and will be their friend, increasing the good that he planted and perfecting what he began. Certainly it is the case that, when a man sincerely says what David said, "I have lifted up my hands to fulfill your commandments, which I have loved" (Ps 119:48), God puts his eyes and heart where the man puts his hands, to favor him. As one who is infinitely good, God receives under his protection and on his side the one who desires to fight for his honor, making war against himself to give pleasure to God.

Truly, when a man begins to serve God in his own particular vocation and is spurred on to despise all things and to search for the "pearl" of the gospel (cf. Matt 13:45) by the perfection of the spiritual life, the demons, working directly and through evil men, stir up snares and wars against him. They put him in such straits that, as soon as he lifts his foot from the ground and places it on the first of the fifteen stairs to climb to perfection, he feels obliged to say: "In tribulation I called to the Lord and he heard me; Lord deliver my soul from wicked lips and from the deceitful tongue" (Ps 120:1–2).[85] "Wicked lips" are those that openly hinder the truth while "a deceitful tongue" is that which underhandedly wills to deceive. Sometimes there are offered, or so it seems, such great impediments for going forth with what has been begun, that they are like those huge giants that the Israelites talked about: "Compared with them, we are like little locusts. It seems that the walls of the city that we must fight reach in their height to the sky, and that the land devours its inhabitants" (Num 13:29, 33–34). But with all this, you and all the rest of us ought to look, with eyes wide open, at how the Israelites' discouragement and despair about the things already mentioned displeased God. The sins they had committed in the desert were many and great, and one of them was to adore the calf instead of God (cf. Deut 1:27–33). Though it seems that the evil could not increase, God endured all this from them and gave them his favor to continue the undertaking they had begun. But he did not tolerate their distrust and despair toward his mercy and power. As David said, "He swore to them in his wrath that they would not enter into his rest." And as he swore, so he fulfilled. Does it not seem to you that we are right in condemning this vice of despair that so dishonors the divine goodness? As God surpasses man in greatness, so his goodness surpasses our wickedness.

Be certain that the way of perfect virtue is an exceedingly bitter battle against very strong enemies within and outside us. There is nothing more harmful for one entering this war than to take along pusillanimity of heart. Whoever has this will flee even from shadows.

With good reason God had commanded in former times that, when his people were at war, his priests should strengthen them before they began to fight. This was not to be done with human calculations, like the number of people or arms, but with the protection of the Lord of hosts, in whose hand is the victory. For the glory of his holy name God frequently conquers the tallest giants with the smallest locusts (cf. Josh 6:4–5). In keeping with God's command, that valiant man Saint Paul says to those who wish to enter into the spiritual combat: "Be strengthened in the Lord and in the might of his power" (Eph 6:10), so that strengthened thus, they might fight the battles of God with joy and valor. As is read of Judas Maccabeus, "he fought with cheerfulness," and thus he conquered (1 Macc 3:2). Saint Antony, a man tried in spiritual struggles, used to say that "spiritual joy is a wonderful and potent remedy to conquer our enemy."[86] It is certain that delight taken in work increases strength for accomplishing it. Because of this, Paul warns us: "Rejoice in the Lord always" (Phil 4:4). We read of Saint Francis that he reprimanded brothers he saw going about sad and gloomy. To them he said, "One who serves God ought not to be like this unless it is because he has committed some sin. If you have committed one, confess it and return to your joy." Of Saint Dominic we read that there appeared on his face a joyful serenity that testified to the kind of interior joy that often arises from love of the Lord and lively hope for his mercy. With these, they can carry the cross on their backs, not only with patience but also with joy, as did those who "were robbed of their goods but remained joyful" (Heb 10:34). The reason was that "they had asserted in their heart that they had a better dwelling in heaven" and were, as Saint Paul said, "joyful in hope;

patient in tribulation" (Rom 12:12). Without the first, it is hard to have the second.

But when this vigor and joy is missing in people, it is worthy of compassion to see what those walking along the way of the Lord experience. Full of unprofitable sadness and without taste for the things of God, they are harsh with themselves and with their neighbors. They have so little confidence in God's mercy that they are close to having none. There are many like this. They do not commit mortal sins, or very rarely do. But they say that they are like this because they do not serve God as they ought and because of the venial sins they commit. Since truly such are the effects that follow upon excessive affliction, they cause more harm than the fault committed. Such persons foster the growth of what they could cut off, if they had prudence and courage. Thus they fall from one evil into another.

People like this ought to labor to serve God with all diligence and, if they see that they have fallen, let them weep. But let them not distrust. Recognizing that they are weaker than they thought, let them humble themselves the more. Let them beg for more grace and live with greater caution, having learned a lesson from this fall for another time. Many do the reverse of this. They are careless and lazy in serving God, and once they fall into sin, they do not know what to do. Thus they throw themselves into the pit of distrust and greater negligence. In fact, the best way for avoiding despair is to avoid mediocrity and carelessness in God's service. When these roots are present, whether a man wants to or not, he cannot possess that vigor of heart and courage that follow from a good and diligent life. Such people should consider that they suffer greater trouble from these gloomy and despairing sentiments that follow from sadness than they would experience if they cut out by the roots the evil affections and dangerous occasions that prevent them from serving God fervently. Inclined as they are to flee labors, they should choose the labors that perfect virtue brings in order to escape those that follow upon its lack.

Saint Paul says, "The end of the commandment is the charity that proceeds from a pure heart and a good conscience and an unfeigned faith" (1 Tim 1:5). By "good conscience," he means "hope," as Saint Augustine says.[87] This makes us see that, without a good conscience and the faith, love, and good works that proceed from it, the lively hope that gives us joy will not exist. Any deficiency in the good conscience will also exist in the consolation and joy that perfect hope causes. This is because, even though such a man is not dead but in grace, yet, in the end, he will only work in a feeble way.

Anyway, those who say, "Believe that God pardons you and loves you, and you shall be pardoned and loved," and other similar words, are very gravely deceived. They give testimony that they speak from their imaginations and not from experience, nor according to the faith. Such efforts as these, since they are not from God, cannot keep a man standing when real tribulation comes. Courage of heart and the joy of a good conscience are fruits of a good life that grow together, and those who live well find them within themselves even without searching. From a contrary cause a contrary effect follows, as it is written: "An evil heart will produce sadness" (Sir 36:20), from which is born distrust and other evils.

## CHAPTER 24

The conclusion to be drawn from all this is that, since it is so helpful to go your way comforted by strong hope and cheerful in God's service, you need to obtain two things. One is the consideration of the divine goodness and love that God has manifested in giving us Christ Jesus as our own. The other is that, casting aside all negligence and tepidity, you serve our Lord with diligence. Whenever you fall into any fault, do not be dejected through distrust but seek a remedy and hope for pardon. If you should fall many times, seek many times to rise. There is no valid reason for you to weary of receiving pardon since God does not weary of giving it. He commanded that we should pardon our neighbors not only seven times a day, but seventy times seven times, which is to say that we should pardon without limit. Much more will the Lord give his pardon as many times as he is asked, for his goodness is greater than ours and an example for us to follow (cf. Matt 18:22).

If integrity of life and the remedy you desire do not come as soon as you would like, do not for that reason think that they will never come. Do not be like those who said, "If the Lord does not send a remedy within five days, we will surrender to our enemies" (Jdt 7:31). Very rightly did holy Judith admonish these people, saying, "Who are you to tempt the Lord?" (Jdt 8:11). Words such as these do not move him to mercy but awaken his wrath and enkindle his fury. Have you assigned the time for the Lord's mercy? Have you assigned the day in accordance with your will? Learn to hope in the Lord until he comes with his mercy. Do not weary of suffering, for your life depends on it. If great afflictions weaken your hope, let them also encourage you, since usually they come on the eve of the remedy. The hour of the Lord's deliverance is when the affliction has lasted a long time and is oppressing greatly. This appears with the disciples whom he let suffer three watches of the night and consoled them in the last part (cf. Matt 14:25). Also, he delivered his people from captivity in Egypt when the tribulation they were enduring had greatly increased. Thus he will also do for you when you are not expecting it.

If it seems to you that you desire to lead a very holy and perfect life, completely for the glory of God, realize that there are persons, so proud and stubborn that they cannot be humbled other than by temptations, distress, and even falls. They are so weak that they do not walk God's way with diligence unless they are spurred on constantly. Their hearts are so hard that it takes many misfortunes to break them. They are unable to have discretion or caution without having made many mistakes. In short, their hearts are puffed up by a few graces and rendered vain. Such people need many afflictions to make them walk humbly before God and neighbor. You see already that these evils can only be cured by cauterizing them with fire. Thus God permits desolation, darkness of mind, and even sins, so that those so afflicted may humble themselves and be free of the miseries already mentioned. The prophet Micah says, "You shall come even to Babylon, and there you shall be freed, and God will redeem you from the hand of your enemies" (Mic 4:10). Confused at these falls and at this kind of life, people usually are humbled and then have to seek and find a remedy from God. Had they not fallen, they might have lost the remedy through pride, or might not have sought it with diligence and grief.

Eternal thanks to you, Lord, for drawing heavenly benefits from such harmful evils and for being as greatly glorified by pardoning sinners as you are in making and keeping them just. By means of a heart contrite and humbled (cf. Ps 51:19), you save the one who was not disposed to serve you with fidelity. You cause a person's sins to be the occasion for humility, discretion, and diligence. As you said, let the one who is forgiven more, love more (cf. Luke 7:47). Thus are fulfilled the words of your apostle that mercy in justice makes your justice appear more glorious (Jas 2:13), since pardoning and saving repentant sinners manifests the greatness of your goodness. In another place it is said that for those who love God, all things turn out to be good (Rom 8:28)—even the sins they have committed, according to Saint Augustine.[88] None of this should be taken as grounds for tepidity or carelessness in sinning, which is never right. But it is said so that, if you should fall into the misfortune of offending our Lord, you may not commit another worse sin by failing to trust in his mercy.

## CHAPTER 25

At other times the demon is accustomed to discourage us by bringing thoughts against faith or foul and abominable ones against the things of God. He makes the one who has them think that they have their origin in himself and that he consents to them. In this way the demon causes such tribulation that he deprives the soul of all joy, making it think that God casts aside and condemns it. He causes it to despair by saying that the soul cannot end up anywhere but in hell since it already utters blasphemies and things similar to those found there. The demon is not so foolish as to think that a Catholic Christian is going to consent to things so abhorrent to a Christian heart, but his intention is to discourage the soul so that it loses its confidence in God. Worn out by such annoyances, the Christian may lose patience and go about with an agitated and despondent heart. From this the demons usually draw much gain because it prepares the way for them to imprint any evil on such a heart.

The first thing we ought to do, if it is not done already, is to examine our conscience carefully and very calmly, and then, by confession, to cleanse it of all the evil we may see in it. We should put it in order not more or less than if we were to have to die that day, and from then on, live with greater care than before in serving our Lord. Sometimes it happens that the sovereign Judge permits these frightening things to come to us against our will as punishment for other things in which we fall by our own will and because of our carelessness in his service. The Lord wants to heal this with blows that hurt so much, so that, wounded by them, we may stop eating forbidden things and be spurred along our way, as an animal without reason is when it is struck by the one behind him. At other times the Lord sends this torment for other purposes that his high wisdom knows. But now, whether the scourge is sent for one reason or another, each one should do what has been said about purifying his conscience and walking diligently in the service of God. This remedy harms nothing and is beneficial for everything.

Afterward, although he has trusted in God's mercy and asks his help, the man still cannot stop hearing this speech. This is because the demon, even though we do not consent, is able to bring us thoughts and interior sayings. At least, let the man act as though he does not hear them and remains in peace, without being discouraged over them and without discussion with the enemy with reasons and responses. As David says, "I, as a deaf man, did not hear, and as a dumb man, did not open my mouth" (Ps 38:14). This is quite difficult to believe for those who know little about the wiles of the demon. These, if they do not stop thinking and doing the good they were doing, are occupied with hearing and killing the flies that such thoughts are. They think that through this very thing they have consented. They do not know that there is a great deal of difference between sensing them and consenting to them. They do not know that the stronger these abominable thoughts are, the more they can confide in our Lord. He will protect them from consenting to such great evils for which they have no inclination but rather horror. So the best remedy is not to be worried about them and to be calm in demeanor, since there is nothing that annoys the demon more than that we pay no attention to him or to what he brings to us. Neither is there anything so dangerous as to begin giving reasons to one who can so quickly deceive us. The least evil that can happen to us is to make us lose time and cease from continuing in the good that we were doing. For this reason, we ought to close the door of our understanding to him as strongly as possible, so that we may be united with God and not respond to our enemy.

For our consolation and satisfaction we must say many times a day that we believe what our holy mother the church believes, and that it is not our will to consent to false or foul thoughts. We must say to the Lord what is written, "Lord, I suffer violence; answer for me" (Isa 38:14), and trust in his mercy that he will do so. Victory in our combat does not depend on us swinging our arms alone. Rather, the most important thing is in calling upon the all–powerful Lord and to take refuge in him. But, if we are going to have much reasoning and many responses to our enemy, how are we to ask God to respond for us? "Be silent," scripture says, "and the Lord will fight for you" (Exod 14:14). In another passage Isaiah says, "In silence and in hope shall your strength be" (Isa 30:15).

By failing in either of these two things, a man is immediately weakened and disturbed. By keeping quiet, by dissimulation, and by hope, I have seen many persons healed in a short time from this painful disease. They have silenced the demon by letting him see that they were not listening or responding to him. It is as puppies that bark usually do. If a man passes by quietly, they are also quiet. Otherwise, they bark all the more.

## CHAPTER 26

But a weak person will say: "These bad thoughts take away my devotion, and they usually come to me when I approach devotion and good works. Sometimes they make me feel like stopping the good that I have started so that I do not hear such things."

But the answer is clear. This is the very thing that the demon went about looking for, even if he was circling around giving you a different kind of thoughts. Instead of decreasing, you must rather increase in the good, as a person who acts deliberately to cause the demon to go out with a loss from a place where he thought that he would draw gain.

If you are lacking tenderness in devotion, do not be troubled, for our service is measured only by love. Love does not consist in tender devotion but in a free offering and intention of the will to do what God and his church want us to do, and to suffer what he wills that we suffer, in order to please him. If those who seem to have left what they have in the world to serve God were also to leave the disordered desire for sweet feelings in the soul, they would live more happily than they do. The devil would not find certain hairs of appetites by which to take hold of their heads and turn them about, thereby harming and even deceiving them. Jesus Christ died naked on the cross; naked, we have to offer ourselves to him. Our only clothing is to be doing his holy will according to the commandments of God and of his church, receiving with loving obedience whatever he wills to send us, no matter how hard. Likewise, we are to receive from his hand temptation and consolation and to give him thanks for the one and the other.

Saint Paul says "we must give thanks to God in all things" (Eph 5:20). The sign of the good Christian is, for the love of God, to love the one who does him wrong as one loves a benefactor. In the same way, giving thanks to God in adversity, not focusing on what looks hard from the outside but on the hidden gift that God sends underneath it, is the sign of a man who has other eyes than those of the flesh, and who loves God. This is because, in what hurts him, he remains in conformity with God's will. Thus we must not cling to the weak branches of our desires, even though they may appear good to us, but to the strong column of the divine will. Obeying it, according to what has been said, we may participate in our own way in the peace and immutability of that will and avoid the many changes we necessarily feel in our heart if avarice is within it.

Certainly, there is little difference between serving Christ for money and serving him for consolations and pleasant feelings in the soul, for heaven or for earth, if the ultimate purpose is my avarice. Lucifer, according to many doctors, desired blessedness. But he did not desire it as he should have, or from the one he should have, or that it should be given to him when God wanted. Therefore, he did not enjoy it. Even though what he desired was good, he sinned by not desiring it well. Thus it was avarice and not holy desire. By this, I am telling you that we ought not to be attached with inordinate intensity to spiritual pleasures. Rather, offering ourselves to the cross of the Lord, let us willingly accept what he sends us, whether it is sweet honey or gall and vinegar.

I have not said this because these things in themselves are evil or without advantage, as long as one knows how to use them and receives them, not to remain in them, but to have more nourishment in God's service. This is especially so for those who are beginning, who ordinarily, in conformity with their age, need the milk of infants. Anyone who wanted to nourish them with adult food in order to make them perfect in one day would be very wrong and, instead of helping, would cause great harm. Each age has its condition and its strength and, in accord with this, nourishment is given. As the experienced Saint Bernard says, "The way of perfection is not traveled by flying but by walking."[89] Let no one think that understanding perfection is the same as possessing it. Therefore, if the Lord gives someone consolations, let him accept them in order to carry his cross with greater strength, since the Lord's way is to console his disciples on Mount Tabor so that they may not be disturbed in the persecution of the cross. Ordinarily, before the gall of tribulation is presented, he sends the honey of consolation. Never have I seen anyone who did not enjoy these consolations or who held them of little value, unless it was someone who had no experience of what they are. But if the Lord wants to lead us by paths of desolation and wants us to hear the painful language of which we are speaking, we should not be discouraged by anything that he sends. Rather, we should drink with patience the cup that the Father gives us, because he gives it, and we should ask him for strength that our weakness may obey him.

Do not think either that I am teaching you that it is possible to do away with joy when the Lord visits us or to prevent the feeling of his absence and being handed over to our enemies to be tempted and afflicted by them. But what I mean to say is that we should try, with the strength God gives us, to conform ourselves to his holy will obediently and quietly, and not to follow our own, from which necessarily there follow desolation, distrust, and the like. Beg the Lord that he open our eyes so that we may see more clearly than we see the light of the sun, that the things of the earth and the heavens are too base to desire and rejoice in, if they separate us from the Lord's will. There is nothing, however small and bitter it may be, that is not of great value if it is in accord with the Lord's will. It is incomparably more valuable to live with hardships if the Lord commands it, than to be in heaven without his willing it.

If at some point, we truly banish from ourselves our secret greed, many evil fruits that come from it would fall with it. We would gather other more precious fruits of joy and peace that are usually born of union with the divine will, and they would be so firm that not even tribulation itself would be able to take them from us. Though such people may feel themselves in tribulation or abandoned, they will not because of this feel themselves in despair or agitation. They know that this is the way of the cross to which they have offered themselves, and that Christ walked along it. This is apparent from what he said to his Father when he was on the cross: "My God, why have you forsaken me?" (Matt 27:46). But a little afterward he said, "Into your hands, Father, I commend my spirit" (Luke 23:46). The Lord said, "I will see you again, and your heart shall rejoice, and no one will take away your joy" (John 16:22). This is because, for a person in this state of rejoicing, there is no tribulation in the inmost part of his soul that may significantly upset him, since there he is totally united with the will of the one who sends him the joy. Acting in this way we would deceive the deceiver, the demon. If we are not discouraged and do not turn back from the good begun despite his evil language, but accept what God sends us with obedience and thanksgiving, we shall emerge from this struggle unharmed, even if it lasts throughout life. We shall have even greater profit than before, since it has given us an occasion to win crowns in heaven as a prize for our conformity with the will of the Lord, without care for our own, even in what was very painful for us.

## CHAPTER 27

The conquest of which we have spoken comes about more through the habit of patience than through the force of our wanting it to come to us. Thus, the Spouse says in the Song of Songs: "Hunt for us the little foxes that destroy the vines, for our vineyard has flourished" (Song 2:15). The vineyard of Christ is our soul, planted by his hand and watered with his blood. It flourishes when, the time of sterility having passed, it begins a new life and bears fruit for the one who planted it. But in such beginnings, these and other temptations of the clever demon usually lie in wait for us. For this reason, Christ, the best of spouses, admonishes us that now that our soul, his vineyard, has flowered, we should try to hunt down such temptations. Saying this, he shows us that the thing has to be done with skill, as we have said. In saying that the temptations are "foxes," he teaches that they come slyly, and when they appear to strike on one side, they wound on the other. By saying that they are "little," he shows that they are not to be feared by one who knows them, because to know them is to conquer them completely or to weaken them. In saying that "they destroy the vines," he means that they do a lot of harm in those who do not recognize them. This is because, frightened and without confidence for going on with their business, they leave their way, and following worthless advice, they yield themselves openly to sin. They do this because it seems to them that they encounter greater peace along the wide path that leads to destruction than along the narrow way of virtue that leads to life. The end of such people, unless they return to the right way, is often such that it bears many very sure signs of eternal perdition. Scripture says, "For the one who passes over from justice to sin, God has prepared for the sword" (Sir 26:28). This means for hell.

These should consider the Gibeonites who, having made friendship with Joshua, were surrounded and persecuted by enemies. When they called Joshua to come to their aid, he helped and delivered them, taking their cause as his own, since they were persecuted by enemies for having made peace with him (cf. Josh 10:1–27). Likewise, when those who serve God begin to be on his side, they start to be persecuted by the demon as never before. This is clear in that, if they decided to leave the band of Christ, the persecution begun against them would cease. If they suffer it, they do so when they keep themselves firmly in the band of Christ. This is a very special gift that God gives. As Saint Paul says, "To you, Christ has given the gift not only that you should believe in him but also that you should suffer for him" (Phil 1:29). If the angels of heaven were able to envy the men of earth, it would be for the fact that men suffer for God.

The word of God promises "the crown to the man who endures temptation and is proved in it." It is good for us to consider and desire this reward so that, having greater nourishment, we may not be lukewarm in working nor weak in suffering. It was said of Moses that "he was looking toward the reward" (Heb 11:26). The same was said of David (Ps 118:112). But true and perfect love for the crucified Lord so esteems conformity with him that it regards suffering for God as a very great gift and reward. As Saint Augustine says, "Blessed is the injury of which God is the cause."[90] Nobody fails to protect one who is suffering because of having entered into his service. Much more should this be expected of the divine goodness, which will take your cause as his own, in accord with David's prayer: "Arise, Lord, and judge your cause; remember the insults that the fool speaks against you all day long" (Ps 74:22). To God pertains the business that his servant undertakes. Therefore, God watches over it with great fidelity. With hope in him rather than in ourselves, we must dare to undertake the endeavor of the service of God.

**CHAPTER 28**

Often those who have temptations experience great difficulty in having to speak openly about them to their confessor, because the things are so ugly and evil that they are scarcely to be mentioned. Even to name them causes distress. But on the other hand, if these people do not tell these things at length, and do not tell every thought, however little it is, it appears to them that they have not made a good confession. Thus, whether they speak or whether they are silent, they never go away satisfied but with greater sadness than they bore before. Such persons must seek a wise and experienced confessor and let him understand the roots of their temptation so that he is satisfied and understands the matter. The penitent must trust completely what the confessor says, for this is the remedy for those who, because of their little knowledge or their great passion, are not able to be good judges of themselves.

The confessor must pray much to the Lord for the health of his patient. He should not grow weary if the penitent asks him the same thing many times or has other weaknesses that such penitents usually have. He should not be afraid of these or despise the penitent for them. Rather, with heartfelt compassion "let him correct such a one in a spirit of gentleness," as Saint Paul says, "lest he also be tempted" (Gal 6:1) in the same thing or in something else, and thus come to experience, at his own cost, how great human weakness is. He must recommend to his penitents the amendment of their lives and the use of the remedy of the sacraments. Make them understand that there is no thought so impure or wicked that it can defile the soul if consent is not given. Give penitents firm hope in the mercy of our Lord, who will deliver them in his own time. Meanwhile, let them suffer this fierce torment to make up for their sins and to imitate the sufferings of Jesus Christ. Thus comforted, penitents will carry their cross patiently and offer themselves to the will of our Lord to carry it throughout life, if that pleases God. In this way they will gain more by the vinegar and gall administered by the devil than from the honey of devotion that they themselves desired.

From all this, our soul, being in the flower of its beginnings, starts to yield the fruit of the perfect. Whereas before we were sucking the

101

milk of tender devotion, we now eat bread with crust. We sustain ourselves with the hard stones of the temptations that the devil brought upon us to test, as he did with our Lord, "whether we are children of God" (cf. Matt 4:3). Thus we draw forth honey from poison and health from our wounds, and we emerge from temptations having been tried and with millions of other blessings.

For these blessings, we do not have the devil to thank, for his will is not to make us crowns but chains. Rather, we must thank God, the supreme and omnipotent Good, who will never permit any evil except to bring good from it by a higher means. Nor would he permit our enemy and those who belong to him to afflict us, unless it is for the great confusion of the enemy and for the good of the one afflicted. This is in accord with the scripture that "God will deride those who deride and that the one who dwells in heaven will mock them" (Ps 2:4). For although this dragon plays and mocks in the sea of this world, tempting and striking the servants of God, God mocks him (Ps 37:13) by drawing good from the devil's wicked deeds. When the devil thinks that he is doing most harm to the virtuous, he benefits them most. Because of this, he ends up so confounded and ashamed that, in his pride and envy, he would prefer that he had not begun this game that turned out so well for those he wanted to harm. The wickedness and the snare that he stretched out for others fell upon his own head (cf. Ps 35:8). He ends up dead with envy, seeing those whom he tempted go free, singing with joy: "The snare has been broken and we are free; our help is the Lord who made heaven and earth" (Ps 124:7–8).

## CHAPTER 29

The demons envy our well–being so much that they try all sorts of ways to keep us from enjoying what they have lost. When, in a battle, they are overcome by us, or to put it better, by God in us, they stir up other battles to see if at some time they can find someone careless to devour. They change their weapons and strategies, thinking that those they cannot overcome in one way, they will overcome in another. Christian doctrine teaches us to place ourselves within the most just will of the Lord and to suffer patiently what he sends us, interior or exterior. When they have seen that, because of this, they have been unable to ruin us by cunning, they try more open war, in which the one that was before a hidden dragon becomes a ferocious lion (cf. 1 Pet 5:8). No longer does he tempt in one thing in order to end up in another, but rather, he clearly wants to make himself feared and plans to achieve by fear what he could not achieve by cunning. Here he will not be seen as a fox but as a fierce lion that wants to inspire fear by his roaring. As Saint Peter says, "Brothers, be sober and watch, because your enemy the devil, as a roaring lion, goes about seeking someone to devour. Resist him, strong in faith" (1 Pet 5:8–9). Those who have such an enemy cannot be immoderate or careless. It is very fitting that the lambs approached by such a ferocious lion should watch and pray to the true shepherd, Jesus Christ. But what are the arms by which this enemy may be vanquished and go away confounded from this war as from the previous one? These are, as Saint Peter and Saint Paul say, "faith." This is because, when a soul, by the love of God that is the life of faith, despises the prosperity and adversity of the world, and believes and trusts in God, whom it does not see, there is no way by which the demon may enter. Also, the light of faith teaches us to trust in God's mercy when there are dangers. If the one under attack wants to take advantage of this mercy, he may gain a lot of courage to struggle against the demon, a thing that is very necessary for this war. If the fainthearted man was not fit for war against visible enemies, and so God ordered that "he return from the war" (cf. Deut 20:8), how much less will he be fit to fight, "not against flesh and blood, but against" the demons, "rulers of darkness," as Saint Paul says? (cf. Eph 6:12). Although in God's presence we ought to prostrate, fearing that he may abandon us because of our sins, yet when our enemy wages war against us, we should, in all events, be strengthened in courage, despising the demon and invoking our Lord. Thus, we read that before his arrest, the Lord, prostrate and with anguish of heart, prayed to his Father. From there, he went out so strengthened that he went to receive his enemies (cf. Mark 14:34–36).

The principal intent of the demon in this battle is to take away the heart's courage so that the good already begun may be abandoned. This he manages at times by taking the form of a dragon or a bull or other animals, by disturbing prayer with turmoil, and by hindering the repose of sleep, as it is read that he did to holy Job (cf. Job 7:14). He infuses profound fear into a man so that, even if he is valiant, it causes him to tremble and, at times, to sweat in anguish. He does other similar things that give testimony that this infernal wolf is prowling nearby. Clearly, since the trickery of his war proceeds by way of fear, the principal arms we must have are in courage of heart. We must be strengthened, not by confidence placed in ourselves, but by the firm hope we place in our Lord. This is what makes us victorious in this war, since firm hope conquers fear, as it is written, "I will act confidently and will not fear" (Isa 12:2). Be certain that you will not regret having placed your firm hope in God, nor will you say, "He has deceived me, for it has not turned out for me as I thought." As Saint Paul says, "Hope will not leave you ashamed" (Rom 5:5). "Whoever hopes in the Lord, will not be confounded" (Ps 25:3). Hope never fails the man who does not fail it. It fails him only at the time that he loses charity, the life of hope and of every virtue.

The ancient fathers of the desert knew how necessary it was to have a courageous heart so as not to be overcome in these battles with the demon that were very common among them. Therefore, they used to go alone to pray at the tombs of the dead in order to obtain freedom from the fear whose dominion is very harmful. We shall live very safe from this fear if we accept the counsel that Christ left us when he said: "I will show you the one you must fear. Fear him that, after having killed the body, has power to cast it into hell. Fear him" (Luke 12:15). Whoever does not fear God must, because of his bad conscience, fear the world and the demon. But whoever fears God is not afraid of the demon, because fearing him is a certain kind of subjection as though he can harm us in some way. Since he cannot touch even a hair of our head without God's permission, there is no reason to fear him, but there is reason to fear God, who can give him permission. Therefore, we ought to be humble and full of holy fear in God's presence. But with the demon we should be very valiant, with our hope placed in God, and full of a holy pride. The more ferocity the demon demonstrates, so much the more you ought to fear God and commend yourself to him, and so much the less you ought to fear the demon.

Thus we read of that great conqueror of demons, Saint Antony, that when he was surrounded by demons in the form of fierce animals that seemed about to devour him, he would say, "If you had any strength, one of you alone would be enough to fight with one man. But, since you are weakened because God has abandoned you, many of you attempt to join together to frighten. If the Lord has given you power over me, you see me here. Devour me. But if you do not have it, why do you labor in vain?"[91] So this saint used to say that, against the demons, the sign of the cross and faith, sometimes meaning confidence, are for us an impregnable wall. Even though our forces, compared with those of the demon, are quite small and weak, yet faith tells us, if we are not deaf, that the Lord is "the protector of all those who trust in him" (Ps 18:31). God is so good that he promises to protect and help us and to fix "his heart and his eyes" in his church, symbolized by the Temple of Solomon. He is faithful and powerful in fulfilling his promises, without anyone in heaven or on earth being able to resist

104

him, nor even the one whom he aids. The Christian would not be thinking of God and his truth, goodness, and power as a Christian should, if he did not believe that God, for his part, fulfills very well his promises to help us.

These and other similar promises of God are understood as having the condition that a man be in the state of grace, or prepared to be so, not only by believing in the promises in general, or believing that they apply to him in particular, but through penance and the means taught by the Catholic Church. We believe as certain that many in the Christian Church are in the state of grace, and that for them, without doubt, God fulfills his promises of being the protector of those who hope in him. Yet no one is certain without a special revelation that he is in the state of grace. He must believe, because it is of the Catholic faith, that the failure of the fulfillment of promises is never God's. But he can and must fear that perhaps they do not take effect in him through his fault or negligence in not doing what he ought to do. Thus, with some fear of himself and with confidence in the Lord, he will endeavor to try hard and to benefit from God's words that promise his help to those who fight for him.

God has left us in the fear and uncertainty of not knowing with certainty where we stand with regard to his friendship. Although this uncertainty appears difficult, it is advantageous. It is a guard for our humility; it prevents us from despising our neighbor; it spurs us on to work well. The less we know whether or not we are pleasing to God, the greater should be our caution and care. But do not think that, because of this, you are to go about with your heart discouraged by vain fear. Though what I have said is true, it does not prevent David from saying, "If armies in camps should rise up against me, my heart would not fear. If they made war against me, I would place my hope in God" (Ps 27:3). So, Saint Paul warns us that we ought to profit from the words that God spoke: "I will not leave you; neither will I forsake you" (Heb 13:5–6). So we may confidently say, "It is the Lord that helps; I will not fear what man can do to me." These and similar words do not at all take away the fear that a Christian must have for himself, but they do remove an excessive fear, by the confidence in God that he must have. So he walks between these two things, fear and hope.

The more love increases, the more hope also increases, and this fear continues to increase. Therefore, if you want to feel the great courage and the little fear that perfect men feel, cast away mediocrity and take to heart the business of virtue. Then you will read in your heart the courage and security that you read about in books. Then you will fight against the demon with daring, even if "he surrounds you like a lion to devour you" (1 Pet 5:8). You will have the hope that Jesus Christ, the mighty lion of Judah (cf. Rev 5:5), will defend you. He always conquers in us if we do not lose confidence in him and, like cowards, surrender to our enemies with hands tied, without desiring to fight.

The Lord does not allow these wars and temptations to come upon his own except for a greater good. As it is written: "Blessed is the man who suffers temptation, because, when he has been tested, he will receive the crown of life that God promised to those who love him" (Jas 1:12). He wanted patience in trials and standing for his honor in temptations to be the tests by which his friends would be proven. This is because being a companion in a time of peace is not the sign of a true friend, but being faithful to one's friend in time of tribulation is. Just as any man rejoices to have friends from among those he knows by experience are present in time of his tribulation, regarding it as their own, so does God rejoice to have such. As one who is grateful, he says to them, "You are those who have continued with me in my temptations." As one who rewards copiously, he says to them, "I prepare a kingdom for you, as my Father prepared it for me, so that you may eat and drink at my table in my kingdom" (Luke 22:28–30). Companions here in the midst of trials and afterward in the kingdom, you must exert yourselves by struggling manfully in the wars waged against you for the purpose of separating you from God. But he is your help on earth and the one who will reward you in heaven.

Remember Saint Antony when he was severely beaten and kicked by demons. Raising his eyes above, he saw that the roof of his cell was opened and that a ray of light so wonderful entered through there that with its presence, all the demons fled, and the pain of his wounds was taken away. With profound sighs, he said to the Lord, who then appeared to him, "Where were you, good Jesus? Where were you when I was so mistreated by your enemies? Why were you not here at the beginning of the fight so that you might prevent or heal all my wounds?" The Lord answered him, saying: "Antony, I have been here since the beginning, but I was watching how you were behaving in the fight. Because you have struggled manfully, I will always help you, and I will make you famous in the whole world." By these words and by the strength of the Lord, Antony arose so encouraged that he learned by experience that he had recovered more strength than he had previously lost.[92]

In this way the Lord treats his own. Many times he leaves them in situations of such danger that they find no place to stand and do not find within themselves one hair of strength on which to depend. They are not able to benefit from favors they received from God in times past. They remain as though naked and in deep darkness, handed over to the persecution of their enemies. But suddenly, when they are not expecting it, the Lord visits and frees them. He leaves them stronger than they were before and puts their enemies under their feet. The soul, though naturally weaker than the demon, senses within itself strength so powerful that it seems to tear the demon to pieces, like something very weak and without resistance. It would dare to fight with a great number of devils, not only with one. Such is the strength that the soul feels has come to it anew from heaven, that it not only defends itself, but it also says like David: "I will pursue my enemies and will overtake them, and I will not return until they are overcome. I will break them and they shall not be able to stand, and they shall fall beneath my feet" (Ps 18:38–39).

What is more beneficial than what Saint Augustine requests when he says, "Lord, let me know you with loving knowledge, and let me know myself"?[93] What is more helpful for a man's self–knowledge than to see himself by experience in such situations? He touches with his own hands, as they say, his own weakness, and it is so real that he ends up disillusioned of his self–esteem. On the other hand, he experiences how faithful God is in fulfilling his promises of help in time of necessity and how strong he is in delivering his own from such great weakness and giving them so suddenly a marvelous fortitude. He experiences how full of mercy God is as he visits and has pity on those who are so extremely worn out by fatigue. At this, a man falls prostrate on the earth, recognizing his littleness and his misery. He adores his God, loving him and hoping for his help if he should find himself in another danger. Saint Paul affirms that it had happened this way to him: "I do not want you to be ignorant, brothers, of the tribulation that we suffered in Asia. In it we were distressed beyond measure and beyond our strength, to the extent that living was weariness for us, and we were interiorly certain that we would not escape death." This happened "in order that we would not have confidence in ourselves, but in God, who gives life to the dead. He delivered us from such great dangers, and we hope in him, that he will also deliver us from now on" (2 Cor 1:8–10).

## CHAPTER 30

According to Saint Gregory, "the fulfillment of past things gives certainty about those of the future."[94] Since men trust on the basis of pledges, it does not seem that much is done in hoping that God will free us from future tribulation, since he has freed us often in the past. It is clear that if a man had shown us his love and his favor by helping us in our needs and difficulties ten or twelve times, we would believe that he loved us and would help us if we needed him in other difficulties. Well then, why do we not have this conviction that God will protect us in our dangers since we have experienced his help in tribulations, not a dozen times, but many more times? Remember well how many times he has drawn you victorious from bitter battles with our adversary. You were grateful for that and began to believe and trust that he loved you, since after the storm he had sent you fair weather, and after tears, joy. He has been a Father and a refuge for you. Now, he wills to try your confidence, love, and patience by present tribulation, and he acts as if he is hiding and does not answer your cries. Why do you get so discouraged that a present trial makes you lose the confidence you had gained in many other trials?

You already know that we feel more what we deal with in the present. If you look at the pressure you have at present, and how the Lord does not draw you out of it, you will probably judge that the Lord no longer has the care he once had for you. You will say what the apostles said to the Lord, who was sleeping during a great storm at sea: "Master, do you not care that we are perishing?" (Mark 4:38). Thus the reprimand of scripture will apply to you: "The fool changes like the moon" (Sir 27:11). That is to say, it is sometimes one way and sometimes another. He will be like the weather vane that even in one day changes as many times as the wind changes. You thought that the Lord was caring for you and protecting you in your afflictions, because then the winds of the mercy and consolation by which he was delivering you were blowing over you, and you gave him thanks. Now, because another wind blows over you, one by which the Lord wills to test and distress you, you do not have the conviction or the confidence you had before. Consequently, you only believe what you see. You are aware of the Lord only with regard to his present way of dealing with you, and you do not profit from what you have often experienced so as to be strengthened in the Lord in the present trial. Strange was the unbelief of those who had seen the marvels of God in Egypt and the victories and favors God had worked for them in the desert. Yet they did not believe in his word, by which he had promised them entry into the land of promise. Because of this, as Saint Paul says (cf. Heb 3:19; 4:6), they did not enter there. Thus, similarly though not equally, a man's distrust and cowardice are great when, although God has delivered him often from past dangers, he does not acquire confidence that he will not be abandoned or confounded in the present danger, nor even in future ones. This is because, as we have said, hope placed in the Lord, if a man does not fail it, will fail no one, nor will it be a motive for anyone to say: "I have been deceived."

It is important to realize that sometimes *believe* is taken as what the understanding does, affirming itself in the truths of the Catholic faith with complete certainty, as was said above. Anyone who believes against this faith is called, and is, in the fullest sense of the word, a heretic and an unbeliever. The error that is believed is called heresy and unbelief. Thus, this man without confidence of whom we are speaking is not an unbeliever and does not hold unbelief, for he does not have the obligation of believing as an article of the Catholic faith that God will deliver him from this difficulty. He is not bound, as those in the desert were bound, to believe that God would give them the victory if their enemies in the Promised Land should fight against them. But other times the saints and common usage are wont to use *to believe* to mean "to hold an opinion" through reason or conjecture. They call this credulity, and if it is strong, it is called faith.[95] One has this kind of credulity who, through probable conjectures, believes that he has been pardoned by God and is in the state of grace, and that God will help him in future need. This, which is in the understanding, helps confidence or hope, which is in the will. Because of this, incredulity is taken for lack of confidence and credulity, or faith, is taken for confidence. Therefore, it can be said that, because God had delivered him from other dangers, and for other motives, this man had reason to believe, though not with certainty, that God would also deliver him in this danger. He is not incredulous against the Catholic faith but against what results from conjectures. But because the Lutherans are accustomed to take some of these words for others, we Catholics must speak distinctly, calling faith and confidence by their proper names and declaring how belief and incredulity are understood. What in one epoch can be safely said in certain words must be avoided in other.

Returning then to our subject: flee distrust and the inconstancy condemned by the scripture when it says that "the fool changes like the moon" (Sir 27:11). Strive to participate in the stability for which the just man is praised: "He endures like the sun." This means that he is always the same. Learn from some times how to conduct yourself in others. Scripture says: "In the day of good things, do not forget evils; and in the day of evils, do not forget good things" (cf. Sir 11:25). Do this so that, tempering prosperity with adversity, you may live in equanimity, not being thrown down in time of tribulation by the weight of distrust and sadness, and not having the head carried away by excessive happiness in the time of spiritual consolations. We read this about that holy woman, Anna, mother of the prophet Samuel. After she had prayed in God's Temple, "she did not move her face to other things" (cf. 1 Sam 1:18), which means that she preserved equanimity of heart. Isaiah says that "he had to have a dwelling that would give shade from the sun and serve as a defense against the whirlwind and the rain" (Isa 4:6). It would be good for us to try to live in this dwelling so that, having strength of heart by trusting in God's mercy, we might procure this security even in times and places where there is usually danger. This is according to what is prophesied concerning the New Law that "in the woods men would sleep secure" (cf. Ezek 34:25). Even though it seems strange to have peace and security in this exile, yet, in comparison with what is in heaven, it is very small, and in comparison with the fears of the wicked it is very great and worthy of esteem. Job says this when he wants someone to cast evil away from him (cf. Job 11:14–15).

Saint Paul in particular says that "the virtue of hope is like a firm and secure anchor of the soul" (Heb 6:19). This is because, though we have the demon as an enemy who wants to intimidate us by these battles and make us lose trust, we also have a friend who is stronger and wiser than he is. If the demon hates us, Christ loves us incomparably more. If the demon does not sleep as he looks for ways to harm us, the blessed eyes of God watch over us to help us to be saved, as over the sheep for whom he gave his precious blood. We have with us the arm of the omnipotent One. Why do we fear the demon whose power is weakness compared with the divine power? How shall one fear the devil if he really believes and wills to benefit from his faith that the demon can harm us in nothing without God's permission, as was said above? Were the demons able perhaps to touch Job or anything belonging to him without first having this permission (cf. Job 1:12; 2:6)? Were they able to drown the swine of the Gerasenes (cf. Matt 8:31–32)? Well, will one who is unable to touch swine without permission be able to touch the children of God?

"Be strengthened then in the Lord," says Saint Paul, "and in the power of his strength. Take up the arms of God so that you may stand against the snares of the demon." After enumerating some particular weapons, he continues, saying: "In all things, take up the shield of faith with which you may be able to extinguish all the darts burning with fire" (Eph 6:10–11, 16). Since this enemy is more powerful than we are, we ought to take advantage of the supernatural "shield of faith," shielding ourselves with something from our faith such as with a word of God, reception of the sacraments, or a doctrine of the church. We ought to believe firmly with the understanding that all power is from God, to be strengthened "with the helmet of hope" (1 Thess 5:8), and to be offered to God with love, accepting willingly what he sends us, however it may come. Thus we shall mock our enemies and adore the Lord who gave us victory against the enemy, not only by himself, but also through the help of his holy angels who fight on our side. This was shown to the servant of Elisha who was exceedingly afraid of a large army of people who were coming to capture his lord. Elisha said to him: "Fear not, for there are more with us than against us." Elisha prayed, saying, "Lord, open the eyes of this young man that he may see." Then God opened the eyes of the youth, and he saw that around Elisha there was a mountain full of horsemen and chariots, and that the angels of the Lord had come to defend the prophet of God (2 Kgs 6:16–17). Therefore, if we choose to be on God's side, we shall have multitudes of angels on our side, one of whom can do more than all the powers of hell. What is more, we have on our side the Lord of the angels, who alone is more powerful than all infernal and celestial powers. Consequently, such favor should be enough to make us despise the demon and, having left behind all vain fear, to become strong lions against him in the power of Christ. Christ was a meek lamb when he handed himself over to death for us, and he was a lion when he despoiled hell, conquering and binding the demons and defending his beloved sheep with his arm.

If it seems to anyone that I have been lengthy in this material, attribute it to my desire that you not be one of the many I have seen who, through fear of the demon, abandon God's service. I know well that there are other wars with this enemy, crueler than those mentioned. I also know that in extreme tribulation, there is no longer strength in the one who suffers, or wisdom in the one directing the ship, and the lion and the infernal bear think that they have swallowed the sheep. Then, there comes the valiant and compassionate David [Jesus Christ] and he draws the sheep free and saves it from the mouth of the lion, tearing in pieces the one that had it (cf. 1 Sam 17: 34–35). I am a witness of greater tribulations that I could not have believed had I not seen them. I am also a witness of the marvelous and merciful providence of God, who does not, in time of tribulation, abandon those who seek him, even though they seek weakly and with faults. Although I have seen that many who fear God have been seriously distressed in these struggles, I have seen none that has come out harmed.

111

Consequently, whoever sees himself in these situations, as placed in the belly of the whale (cf. Jonah 2:1), let him call upon Jesus Christ from there, and let him be helped by the good advice that his spiritual director gives him. Let them both have firm hope in the Good Shepherd who gave his life for his sheep (cf. John 10:11) and who "kills and gives life, puts in hell and draws forth from there" (1 Sam 2:6). If at one time he sends afflictions, at other times, he removes them with great gain to the one in tribulation.

# B. God's Voice to Be Heard through Faith (chaps. 31–44)

## Introduction: Faith as the Principle of the Spiritual Life (chap. 31)

### CHAPTER 31

Everything to this point has been said so that you might know to whom not to listen, and, for this purpose, I have given you the counsels that you have read. It remains to tell you to whom you must listen in order to fulfill the first word of the Prophet: "Listen, O daughter" (Ps 45:11).

Know that the one who deserves to be heard is the one who alone is Truth. But there are many truths to be heard and known that have little to do with our purpose here, which is to speak of the Catholic faith that we Christians hold. I tell you that you are to hear and to learn what God says in his holy scripture and in his Catholic Church.

This faith is the beginning of the spiritual life. Therefore, as I said before, with good reason, we are first admonished by the Prophet to do that which it is beneficial to do first, for as Saint Paul says, "Faith comes to us through hearing" (Rom 10:17).

This faith is the first reverence by which the soul adores its Creator, thinking of him in all his grandeur, as is fitting. For, even if one can know some things about God through reason, the things that Saint Paul calls "what is manifest about God" (Rom 1:19), nonetheless reason cannot attain to the mysteries that faith believes. Therefore, it is said that faith believes what it does not see and adores firmly what is hidden to reason. We are shown this by the fact that the two seraphim covered the face of the great Lord whom Isaiah saw in the temple (Isa 6:2). Also when Moses approached to deal with the Lord on the mountain, the scripture says that he entered into darkness or a cloud where the Lord was (Exod 24:18). It seems very strange that God, the brightest Light in whom, as Saint John says, there is no darkness (1 John 1:5) would put his dwelling in darkness. But he is said to dwell in darkness because he is Light, so bright and so excellent that, as Saint Paul says, he dwells in a light that no one can reach (1 Tim 6:16). No created eye, human or angelic, can arrive at his mysteries through reason. Therefore, for such an eye, the light is called darkness. It is not that the light is dark, but that it is a light that in every way exceeds all understanding. It is the same as when we see a wheel moving at the highest speed. We usually say that the wheel is not stirring. We speak in this way because our eyes cannot take in such rapid motion. It is not that there is not enough motion, but rather that it is too rapid for our human sight.

Not only does our faith reverence God by believing what reason does not attain, but it also tells us that he is so high that, even if God is seen clearly in heaven by his own light, no human or angelic understanding can see all that is to be seen in him. No will and no desire, even if all are joined together, can love him and rejoice in him to the extent that he can be loved and enjoyed. God is the only one who understands himself. Let others see, love, enjoy, and praise him with all the strength of their hearts. Let them reverence him knowing that in comparison with what he is and what can be said of him and the service due him, all that they know of him and do for him is very little. Thus, falling prostrate, they adore him in profound silence, confessing that it alone is that perfect praise which they cannot attain. This silence is a very appropriate honor for God because it is the confession that the praises owed him are beyond expression by any creature. About this honor, David speaks: "To you, O God, praise is due in Zion" (Ps 65:2).

Therefore, even though in heaven the voice of divine praise is unceasing saying, "Holy, holy, holy is the Lord of hosts" (cf. Isa 6:3), and other wonderful praises that they give to him there, they also confess by silence that he is the Lord, greater than anything they can understand or say. "He ascended upon the cherubim and he flew upon the wings of the wind" (Ps 18:11), and no one, however much learning he may possess, is able to understand him. All who know or see him have to say what the Israelites said when they saw the bread that came down from heaven: *Manhu*, which is to say, "What is this?" (Exod 16:15). At that infinite abyss of light, they are overwhelmed with admi-

113

ration, as was the queen of Sheba (cf. 1 Kgs 10:1–10). Even if in heaven they understand more of him than they heard on earth, they cannot understand all that is in him. Such is our God and such our faith proclaims him to be, singing the words of David: "the heaven of heaven is the Lord's" (Ps 115:16). This secret concerning his being is, as has been said, for him alone, for he alone understands himself.

# 1. The Credibility of Christian Faith
## (chaps. 32–42)

**CHAPTER 32**

You have heard that in our faith we believe things that, though not contrary to reason, are unattainable by reason. You need to be warned not to think that this means that to believe in these things is contrary to reason or without reason. Just as it is very far from a believer to understand clearly what he believes, so it is far from Christian faith to be superficial in believing. We have such reasons for believing that we dare to appear and "give a reason for our faith" before any tribunal, no matter how exact it may be, as Saint Peter warns us Christians that we must be "ready" to do (1 Pet 3:15). You will understand this easily through the following comparison. If you heard it said that a man blind from birth had suddenly recovered his sight, or that a dead man had been raised, clearly your reason would not be able to understand how this can happen, because it is beyond nature, and the reason cannot arrive at the supernatural. So many reliable witnesses could affirm for you that they had seen it that, not only would it not be naiveté to believe, but it would be incredulity and hardness of heart not to believe it. Though reason cannot arrive at knowledge of how a blind man can see or a dead man return to life, it does at least arrive at the reasonableness of believing such and so many witnesses. If these witnesses were to die in confirmation of what they affirm, there would be yet more reason for believing them. If they were to perform other miracles as great as or greater than the other that they are affirming and in confirmation of it, then it would be a great fault not to believe, even if what they said had happened were something very new and exalted. Just so you ought to understand that there is nothing that reason attains less than a clear understanding of what faith believes. But neither is there anything so in harmony with reason as to believe it, and it is a very great fault not to do so.

It is certain that through the authentic miracles that Moses performed, the people of Israel believed that he was God's messenger, that he spoke with God, and that he received the Law as a thing given by God (cf. Exod 14:31). Likewise, through a few false miracles that Mohammed performed, the Arabs, a barbarian people, believed that he was God's messenger, and considering him such, they received the crude law that he gave them. Look then at the miracles done by our Lord Jesus Christ and his apostles and other holy men, miracles done in confirmation of our faith from their time till this very day. You will find that you can sooner count the sands of the sea than the multitude of miracles that, beyond any comparison, exceed all that have been done in the world in both quality and quantity. Only three dead persons were raised in the whole course of the Old Law that lasted some two thousand years. In the New Law, Saint Andrew alone raised forty dead people at one time. This was so that what the Lord said would be accomplished: "Whoever believes in me will do even greater works than I" (John 14:12). Thus his great power may be seen, not only in what he does, but by means of those who belong to him and in whom he works. He can do whatever he wants, no matter how marvelous it may be. I have told you about what one apostle alone did at one time so that through it, you may understand the innumerable miracles done by this apostle and by the other apostles and saints in the Christian Church.

Even in the beginning of the church there were so many and so great miracles in confirmation of the faith that proof abounds. But so great is "the desire that the Lord has that all be saved and come to knowledge of the truth" (1 Tim 2:4) and that those who already know it may be consoled and confirmed more in it, that his providence takes care to renew this proof and to be witness of this truth by new miracles. Thus, it would be strange if there were an era in which there were no Christian canonized a saint, something that is not done without sufficient proof of a perfect life and of many miracles. If anyone is curious and wants to search for them, miracles will not be lacking, even in our own times and among us, and in greater abundance, in the East and West Indies.

## CHAPTER 33

Possibly someone may doubt what our witnesses have said in speech or in writing about the multitude of miracles that have been performed in the Christian Church. Since they abhor the faith, they think that if these witnesses are true, they cannot avoid acknowledging that we have much greater reason for believing our truth than they have for their deception. But I ask, if they do not believe our witnesses,

115

and thus are unwilling to receive our faith, why do they believe their own witnesses and receive their false belief? It is certain and manifest, if they will take the trouble to consider it, that our witnesses exceed theirs in every kind and measure of authority. There have been men in the Christian Church whose lives have been so manifestly good as to testify that they were free from all greed, from every desire for honor, and from all that is valued and prosperous in this world. They were full of every virtue and of truth, even to the point of dying in order not to lose them. What interest can he claim with his testimony, when he claims nothing in this world, and even what he possesses, he casts away? What interest can move him to be a false witness when he gives his life in the gravest torments to confirm what he says? Under torment, some are wont to say what the judge demands of them even if it is contrary to the truth. If ours had said what the judge demanded, not only would they not have lost their possessions or their life, but they would even have been left more prosperous in everything by all that the judges were promising them. But, despising all this, they died so that they would not lose the faith or virtue that the judge wanted them to lose. Thus, they did not love or fear anything temporal, no matter how difficult. For this reason, no fault can be found in what they say.

Someone might think that these proofs are sufficient to hold these men to have been good and not to have deceived anyone knowingly, but that perhaps they were deceived and deceived others without meaning to. The answer to this is that there have been such people in the church who have shed their blood for Christ. They have been so manifestly full of wisdom that it cannot reasonably be believed that they were deceived in a matter so well considered and supported, even to the point of losing life for it. Great interest in these things makes men consider and reconsider what they affirm. Such a one is not likely to lay down his life in confirmation of a truth if he is not sufficiently sure of it. It is well known that there has been, and there is, such wisdom in the Christian people that they surpass other generations as very wise teachers surpass their uneducated disciples. That there have been not one or a hundred of these, but a very great number, is a very powerful testimony to the truth of our faith, in confirmation of which they lost their lives. Even if we read of some that have died to confirm their error, our witnesses are incomparably greater in number, virtue, and wisdom.

## CHAPTER 34

Since we have mentioned the goodness and virtues of the Christian martyrs, there is no reason for me not to tell you here what a great testimony to our faith is the perfect life of those who believe it. Since God is good and the author of all that is good, reason says that God is a friend of those who are good. This is because each one loves the other who is like him, and each cause loves its effect. If God is a friend, he must help the good in their necessities, the greatest of which is the salvation of their souls. They cannot be saved without knowing God, and they cannot know him in order to be saved if he does not reveal himself to them. Since none of these things can be denied, it remains that, if there is knowledge of God on the earth through which men are saved, God gives it to Christians. This is clear, since among them there have been, and are, people of higher life and more perfect morals than have been in any other time or generation.

It seems that the philosophers were the very flower and beauty of Nature, where apparently, she put all her forces into what concerns living well in conformity with reason. Passing over the vile evils Saint Jerome tells concerning the principal philosophers, we speak of some who apparently had more virtue than the others.[96] But those of the Christian Church exceed them so much that our weak women and young people have greater virtue than those who were there esteemed as heroic men. No one can equal the fortitude and joy with which the saints—Catherine, Agnes, Lucy, Agatha, and many like them—offered themselves to the harshest torments and to death for love of truth and virtue. These women surpassed the men considered heroic among the philosophers in a strength that seems foreign to feminine weakness. They did this both by the number and greatness of their torments and by their joy in suffering. How much greater, then, will be their excellence in humility, charity, and other virtues that are not as uncommon to women! We have put these women forward as examples, but you see the countless number of men and women in every state of life who have served the Lord with a perfect life in the Christian Church. Some of these, being very high in the world and abounding in every kind of wealth and human prosperity, expecting to inherit estates and kingdoms and possessing much in the present, have despised all of this. To please God more, they have chosen the life of the cross, in poverty and labors, and in obedience to God and men. All of this they did with such a great testimony of interior and exterior virtue that they roused admiration in those who dealt with them. There have been people in the church who, as Saint Paul says, "shine in the world as lights" of heaven (Phil 2:15). Compared with the rest of the world, they excel beyond comparison. This no one will be able to deny, however stubborn he may be, if he considers the life of a Saint Paul and the other apostles and apostolic men there have been in the church. Since in this Christian people there has been very great goodness, as is clear in their actions, what room is there for doubt? Rather, we must either say that there is no knowledge of God on earth, or that these men as a people more beloved by God, have it, and that they made better use of the knowledge by using it to better please the one who gave it to them.

In no way should it be said that the earth lacks the knowledge of God needed for salvation. That would be to say that the principal creatures that God created under heaven, and for whose love he created all things, are all lost because God has not given them the means to be saved. God is not such that he closes the door of salvation. Nor is it in keeping with the depths of his goodness and mercy to be without friends to whom he gives great gifts here, and greater ones in heaven.

This proof of our faith, the good life of Christians, was highly esteemed and recommended by the holy apostles at the beginning of the Catholic Church. Among these, Saint Peter says: "Let wives be subject to their husbands," so that, "if some do not believe the word of God, they may be won without the word of God, by the good conduct of their wives, seeing your holy conduct in the fear of God" (1 Pet 3:1–2). Here appears the power of a good life. It was powerful to convert nonbelievers, who could not be won by the apostolic preaching, even though it was carried on with great efficacy and even with miracles. Saint Paul says that for him to go from one land to another, it was not necessary that those to whom he had preached should give him favorable letters to recommend him to those to whom he was going to preach. He tells the Corinthians, "You are my letter, which is known and read by all" (2 Cor 3:1–2). He says this because the good conduct that they have through his preaching and labors was enough of a "letter" to declare who Saint Paul was and how beneficial his presence was. He says that all know and read this "letter" because anyone, no matter how barbarous, even if he does not understand the language of the word, understands the language of good example and virtue that he sees put into action. From this, people come to high esteem for what such disciples possess. Therefore, the same apostle says in another passage: "Let Christian servants serve their masters in such good faith that in all things they may make attractive the doctrine of God our Savior." He means that "their life should be such that it gives testimony of the way in which Christian doctrine may be held as true" (1 Tim 6:1).

The Lord, who knows all, teaches us very well how important this point is. Praying to his Father, he said these words praying for us

Christians: "I ask you that all may be one as you, Father, in me, and I in you, that they may be one in us, so that the world may believe that you have sent me" (John 17:21). Certainly, he who is the supreme Truth speaks a great truth. If we Christians would keep our law perfectly, the principal commandment of which is that of charity, how great would be the admiration that we would cause in the world to those who would see us equal to them in nature but much greater in virtue. They would then yield to us as the weak do to the strong and the lowly to the great. They would believe that God dwells in us, because they would see that we are able to do what their strength cannot attain, and they would give glory to God who has such servants. Then it would be fulfilled that we are a "letter" of Jesus Christ in which all may read his teachings (cf. 2 Cor 3:2). "We are the adornment of doctrine." We are the "good odor" of Christ (cf. 2 Cor 2:14–15). Because of our life, all would speak well of him.

You, Lord, know that there have been in your church a great number (and there are always some) whose lives are resplendent with a great light, by which they were able to touch any infidels who were willing, so that they might know the truth and be saved. But you also know, Lord, how many there are in the church (which includes both good and evil Christians), who not only are not a means by which unbelievers may know and honor you, but are a means by which they may be more separated from you and blinded. Instead of the honor that they should give you when they hear the Christian name, they blaspheme you very harshly, thinking in their deceived judgment that one who has servants who live so badly cannot be true God and Lord. But you, Lord, have a day set aside to protest this offense and to say, "My name is blasphemed because of you among the Gentiles" (Rom 2:24). On that day you will punish severely anyone who was supposed to gather with you what had been scattered, but instead, scatters what had been gathered (cf. Luke 11:23), or is an impediment to the gathering. Then you will make all understand clearly that you are good, even if your creatures are evil. The evils they commit displease you; you prohibit them in your commandments and punish them severely.

## CHAPTER 35

The nearer and better known the witnesses are, the more people believe their testimony as the truth. Therefore, since you have already been told of some ways of witnessing to the truth, listen now to others. These are not from the past but present and so near to you that, if you want to receive them, they are in your heart. You have particular knowledge of these as you have it of what takes place in your heart. This is based on the word that the Lord spoke: "If anyone wants to do the will of my Father, he will know that my doctrine is of God" (John 7:17). Blessed may you be, Lord! So sure are you of the justice of your cause and the truth of your doctrine, that you leave judgment of it in the hands of anyone at all, friend or enemy. The only condition is that the one who wants to be its judge should desire to do the will of God, which is that man be virtuous and be saved.

It is certainly so that if a man really desires to be good toward God, himself, and his neighbor, he also desires to search for the best teaching there is for him to be good. Imagine that all the laws and doctrines in the world, true and false, are placed before such a person, and that he had no enthusiasm or passion for any of them but was only looking for the truth. Such a man, having left aside all the others, would lay his hand on the gospel and the Christian doctrine, if he understood it, as a thing that better than any other can direct him to what he desires. Insofar as he continues practicing the virtue that he desires, he will continue experiencing the efficacy of this doctrine: how fitting it is for what fulfills the soul; how suitable it is to remedy its needs; in how little time and with what clarity it helps him to be virtuous.

Thus, this man will come, by the very experience of the power of this doctrine, to confess in the Lord's words that "it is a doctrine come from God." He will say what some said that heard Jesus Christ our Lord preaching: "Never has any man in the world spoken so well" (John 7:46). It may happen that those who do not know Christ by faith would hear that admirable and loving voice with which the same Lord cried out with a great shout, "If anyone thirsts, let him come to me and drink" (John 7:37). If, then, desirous of being virtuous, they wanted to taste the satisfying experience of this doctrine, certainly they would not remain in their blindness and infidelity.

But since they are friends of the world and not of true and perfect virtue, and do not seek the certainty of the truth and knowledge of God, they remain without hearing and receiving it. Even if they heard it, some would not receive it, because it is contrary to the things that they desire. Therefore, the Lord said to the Pharisees the words that we have already said before: "How can you believe since you seek honor from each other, and you do not seek the honor that comes only from God?" (John 5:44). Not without great seriousness did Saint Paul say that "some had lost the faith by following after covetousness" (cf. 1 Tim 6:10). Faith is not lost immediately when a man commits any sin at all, unless it is heresy. But a heart may be inclined toward the things of the world and inclined away from virtue. As soon as a person finds truths in Christian doctrine contrary to the heart's evil desires and condemns them with great penalties, he looks, little by little, for other doctrines that do not give a bad taste or bark against his evil desires and deeds. So the heart that is inclined to evil is usually the cause for the blinding of the understanding. It follows that the person abandons the faith that barks against evil and follows or creates other doctrines with which he may be at ease and live as he wants. Bad will sometimes causes one who has faith to lose it, as it will also cause one without faith not to receive it. To both believers and unbelievers, perfect virtue causes repugnance, for no other reason than that it is unpleasant or that it is very good. Thus, the truth of the faith also causes repugnance because it is so contrary to the evil that these people love.

## CHAPTER 36

How much more liberated are those who, with the desire of serving God, have chosen the truth! Although all who serve God rejoice if they are attentive to the many testimonies that faith gives them in their hearts, those who serve him with industrious virtue are the ones who principally rejoice. Many of these were previously in a very miserable state, having become slaves of wickedness and so attached to it that it seemed that their hearts were transformed into it. They had such great determination to do evil that they would face an army with lances ready for battle, as they say, in order to commit it. They were miserable captives, so weak that they could not liberate themselves from so strong a tyrant. Sometimes when they heard a sermon or made their confession or by God's inspiration alone or by other means that are in the Catholic Church, they felt within themselves a most powerful hand that captured their captors and drew them from the wickedness in which they were living. It changed their hearts so truly that many times, in less than a month or a week, they were detesting wickedness more than they had loved it before, saying from the heart: "I have hated and abhorred iniquity, but I have loved your law" (Ps 119:163). They are truly determined not to commit a sin for life or death, nor for heaven or earth or any creature, as Saint Paul says (cf. Rom 8:38–39). Who wrought such a marvelous and good change in such a short time? Who drew water from so hard a rock? Who raised such a miserable dead man, giving him such an excellent life? Certainly, it was no other than the hand of God, believed in and loved as the Catholic Church believes in and loves him, and it was through the means that Christian doctrine holds and teaches.

It may be that this relationship, having begun thus, continues to go forward. This happens with many who, having left everything, are occupied in dedicating themselves totally to their God who "broke their bonds for them" (cf. Ps 116:16), so that they began to travel through the desert of the spiritual life and along the "narrow way that leads to life" (cf. Matt 7:14). Many times they have found themselves in great straits and in storms so fierce that, as David says, "they make the navigators lose their skill and they swallow up their wisdom" (Ps 107:27). But by calling upon their Jesus, the guide of their journey, or other times by receiving the help of the sacraments or by hearing or reading God's words or by other means that are in the church, they have found themselves marvelously succored in tribulation. Therefore, seeing the sudden calming of the sea of their heart, they say what the apostles said: "Who is this whom the winds and the sea obey?" (Matt 8:27). "Truly this is the holy Son of God" (cf. Matt 14:33; 27:54).

Saint Bernard tells of what he had experienced many times: Jesus, when he is truly invoked, is the remedy and the medicine for all the infirmities of the soul.[97] What this saint said, experienced, and demonstrated has happened to many others before and after him. Among such is Saint Jerome, a witness worthy to be believed. As we said above, he tells of finding himself tormented by the flesh and finding no remedy in anything he did. Not knowing what else to do, he found the remedy in throwing himself at the feet of Jesus Christ and calling on him with devout prayer. He received such a calming of the storm that it seemed to him that he was among the choirs of angels.[98] This favor that God is wont to give does not consist only in the cessation of the tribulation being experienced, as can happen when a person diverts his thought elsewhere or takes some similar measure. But the favor that God gives is to communicate a disposition completely contrary to what they were feeling before. This sudden change and perfect liberation is not in the hands of men, as anyone who wants to prove it will come to understand. It comes from outside; it comes from God; it comes through Christian means. It is the experience of what Saint Paul said: "Jesus Christ crucified is the power of God and the wisdom of God for those called by God" (1 Cor 1:23–24). When they invoke him on the day of tribulation, he gives light and strength so that, having overcome hindrances, such men may continue along their journey, singing along the way in the words of David: "Great is the glory of the Lord!" (Ps 138:5). They feel within themselves what the same prophet says: "When I call upon you, I shall know that you are my God" (Ps 56:10). Being healed swiftly and powerfully is a great testimony for them that God is the true God and that he cares for them. We are not speaking of heavenly visions and revelations because these can be counted as miracles. Rather, we are speaking of more common things for which there is more testimony.

## CHAPTER 37

Those who follow diligently along the path of perfect virtue do not merely experience the joy of being liberated by Christ in the midst of the dangers presented to them. They also experience the joy of obtaining and possessing such blessings in their souls that they can say with much truth: "The kingdom of God is within you" (Luke 17:21). As Saint Paul says, this kingdom "consists" in having within oneself "justice, peace, and joy in the Holy Spirit" (Rom 14:17). Such persons as these are so enthusiastic about what is just and good, and they love it so much that, if the laws of virtue were to disappear from books, "they would be found written in their hearts" (cf. Rom 2:15). This is not because they know them by memory but because the resolute love of their hearts is exactly what the law speaks from outside. Their will is already so transformed by love of the good, and through putting it into practice with such love and delight, that to follow their heart's desire is to follow virtue and to flee from vice. They have become the living law and measure of human actions that Aristotle was aiming at. From here there is born a peace and a joy so complete that no one can understand them except the one who tastes them. This is because, as Isaiah says, "the peace of such as these is like a river and like the waves of the ocean" (cf. Isa 48:18). Saint Paul says that "this peace of God surpasses all understanding" (Phil 4:7), and Saint Peter says that "this joy is unspeakable" (cf. 1 Pet 1:8). It is "hidden manna" that is given to the one who manfully overcomes himself. "No one can taste it except the one who receives it" (cf. Rev 2:17).

From where, then, shall we say that such perfect virtue comes, and from where comes this rest that is the pledge and principle of eternal happiness? It certainly does not come from the demon. Sometimes, as we have said, the demon has advised some persons to do some particular good. He does this to win credit by these counsels so that afterward he may deceive them. But to make a man perfectly good and an observer of the natural law (which undeniably is good because God is the author of nature), such a work as this, the demon does not do, nor can he do it. He cannot give the good that he does not have. Neither is it a work of man alone. To have virtue, and even more to have "perfect virtue," with which God is perfectly served, "is a gift from the

Father of lights from whom comes down every perfect gift" (cf. Jas 1:17). The same man experiences not once but many times that he is free from evils from which he could not depart, and he is favored with blessings that he was unable to attain. Since this perfect virtue is neither from the demon nor from the human spirit, it remains that it is infused by God, invoked and served as the faith of the church teaches. Man experiences that this virtue comes to him by the means of faith, in testimony of its truth. Knowledge so advantageous for perfect virtue and for invoking God's help could not come from the lie.

Saint Paul uses this proof when he speaks with the Galatians. "I only want you to tell me this: Did you receive the Holy Spirit by means of the Law or by means of faith?" (Gal 3:2). It is as if he had said: "You received the Holy Spirit when I preached faith, not the Old Law to you, and when you believed and willingly disposed yourself to it. Why are you now returning to the Old Law, since you have experienced that without the Law, by means of faith and penitence and upon receiving baptism, you obtained the Holy Spirit and his grace and his gifts?" Thus, returning to our subject, the perfect virtue obtained by making good use of faith, and of the other means that faith teaches us, is testimony that faith is true, since it has been a means for so good a thing and has taught us the means. So these men, so rich with the blessings that come from Jesus Christ, are so dependent upon him and so rich with him that, certainly, they have no desire to wait for the Messiah that the Jews await or to rejoice in the paradise that Mohammed promises. Since they despise the bestial delights of the flesh that Mohammed promises in his paradise and the other perishable goods of the earth that the Jews await with their Messiah, they willingly leave behind the one and the other, even if they coax them with these things. They recall that it was prophesied that, in the time of the Messiah, they would know that the Lord was God, "when he had broken the bonds of the yoke from his shoulders," and that "God would give them new hearts" (Ezek 36:26). "He would write his Law in the hearts of those who received it" (Jer 31:33). The fact that they have very great signs that they share in these blessings serves them as testimony that Christ has come. By these and other effects within them that cannot be mentioned, they are full of joy and peace and secure in Jesus Christ. Therefore, if anyone told them that "another Christ is in the desert or on the threshold of your house" (cf. Matt 24:26), they would not go far or near to look for him. There can only be one true Christ, and in him they believe that they encounter the qualities of the true one.

Consequently, by one and the same faith, they accept the one and reject the others.

I am not telling you this so that you may think that Christians believe for these motives or experiences that they feel within themselves. They only believe because of the faith that God infuses into them, as will be said later. But I have told you this so that you may know the many motives we have for believing, since we are speaking of this matter. One motive is these experiences that the perfect feel in their souls. Since they are of things that take place in the heart, you do not have to look for them in books or in the lives of others. Instead, you look for them in your own consciousness, as you exert yourself in perfect virtue, so that, as I said at the beginning, you have witnesses nearby and known to you since they are within you. You may fulfill what scripture says: "Drink water out of your own cistern" (Prov 5:15). You will see such marvels within yourself that the desire to look for others outside you will be taken away.

## CHAPTER 38

Anyone who had light to see and a scale to weigh the very act of believing would not need to look for other witnesses for accepting the faith but would find within it beauty to love and reason to accept it.

Who is there who does not understand that it is very just that the creature should serve his Creator with all his strength and with all his possessions? All know that we owe him this service with all these things. But the principal service we must especially render him is with our spirit, because of its likeness to God, since God is Spirit (cf. John 4:24). Since in our spirit there are reason and will, and it cannot be denied that man must serve God with the will, neither can it be denied that man must serve God with the understanding. It is not reasonable that man should serve God with lesser things that he has in himself, but should not serve him with what is most important in him, namely, his understanding and will. Nor is it reasonable that, since the will renders to God the service of obedience, the understanding would remain without obeying God. Just as the obedience of the will consists in denying oneself in order to do God's will, so the service that the understanding must render is to deny itself by believing according to the mind of God. If the service of the understanding were merely to think or consent to something that the person can attain through his own reason, either it should not be called service, or it would be a very low service, since there is no obedience in it. Or if there were obedience in it, it would be of the will, which God commanded to direct the understanding in its thinking. But that the service and obedience of the understanding be proper to man, it is fitting that he consent to something that, by himself, he does not understand. Then he is humbled and truly denies himself; he obeys and is captured and reverences the most high God. He fulfills Saint Paul's words that we must "capture the understanding in the service of faith" (cf. 2 Cor 10:5). In another passage he calls this the "obedience of faith" (Rom 1:5).

As the goodness of God asks us to give him love, and his generosity asks us to hope for more from him, so also his truth asks that we believe him, since one is not less reasonable than the other. The obedience we give to God in love presupposes that we deny our self–love, and the dependence that we place on him is had by not depending on ourselves. So the obedience we must give to his truth is to leave our own opinion and to believe his truth with greater firmness than if we understood it. Otherwise, what thanks would be due to someone who believes what the other says, not because the other says it, but because he himself understands it? But believing without understanding is a praiseworthy work that bears some difficulty within it. It is like trusting without a guarantee or walking without a staff or loving one's enemy for God's sake. If, then, it is done for God, it will be true virtue, worthy of being offered to God and of being rewarded by him.

Since the will of man is dedicated to God and is sanctified by denying itself, the understanding must not remain as if profane, believing in itself without obeying God, because it is to be blessed in heaven by seeing him with all clarity. As Saint Augustine says, "the reward of faith is seeing."[99] Therefore, no reasoning will allow the understanding to abandon its service upon the earth, and its proper service is to believe.

## CHAPTER 39

Moved by these or other reasons, someone will probably say that it is right for a man to believe what he does not understand because God says it. But, he says, this may also be done with regard to believing other things, and therefore there is no reason for believing what we Christians believe.

But tell me, blind men: What defect do you find in what we Christians believe? If you cannot express what you think, I will tell you. The exalted things that we believe about the majesty of God seem so high to you that, because they are high, you do not believe them. The lowly things that we believe about the humility of God seem so lowly to you that, for this reason, you do not consider them worthy of God, and you do not believe them. Tell me: What offends you in the highest mystery of the Most Holy Trinity other than that it is so incomprehensible? When the eyes of your understanding reflect the abyss of that infinite light and the height of such a mystery, you close your eyes and say, "how can this be"? Do you cease to believe, even though it is completely reasonable that we would think most highly of the Most High and that we attribute to him the highest and the best being that our understanding can reach? When we have arrived at very high things about him, we must believe that in him, there are things yet greater and that they completely exceed our understanding. This is to honor God and to consider him as God and as great. If our understanding were able to understand all the height of God, God would be quite small. Therefore, he would not be God, for he could not be so if he were not infinite, and the infinite is incomprehensible for the finite being.

It is better that there be in God the highest communication, and the highest communication is fitting for the highest Good. Therefore, if this is so, the highest Good has to communicate his own total essence. Thus, as is fitting, there will be in God the highest fecundity, and not sterility, a thing completely foreign to him. He says this through Isaiah: "Shall I, who give power for generation to others, remain sterile?" (Isa 66:9).

By creating angels and men and the universe and by giving gifts, God communicates himself. However, this is not the fecundity or communication of the infinite Good, because he does not give them his essence but only their being and power. Nor does God cease from being God alone, no matter how many creatures might accompany him, because there is an infinite distance between them and him. In the same way Adam did not cease being alone, no matter how many beasts and other creatures there might be in the world, and even though he had many of these around him (cf. Gen 2:18–20). So that the man would not be alone, God gave him a companion who was like him and his equal. Likewise, God is not alone because, in the unity of his essence, there are three divine Persons. Nor is he sterile or covetous, because there is communication of the infinite Godhead.

Just because you do not understand how all this is so, you ought not to cease believing in it. Precisely because it is so high, it bears a sign and scent of being a thing of God. It is better that this be so than that it not be. Therefore, it is fitting that God should have, and that we should believe. When we think of God, we ought to think in conformity with God, which means the highest that we are able to think.

## CHAPTER 40

Neither is there any reason to stumble over the humility that the most high God assumed by lowering himself to be man, to live in poverty, and to die on a cross. Not only are these things not unworthy of God, but they are very worthy, if they are understood.

Indeed, if he had abased himself because he could do nothing else, or if in abasing himself he had lost the height that he had before, or if his own interest moved him, there might be some suspicion of his lowering himself. But he did not cease to be what he was by assuming what he was not; nor did he come forcibly from heaven to earth; nor did his own interest move him, for God cannot grow in wealth. Rather, his goodness alone and his love for men moved him, together with his desire to save them in the way that would be most glorious for him and most advantageous for us.

Such is the way that he took in becoming man and dying on the cross, for, "there is no greater sign of love than that a man should die for his friends" (cf. John 15:13). The Lord even died for his enemies in order to make them his friends. Such surpassing love did not come about from their merit but from his supreme goodness. Likewise, his abasement and his death do not indicate any lack of power or knowledge in him, for since he is omnipotent and all wise, he could have saved us by many other means without this. Rather, they indicate the very great excess of goodness and love in him. This is all the more so insofar as the God who loves and suffers is greater, and what he suffers is more grievous and painful, and those for whom he suffers are more unworthy and base. Since in loving, and in loving such men, his surpassing goodness is manifest, it should be said that this work is a very high one. This is because in the spiritual realm, the good and the high are one, and the better a thing is, the higher and greater it is. The greatest honor we can bestow on anyone is to consider him not strong or wise, but good, and there is no one who desires honor who does not want it in this way. Therefore, it is clear that, since these works manifest his goodness and his love more than all others, they give him more honor, and they give it better than all other works. If it seemed to the ignorant that in lowering himself God took away honor from his greatness, it should appear to the wise that the honor of his goodness increases, and consequently, so does that of his majesty and greatness. Thus he loses neither the one nor the other.

Not only does his goodness shine forth in these works more than in others, but also his wisdom and power and other great wonders. Among all the works that God has done or will do in time, there is no other equal or so marvelous, nor is there a miracle so great, as that God should become man, and that afterward he should suffer for men. Whoever does not believe this takes away from God (as much as it is in his power) the greatest honor that he can, even if he were to take away all God's honor for all the other works that he has done or will do in time. Attend well to this and you will see how God's omnipotence and wisdom shine forth in his joining two such distant extremes as God and man in unity of person. Consider how his power is manifest more by fighting and conquering our sins and death with the weapons of our weakness, than if he conquered with the weapons of his omnipotence, as was said above when we were speaking about despair. Consider how, when God abided in his majesty, he had a small people that knew him and that almost every day left him to adore foreign gods. When they were not doing this, they were serving him with great weaknesses. But, having lowered himself to become man and to die, he impressed men so much that the great lowered themselves, the weak became strong, and the wicked good. Finally, there was great change in the world, as much through the suppression of idols as through the transformation of morals. Consequently, the fulfillment of the Lord's word was clearly seen: "When I am lifted from the earth," placed on a cross, "I will bring all to myself" (John 12:32). So it becomes clear that he achieved the victory over human hearts by his abasement, weakness, torments, and death, the victory that he did not achieve in the height of his majesty. Thus, what Saint Paul said is fulfilled, "that the weakness of God is stronger than men" (1 Cor 1:25). Thus also, it seems clear that God does not win honor only by being good, but also by being wise and powerful in taking our lowliness and working in it what he did not work by his greatness.

Because of this, Saint Paul says "he is not ashamed to preach the gospel, for it is the power of God for the salvation of men" (Rom 1:16). Even if humanity, hunger, dishonor, torments, and death are attributed to God, the Christian has no reason to be ashamed. By means of these things God overcame things as strong as sin and death; he brought it about that man might reach the grace of God and his reign, the greatest things that man could come to. Thus God won more honor than for having created the heavens and the earth and all that is in them. Therefore, this work is called the work of God par excellence. As the Lord said, "This is my food, to do the will of my Father, completing his work" (John 4:34), which is the redemption of men. It is not that God has not done other works, but that the incarnation, together with the redemption following from it, is the greatest work of all. It is the thing he finds most precious and that gives him most honor. Although, as Isaiah said, God gained honor by scourging Egypt for love of his people and by bringing them out and guiding them through the desert (cf. Isa 63:12), you already see which is the greater feat of love. Is it that God scourges the enemy out of love for his people, or that God permits himself to be scourged in his own flesh for love of his own? It is one thing for God to lead his own through the desert, "like the eagle that teaches its young to fly and takes them on her shoulders" (Deut 32:11) when they are tired, so that they may rest, since God does not tire. It is another thing to bear on his shoulders a heavy cross (that was removing the skin from them) and all the sins of the world. These crushed him "like the heavy beam of a winepress" (cf. Isa 63:2), to the point of taking his life on the cross, so that men might find rest. Who would not see that this is a most excellent feat of love, and of a love never before seen, and that it gives God greater honor than what was done in the past? What was done in the past was a more common thing, and a little love suffices to do it. But Christ's passion is a thing for few, and hardly will there be found on the earth anyone who would suffer to be beaten publicly or to die for the sake of some good man or friend. If such as this were found, it cannot be compared with the Lord's love and suffering, because he has no equal. It is not so wonderful that a lion act like a lion, but if he should suffer like a lamb for the sake of love, that would be a marvelous feat and worthy of perpetual honor. Of old it was said, "Let us sing to the Lord for he has been gloriously magnified" (Exod 15:1). With profound gratitude, we would say: "Let us sing to the Lord, who has been magnified" in his humility. In the Old Testament, God did not lower himself, nor did he labor in the rest that he was giving, nor did he impoverish himself, although he gave riches. But here, he impoverished himself, he sweat, and "he humbled himself unto death, death on a cross" (Phil 2:8) in order to raise his own from sin and to lead them to heaven. He achieved that and fulfilled what Isaiah said: "Instead of the shrub, shall come up the fir tree, and instead of the nettle, shall come up the myrtle tree, and the Lord shall be named an everlasting sign that shall not be taken away" (Isa 55:13). The honor that God gained by placing himself on the "sign" that is the cross, and by dying on it to make good men from bad, shall last forever without anyone being able to prevent it.

## CHAPTER 41

Not only does his honor shine forth in an excellent way in the works of God's humanity and humility, but a very great profit and

esteem for man also result. There is nothing that exalts man so much
as that God should become his brother. Nor is there anything that so
strengthens his heart against the despondency caused by sin as seeing
that God died as its remedy and was given to him to be his own. Nor
is there anything that so moves him to love God as seeing that he is
beloved by him even to death. Nothing so moves him to despise success, suffer adversities, humble himself to God and his neighbor, or
anything else, however small or grand it may be, as to see God humbled and made human. He passed through these things, giving man
commandments to obey, examples to consider, and help to fulfill them.

Since saving us through humility and lowliness is more fitting for
God's honor and men's good, it is a sign that this is a work of God. In
his work God intends the manifestation of his glory and the advantage
of men. Therefore, one who does not want this work to be or who
denies it is an enemy of God and of all men. He wants to deprive God
of the greatest honor that can come to him through his works, and he
wants to deprive men of the highest honor and advantage that can be
imagined. Since he declares himself an enemy of God and of creatures,
he rightly merits the punishment and death of hell.

The reason he can give when God asks him, "Why did you not
believe exalted things about me?" will be this: "They seemed to me,
Lord, so high, and I did not believe that you were so high." Asked why
he did not believe things about God's humanity and humility, since his
goodness and love were witness to them, he will answer that he did not
think that the Lord's goodness and love were great enough for him to
do and suffer so much for love of men. Thus he stumbles over what is
high and what is low. The root of this lies in his thinking basely of God,
considering him limited in majesty and goodness. This root, and what
proceeds from it, will rightly burn in hell, since it is insulting to the
most high God, because it desires to reduce and limit him.

How much better a response will be that of the one who says:
"Lord, I have believed as much as I could of your majesty and your
goodness, because I hold you to be Lord, infinite in all things. Because
they possess an excess of goodness and love for me, do not allow your
works to seem evil, as they do to the unfaithful, who find no other
defect in you than that you are very good and very loving. It is right
that, for this very reason, we should come to you and take you as God."
Everyone wants a lord who may be for him more a loving and forgiv-
ing father than a rigorous judge who makes him tremble with rigorous
punishments. If the manner of God's dealings with us and of remedy-
ing our sins were placed in the hands of a man, he would not choose

131

other than the one that God chose, the most honorable to himself and the most beneficial for man, and full of all gentleness.

## CHAPTER 42

Let us add to what has been said a discussion of how this faith and belief was received in the world, not by armed force or human favors or human wisdom. Rather, the truth of God fought alone through a few fishermen without learning or resources, against emperors, priests, and all the wisdom of men. That truth turned out so victorious that it caused people to leave their former false belief and to believe a truth beyond their reason, and to believe it from the heart. It is a marvelous work of God that such firmness is had in assent to such lofty matters. It is also marvelous that the very ones who before were killing believers stopped killing them afterward because of the truth of the same things. They did this with more vigor and love than previously they had not believed them and had persecuted them.

A law was preached to them and some very clear commandments. These were so contrary to the inclination of their hearts that it is impossible to think of things more contradictory to each other than the law of the gospel and man's inclination to sin. As Saint Paul says, "The law is spiritual, but I am carnal, sold to sin" (Rom 7:14). Nevertheless, this law was received. By the very power of Jesus Christ, their hearts and works were so renewed to fulfill it that it was clear that he himself was the one creating these men anew in every kind of virtue, as before he had created them in their natural being.

If this had been preached among the uncivilized people of Arabia, where Mohammed preached his lie, or among other peoples likewise easily deceived (such as those bearing lies look for), they might have had some suspicion of the beliefs of these men. But, what shall we say? This truth was preached in Judea, where there was knowledge of God and his divine scripture; it was preached in Greece, where the summit of human wisdom resided; it was preached in Rome where the imperial authority and the government of the world were located. Everywhere, even though it was persecuted, in the end, it was believed. The triumphal title over the cross, "written in Hebrew, in Greek, and in Latin" (John 19:20), was verified, to show that in the principal languages of the world, Christ was to be confessed as king. If then these believed, having sufficient motives, we have a reason to follow them. If they did not have sufficient motives, it is clearly seen that they believed because of light from God. They were a well–informed people, attached to their own belief and strong in human power. It would not have been possible to plant a tree of faith, so lofty and so deeply rooted, in a people so contrary to this truth, unless the powerful hand of God were involved in it. Considering this, Saint Augustine says that the one who sees that the world has believed but does not believe or ask for new miracles in order to believe, is himself a frightening prodigy or miracle for not wanting to follow what so many well–born and wise men have resolutely embraced.[100]

We, who are Christians by God's grace, have good reason to believe. As long as the world has existed, there never has appeared in it a man with such heroic teaching and virtue, and of such marvelous deeds and miracles, as Jesus Christ our Lord. He preached that he was true God and proved it with divine scripture and a host of miracles, and with the testimony of Saint John the Baptist, a witness credited by all. Christ has also been preached and proven by a host of miracles in the Christian Church. There has appeared no faith that so honors God as the faith of the church, or any law that so teaches how to serve him as the gospel. Anyone who understood the gospel well would need no other motive to believe. Neither have there appeared in the world men of such sanctity as those of the Christian people. Nor have such great and high rewards been preached for those who follow virtue, nor such frightful threats against the wicked. These are testimony that our God is a great friend of good and a great enemy of evil. Neither have so many and so great miracles been performed in confirmation of any– thing as those done in confirmation of this faith. If it were not true, it would be very insulting to the honor of the true God, because it attrib– utes to a man equality and unity of essence with God himself. Nor would it have been permitted to last so many years; nor would he have punished the Jews who crucified such a man; nor would he have per– formed so many great miracles as a proof of this belief. Therefore, with reason we can say to God, as Richard says, that if we are deceived in what we believe, God has deceived us.[101]

This truth possesses such great light within itself, and such great things and miracles have been done in confirmation of it, that no one else but God could have done them. But as God is far from being a deceiver, we are far from being deceived. Glory be to God forever!

# 2. The Supernatural Quality of Faith
## (chaps. 43–44)

**CHAPTER 43**

Up to this point, you have heard some of the reasons for determining that the Catholic faith is the true one and for giving an account to anyone who may ask it. We are not weak in faith, since we have more motives for belief than any people of the world do.

But, with all this, you should be convinced that the Christian faith is so high that, even if a man had these and other motives that could be mentioned, and even if among these were included seeing miracles confirming the faith with his own eyes, he cannot, through his own strength, have the capacity to believe as the Christian believes and as God commands him to believe. This is because, just as God alone declares through his church what must be believed, so he alone can give strength to believe it. God is the interior Master of this teaching, infusing into the understanding this faith by which man is instructed and fortified for this belief. As Christ says, "It is written in the prophets that all shall be taught by God" (John 6:45). The same Lord, after Peter had confessed him as the true Son of God and the Messiah promised in the Law, gave him to understand that he ought not to credit such faith and such a confession to his own strength but to the gift of God. "Blessed are you, Simon, son of Jona, because flesh and blood has not revealed these things to you, but my Father, who is in heaven" (Matt 16:17). In another place he says, "Everyone who hears my Father and learns from him, comes to me" (John 6:45). This is the supreme school, where the teacher is God the Father, and the doctrine he teaches is faith in Jesus Christ his Son and the way to him is by steps of faith and love.

This faith is not dependent on any reasons or motives that could be brought forth. Whoever believes because of these does not believe in such a way that his understanding is persuaded with no doubt or scruple remaining. But the faith that God infuses is dependent on the divine Word and makes one believe with greater firmness than if he had seen him with his own eyes and touched him with his own hands. He has greater certainty than that four are more than three, or any other such thing that the understanding sees with such great clarity that it has no scruple and cannot doubt, even if it should want to. Then such a man says to all the motives he had for believing, what the Samaritans said to the Samaritan woman: "Now we do not believe because of what you told us, because we ourselves have seen and known that this is the Savior of the world" (John 4:42).

Although it says, "we have known," do not understand that those who believe have the clarity of evidence that philosophers call science. As was said above, the understanding cannot arrive by its own reason at this clarity regarding the things of the faith, nor does faith consist in having evidence, because then it would not be faith and there would be no merit. Faith in the understanding is called sight. But because we do not have the clarity of evidence, Saint Paul says that "we see now as in a mirror, and afterward in heaven, we shall see face to face" (1 Cor 13:12). However, the Samaritans say they "know" that Christ is "the Savior of the world," to make it understood that they believe with firmness as great as when something is known more clearly, even much more clearly. This is because, as we have said, one who has faith infused by God believes because the truth of God says it. This truth is infinite and more certain than all other truths, because they receive firmness from participation in infinite truth. Therefore, the believer is as certain that he cannot be deceived in what he believes, as he is certain that God cannot cease being true. This certainty exceeds any other that can be had in any other way. It causes the man to be so peaceful in this regard that, not even in thought, does he suffer anything against the faith, and if it does happen, it is so passing that it gives him little trouble. Even though he may be attacked with scruples or with false thoughts in the interior of his understanding, he is very firm and calm because his faith is built upon the firmest rock, which is the truth itself. This, he believes for itself and not for other motives. Therefore, neither winds nor waters nor rivers will be able to bring it down.

Perhaps you wonder that in a human understanding, so various and changeable in its opinions, and with so little firmness settled in the things of reason, there is such great certainty and calm firmness. Because of these, the person is not moved from what he believes through arguments or torments or seeing that others lose their faith or by anything high or low. I tell you that it is enough for you to understand that this business and this building are not a thing of our strength, which cannot obtain so much. "It is a gift of God" (Eph 1:8), as Saint Paul says. It is not inherited or merited or achieved by human strength. Consequently, let no one boast in himself for having it, but let him be faithful in recognizing that it is a gift of God, given through Jesus Christ, his Son. As Saint Peter says, "You were faithful through him" (1 Pet 1:21). Do not wonder, then, that upon the miserable sand of human understanding there is an edifice of such firmness, because the Lord says: "This is the work of God: that you believe in the one that he sent" (John 6:29). Therefore, as God leads man to the supernatural end of seeing him clearly in heaven, so he is not content that man should believe as man, on the strength of motives or miracles or reasons. Rather, raising man above himself, he gives him supernatural strength with which to believe, not with fear and scruple as a man, but with certainty and security as befits the things of God. Concerning this faith, it is understood that "no one can call Jesus Lord except in the Holy Spirit" (1 Cor 12:3). Even though it may not be necessary to be in grace in order to believe, nevertheless it cannot be done without the inspiration of the Holy Spirit, as will be said later. It is of such works or graces, which are described as "freely given," that Paul is speaking in that passage.

Faith inclines the understanding to believe the supreme truth in what the Catholic faith teaches, as love inclines the will to love the supreme good. As the needle of the compass is attracted by the force of the North to be pointed toward it, so, by the faith that he infuses, God moves the understanding so that it goes toward him with an assent that is firm, tranquil, and full of satisfaction. When this faith is perfect, it carries with it a light by which, though it does not see what it believes, it does see how worthy of belief are the things of God. Not only does it not experience difficulty in believing, but it experiences a very great delight, such as perfect virtue usually produces as it works with ease, strength, and delight.

This is the faith that very rightly must be appreciated and honored, for by it we honor God, as Saint Paul says that Abraham did, "giving God honor for being so powerful that he can do whatever he says" (Rom 4:20–21). You should understand here that faith is an honor to God since it believes and preaches his infinite perfections. This is the faith that God constructed in the soul like a tower, so that having climbed it, we may see, although "as in a mirror," what there is in heaven and in hell, and what happened at the beginning of the world and what will happen at its end. As hidden as this may be, it is not hidden from the eyes of faith. This is apparent in the good thief who, seeing such exterior contempt and baseness in Christ crucified, entered by faith into what is hidden and recognized him as the Lord of heaven. As such he confessed him with great humility and firmness (cf. Luke 23:42).

By this faith, we believe that what the church declares to us to be scripture and the divine word is such. Even if it is spoken by the mouths of men, we hold it to be the word of God. Therefore, we do not believe less the evangelist or the prophet who did not see what he wrote than the one who saw what he wrote. This is because this faith does not look to human testimony that rests on human means, but on the fact that God inspires the prophet or the evangelist to write the truth. God assists him so that he may not be deceived in what he thus writes. Saint Peter heard with his own ears the voice of the Father that sounded on Mount Tabor: "This is my beloved Son" (2 Pet 1:17); he saw with his own eyes that Jesus Christ was resplendent as the sun. But it is certain that, if we see him only as a man who gives testimony of what he saw and heard, "more firmness and certainty the scripture has, or the word of the prophets" (cf. 2 Pet 1:19). These give firmer testimony that Jesus Christ is the Son of God, even if they neither saw nor heard him with the eyes and ears of the body, than what Peter said about what he had seen and heard. But, the church has declared that the letter of Saint Peter, where this is written, is divine scripture. Consequently, what Saint Peter says in it is the word of God. It is clear that God assisted him that he might say it. He assisted him so that he might not be deceived concerning what he saw and heard on Mount Tabor, nor in what he wrote, when he recounted what had happened there. Therefore, the word of the prophets "is not firmer or more certain," because they and he spoke through one and the same Spirit, which is one and the same Truth.

This habitual faith God infuses into children when they are baptized, and as habitual and actual faith in those who are older and do not have it, when they dispose themselves for it. "He desires that all be saved and come to knowledge of the truth" (1 Tim 2:4). Since without faith they cannot please God (Heb 11:5–6) or be saved, he does not cease giving it to anyone who has not abandoned him.

**CHAPTER 44**

It is very reasonable, my daughter in Christ, that all of us Christians should give heartfelt thanks to the Lord who has graciously bestowed on us the gift of faith. There is no reason why we should let a day go by without confessing this faith by reciting the Creed at least twice—in the morning and at night—or without giving thanks to the one who gave us the gift of this faith. We must endeavor to preserve it in its purity and integrity as something of great importance to us. We must consider the end for which it has been given us, so that we might neither cease to practice it as it is nor attribute to it what does not pertain to it. Faith has been given to us so that we might believe what God commands us to believe, and that it might be a light for the knowledge that helps move our will to love God and keep his commandments, by which man is saved.

But, if anyone should say of this faith that through it alone justice is obtained and the pardon of sins, he will grievously err, as have those who have affirmed this. As has been said above by the authority of Saint Paul, "No one can say that Jesus is Lord, except through the inspiration of the Holy Spirit" (1 Cor 12:3). By this it is understood that the same inspiration is required to believe the other mysteries of our faith. We know that the Lord said to some of those who heard him: "Why do you call me Lord, Lord, and not do the things that I tell you?" (Luke 6:46). Since they called Jesus "Lord," they had faith, as Saint Paul says, but since they did not do what the Lord commanded, they were not in grace. From this it clearly follows that a man may have faith without having grace. Paul affirms this in another passage. There he says that "if a man has the gift of speaking tongues, and knows and possesses all knowledge and prophecy and all faith, and even moves mountains from one place to another, but does not have charity, he is nothing" (1 Cor 13:1–2). Since Paul is certain that the gift of tongues and the others he lists here are compatible with being in mortal sin, it is not right for anyone to wed charity with faith in such a way that faith cannot exist without charity. However, it is true that charity cannot exist without faith.

It is a word of the divine scripture that justice is given through faith. But that it is given by faith alone is a human invention and a very ignorant and perverse error (cf. Gal 2:16). The Lord warned us of it when he told the Magdalene that "her many sins are forgiven her because she has loved much" (Luke 7:47). These words giving testimony that love is required are as clear as those in the whole of scripture that give testimony that, for the justification of the sinner, faith is required, not just love. The two things go together because love is the cause and disposition for pardon, and so is faith. The Lord mentioned both in the case of the Magdalene when, at the end of the discussion, he said: "Your faith has saved you; go in peace" (Luke 7:50).

The Lord said that "her many sins are forgiven her because she has loved much"; he did not say, "because she has believed much." This would have been to call the effect by the name of the cause. It is clear that, having asked which of the debtors most *loved* the one who pardoned him, the one pardoned less or the one pardoned more, the Lord had to conclude his discourse by speaking of love, not of faith. One may take the liberty of saying that he meant faith when he said love and was calling the effect by the name of its cause. We will then take the liberty of saying that, in the places in scripture where it says that "man is justified through faith," the word "faith" is to be understood as meaning love, since the effect is understood in the cause. All this presupposes that it is a frequent and reasonable manner of speaking to call the effect by name of the cause and the cause by the name of the effect.

The Lord spoke clearly here, except for anyone who chooses to be blinded by the light. He called faith and love by their own names. Both are required for justification, as we have said. The Lord affirms the same union when he says to his disciples: "The Father himself loves you, because you have loved me, and have believed that I came forth from him" (John 16:27). Since faith and love are required, there shall certainly be sorrow for sins, for the one who loves God above all things, does not cease grieving over the grave offenses he has committed against him. This appears in the Magdalene and in other sinners who are converted to God.

Because these things are required (and others that follow from them) to obtain justice, the divine scripture sometimes speaks of faith, other times of love, and other times of the sighing and sorrow of penance. Sometimes it gives the humble prayer of the penitent who says, "Lord, be merciful to me a sinner!" (Luke 18:3). At other times it gives the recognition of sin. "I have sinned against the Lord," said David, and he immediately heard the word of pardon from God. But whoever moved by this would say that sin is pardoned by the recognition of sin alone would commit no small error (2 Sam 12:13). Cain, Judas, and many others, including Saul, all recognized their sin but did not obtain pardon. It would be as baseless to say that it is obtained "by faith alone" because in some passages of scripture it mentions nothing but faith. Following this reasoning we would be able to throw faith out of this affair on the grounds that in other passages the scripture speaks of sins being pardoned by penitence or other things without any mention of faith. But the Catholic truth is that the one and the others are required as dispositions for obtaining pardon and grace.

Someone may think that faith is named many times: justice is attributed to it; by faith we are made sons of God and participants in the merits of Jesus Christ; faith has other similar effects that are in harmony with grace and charity. This is not because faith alone suffices for this. Rather, it is because the meaning of the scripture when it attributes these effects to faith is that it is understood as "faith formed by charity" (cf. Gal 5:6), that charity which is the life of faith.

Do not attribute these effects to faith on the grounds that having it, love is necessarily possessed. As has been said, true faith can subsist when grace and love have been lost. As Saint Paul puts it, love "is greater than faith and hope" (1 Cor 13:13). When the Lord spoke of faith and love, as in the case of the Magdalene, and in what we said about his disciples, he named love first before faith. He thus gave the first place in perfection to an act of the will that, in a certain way, comes after, when compared with the act of the understanding, to which faith pertains.

It must also be seen that it is necessary to receive the sacraments of baptism and penance (the first for unbelievers, the other for believers who have committed mortal sin after baptism), or to have the intention of receiving them, to obtain the grace that has been lost. But scripture does not mention them as many times as it mentions faith. We will speak shortly about the reason for this. But neither does it omit speaking of them lest anyone should think they are not necessary for obtaining justice. Saint Paul says that "through the baptism of regeneration and renewal of the Holy Spirit, God saved us" (Titus 3:5). He also says that Christ "cleansed his church with the baptism of water, in the word of life" (Eph 5:26). If because the scripture says that we are justified by faith, the sacraments have to be thrown out, it would also be possible to throw out faith, since scripture says that "salvation and purification are given by holy baptism." But the Lord unites both things, saying, "Whoever believes and is baptized, will be saved" (Mark 16:16).

Also, the same Lord said to his apostles when he instituted the sacrament of penance: "Whose sins you shall forgive, they shall be forgiven them" (John 20:23), and so on. Consequently, grace and justice are given by means of this sacrament, for no one can have pardon of sins without grace being given. This is signified and contained in all seven sacraments of the church. It is given to anyone who receives them well, and in greater abundance according to the disposition of the one receiving them. This is because they are privileged works that, by the very performance, give grace. Therefore, they must be reverenced and used extensively, as the Catholic Church believes and teaches us.

If faith was so frequently preached and named in the beginning of the church, it was fitting that it should have been. Then it was being planted, and it was being suggested that unbelievers should receive it and should enter through it as through the first door to salvation. After having entered, they would be informed more specifically of what they had to believe and to do.

Likewise it was fitting in those times to manifest particularly the mystery and value of the passion and death of Jesus Christ our Redeemer, who had been crucified in those times in extreme dishonor.

Faith in this mystery makes people believe and confess that on that wood, so dishonored in external appearance, was hung the divine life, and that there, "in the midst of the earth, God worked salvation" (cf. Ps 74:12) and the remedy for the world by his death. Such a faith honors the dishonor of the cross and is the exaltation of the lowliness that was exercised there to the utmost. Thus, it was fitting that faith should be named many times and with great honor, since it redounds to the honor of Jesus Christ our Lord. To his person and merit, faith testifies by preaching his eminence.

When scripture says that "through faith men are justified" (cf. Gal 3:8), it attributes this to it, not because it is sufficient by itself, but as the principle and foundation and root of all that is good, as the Council of Trent says. Those who attribute justification to faith alone, do it as a means of finding consolation for their mediocrity or for the wickedness of their lives. They desire to assure themselves by the way of believing so that they may have broader license. Without the difficulties that perfect virtue demands, they want to obtain the peace and the confidence of a good conscience, which is the cause of perfect charity. They are not even content with this, since, according to the truth, "there is no one" in this life completely "sure whether he is worthy of love or of hate" (cf. Eccl 9:1). However, depending on whether they have greater or lesser virtue, they will have more or fewer reasons for confidence. But there are those who, according to their own imaginations, want to give the same certitude to the believer that he is pardoned by God as that given to what the Christian believes as an article of the faith. These are deceptions of the devil, believed by people who possess neither assent in faith nor sanctity in life. They are enemies of obedience who, as they say, go along blindly, groping their way in the things of God. If this were not so, the demon would not so quickly deceive them.

# PART TWO

# "Incline Your Ear!"

(CHAPS. 45–55)

# A. Submission to God's Revealed Word (Chaps. 45–49)

## CHAPTER 45

The word order of this treatise requires that after the first word, "listen," I would explain the second word, "look." But the logical order of thought by which the first and third are related requires that I postpone discussion of the second word in order to deal with the third, which reads, "Incline your ear."

To understand this, you must note that the things of God are so lofty, and our reason is so lowly and subject to deceit that, for the security of our salvation, God arranged to save us through faith and not through our knowledge. This, he did not do without very just cause. For since the world, as Saint Paul says, did not know God through wisdom (1 Cor 1:21), people were deceived through various errors, attributing the glory of God to the sun, the moon, and other creatures. Others, knowing God through the traces of his creatures, became so proud by searching into the knowledge of something so exalted that through their pride the light that the Lord in his goodness had given them was taken away. Thus they fell into the darkness of idolatry and a host of other sins, just as those who had not known God (cf. Rom 1:21–32). After the wicked angels sinned (cf. Rev 12:7–9), God, "having learned his lesson," as they say, did not allow any creature able to sin to live in heaven. Similarly, having seen how poorly human beings availed themselves of reason, and that the world, as Saint Paul says, did not know God through wisdom (1 Cor 1:21), he refused to leave in the hands of their wisdom either knowledge of himself or their own salvation. Instead, through the preaching of that which reason could not attain, he preferred to save, not the learned, but simple believers. Thus, after the Holy Spirit admonishes us by the two words already mentioned, "hear" and "see," he gives a third admonition: "Incline your ear." In this he shows us that we must subject our reason most profoundly and not be inflexible in it, if we do not want the "hearing" and "seeing" that were given for our good to become for us the occasion of eternal perdition.

Certainly, many people have heard God's words and have possessed excellent knowledge of subtle and lofty matters. But because they drew near to see, more through curiosity to see, than obediently to "incline" the ear of their reason, their seeing became blindness, and they stumbled about in the noonday light as if it were darkness. Therefore, if you do not want to stray along the path to heaven, "incline your ear," which is to say your reason, without any fear of being deceived. Incline it with the most profound reverence for the word of God, spoken in the whole of Sacred Scripture. If you do not understand it, do not think that the Holy Spirit made a mistake. Rather, subject your understanding and, as Saint Augustine says that he did, believe that because of the loftiness of the word, you are unable to attain it.

You must incline your ear with the same consent of faith to all the scripture of God, because all of it is the word of one and the same supreme Truth. But you have to be particularly careful to profit from the blessed words that the true God–made–flesh spoke upon the earth. With devout attention, open the ears of your body and soul to every word of this Lord, who was given to us as our special teacher by the voice of the eternal Father, saying, "This is my beloved Son in whom I am well pleased; listen to him" (Matt 17:5). Apply yourself to reading and hearing these words. Without doubt, you will find in them a unique medicine and a powerful efficacy for whatever has to do with your soul, such as you will not find in all the other words spoken by God since the beginning of the world. There is good reason for this. For in what he said in other places, he has spoken through the mouths of his servants. But what he spoke in the humanity that he assumed, he spoke in his own person, "opening his own mouth" (cf. Matt 5:2) to speak. He is the one who at first opened the mouths of those who spoke in the Old Testament and afterward opened the mouths of those who spoke in the New Testament. Watch out that you are not ungrateful for this great gift that God has given in wanting himself to be our teacher. The One who gave us being so that we might exist, gives us the milk of his word to sustain us. This is a grace so great that, if there were a scale to weigh it, and if we were told that, at the end of the world, there were words of God for the instruction of the soul, we would suffer every difficulty and danger to hear a few such blessed words of the highest wisdom and to become his disciples.

Take advantage of this grace for God has placed it near at hand. Ask the one in charge of guiding your soul to look in Sacred Scripture, in the teaching of the church, and in the words of the saints, for words appropriate to the necessities of your soul. Now it may be to defend you from temptations according to what the Lord did, when he was fasting in the desert (cf. Luke 4:1–2) as an example to us, or to encourage you to have the virtues you lack. At another time it may be so that you may conduct yourself as you ought to with God, yourself, and your neighbors, whether those in charge, subjects, or peers, or how to conduct yourself in prosperity and in tribulation. In short, scripture is for any necessity that you find along the way of God so that you can say: "In my heart, I have hidden your words so that I may not sin against you. Your word is a lamp for my feet and a light on my paths" (Ps 119:11).

Take care that you do not fall into the curiosity of wanting to know more than you need, either for yourself or for those in your care. The rest you ought to leave to those who have charge of teaching God's people. As Saint Paul cautions: "Let our wisdom be with moderation" (Rom 12:3).

## CHAPTER 46

You should be aware that the exposition of divine scripture is not to be done according to the mind or ingenuity of each person. If it were, God's word, which is most certain in itself because it is God's word, would be very uncertain as it applies to us, since there are usually as many opinions as there are heads. It is very fitting for us to have the highest certainty about this word that we are to believe and follow and, for the sake of confessing and obeying it, to lay down all that we have, even life itself. The matter would not be well provided for if the diverse opinions of men did not permit the word to have certainty in the heart of the Christian. Only the Catholic Church has the privilege of interpreting and understanding the divine scripture, because the same Holy Spirit who spoke in the scripture dwells in her. Where the church does not determine anything, we must follow the unanimously agreed upon interpretation of the saints if we do not want to err. Otherwise, how can the human spirit and ingenuity understand correctly what the divine Spirit spoke, for every scripture must be read and declared by the same Spirit by which it was made?

You also must know that to declare which scripture is the word of God that all must believe to be such pertains to no one except the same Christian Church, whose head on earth, by divine ordering, is the Roman pontiff. Hold as certain, as Saint Jerome says, that "any person, who, outside this church and house of God, should eat the Lamb of

God, is a profane person, not a Christian."[102] Whoever is found outside of her must necessarily perish, just as those who did not enter into Noah's ark were drowned in the flood (cf. Gen 7:23). This is the church that the gospel commands us to hear and to regard anyone who does not hear as an evil and unbelieving person (cf. Matt 18:17). This is the church that Saint Paul says, "is the pillar and ground of truth" (1 Tim 3:15).

The very faith infused by God, of which we have spoken above, inclines and enlightens us to believe that this is so, as one of the articles of faith, and with the same and equal certainty. Up to this point, the church has so believed. Because a people, full of pride and thus deceived by the devil, has separated itself in our time, the church does not cease being what she has been, and neither should we cease believing what we have believed. Therefore, against this church, let no revelation move you or any sentiment of spirit or anything greater or less, even if it should appear that the one who speaks against her is "an angel from heaven" (cf. Gal 1:8). For it is not possible that this would be the truth. Even less should the teaching of past, present, or future heretics move you. Abandoned by God by his just judgment, they follow a false light as if it were true. Being lost themselves, they cause perdition to all who follow them. Consider the end of those who departed from the faith of the church in times past and how they were like a gust of wind that passes immediately and then is forgotten. Consider, on the other hand, the firmness of our faith and the church, and how it has ever remained victorious. Even though it has been attacked from its birth, it has never been conquered, "for it is founded upon a firm rock" (cf. Matt 7:25). Against it, neither rains nor winds nor rivers "nor the gates of hell can prevail" (cf. Matt 16:18).

Close your ears, then, to all doctrine alien to that of the church and follow the faith practiced and preserved for such a multitude of years, since it is certain that in her a great multitude of people have been saved and sanctified. I see no greater madness than that a man leave a road by which very wise and holy persons have traveled and gone to heaven, to follow some who are incomparably inferior in every kind of good. They are greater only in the pride and shamelessness of wanting, without any proof other than their own opinion, to be believed more than the multitude of those of the past who had divine wisdom, an excellent life, and a multitude of great miracles. These deceived people principally follow a certain Luther. He was so weak in his flesh that, according to what he himself said, he could not live without a wife. When she died, he could not live chastely without taking another.

Many have been content with one wife, and others have decided not to have even one in order to dedicate themselves completely to God with greater purity and liberty. How can we call good the spirit that lived in that evil man, since it did not have strength to give him even the most common kind of chastity? He had promised the highest kind of chastity such as many possess. It would have been right for him to follow these as his betters. The Lord said that "by their fruits we shall know the tree" (Matt 7:16). Since Luther gave forth such fruits and other worse ones, there dwelt in him the spirit of the earth, of weakness of the flesh, and of the devil. Wait a little and you will see the end of the wicked, and how "God will vomit them" (cf. Rev 3:16) in extreme dishonor, declaring their error with clear punishment, as he has done with those of the past.

## CHAPTER 47

Anyone with light to judge that the true goods and evils for man are spiritual, already in the present sees the severe punishment of God upon this heretical people. It is a punishment such that there is none greater except hell. "Who shall not fear you, O King of the nations?" (Jer 10:7). "Who has not known the power of your anger, or will be able to count it with the great fear of it?" (Ps 90:11). The great chastisements of God, that ought to be feared above all, are not misfortunes with regard to possessions, honor, or life. Rather, they are that God allows the will of man to be hardened in sin or the understanding to be darkened by error, especially in matters of faith. These are the wounds of divine wrath. They are not the wounds of a father but of a just and rigorous judge. What God says in Jeremiah is rightly understood of them: "With a wound of an enemy, I have wounded you, with rigorous chastisement" (Jer 30:14). However, he does not use the rigor of a judge without having first used the mercy of a father.

If you consider well, blindness of the understanding involves a particular evil, greater than hardness of the will. Though this latter is serious, there is still some hope of obtaining a remedy. This is because his faith remains in the man even if it is dead, and therefore he has knowledge that there is a remedy in the church for his sin. This is a great help for his rising and mending his ways. But how will one who errs in faith seek or find a remedy? One who is outside the church will not find one because there is none outside the church. But one who is inside the church does not look for a remedy because he does not believe in it. Thus he ends up lost. "It is a thing that God does in Israel. Whoever hears of it, his ears will tingle from pure fear" (1 Sam 3:11).

But such great chastisement does not come without great justice. Saint Paul declares this, saying, "The wrath of God is revealed from heaven against all wickedness of those men that detain the truth of God in injustice" (cf. Rom 1:18). The intention of the Apostle in this passage is to say that there were men who, "although they knew God, they did not serve him as God but were puffed up with blind pride" (cf. Rom 1:21). Possessing the truth in the understanding, they committed evil with the will. Thus, the truth of God was "detained" or imprisoned in them, since they did not do what it taught but did what their evil will desired. The truth of God is a very excellent thing, and he gives it as a great gift in order that the man who follows it with affection may honor it, arrive at virtue, and be saved. But if such a man does not see this and treats the truth in such a way that he neither does what it teaches nor keeps it in a pure place, as it deserves, he thus greatly dishonors both God, who gave it, and the truth that he gave. If the truth had a tongue, it would loudly cry out for justice against such a man. For, though it is so precious a jewel and can so benefit man, it is "detained," without him hearing it or doing what it says; it is lodged amid the filth of the sins that such a man has in his will. So, as it can, it cries like the blood of Abel seeking vengeance (cf. Gen 4:10). Such a one does not deprive the truth of life, since true faith can coexist with an evil life. But it does deprive it of the efficacy that it would have in action if, instead of hindering it, the man were helping it by his will to do what it teaches. God hears these cries, and he is the one who says, "The servant who knows the will of his Lord and does not do it, will receive many stripes" (Luke 12:47). Among these, the greatest that he gives in this world, as we have said, is to permit that such a man fall into error in punishment for his sins. So were those punished that fell into idolatry so blind that "instead of God they came to adore birds and serpents, and beasts" (cf. Rom 1:23). They took from God the honor owed to him as God and gave it to those to whom it did not belong. Therefore, God again chastised this sin of idolatry by permitting them to fall into sins so foul that it is frightening to think of them and shameful to speak of them.

Even though those chastised with this chastisement will, without doubt, fall into sins, their fall is as free as in their other sins, in that they fall by their own will. As many as their earlier and later sins are, God's mercy is not closed to them if they desire to take refuge in his merciful heart. The power of God is manifest in the first, his wisdom in the second, and his goodness and mercy in the third. For the same purpose that the sovereign judge punished these proud Gentiles, he also punished the ungrateful Jews, and with good reason, for he had given them more knowledge than he had given to the Gentiles. They used it so badly that they unfaithfully rejected the true light itself, who is Jesus Christ, and they crucified him by the hand of the Gentiles. Because they wanted to extinguish that sovereign light, without which there is neither light nor truth, they ended up in obscure darkness and eternal perdition, unless they were converted to the service of the God they had rejected. But let us see the motive that led them to so great an evil, the denial of credence to the light that was present to them. Saint John responds, "Men loved darkness more than the light because their works were evil; and everyone who does evil hates the light" (John 3:19–20). Thus, because the Lord and his teaching directed them to the fullness of truth and virtue, and they loved the lie and wickedness, they were unable to hear or to see. They would not desire a light of doctrine that would uncover their false sanctity. Nor would they desire an example of a perfect life, in comparison with which their own life was condemned as evil. From the root of this depraved will came forth the fruit that they would deny and kill the heavenly physician who came to heal them. They turned out to be such as the prophet David had painted them a long time before, when he said of them, "Let their eyes be darkened so that they may not see, and their back be always bent down" (Ps 69:24). For their eyes remained without the light of faith and their will desirous of the things of the earth.

## CHAPTER 48

If God had such great zeal for the honor of the knowledge that he gave to Gentiles and Jews, how much more zeal will he give to Christians, since it is incomparably greater than that of either of the others? Given that many make very poor use of such excellent knowledge of the faith, it is not strange that God sometimes wounds such men with the terrible punishment of letting them fall into heresies, as he did with those of the past. Are we not perhaps seeing with our own eyes the fulfillment of what Paul prophesied about the end times, saying that "God would send to some men a deceptive power so that they may believe in a lie," and a lie against the faith (2 Thess 2:11–12)? Everyone knows the unfortunately great success of the Lutheran heresy that so many people have willingly embraced. By this it is obvious that God has sent them this "deceptive power so that they may believe in a lie," as Saint Paul said. But God did not send any of these things, inciting man to believe the lie or to do evil, because "he is not a tempter of the wicked" (Jas 1:13), as Saint James says. But what is said

151

is that he sent a "deceptive power," when with just judgment he allows the understanding of man to be deceived by false reasons or false miracles, done by another man or by the perverse devil. Thus the man feels within himself "a potency to believe that lie." It seems to him that he is moved to believe it as a very great and beneficial truth. This is a severe judgment of God, and since he is just, the fault for which it is the punishment must be great. What this sin is, Saint Paul himself tells us, saying that "they did not receive the love of the truth, that they might be saved" (2 Thess 2:10). If you consider how powerful the truth that we believe is for helping us to serve God and to be saved, you will realize that it is a grave fault not to love this truth and its teaching. It is an even greater fault to commit foul deeds against all that the truth teaches. How far from offending God would be one who believes that there is an eternal fire for the offender and countless other torments with which he will be punished, as long as God is God, without hope of any remedy! How would one dare to sin who believes that when sin enters the soul by one door, God leaves by the other? And what man is like without you, Lord, that man knew who begged, "Lord, depart not from me" (Ps 35:22). Once God has left, we remain in the first death of sin and on the eve of the second death of sin and infernal punishment.

Rightly was Job amazed when he said, "Who will be able to taste that which, after it is tasted, brings death with it?" (cf. Job 6:6). Certainly we would not taste a dish that a trustworthy physician has told us is lethal. Let us not with perverse consent taste sin, since God has said, "The soul that sins, that one shall die" (Ezek 18:20). Why does your faith in God's word not work in you what the physician's word works, since the latter can and often does deceive, but God never does? Why does God's word that he is the eternal reward for those who serve him not make all of us serve him with great diligence and effort, even if, in doing this, we should suffer many troubles and it should cost us our life? Why do we not love our Lord, whom we believe to be the highest good and the one who first loved us even to the point of dying for us? It is the same with everything else that this sacred faith teaches and invites us to for its part. With grave fault we stop following and go after contrary works. Is there a greater monstrosity than a Christian believing what he believes and yet doing the evil deeds that many do? As punishment for "not having love of the truth" by which they were saved, and for not putting into practice what it taught them, it is a very just judgment of that Lord, who is "terrible in his counsels over the sons of men" (Ps 66:5), that he should leave them, permitting them to believe in error. If you see where God set the trap by which the Jews and heretics were punished, as we have said, you will think that it is a thing more to tremble at than to talk about. Ask these men on what they were relying to follow their error with such stubborn persistence. Those in the first group will tell you they were relying on the Sacred Scripture of the Old Testament, and those in the second group will tell you that they were relying on the New Testament. You will see clearly fulfilled the prophecy of the prophet David in which he says, "Their table shall be changed into a snare, a punishment, and a stumbling block" (Ps 69:23). Have you ever seen anything so backward? The table of life is converted into a snare of death; the table of consolation and pardon becomes punishment; the table where there is light to know how to follow the path that leads to life is changed into a stumbling block, causing one to lose the way and to fall into death. Certainly the fault is great that merits the punishment that a man should be blinded in the light and that his life should become death.

"You are just, Lord, and your judgments are just" (Ps 119:137), and there is no wickedness in you. But there is wickedness in them who use badly the goods that come from you. Because of this, it is just that they stumble over them and that they be punished for dishonoring the goods and you. Faith in you, Lord, is a great good, indeed a very great good. It is reasonable that it be respected, obeyed, and put into action. Great are the gifts you have made to us in giving us your divine scripture, so beneficial and necessary for serving you. But, because the wind blowing on this sea is from heaven, and some preferred to sail the sea by winds of the earth (their own talents and studies), they drowned in it, and you permitted it. In the parables that you preached on the earth, Lord, those with the disposition for it were secretly taught, while others were blinded by the same parables, by your just judgment (cf. Matt 13:11ff.). In the same way you deal with the deep sea of your divine scripture. It is charged with showing mercy to the lambs of your flock, so that they swim to their own advantage and that of others. But it is also charged with executing justice by which the proud elephants may drown themselves and drown others. Fearsome, and very fearsome, must the entrance into the divine scripture be, and no one should hurl himself into it without much preparation, as in it there is much danger. Let anyone who must enter it take along the sense of the Roman Catholic Church and he will avoid the danger of heresy. So that he may profit from the scripture, let him take along purity of life, as Saint Athanasius says in the following words: "Goodness of life is necessary, and purity of soul and Christian piety, for the investigation and true knowledge of the scriptures." Afterward, he says: "Without purity of spirit and without a life imitating sanctity, it is impossible to understand the sayings of the saints. It is as if someone wants to look at the light of the sun. He cleans his eyes and, by so doing, becomes clearer, almost in likeness to the sun that he wants to see. Thus the eye, having become light, is able to see the light of the sun. Also, if someone should desire to see some region or city, he draws near to see it. So it is fitting for one who desires to know the saints to first wash and cleanse his soul. Then, by similarity in life and behavior, he may come near those same saints, and, in this way, may be united to them by desires and life. Thus, he may understand those things that God has revealed to them, and having become almost one of them, escape the danger of sinners and the fire prepared for them on the last day."[103]

It is very helpful to act in accord with what Saint Athanasius says in order to draw benefit from the divine scripture. Without this purity of life, one is well able to know through scripture what God wants in general. But to know in particular the guidance of God, and what he wills, cannot be known by human study, as the Sage says: "Who shall know what you think, Lord, if you do not give him wisdom and send your Holy Spirit from on high?" (Wis 9:17). This wisdom teaches what is pleasing to God in particular, and it does not dwell in the wicked. But when this wisdom endures in a man together with the experience of holy labors, humble prayers, and the fruit of good works, it makes him truly wise. Then, by the reading of scripture and long experience, he is able to teach others in the manner of an eyewitness; he is able to penetrate to the depth of another's heart, having been taught by what takes place in his own. Without this, if he hits the target once, he will miss it many times. He will be one of those of whom Saint Paul says, "Though they desire to be doctors of the Law, they do not understand the things they talk about" (1 Tim:1:7).

It is also helpful that the man who desires to study divine scripture be helped by the aid and exposition of the saints, and even of the Scholastics. What is drawn from the study of the divine scripture without following these, Germany has experienced to its harm.

## CHAPTER 49

Do not take any pride of heart upon hearing of the falls of others, by which you say, "I am not like those who have so disgracefully lost the faith." Recall those men who told our Lord that "Pilate had killed certain people of Galilee in the midst of some sacrifices" they were offering (cf. Luke 13:1). Those who were recounting this event bore a certain slight complacency in their hearts, by which they considered themselves better than those who had deserved that Pilate should kill them. The sovereign Master would recognize this pride without them declaring it. Desiring to open their eyes, he spoke thus: "Do you think that those Galileans were greater sinners than all the men of that province, because that punishment came upon them? Or do you think that the eighteen who were killed when the tower of Siloe fell on them were greater sinners than all the others were who were living in Jerusalem? No, I say to you, and if you do not do penance, you shall all likewise perish" (Luke 13:2–5). Saint Paul means the same when he says: "Because of unbelief, the Jews, who were branches on the olive tree of believers, were cut off, while you are standing through faith. Do not become proud, but rather fear, because otherwise, you also will be cut off" (Rom 11:19–21).

The punishments that God has inflicted on others ought not to make us proud but humble and cautious. Wherever we look in these unhappy times of ours, we must weep and say with Jeremiah, "If I go into the countryside, I see those slain by the sword; if I enter into the city, I see those dead and consumed by famine" (Jer 14:18). The first are those who have left "the city," which is the church. They are people without a head because "the sword" of incredulity has taken away the head that God has given to Christians, that is, the Roman pontiff. The second are many of those "in the city" of the church, who keep the faith intact. But they are miserably "dead from hunger" because they do not eat the food of obedience to the commandments of God and of his church. If we have the feeling of Christ, we should feel these things and weep over them in his presence and say to him: "How long, Lord, will you not have mercy on those for whom you shed your blood and lost your life on the cross with so many torments? Since the business is yours, let your hand also be the remedy, since it is not possible that it should come from any other hand."

Be careful, daughter, to feel and to ask this, since, if you love Christ, you must have within your heart a deep compassion for souls because Christ died for them. Also, it is very important for you to consider how you are living and how you profit from the faith that you have, lest God punish you by allowing you to fall into some error by which you lose it. You have heard with your own ears how many people have lost it through the heresy of the wicked Luther. There are others who have denied Christ in a land of the Moors by living according to the bestial law of Mohammed. In this, you see fulfilled what Paul said: "Some, by having cast aside a good conscience, lost the faith" (1 Tim

1:19). As we said before when we were speaking about the motives for believing, it may be because the bad conscience little by little causes the understanding to be blinded, so that it looks for a doctrine that does not contradict its wickedness. Or it may be because the sovereign judge, in punishment for their sins, allows them to fall into heresy. Whatever the reason, it is a thing to fear and to take care to avoid.

This does not happen to all bad Christians since, even if they are in mortal sin, they do not lose the faith for that reason, as we have said. But in a thing of such importance, what may have happened to only one person is a reason for all to take care and to fear in order to flee from that occasion. Certainly, the hearts of the eleven apostles were quite far from handing over Jesus Christ our Lord to death. But because he said that one of them was going to betray him, they all feared and said, "Is it I, Lord?" (Matt 26:22). They were afraid that they could fall through weakness into betraying him, an action that, in the present, they felt themselves free of.

For all of this, the passage that we have in hand will be very beneficial: "Incline your ear," obeying God and his church with faith and not having an inquisitive understanding "that may be oppressed by Majesty," as is threatened in scripture (Prov 25:27). Some desire to measure the ineffable things of God with the smallness of their understanding and reason. What happens to them is what happens to those who look fixedly at the sun. Not only do they not see it, but, to the contrary, they lose their sight. The excessive light they look at is too much for the eyes with which they are looking. It is the same with those who seek satisfaction along the path of understanding and inquiry but meet doubts and disquiet. This is because the wisdom of God is only communicated to the little and the humble who approach him with simplicity, "inclining their ear" to him and to his church. These receive very great gifts from his goodness that leave the soul satisfied and beautiful with faith and with works as the lovely Rebecca, to whom Isaac gave earrings for her ears and bracelets for her wrists (cf. Gen 24:22).

So that this simple subjection of our understanding might commend itself more to us, the Holy Spirit was not content with counseling us in the first passage by saying, "Listen, O daughter." Rather, he counseled us in this other one that says, "Incline your ear." He did this so that men might know that, since God does not say idle words, when he speaks a saying with several words, he greatly desires to commend this simple and humble believing, the principle of our salvation. If love is joined to it, we possess salvation in all its perfection.

# B. DISCERNMENT OF FALSE REVELATIONS (CHAPS. 50–55)

**CHAPTER 50**

It is not right to go on without warning you of a great danger that comes upon those who travel along God's way and has caused many to fall. The principal remedy against it consists in the advice that the Holy Spirit gives us through this word, "Incline your ear." The danger consists in the revelations, visions, or other spiritual sentiments offered to some devout persons. Many times the devil, by God's permission, brings these things about for two reasons: one is to discredit true revelations from God by these deceptions, just as he has managed false miracles in order to discredit true ones; another is to deceive a person under the appearance of good since he is unable to do so in another way. We read about many such things in the past and have seen many in the present. They ought to serve as a lesson and a warning to any person desirous of his salvation so that he will not easily believe in these things. The very ones who previously gave such credit to them, after having been freed from such deceptions, have advised others to guard themselves from falling into them. Gerson says that many of these deceptions happened in his time and that he had known of many who said and held as certain that God had revealed to them that they were going to be popes. One of them had written of this and, by conjectures and other proofs, affirmed that it was true. Another had the same persuasion that he would be pope, and then afterward, the thought settled in his heart that he would be the Antichrist, or at least, his messenger. Later, he was grievously tempted to kill himself in order not to bring such great harm to the Christian people. Finally, through God's mercy, he was drawn out of all these deceits and left an account of them in writing as a warning and teaching for others.[104]

There have not been lacking in our time persons who have held it as certain that they were to reform the Christian Church and bring it to the perfection it had in its beginning, or to another greater. Those who have died without doing this have been enough proof of their deceived hearts. It would have been better for them to have dedicated themselves to their own reform. That is a thing that, with God's grace, would have turned out to be easy, rather than, forgetting their own consciences, to set the eyes of their vanity on a thing that God did not want done through them.

Others have desired to search for new paths that seemed short and quick for arriving soon to God. They thought that, by surrendering themselves perfectly to him and abandoning themselves in his hands, they were so taken by God and directed by the Holy Spirit that every-thing that came to their minds was nothing but a light and an impulse from God. This deception reached such a point that, if this interior motion did not come, they would not move themselves to do any good work, no matter how good it was. But if the heart moved them to do any work, they had to do it, even if it were against God's command-ment. They believed that their heart's desire was an impulse from God and the freedom of the Holy Spirit who was freeing them from all obli-gations to the commandments of God. They said that they loved him so truly that, even breaking his commandments, they did not lose his love.[105] They did not consider what the Son of God had preached con-trary to this with his own mouth: "He who receives my command-ments and keeps them, he it is who loves me." Again, he said: "If anyone loves me, he will keep my words," and, "He that does not love me, does not keep my words" (John 14:21–24). He teaches clearly that whoever does not keep his word has neither his love nor his friendship. As Saint Augustine says, "No one can love the king if he hates his com-mandment."[106]

Saint Paul says: "The law is not imposed on the just man" (1 Tim 1:9), and, "Where the Spirit of the Lord is, there is liberty" (2 Cor 3:17). This is not to be understood as saying that the Holy Spirit frees anyone, no matter how just he may be, from keeping the command-ments of God or his church or those of superiors. On the contrary, the more this Spirit communicates himself, the more love does he place within them. When love grows, care and desire for keeping ever more perfectly the commandments of God and of his church also grow. Since this Spirit is entirely efficacious, he makes a man love the good truly and fervently. When the Spirit is given abundantly, it places such a disposition in the soul that the keeping of the commandments is not a heavy burden but very easy and delightful. As David says: "How sweet are your words to my palate! They are sweeter than honey to my mouth" (Ps 119:103). The Spirit places in man's will a most perfect conformity with God's will, making it to be "one spirit with him" (cf. 1 Cor 6:17). This means, as Saint Paul says, that he holds it the same to will and not to will. Necessarily, keeping the will of God must be delightful for a man because to do what one likes is delightful for everyone. Therefore, if the law of God were lost, it would be found written by the Holy Spirit on their hearts. As David says, "The law of God is in the heart of the just man" (Ps 37:31), which means, in his will insofar as it is conformed to God's will. God himself had said, "I will place my law in their hearts" (Jer 31:33). From this it follows that, even if there were no hell to threaten, no paradise to invite, no commandment to compel, the just man would do what he does solely for the love of God. In man's relationship with God, the Holy Spirit works what human generation works in the Son's relationship with his Father, since through him and his grace, we receive the adoption of sons of God. Thus, a man comes to reverence and serve God through filial love, with which there come perfect hatred for all sin and the perfect hope that casts out sadness and fear, as much as they can be cast out during this exile. All this makes a man suffer difficulties patiently and joyfully. Because of the freedom he has with regard to sins and trials, hating the one and loving the other, he is called "free," and on such a just man, "the law is not imposed." It is similar to the case of a mother who loved her son very much and did a lot for him. The law commanding her to do for her son what she does through her maternal heart would not be a burden to her. Thus, such a mother would not be under the law or its burdens, but would be above the law, as a free woman, since she does with delight what the law commands with authority. Those we have been discussing act in the same way when they fulfill the law with love. Many even do things for which they have no obligation, because their hearts burn with a fire of love greater than the obligation the law imposes. In this way we are to understand Saint Paul when he says that "if you are led by the Spirit, you are not under the law" (Gal 5:18). Since they hate sin and are full of love with regard to the law and joyful in difficulties (all of which come from being guided by the Spirit), the law is not a burden to them, as has been said.

But, if anyone breaks even one of the commandments of God or of his church, in that instant the Spirit departs. As it is written: "He withdraws himself from thoughts that are without understanding, and will leave the soul when iniquity enters it" (Wis 1:5). Since these men are not led by the Holy Spirit, they must remain subject to the affliction that the law imposes on those who do not love it, weak in supporting troubles, and subject to falling into sin. Let no one, then, say that, breaking a commandment of God or of his church, he can possess justice or liberty or love for him. The Lord declares that "the one who commits sin is a slave," not free (cf. John 8:34). As "there is no participation between light and darkness" (cf. 2 Cor 6:14), there is none between God and the one who works iniquity. As it is written: "The wicked man and his wickedness are hateful to God" (Wis 14:9).

I have told you about this blind error as an example from which you may draw many other examples just as foolish and senseless. Into such errors those of past and present have fallen, who have indiscreetly believed that the sentiments and impulses in their hearts were from God.

## CHAPTER 51

Desiring that your soul not be one of these, I recommend strongly that, as they say, you learn your lesson in the head of another. Be very careful not to allow in yourself any desire, small or great, for singular and supernatural things, because this is a sign of pride and dangerous curiosity. Saint Augustine was once tempted with this. These are his words: "With how many crafty temptations has the enemy tried to get me to ask you, Lord, for some miracle! But I beg you, through the love of our king Jesus Christ, and of our chaste and simple city, the heavenly Jerusalem, that just as consent to this temptation is now far from me, so it may be ever farther and farther away."[107] Saint Bonaventure says that many have fallen into madness and errors as punishment for having desired the things already mentioned. He adds that these things should be feared rather than desired.[108] If they come to you without your wanting them, be afraid, and do not give them credence. Instead, run immediately to our Lord, begging him to be pleased not to take you by this road, but to let you "work out your salvation in holy fear of him" (Phil 2:12) and by the ordinary and level path of those who serve him. You have to watch especially when such a revelation or impulse invites you to admonish or inform a third person of something secret, all the more if the person is a priest, prelate, or someone similar, to whom particular reverence is due. Expel these things then from your heart, and depart from them saying what Moses said: "I beseech you, Lord, to send the one you will to send" (Exod 4:13). Jeremiah said, "I am a child, Lord; I do not know how to speak" (Jer 1:6). Both considered themselves inadequate and fled from being sent to correct others. Do not fear that you will offend God by this humble resistance or that he will be angry or absent if the affair is his. On the contrary, he will approach and clarify the matter. The one who "gives his grace to the humble" (cf. Jas 4:6) will not take it away for an act of humility. But if the thing is not of God, the demon will flee, "wounded by the stone" of humility, a blow that "breaks his head" like that of Goliath (cf. 1 Sam 17:49).

It happened to a desert father that, when an image of the Crucified appeared to him, not only did he refuse to adore it or believe in it, but he closed his eyes and said: "I do not want to see Jesus Christ in this world. It is enough for me to see him in heaven." At this response the demon, who had wanted to deceive him under another form, fled. Another father responded to one who said that he was an angel sent to him by God: "I have no need of messages from angels, nor am I worthy. Therefore, look for the one to whom you were sent, for it is not possible that you were sent to me, and I do not want to listen to you." At this humble response the proud demon fled. Through the way of humility and by wholeheartedly rejecting these things, many persons have been freed by God's hand from very strong bonds that the devil had forged for them. So they experienced in themselves what David says: "The Lord keeps the little ones; I humbled myself and he delivered me" (Ps 116:6). On the other hand, if the false revelation or impulse of the demon finds any desire or vain satisfaction in the heart of the one who receives it, it takes root there and gathers strength to deceive him completely. God's judgment is just in permitting this for, as Saint Augustine says, "pride deserves to be deceived."[109]

You, then, ought to be so free from vain satisfaction and from thinking that you are something because of these revelations, that your heart is not moved in the least degree from the humble place where you were before, under the holy fear of God. Conduct yourself in them as though they had not come to you. If when you respond in this way the thing continues, give an account to one who may counsel you what you should do. It would be better for you to give this account immediately after it happens to you. Also, you should help the one who is to counsel you by prayers, fasting, and other good works, so that God may clarify the truth to him, since the matter is full of difficulty. It is a great blasphemy for us to take the good spirit of God for the evil spirit of the demon. In that case we are like the miserable Pharisees who contradicted the truth of God and attributed to the evil spirit, the works that Jesus Christ our Lord was doing through the Holy Spirit (cf. Matt 12:24). But if we credulously accept the impulse of the evil spirit as a thing from the Holy Spirit, what greater evil can there be than to follow darkness as light, deception as truth, and what is worse, the devil as God? On both sides there is a great danger, either taking God for the devil, or the devil for God. No one, no matter how blind, fails to see the great need of being able to distinguish and value each of these things for what it is. But as the necessity is clear, so is certainty and light in this doubt fraught with difficulty and hidden. Not all prophesy and perform miracles and other similar graces, but only those to whom they are distributed by the Holy Spirit. So it is not given to the human spirit, however wise, to judge certainly and truly the difference of spirits, unless it is in some very clear thing against the scripture or the church of God. Necessary then in every case, is the light of the Holy Spirit, which is called *discernment of spirits*. By this profound inspiration and illumination, the man who has this gift judges without error which is the spirit of truth and which that of the lie. If the matter is of substance, it ought to be told to the bishop and his determination accepted as certain.

## CHAPTER 52

Yet another thing to consider is what benefit or edification these things leave in your soul. I do not tell you this so that by these or other signs you may judge what takes place within you. My purpose is rather that, when you give an account to the one who counsels you, you give it more particularly, so that he may better be able to understand with certainty and to show you the truth.

Consider, then, whether these things benefit you as a remedy for some spiritual necessity or as something of outstanding edification for your soul. If a good man does not speak idle words, even less will God speak them. He says, "I am the Lord who teaches you profitable things, and I lead you along the way that you walk" (Isa 48:17). When it is seen that there is nothing of profit, but only tangled and unnecessary things, take it as the fruit of the demon. He goes about trying to deceive the one to whom he brings them, or to make that person waste his time, and the time of others to whom they are told. When he can do no more, he is content with this waste of time.

Among the things worked in your soul that you are to consider, the principal one is whether they leave you more humble than before. For, as a doctor says, humility puts so much weight in the spiritual coin that it sufficiently distinguishes it from the lack of weight of the false coin. As Saint Gregory says, "The most evident sign of the elect is humility and that of the reprobates is pride."[110] See, then, what trace remains in your soul from the vision or consolation or spiritual feeling. Do you see that you are left more humble and ashamed of your faults and with greater reverence and fear of the infinite greatness of God, and that you do not have frivolous desires of communicating to others what has happened? Do you avoid occupying yourself a great deal in looking at it or paying it a lot of attention and forget about it as a thing that can bring you self–esteem? If at times it comes to your memory, do you humble yourself and marvel at God's great mercy that gives such gifts to those who are so base? Is your heart more tranquil in its self–knowledge than you were before it came to you? It has some sign of being from God if it is in conformity with the Christian teaching and truth that a man is to be humbled and despised in his own eyes, recognizing himself as more obliged and ashamed for the goods that he receives from God and attributing all glory to the one from whose hand comes all good. Saint Gregory agrees with this when he says, "It is fitting to know that the soul, filled with divine understanding, has truth and humility as its most evident signs."[111] If these two are joined perfectly in a soul, it is well–known that they give testimony of the presence of the Holy Spirit.

But, with a deceit of the demon, it is completely the reverse. At the beginning or the end of the revelation or consolation, the soul feels lighthearted and desires to tell what it is experiencing. It possesses some esteem for itself and its own judgment and thinks that God is going to do great things in and through it. The soul does not feel like thinking about its defects or of being corrected by others. Instead, the only thing it does is talk about its experience and turn it over in its memory. It would also desire that others would talk about it. When you see these and other signs that demonstrate frivolity of heart, you can say without doubt that the spirit of the demon is walking there.

However good a thing that happens to you may appear (tears, or consolation, or knowledge of the things of God, or even that you have ascended to the third heaven), if your soul does not remain in profound humility, do not trust in or receive it. The reason is that, the higher the thing is, the more dangerous it is, and it will cause you a greater fall. Ask God for his grace so that you may know and humble yourself, and above all this, that he grant you what would be most pleasing to him. But, if this is lacking, all the rest, no matter how valuable it may seem, is not gold but tinsel, and is not flour that sustains but ashes without substance. Pride has this evil, that it despoils the soul of the true grace of God. If it leaves any of its goods, they are falsified so that they do not please God and are the occasion for a greater fall for the one that possesses them. We read that our Redeemer, when he appeared to his disciples on the day of his ascension, first "upbraided them with their incredulity and hardness of heart" (Mark 16:14), and afterward commanded them to go preach, giving them power to perform many great miracles. By this, he showed that the one he is going to lift up to great things he first humbles, giving him knowledge of his own weaknesses. This is so that, even if they soar above the heavens, they may remain rooted in their own lowliness, without power to attribute anything to themselves except their unworthiness.

The summary of all this is that you should take account of the effects that these things work in you, not in order that you be the judge of them, but so that you may inform the one who is going to counsel you, and that you may follow his counsel.

## CHAPTER 53

You must realize that many feel within themselves their own vileness and nothingness, and they think that they attribute to God alone the glory for all their good, and they perceive many other signs of their own humility. But with all this they are filled with pride and trapped in it in the measure that they think that they are freer. The cause is that, since they live in the truth by not attributing good to themselves, they live in deception by thinking that their goods are more and better than in fact they are. They think that they have such light from God that they are sufficient to direct themselves and others along the way of God. In their eyes there is no one competent to direct them. To a large extent they are friends of their own opinion, and they even hold in little regard what saints of the past have said, as well as the opinion of servants of God living in their own time. They boast of possessing the spirit of Christ and being directed by him and of not needing human counsel, since God and his unction satisfy them with such great certainty in their prayers.

They think, as Saint Bernard says, "of the houses of others, but that only in their own does the sun shine."[112] They distrust and despise all wise men, as Goliath did the people of God (cf. 1 Sam 17:8–10). The only one who is good in their judgment is the one who is conformed to them, and nothing annoys them more than to be contradicted. They want to be masters of all and believed by all, but they are not willing to believe anyone. The cautious discretion of people with experience they call tepidity and fear; unbridled passions and novelties full of singularity and causing riots they call liberty of spirit and fortitude from God. They have in their mouth almost continually: "My spirit tells me this," "God satisfies me," and similar words. At other times, they quote the scripture of God, but they refuse to understand it as the church and the saints understand it. Instead, they understand it as it seems to them, believing that they have no less light than the saints of the past. They even believe that God has taken them as an instrument for greater works than those saints. So, making idols of themselves, and, with abominable arrogance, placing themselves above all heads, their deception is so miserable that, although they are extremely proud, they take themselves to be perfectly humble. They believe that only in them does God dwell. But God is very far from them. What they think is light is the deepest darkness. Of these, or of those like them, Gerson says:

> There are some who are pleased to be directed by their own opinion, and they walk amid their own inventions, guided, or better said, driven by their own opinion, which is a most dangerous guide. They mortify themselves excessively with fasts and keep many vigils; they disturb and confuse their brain with too many tears. In the midst of these things, they do not consider the admonition or the counsel of anyone. They are not careful to ask counsel of those wise in God's law, nor do they care to listen to them, and when they do hear them or seek counsel, they despise their words. The cause is that they have come to think of themselves as being already something, and as knowing better than all others what is fitting for them to do. Of such as these, I declare that they will soon fall into the illusion of demons. Soon they will fall on the stumbling block because they are carried along with blind haste and excessive levity. Therefore, be suspicious of anything they may say about unusual revelations.[113]

## CHAPTER 54

You are to understand that some that I have mentioned in the last chapter are people without learning and cordial enemies of the learned. They may, by chance, know a little Latin so as to read and carry with them the New Testament. They believe a great deal in themselves while they think they believe in God. They rely upon some very superficial ideas and tangle themselves up in them so blindly that, however clear the ideas are, these people do not know how to shake themselves free of them. They are so bold and so beyond persuasion that, as scripture says, "it is better to meet a bear robbed of her whelps, than a fool trusting in his own folly" (Prov 17:12). They keep very much in mind and on their tongues the saying of Saint Paul: "Knowledge puffs up; charity builds up" (1 Cor 8:1). With this, they think they have a license to despise the learned as people who are puffed up, and to pride themselves on being people full of charity. They do not notice that they are puffed up with pride in their own sanctity. This is more dangerous than pride in learning, because it arises from something better and is, therefore, worse. Indeed, neither learning nor good works of themselves produce this destructive moth, but the wickedness of the wicked that seizes the occasion of the good to swell with pride. Since this is so, they ought not so quickly to despise the learned, since wisdom in itself does not prevent them from being humble and holy. To the contrary, wisdom has been and is for many a grand occasion for being so. It is great pride and an offensive judgment to judge that the wise are not humble and holy. But if they are not, remember that it is written: "The scribes and the Pharisees have sat on the chair of Moses. Do what they tell you, but do not do as they do" (Matt 23:2–3). These people do the reverse. They do not accept the good teaching that the wise give, and they do the evil that they say the wise do, which is to be proud. They despise the wise without care for the natural and divine order by which the less wise are directed by those who are wiser.

This is not contradicted by what Saint John says: "The anointing teaches all things" (1 John 2:27). This saying means that God's grace and light sometimes teach man interiorly within himself, and at other times instruct him to seek the counsel of another, and even tell him from whom he must seek it. So God teaches all, but he does not teach all interiorly. Saint Augustine addresses this subject:

> Let us flee from such temptations, which are exceedingly proud and dangerous. Instead, let us think like the Apostle Saint Paul. Even though he was cast down and taught by a heavenly voice, he was in spite of that sent to a man in order to receive the sacraments and be incorporated into the Church (cf. Acts 9:4, 17). The centurion Cornelius was sent to Saint Peter (cf. Acts 10:5ff.), not only to receive the sacraments, but to hear from him what he had to believe, hope, and love. For, if God had not spoken to men by the mouth of men, the condition of men would be most despicable. How would what is written be true, that "The temple of God, which you are, is holy" (1 Cor 3:17), if God had not responded from this temple, which is men, but had said all that he wanted man to learn from heaven by means of angels? Neither would charity itself have had an entrance, so that the hearts of some would communicate with those of others, if men had not learned through other men. Saint Philip was sent to the eunuch; Moses received the advice of his father–in–law Jethro (cf. Ex 18:24).[114]

Likewise, Saint John Climacus says that "the man who believes in himself does not need to be tempted by the demon, because he himself is his own demon." Saint Jerome also says, "I decided not to follow my own opinion, because it is wont to be a very bad adviser."[115] Saint Vincent also says and advises often that anyone who wants to be spiritual should have a master to direct him. If he is able to have one and does not accept him, then God will never communicate his grace to him because of his pride.

Saint Bernard and Saint Bonaventure give the same advice at every step. The scripture of God is full of the same thing. Sometimes it says, "Woe to you that are wise in your own eyes and prudent in your own sight" (Isa 5:21). In another place it says, "If you see anyone who considers himself wise, think that even the ignoramus will turn out better than he" (Prov 26:12). Saint Paul warns us, "Do not desire to be wise in your own estimation" (Rom 12:16). The wise man says, "Unless you tell the fool things that are in his own heart, he will not receive prudent words" (Prov 18:2). In another place, he says, "If you incline your ear, you will receive instruction; if you desire to hear, you will be wise" (Sir 6:33). So as not to be too long, I say that the divine scripture, the warnings of the saints and their lives, and the experiences we have seen, all with one voice recommend that we do not rely on our own prudence, but that we incline our ear to the advice of another.

Otherwise, what would be more disorderly than the church or any congregation, if each one followed his own opinion, thinking that he is right? How can it be that the Spirit of Christ, a spirit of humility, peace, and union, moves one to be opposed to all the others, in whom dwells the same God? How can it arise from this Spirit that a man hold himself in such esteem that no one is found in the assembly of men to teach him or judge if his spirit is good or evil? For, as Saint Augustine says, this man would not refuse to take advice from another and to obey him, except that, in his own pride, he thinks that he is better than the one who counsels him. Since his pride is so great that he believes himself better than others, he ought to consider that one person can be less good than another and yet have the gift of prophecy, healing the sick, and similar gifts that are lacking in one who is better than he. Likewise, one may have fewer of some gifts and yet possess more counsel and discernment of spirits than another who has more of the other gifts. God is a great friend of humility and peace. Therefore, let no one fear that what he has from God may depart or be lost when he subjects himself to the opinion of another for the sake of the same God. Rather, it will be more and more confirmed, and if it is from someplace else, it will flee away. Consider that one of the conditions for the wisdom infused by God is that, according to Saint James, it "allows itself to be persuaded" (cf. Jas 3:17). Consider also that Saint Augustine calls these thoughts "very proud and dangerous."[116] Pride and disobedience of the will, manifest in refusing to obey the will of another, are dangerous, but much more dangerous is pride of the understanding. In this a person does not subject himself to another because he believes in his own opinion. The proud of heart will obey whenever he holds the other's

167

opinion to be better. But who will cure the one who has determined within himself that his own opinion is best? How will he obey one whom he does not consider to be so good? If "the eye of the soul," which is the understanding, by which pride must be seen and cured, "is blind," (cf. Luke 11:34) and full of the same pride, who will cure it? And if the light becomes darkness (cf. Luke 11:35), and if the rule is twisted, what else will come?

The evils that come from this pride are so great that they disturb all who have to deal with them. Who can live in peace with someone who obstinately defends his own opinion and is its friend?

So that you may utterly condemn and flee this vice, you must real- ize that it goes so far as to turn good Christians into perverse heretics. They have not been so, nor are they so, for any other reason than that they believed more in their own view than in that of the church and of their superiors. They thought that they were right and that what took place in their hearts was the work of God, and that if they believed more in the view of another than in what they felt in their hearts, they were leaving God for man. But experience and the truth show us that what they thought was the spirit of truth was the spirit of deception. This spirit, unable to conquer them any other way, attacked them under the appearance of good by "transforming itself into an angel of light" (2 Cor 11:14). Thus it deprived them of the life of the soul because they were unwilling to be subject to the opinion of another.

## CHAPTER 55

Learn a lesson, then, from these things. I warn you that, as you are to be an enemy of your own will, so even more you are to be an enemy of your opinion and of the desire to get your own way, since you see the bad end that following one's own opinion has. Be its enemy outside your house and within, and even if it has to do with trivial things, do not follow it. You will hardly find anything that so disturbs the peace that Christ desires in the soul so that he may communicate with it than stubbornness and the desire to have your own way. It is far better that what you want is not done than that you lose something that you need so much in order to enjoy God in peace. Understand that I enjoin this if you do not have the obligation of running the household. If you do, you must not omit what seems good to you, though you ought to inform yourself well by prayer and taking counsel, according to the importance of the thing.

You already know that those who have to be involved with some- thing that could be embarrassing are wont to practice first with things of no importance, so as to be skillful in those that are really important. Certainly, you ought to know that one who is used to believing himself wise and to esteeming his intelligence, desiring to have his own way in small things, will find himself inexperienced and having difficulty denying his opinion in matters of greater importance. On the other hand, one who exercises himself in small things, considering his own understanding foolish and having little confidence in himself, will find it easy to subject himself to God's will or that of his superiors, and not to easily judge his neighbor.

I have said that in things of little importance you may deny your own opinion and follow that of another without examining a great deal who says or does not say something. So I tell you that in what touches your conscience you must be prudent, so that you do not trust your own opinion or trust that of just anyone. It is helpful to take as guide and father someone who is learned and experienced in the things of God. Ordinarily, the one without the other does not suffice. Learning alone is not enough to provide for particular needs, successes, and temptations that occur in the souls of those who follow the spiritual life. In these matters, as Gerson says, one is to turn to those with experience. Many times, those who only have learning will experience the same thing that happened to the apostles one stormy night at sea. They thought that Christ, who was coming toward them, "was a ghost" (Matt 14:26). Those with learning alone do what the apostles did and take as deception what is a real gift from our Lord. Some of these will burden you with excessive fears, condemning everything as evil. Since, in their hearts, they are very far from experiencing desire for God and illumination from him, they speak of it as of something unknown. They will hardly be able to believe that higher things take place in the hearts of others than those that take place in their own hearts.

You will find others practiced in things of devotion that easily inquire after any spiritual feeling and make much out of it. When someone tells them something about these things, they listen in admiration, and they regard as holier anyone who has more of these. They easily approve such things as if, in them, everything were safe. Since this is not so, many of these fall into error through ignorance, and they allow those in their charge to fall by not giving them enough advice against the cunning of the demon. For this reason they, like the first group, are unfit to give direction.

Be aware that there are some of good judgment who understand that true sanctity does not consist in these things but in the fulfillment of the Lord's will. They have experience of spiritual things and know

169

how to doubt and ask someone to inform them. Such as these you well can trust, even if they are not learned, since for one whose whole occupation is in looking to himself this is enough.

Since it is so helpful to find a good guide, you ought to ask the Lord insistently that with his own hand he place one in your path. Once he is placed in your path, entrust your heart to him with great security. Do not hide anything from him, either good or bad: the good, so that he may direct and warn you; the bad so that he may correct you. Do nothing important without his opinion, trusting that God, who is a friend of obedience, will place in the heart and on the tongue of your guide what will be helpful for your salvation. In this way you will flee from two evil extremes. One is that of those who say, "I do not need advice from men; God teaches me and is enough for me." Others are so subject to men that they are included in that curse that says, "cursed be the man that trusts in man" (Jer 17:5). Subject yourself to a man, and you will have escaped the first danger. Do not trust in the knowledge or strength of a man, but in God, who will speak to you and strengthen you by means of a man. Thus, you will have avoided the second danger.

You can be certain that even if you search much, you will not find any other path as certain and safe for finding God's will as this one of humble obedience, so much advised by all the saints and so well practiced by many of them. The lives of the holy fathers bear witness to this. Among them, being subject to one's elder was regarded as a very great sign that one had arrived at perfection. Among the many good things in religious life, you will hardly find another as good as that all live under a superior whom they obey, not only in external actions but also internally in opinion and in will. These religious, if they have confidence and devotion in their obedience, will lead a well–directed and very tranquil life.

# PART THREE

# *"See!"*

## (CHAPS. 56–96)

# INTRODUCTION:
# EXTERIOR AND INTERIOR
# VISION (CHAP. 56)

## CHAPTER 56

If you have paid attention to what has been said, you will have seen how necessary hearing is to listen to please God. Now listen to the second word, "see." It is not enough to be attentive to the divine words that come from outside and to inspirations that come from within through hearing. It is also necessary to keep the sense of sight healthy. Christ blames the blind who do not see the light just as much as the deaf who do not hear the truth.

But do not think that his advising you to see means that you are to set your eyes on festivals or on the world. What else is such seeing than blindness, since it hinders the vision of the soul? It is enough for the bodily eyes to see the earth to which they must return and the heavens where the heart's desire is lodged. As David says, "I will see your heavens, the work of your fingers; the moon and the stars which you established" (Ps 8:4). If these eyes want to look upon more creatures, I do not object, as long as their sight passes from the creatures to God and does not lose and forget God in the creatures. Concerning the sight of creatures David says to the Lord, "Lord, turn away my eyes that they may not behold vanity; enliven me along your path" (Ps 119:37). Well did this holy king know that to "see" too much is an impediment to running lightly along the way of God, and that it usually makes the enkindled heart grow lukewarm. For this reason he says, "Enliven me along your path." It is clear to those with experience that, the more recollected their exterior eyes are, the more they see with their inner eyes, and this sight is happier and more helpful. It is right that a Christian should easily believe this, since we read that some philosophers tore out their bodily eyes so that their understanding would be more recollected for contemplation. Aware of this fact, we ought to avoid their error in tearing out their eyes but benefit from their worthy desire of being recollected in their use.

Thus, we ought to guard our eyes with every kind of guard, so that the evils that usually come from their wandering do not happen to us. From where do you think the beginning of the world's perdition came? It is certain that it came from one disordered look. Eve looked at the forbidden tree. This gave her the desire to eat of its fruit, because it seemed to her beautiful and delicious. She ate it and gave it to her husband to eat. That food was death for them and for all who came from them (cf. Gen 3:6). It makes no sense to look at what it is not lawful to desire. This is clear in the holy king David, whose eyes delighted in gazing upon the woman who was bathing in her garden (cf. 2 Sam 11:2). Afterward, he had to weep night and day, watering his bed and his couch with tears (cf. Ps 6:7) so abundant that his eyes were worn out from so much weeping, as though consumed by a moth. David said, "My eyes have shed streams of water because the wicked did not keep your law" (cf. Ps 119:136). He would have done better to shed them for not having kept the law himself. It would have been good advice for his eyes not to take delight in what would afterward cost them so dearly. It will also be good advice for us sinners, for we are so inconstant that where our eyes go, our heart follows. Let us then put a veil between ourselves and every creature, not fixing our sight completely on any of them, lest, occupied with them, we lose sight of the Creator, which is to say, of the devout considerations that we had of him.

One of the surest signs of a recollected heart is mortification in looking at things, and one of the most certain signs of a dissolute heart is dissipation in looking. No pulse shows so accurately what is going on in the body as the eye declares what is going on in the soul, whether of good or of evil. For this reason the Bridegroom praises the eyes of his spouse, saying, "Your eyes are those of a dove" (Song 5:12). This implies that her eyes are pure like those of the dove, which are usually black. Let us then watch how we see, if we do not want to pay with weeping for the sins we commit by seeing. If we must have this care for seeing with the exterior eyes, how much greater care must we have for the interior eyes by which truly one sees well or badly, and by which one is judged as having sight or being blind? It is clear that the Pharisees, with whom our Lord Jesus Christ spoke, had eyes in their heads with which they saw. But because they did not see with those of the soul, he called them "blind and guides of the blind" (Matt 15:14). On the other hand, the patriarch Isaac and Tobias had very clear vision in the eyes of the soul, so that it harmed them little to be blind in the eyes of the body. Saint Antony told a blind man named Didymus that since he was very learned in the divine scriptures, "there is no reason to be troubled at not having the eyes of the body. Even cats, dogs, and other lesser animals have these. But the eyes of your soul are clear, and, with these, God is seen."[117]

Concerning this interior sight, you should understand the advice given in the second word, "see," if you want to carry it out. The eyes of your understanding have been given to you so that you may see God. Do not fill your understanding with the dust of the earth and worldly honors, or block it with the thick vapors of sensual thoughts. Rather, shaking yourself free of trivialities such as these, which occupy your sight, keep your understanding clear in order to employ it on the one who gave it and who asks it from you in order to make you happy in him. Do not think that for nothing Christ freed you from the occupations of this world and kept you from entering into the trials of the married life. The cares of marriage usually trouble the sight of those in that state, unless they have a very special grace from the Lord to fulfill both parts. But the Lord freed you to be completely his own so that your eyes would look only at him, as the chaste spouse looks only at her husband.

# A. SEEING ONESELF: SELF-KNOWLEDGE (CHAPS. 57–67)

**CHAPTER 57**

This is the order to follow with regard to the psalm's command to see: first, look at yourself; then at God; and then at your neighbor. Look at yourself so that you may know yourself and consider yourself little, for there is no worse deception than to be deceived about yourself, considering yourself to be other than you are. You are dust as far as the body is concerned, and a sinner from the point of view of the soul. If you consider yourself to be more, you are blind, and your Spouse will have to say to you, "If you do not know yourself, O fairest among women, go forth, and follow in the steps of the flocks, and feed your kids beside the tents of the shepherds" (Song 1:8). I will explain this passage to you according to the Greek text and the Vulgate version, which the Council of Trent commanded us to follow, although the Hebrew text has a different sense.[118]

Saint Gregory, Saint Bernard, and Origen speak of this passage in this way:

> There is nothing that so makes one tremble as to hear these words from the mouth of God: "Depart and go away." This is the harshest word that a father can say to his son. It is also the harshest word that a husband can say to his wife, whom he had taken care of with great abundance, removing her from his support and wealth saying: "Leave me and leave my house." If this is so, what will it mean for the soul to depart and separate itself from God except to be banished from all goods and to fall into all evils?[119]

"Where shall we go? You have the words of eternal life" Peter said to Christ (John 6:68). Where shall we go since you, and you alone, possess the fountain of life? Where shall we go, our Light and Joy, without whom there is only darkness? Where shall we go, O living bread, without which there is only deadly starvation? Where shall we go, O strongest shelter, without which even safety is a danger? Finally, where shall the sheep go, surrounded on all sides by wolves, if the shepherd casts it off and sends it away? "Depart and go away" is a harsh saying, similar to that which Christ is to say to the wicked on the last day: "Depart, you cursed, into the fire which has been prepared" (Matt 25:41). I say it again. There is nothing that ought to make a person more afraid and nothing that one should labor more to avoid than hearing these words: "Depart and go away." For anyone who dwells in the generous and joyful house of God and is under his most powerful protection, this departure is no light matter but the cause of all ills. What will the person deprived of divine help and left to his own resources do? As Saint Augustine says,[120] he will do nothing but what Saint Peter did when he denied our Lord. Having fallen into sin and forgotten that he was in it, Peter was not even aware of the evil he had done or repentant for it until the help of the divine countenance turned to him. This made him aware of the evil he had done in having fallen and gave him sorrow for it. It also made him aware that the cause of his fall was that he had trusted in himself.

Therefore, the merciful Lord becomes so severe in throwing his children out of his house because they do not know themselves. They think they are something and rely on their own strength. To such a soul, the Spouse says, "If you do not know yourself, go forth and follow in the steps of the flocks." This means that he lets her wander lost, following the works and the tracks of sinners, who walk together in their sins like herds of cattle, helping each other in them. Those who were together in their sins will also be joined together on the last day, like bundles to be cast into the infernal fire. The Spouse speaks to the soul about "your herds" because sin has its origin within us, not in God, whereas the good comes from God and not from ourselves, and by his power we do the good. Indeed, he very much wants us to know that this is so, not so much because it affects him, for his glory does not increase in itself even when we glorify him. Rather, it is because it concerns us, whose greatest good is to know that for every good that we have, honor is due not to ourselves but to him. If we desire to build an idol out of what he has put in us for his own praise, attributing the glory of God to ourselves, corruptible human beings (Rom 1:23), he will not let it go unpunished. Rather, he will say: "Remain with what belongs to you and be lost since you did not desire to remain in me so that you might be saved." How truly are these words fulfilled in the proud! How swiftly do they change from being spiritual to being carnal, from being recollected to being dissipated, from being gold to being mud! Those who used to eat the heavenly bread afterward take delight in eating the food of swine. They find it annoying, not only to do the works of God, but even to hear about him. How do you think it has happened that some, who were chaste in their youth, even though afflicted with strong temptations, arrive at old age and fall miserably into abominations so ugly that they themselves are appalled and despise themselves? In their youth they lived with holy fear and humility, and seeing themselves on the verge of falling, they invoked God and were defended by him. But afterward, with long possession of chastity, they began to become conceited and to trust in themselves. At that point they were abandoned by the hand of God, and they did what was proper to them, which was to fall.

Then is accomplished the words saying that they "feed their kids," that is, their inconstant and indecent senses, "near the tents of the shepherds," which are the bodies of God's servants. They dwell in them as in a tent set up in a field, ready to be moved quickly, rather than in a house or a city, which remains standing. Very rightly, they feed their senses on bodies or on things that have bodies. Because of their pride they lost their true direction and began to think of themselves as something other than sinners who are nothing in themselves. Thus they robbed God of the glory really due to him for all the good that we do, however we do it.

Wake up then, daughter, and learn from other people's mistakes. Profit by the threat so that you do not experience the punishment. Be like the bride to whom these words were said, "Depart and go away."

When she heard such painful words from the mouth of the one who was the source of all her good, she saw and recognized herself and then removed from herself certain presumptions she had held. Having made her humble by this reprimand, the Spouse consoles her saying, "To my company of horses in Pharaoh's chariots have I likened you, O my friend; your cheeks are beautiful as the turtledove" (Song 1:9–10). Through pride, a soul is like the devil who, as the gospel says, "did not remain in the truth" (John 8:44), that is, in God. Instead, the devil decided to take his stand in himself and to lean on himself for support and rest. Consequently, he fell, for the creature cannot subsist in himself, but only in God. But through humble knowledge of self, a soul is like the good angels, who relied on God and let go of themselves. They saw that they were like a broken reed, and so God upheld and confirmed them. They cried out saying, "Michael," which means, "Who is like God?" (cf. Rev 12:7–8). In saying this they were contradicting the unfortunate Lucifer and his followers, who wanted to make idols of themselves, attributing to themselves what belonged to God, namely, to be the beginning, the support, and the repose of every creature. It is not as if they understood that they wanted to be such, for they knew that they were creatures. But it is because they delighted in the prospect as if they possessed it, as the proud are wont to do. Although their mouth or their understanding may cry aloud that they hold and hope for all good from God, yet with the will they exalt themselves and rejoice vainly in themselves, as if the good they possess belonged to them. They confess with their understanding that the glory is due to God while they rob him of it with their will. But the good angels cry out with both the understanding and the will: "Who is like God?" From their hearts they humbled and made little of themselves in accord with what they knew through their understanding. For this reason they were exalted to participation with God that they could never lose. To this cavalry, the angelic army that destroyed Pharaoh and his chariots in the Red Sea, Christ compares his bride when she knows herself and acts in accord with who she is (cf. Exod 14:28).

He also praises her cheeks, where modesty usually shows itself. Why was the bride embarrassed about such a reprimand? Because it asked for things greater than were proper to her littleness. Thus, her pale and colorless cheeks became flushed with modesty and chastity like the turtledove, which is a bashful bird. For this reason that devout man Bernard used to say that he had found through experience that there was nothing so beneficial for attaining, preserving, and recovering grace as living always in fear and holy mistrust of self. When we lack grace, we need fear because we are on the brink of every kind of fall. When we possess grace, we need holy distrust because we have to act in conformity with the talent that has been given us along with grace. When we lose grace, we need still greater distrust, because, through our own negligence, favor has departed from us. For this reason scripture says, "Blessed is the man who is always fearful" (Prov 28:14).

## CHAPTER 58

From what has already been said, and from many other things that the saints have said in praise of self–knowledge, you will see how necessary this jewel is to arrive at knowledge of God. Since you desire to build a house in your soul for such a high Lord, be aware that the humble of heart, not the high and mighty, are his dwelling places.

Therefore, your first care is to dig in the earth of your littleness to the point that, having removed all that is shifting from your esteem for yourself, you arrive at the firm rock that is God. On this, and not on the sand that you are, you will found your house. For this, the blessed Saint Gregory said: "You who plan to build a building of virtues, take care first of the foundation of humility; whoever desires to have virtues without it, is like someone who carries ashes in his hand against the wind."[121] He says this because, not only are the virtues of no benefit without it—since without it they are not virtues—but they are the occasion of the greatest loss, just as a great building upon a small and weak foundation is an accident waiting to happen. That is why the depth of the foundation of humility has to be in conformity with the loftiness of the virtues, and thus the soul may be firm and avoid being knocked down by the wind of pride.

If you ask me, "Where will I find this jewel of self–knowledge?" I answer that, even though it is of great value, you will find it in the stable when you take your eyes off the lives of others and look in the dunghill of your own littleness and defects. Do not involve yourself in knowing curiosities; turn your vision to yourself and persevere in examining yourself. At the beginning you find nothing of importance for knowing yourself, like someone who enters a dark room from the brightness of the sun. But if you persevere quietly, you will little by little see, by the grace of God, what is in your heart, even in the most secret corners. To know the means you must take for something so important for you, listen to what Saint Jerome says to a married woman:

179

Take care of your house in such a way that you also have some rest for your soul. Look for a suitable place, one sufficiently apart from the noise of your family, where you may go as one goes to a harbor, fleeing the great storm of your cares. There consider only the reading of divine things, continuous prayer, and thoughts of the things of the other world, so firmly that you easily balance all the activities of the rest of the day with this period of inactivity. We are not telling you this to take you away from running your house, but so that there you may learn and plan how to conduct yourself in it.[122]

This blessed saint is recommending to a married woman that she leave her household occupations for a while and recollect herself in a quiet place to read and think of the things of God. The spouse of Christ is free from worldly cares and must be conscious that she lives for nothing but to exercise herself in prayer and interior and exterior recollection. With how much greater reason should she search in her house for some hidden and secret place in which she may keep her devotional books and images, a place set aside solely to "see and taste how sweet the Lord is" (Ps 34:9). The state of virginity that you have taken on does not exist that you may be tied up with the passing cares of the world (cf. Col 3:2). But, just as it is like the state of heaven with regard to the integrity and incorruption of the flesh, so you must realize that, as far as possible, no earthly care is to enter into your heart. Rather, you must be a living temple in which continuous prayers are offered and continuous praises sound to him who created you. Let only one care occupy your heart: to thank the Lord. As Saint Paul says, "Consider yourself dead" (Col 3:3) to this world since you have espoused yourself to the heavenly king.

Remember what the Spouse says to the bride: "A garden enclosed is my sister, my spouse, a garden enclosed" (Song 4:12). Not only are you to be pure and protected in the flesh, but also completely enclosed and recollected in the soul. Virginity is embraced among Christians not for itself but so that it may help to give the heart to God with greater liberty. Since this is so, what is the young woman doing who contents herself with bodily virginity and lives without care for progress in virtue, prayer, and the desire for God? What is she doing but stopping on the way and never arriving where she is heading? Would you prepare to sew and embroider but never occupy yourself in them? It is a shameful thing for any Christian not to exercise himself in holy reading and holy thoughts within his soul. But for the religious, the priest, and the virgin, who have given themselves to Christ, it is not only shameful but intolerable. Therefore, if you want to enjoy the fruits of the holy virginity that you have promised to Christ, be an enemy of seeing and being seen. As is suitable for young women, leave the house as little as possible, even for holy places and good works. Do not involve yourself in temporal concerns. Having completed manual labor, which done moderately is a help to body and soul, and having completed occupations of necessity or charity in accord with your plan of life, take as much time as you can for being in your oratory. Even if at the beginning this may be annoying to you, afterward you will experience that you deal with heavenly matters in your cell, and that there is no time of such great satisfaction as that spent there in quiet.

## CHAPTER 59

Once you have found this quiet place, recollect yourself in it at least twice a day: once in the morning to reflect on the sacred passion of Jesus Christ our Lord (of which we will speak later), and the other time during the evening as night approaches, to reflect on the exercise of self–knowledge. Do it in this way.

First, take some book of sound doctrine in which you can see your faults as in a mirror, and, from it, take nourishment to strengthen your soul in the way of the Lord. This reading does not have to be heavy, nor do you have to cover many pages. Raise your heart to our Lord, and ask him to speak in your heart with his living voice through the words you are reading outwardly and to give you their true meaning. With this purpose and reverence, be attentive, listening to God speaking in the words you are reading, as if you were hearing him preaching when he spoke in this world. Even though your eyes are on the book, do not fix your heart on it with so much anxiety that you forget about God. Rather, pay a moderate and restful attention to what you are reading so that it does not captivate you or prevent you from having the free and alert attention you must have for the Lord. Reading in this way, you will not tire yourself out. Our Lord will give you the lively sense of the words, so that it may at times work in your soul repentance for your sins and at other times confidence in him and in his pardon. He will open your understanding so that you know many other things even if you read few lines. Sometimes it helps to interrupt the reading to think on something that came from it and then afterward read again. Thus reading and prayer go along helping each other.

With the heart thus devout and recollected, you can begin to occupy yourself in the exercise of self–knowledge. Kneel down and think of the excellent and sovereign Majesty you are about to address.

Do not think that he is far from you, but rather that he fills the heavens and the earth, and there is no place where he is not present, and that he is more within you than you are. Considering your littleness, make a profound reverence to him, humbling your heart like a tiny ant before an infinite being. Ask permission to speak to him. Begin first by speaking ill of yourself and pray the general confession, recalling especially and asking pardon for anything in which you may have sinned that day.

Afterward, pray some of your customary devotions, not too many lest you weary your head and cause your devotion to become dry. But do not omit them entirely because they serve to awaken the soul's devotion and to offer to God a service with the tongue as a sign that it is his gift. For this reason, Saint Paul teaches us that "we are to pray and sing with the spirit of the voice and with the soul" (cf. 1 Cor 14:15). These prayers are not only to ask our Lord for graces for yourself, but for those for whom you have a special obligation and for the whole Christian Church, whose care you must have fixed in your heart. If you love Christ, it is fitting that anyone for whom he shed his blood should be important to you. Pray as much for the living as for those who are in purgatory. Pray also for all infidels, who are deprived of the knowledge of God, begging him to bring all to his holy faith, since he desires that all be saved (cf. 1 Tim 2:4). Most of these prayers will be directed in two ways: one to our Lady, for whom you must have a very deep love and complete confidence that she will be a very true mother in all your needs; the other, toward the passion of Jesus Christ our Lord, who must also be for you a very familiar refuge in your difficulties and your only hope of salvation.

## CHAPTER 60

After this, cease from praying vocally. Place yourself in the very depth of your heart, realizing that you are alone in the presence of God. Consider how, before you came to this world, you were nothing until the overwhelming goodness of God our Lord drew you from the abyss of nothingness and made you his creature, not just any one, but a rational creature. Think how he gave you body and soul so that with the one and the other you might labor to serve him.

Imagine that you are already in the event of your death, as really as you are able to experience it, saying to yourself: "Someday, this hour of my end has to arrive. I do not know if it will be tonight or tomorrow, but since it certainly will come, it is right that I should think about it." Consider how you will fall into your bed and sweat the sweat of death.

Your chest will rise up; your eyes will be weakened; the color of your face will be lost. With great pains the friendly union of body and soul will be broken. Afterward, they will clothe your body in a shroud, put it on a bier, and carry it to be buried. Some will be weeping and others singing. They will place you in a small grave, cover you with earth, and having walked over you, they will leave you alone, and you will be forgotten immediately.

Consider then all this that has to happen to you. Consider the state of your body under the earth, and how soon it will be such that no person, however much he may love you, will be able to see or smell or be near you. Consider attentively how the flesh and its glory end, and you will see how foolish they are who, though they have to leave the world so poor, go about now anxious to be very rich. Though they so soon are to be trodden underfoot and forgotten, they greatly desire to be put in places higher than others. How deceived are they who pamper their bodies and go after their desires! They have done nothing but act as cooks preparing delicacies for worms to eat, while by their fleeting delights, they gain for themselves never–ending torments. Consider and look with the greatest attention and without haste at your body stretched out in the tomb. Imagining that you are already in it, mortify the desires of the flesh each time that they come to your memory. Mortify desires of pleasing or displeasing the world, or of possessing something that flourishes in it, since so soon and with such great affliction you have to leave it, and it has to leave you. Consider how your body, after being the food of worms, is changed into dust and ashes. Because of this, do not consider it as anything more than a heap of waste covered with snow that disgusts when you think of it. If you think about the body in this way, you will not be deceived concerning the esteem that you should have for it. Rather, you will have true knowledge and will know how you have to rule it in view of its end as one puts his ship's destination in view so as to guide it better.

**CHAPTER 61**

You have heard how your body will come to an end. Now you are to hear what will happen to your soul. In that hour it will be full of anxiety, remembering the offenses it committed against our Lord in this life. Those that previously seemed light will then seem very grave. The soul will be bereft of its senses and unable to use the tongue to ask our Lord for help; the understanding will be darkened and unable even to think of God. Finally, little by little, the hour will approach in which, at God's command, the soul will leave the body and take upon itself the decision either of eternal perdition or eternal salvation. It must hear from the mouth of God: "Depart from me into eternal fire," or "Remain with me in a state of salvation, in purgatory or in paradise." You will be solely dependent on the hand of God, and in him alone will your remedy be. For this reason you must flee in your life from offending the one you will so greatly need in the hour of your death. There will be no lack of demons to accuse you and demand God for justice against your soul, as they accuse you individually of each sin. If the mercy of God forgets you then, what will you do, poor sheep, surrounded by such ravenous wolves, very desirous of consuming you?

Think, then, during your time of recollection, how in this precise instant you will be presented before the judgment seat of God, naked and with nothing, accompanied only by the good or evil you have done. Tell our Lord that you present yourself now voluntarily so that you may attain mercy in that hour when by force you must leave this world. Think of yourself as a thief caught in the act of robbing and handed over to the judge with hands bound, or as a woman whose husband has found her betraying him. Such as these do not dare to raise their eyes, nor can they deny their crime. Believe that God has seen you much more clearly in all your sins than the eyes of any man can see what is done before him. Ashamed of having been so evil in the presence of such great goodness, cover yourself in the shame that you then lost, and feel within yourself confusion at your sins, as one who is before the presence of the sovereign Judge and Lord. Accuse yourself as you ought to be accused. Especially remember your most serious sins. If they are indecent things, it is safer not to linger in thinking about them specifically, but broadly, as of something repulsive that gives you great fright to behold. Judge and sentence yourself as evil and lower your eyes to consider the infernal fires, believing that you have very well merited them.

Place on one side the good things that God has done for you since he created you. Consider your body and your soul, and how you were obliged to reverence and thank him, and to love him with your whole heart, serving him with total obedience and with all your being, keeping his commandments and those of his church. Look at how he has sustained you by a thousand other goods that he has done for you and evils from which he has delivered you. Above all, consider how, in order to invite you by his example and love to be good, the very Lord of the world became man. To remedy your iniquity and blindness, he suffered many afflictions, shed many tears, and later shed his blood, losing his life for your sake. All this will have to be put on a scale on the day of your death and judgment, as you take responsibility for it, acknowledging its receipt. You will be asked to account for the use you have made of such great graces, of how you have conducted yourself in God's service, and of the care with which you have responded to God's great goodness in desiring and arranging to save you. Consider well, and you will see how right it is for you to fear since, not only have you not responded with service equal to your debts, but you returned evils in exchange for goods. You have despised the one who valued you so greatly, fleeing from him and turning your back on the one who was following you for your good.

What thanks do you think ought to be given to the one who, by his infinite mercy, has delivered us from the hell that we have justly deserved? What shall we give to one who so many times has stretched out his hand so that the demons should not choke us and carry us off with them? Although we have cruelly offended his Majesty, he has been for us a merciful Father and a gentle defender. Consider that in hell there may be some with fewer sins than you. Look at yourself in this way and serve God as if you had already entered into hell because of your sins, and he had drawn you forth from there. It is all the same account, whether he hindered you from going there when you deserved it, or, through his great mercy, he drew you out of there after you entered.

Comparing the goods that God has done for you with the evils you have done to God, if you do not feel shame or sorrow as you desire, do not be disturbed, but persevere in this judgment, and place your wounded and indebted heart before the eyes of God. Beg him to tell you who you are and what you ought to feel about yourself. The effect of this exercise is not only to understand that you are evil, but to know and taste it with the will, and to discover your great wickedness and unworthiness, as one who has a dead dog under his nose. For this, you should not make these considerations hurriedly or for only a day. They should be made over a long period of time and calmly, so that, little by little, your will may absorb that contempt and unworthiness that your understanding has judged are your due. You must present this thought before God, asking him to establish it in the depths of your heart. From then on, esteem yourself simply and truly as a very wicked person deserving all contempt and torment, even that of hell. Be prepared to suffer patiently any difficulty or contempt that is offered to you, considering that, since you have offended God, it is very just that all creatures rise up against you to avenge the injury to their Creator. You will occupy yourself in this patience if you really recognize yourself as

185

a sinner worthy of hell. Say within: "All the evil that may be done to me is very little since I deserve hell." Who will complain of the stinging of flies when he merits eternal torments? Walk thus, very amazed at the Lord's goodness and at how he does not cast from himself a repulsive worm but supports and lavishes attention on it. He bestows graces on it in body and in soul. This is all for his glory, not that we might have anything in which to glory.

## CHAPTER 62

To complete this exercise in self–knowledge, two things remain for you to hear. One is that the Christian ought not to be content with entering into judgment before God in order to accuse himself only of past sins but also of those that he commits each day. It would be difficult to find anything as advantageous for the amendment of life as that a man should take account of how he spends his life and of the wrongs that he commits. The soul that is careless about examining its thoughts, words, and deeds is like the vineyard of the lazy man, of which the Sage said that "he passed through it and saw its fence fallen and full of thorns" (Prov 24:30–31).

Suppose that a king's daughter has been entrusted to you so that you may continually watch out for her behavior and, at night, ask an account from her so that you can scold her for her faults and encourage her in virtues. Similarly, look at yourself as a person whom God has entrusted to you. Be convinced that you are not to live without rule or discipline, but under the holy subjection and discipline of virtue, and that you will not do anything bad that you will not pay for. Enter into chapter with yourself at night, judging yourself very particularly, as you would a third person. Reproach and punish yourself for your faults and preach to yourself with much greater care than you would to any other person, however much you love him. Where you think that there are more faults, apply greater remedy. You ought to believe that, if this examination and self–reproach continue, your faults will not be able to last long without your applying a remedy.

You will learn a very salutary "science" that will make you weep and will prevent you from being "puffed up." It will guard you from the dangerous infirmity of pride that enters little by little and undetected, as a person seems fine to himself and is content with himself. Watch out for pride's entrance. Protect yourself carefully from self–satisfaction. Instead, with the light of truth, learn how to reproach yourself and to feel displeasure with yourself. The mercy of God will be near you. To him alone do those who appear bad to themselves appear good. With abundant goodness he pardons the faults of those who recognize them and humble themselves with true judgment and willingly groan over them.

You will also escape from two other vices that usually accompany pride: ingratitude and sloth. Knowing and reproaching your defects, you will see both your weakness and unworthiness and the great mercy of God in putting up with you, pardoning you, and granting you good things when you deserve evil ones. Thus you will be grateful. Looking at the little good that you do and the evils into which you fall, and as you see what little good you have done in the past, you will awaken from the sleep of laziness and begin each day anew serving our Lord.

This and many other goods usually arise from a man's self–knowledge and self–reproach. For this reason one of the ancient fathers, when asked whether one would be more secure in solitude or in company, responded, "If he knows how to reproach himself, he will be secure everywhere, and if he does not know how, he will be in danger everywhere."

Because of our great self–love, we do not learn to know and correct ourselves with that true judgment that truth requires. Therefore, we ought to thank the person who corrects us. We ought also to beg the Lord that he correct us with love, "sending us his light and his truth" (Ps 43:3), so that we may feel what we ought to feel about ourselves, in accordance with the truth. This is what Jeremiah asked, saying, "Correct me, O Lord, in judgment, and not in fury, lest by chance you bring me to nothing" (Jer 10:24). To correct "in fury" pertains to the last day, when God will send the wicked to hell for their sins. To correct "in judgment" is to reproach his own in this world with the love of a father. This correction is such a great testimony to God's love for the one he corrects that no one is so secure, nor is there anyone who bears such good news of being on the eve of receiving great graces from God. So Saint Mark says that when our Lord Jesus Christ appeared to his disciples, "he upbraided them with their incredulity and hardness of heart" (Mark 16:14). After that, he gave them power to do marvelous works. The prophet Isaiah says that "the Lord washes away the filth of the daughters of Zion and the blood from the midst of Jerusalem by a spirit of judgment and a spirit of burning" (Isa 4:4). This shows us that when our Lord comes to wash away our stains, he first shows us who we are. This is "judgment." Afterward, he sends us "a spirit of burning" that causes us pain. This is love. Thus he washes us, giving us his pardon and his grace. We will not dare to attribute glory to ourselves for this, since he first showed us our unworthiness and lack of merit.

Do not understand correction as something that weakens the heart and causes it to be overly sad and discontented. Things of this sort come either from the demon or from one's own spirit and should be fled. Rather, it is a quiet knowledge of one's own faults and a heavenly judgment heard in the soul. It makes the earth of our weakness tremble so with shame and fear and love that it spurs us on to improve ourselves and to serve the Lord with greater diligence. It gives one the greatest confidence that the Lord loves him as a son, since he exercises with him the office of Father, as is written: "I correct those I love" (Rev 3:19).

Take care, then, to watch over and correct yourself, presenting yourself in God's presence. Before him, the humble knowledge of our faults is safer than the proud loftiness of other knowledge. Do not be like some who love to esteem themselves and, in order not to seem bad to themselves, distract themselves willingly, wasting a lot of time thinking about other devout things. They skim over knowledge of their defects because they do not find them to their taste, since they do not love to despise themselves. But, indeed, there is nothing so secure and nothing that so causes God to take his eyes from our sins as our seeing and correcting ourselves with sorrow and penitence, according to what is written: "If we judged ourselves, we would not be judged" (1 Cor 11:31).

## CHAPTER 63

There is a second thing you have to watch with self–knowledge. Even though it is good and advantageous, since through it there comes to us "the contrite and humbled heart that the Lord does not despise" (Ps 51:19), it does have the flaw of being based upon our having sinned. It is not very surprising that a sinner should know and consider himself a sinner, but he would be a very frightening monster if, being that, he were to consider himself just. It would be as if a man full of leprosy would consider himself healthy. Consequently, we are not to be content with having little esteem for ourselves in our sins. Rather, we are to see this much more even in our good works, recognizing profoundly that the fault of our sins does not belong to God, nor does the glory for our good deeds come from us. For all the good there may be in us, the glory is to be given completely "to the Father of all lights, from whom proceeds every good and every perfect gift" (Jas 1:17). Thus, even if we possess the good, let us consider it as something that does not belong to us. Let us treat it so faithfully that we do not exalt ourselves with the glory that belongs to God; nor do we, as they say, let the honey stick to our hands. We are not speaking here of the humility of sinners, as above, but of the humility of the just, both in this world and in heaven. Concerning this, it is written: "Who is as the Lord our God, who dwells on high and looks upon the lowly things in heaven and on earth?" (Ps 113:5–6). Humility kept the good angels standing and disposed them to rejoice in God, for they were subject to him. Its lack brought down the bad angels because they desired to exalt themselves with the glory of God. The holy Virgin Mary possessed such humility. Having been declared happy and blessed by the mouth of Saint Elizabeth, she was not puffed up, and she did not attribute to herself any of the goods that she had in her. Instead, with a humble and completely faithful heart, she taught Saint Elizabeth and the whole world that no glory was due to her for her greatness but to God. With profound reverence, she began to sing: "My soul magnifies the Lord" (Luke 1:42–46).

The most blessed soul of Jesus Christ our Lord possessed this same most perfect humility. Just as in his personal being he did not depend on himself but on the person of the Word, which exceeds all souls and heavenly spirits, so he exceeds them in this holy humility. His soul is farther from giving glory to itself or depending on itself than all of the others together. From this heart went forth what he often preached to the world in complete fidelity, namely, that he had received his words and deeds from the Father. To him he gave the glory, saying, "My doctrine is not mine, but his that sent me" (John 7:16). In another place he says, "The words that I speak, I speak not of myself, but the Father who abides in me, he does the works" (John 14:10). So it was fitting that the one who was offering a remedy to men should be very humble, since pride is the root of all evil in people and in things. Wanting to show us how fitting it is to possess this holy and true humility, the Lord becomes its teacher in a special way. He sets himself as an example when he says: "Learn of me, because I am meek and humble of heart" (Matt 11:29). He did this so that all would labor to possess this virtue, seeing that such a wise master particularly recommended it. Seeing that such a high Lord does not attribute good to himself, no one would be so foolish as to dare to commit such an evil.

Learn this holy lowliness, then, O servant of Christ, from your master and Lord, so that you may be exalted, according to his word: "Whoever humbles himself shall be exalted" (Luke 14:11). Preserve in your soul this holy poverty, because of which it is understood: "Blessed are the poor in spirit, for theirs is the kingdom of heaven" (Matt 5:3). Hold it for certain that, since Jesus Christ our Lord was exalted by the way of humility, the one who does not have it strays far from the way. He ought to set himself straight by taking his direction from Saint Augustine: "If you ask me the way to heaven, I will answer that it is humility. If you ask me a third time, I will answer the same. If you ask me a thousand times, I will reply a thousand times that there is no other way than humility."[123]

## CHAPTER 64

Because I believe that you desire this holy lowliness by which you please the Lord, I want to say something about how to attain it. The first thing is to ask for it with perseverance from the giver of all good gifts, because this humility is his very special gift to his elect. Even realizing that it is a gift of God is no small grace. Those tempted to pride know well that there is nothing further away from our own strength than true and profound humility. It often happens that, through the remedies they undertake to attain such humility, it flees further away, so that even their humbling themselves gives rise to the pride that is its opposite. Therefore, do in this matter what I told you to do about chastity. Take up the exercises to attain this jewel in such a way that you do not cease from them, saying, "What good is it for me to do this since it is God's gift?" Neither are you to do these exercises with confidence in your arm of flesh, but in him who is wont to give his gifts to those to whom he gives his grace, so that they may ask for them with prayer and devout exercises.

This is to be your way. Consider two things in order: the one, being; the other, being that is good. As far as the first, you are to think who you were before God created you. You will find that you were an abyss of nothingness and the privation of all goods. Stay a good while feeling this "nonbeing" until you see and touch your nothingness and your nonbeing. Afterward, consider how God's powerful but gentle hand drew you out of that profound abyss and placed you in the number of his creatures, giving you true and real existence. Look at yourself not as of your own making but as a gift with which God has favored you. Look at your being as just as far beyond your strength as you see another person to be. Believe that you were unable to create yourself, just as you were unable to create another; you were not able to depart from that darkness of nonbeing any more than those who remained in it. For your part, things that do not exist are equal to you in the sense that you must attribute to God the advantage you have over them.

Now that you have been created, try not to think that you stand firm within yourself. You have no less need of God every moment of your life, so as not to lose what you have, than the need you had when you were nothing to attain the being you have. Enter within yourself and consider how you are something that has being and lives. Ask yourself: "Is this creature dependent on itself or on another?" "Does it sustain itself, or does it need the hand of another?" The apostle Saint Paul will answer you: "God is not far from us, but in him we live and move and have being" (Acts 17:27–28). Reflect that God is "the being" of all that is, and that without him there is nothing. He is the "life" of all that lives, and without him there is only death. He is the strength of all that can do anything, and without him there is only weakness. He is the complete good of all that is good, and without him there cannot be even the smallest good of all that is good. For this reason scripture says, "All nations are before God as if they were not, and they are counted as nothing and vanity before him" (Isa 40:17). In another place it is written, "Anyone who thinks that he is something, whereas he is nothing, deceives himself" (Gal 6:3). The prophet David said, speaking with God, "I am as nothing before you" (Ps 39:6). In these passages you are not to understand that creatures do not have life or their own operations distinct from those of their Creator. But it is said that they "are not" because they do not have what they have from themselves but from God, and they cannot preserve them by themselves but in God. This means that they have being and power to act from the hand of God, not from their own hand.

Immerse yourself, then, in the being and strength that you have, and do not stop until you arrive at the first foundation, the strongest one and without deficiency, founded on no other foundation. It is the one that sustains you so that you do not fall back into the deep well of nothingness from which God drew you before. Recognize this support that sustains you and this hand placed upon you that causes you to stand. Confess with David: "You, Lord, made me, and placed your hand upon me" (Ps 139:5). Consider that you are so dependent on God's power that, if it were to fail you, you would, in that moment, also fail. It is just as the light in a room would fail if the lamp lighting it were taken out, or as light is taken away from the earth by the absence of the sun. With profound reverence, then, adore this Lord as the principle of your being. Love him as your constant benefactor and the protector of your existence. Speak to him with your heart and your tongue: "Glory be to you, Mighty Power, by which I am sustained. I have nothing, Lord, to look for outside me, since you are more intimately within me than I am in myself, and I must pass through myself to enter into you." Join your heart with him and unite it with him lovingly. Say to him: "This is my rest forever; here will I dwell, for I have chosen it" (Ps 132:14). From here on, think with all reverence that God is present within you since he is most present to you.

As you have understood from what has taken place within you, that God is the one who has given you being and the power to act, you must understand the same about all other creatures. If you consider God in all of them, they will be to you as a shining mirror that represents the Creator to you. Thus, your soul will be able to walk united with God and devout in his praises, if you do not seek in creatures anything other than God.

## CHAPTER 65

If you have engaged yourself carefully in knowing yourself, in order to attribute to God the glory of the "being" that you possess, you ought with much greater care to be engaged in recognizing that the goodness of your being is not yours but is a gracious gift from the Lord's hand. If you attribute to him the glory of your being, confessing that you did not make yourself, "but his hands made you" (cf. Job 10:8), but you appropriate to yourself the honor for your good works, believing that you made yourself good, then you take for yourself a greater honor than you give to God, insofar as being good is more excellent than mere being. Therefore, it is helpful to occupy yourself with the greatest vigilance in knowing God and holding him to be the cause of your good. Live so that no trace or hint of foolish pride is left on your hands. You recognize that from yourself, you can have no being, however small it may be, unless God gives it to you. So you ought to recognize also that you cannot have the least of goods from yourself, unless God opens his hand to give it to you.

Consider that, just as what is nothing does not have natural being among creatures, so the sinner, however great his state and possessions, if he lacks grace and spiritual being, is considered as nothing before the eyes of God. Saint Paul says this: "If I should have the gift of prophecy and should know all mysteries and all knowledge, and if I should have such great faith that I could move mountains from one place to another, and had not charity, I am nothing" (cf. 1 Cor 13:2). This is so true that the sinner is even less than nothing because being evil is worse than not being. There is no place so low, so distant, so despised in the eyes of God, among all that is and is not, as the man who lives in offense to God, since he is disinherited from heaven and sentenced to hell.

So that you may have something to awaken you somewhat in the knowledge of this miserable state of the sinner, listen to this. When you see something completely contrary to reason and very disordered, think that it is far uglier and more abominable to be in disgrace and enmity with our Lord. Do you hear of some serious robbery, betrayal, or evil that some woman does to her husband, or of the disrespect of some son to his father, or of things of this type, that seem ugly to anyone, no matter how ignorant, because they are contrary to reason? Think that offending God by one sin against his commandment and against the reverence due to him is uglier than all the evil works that can take place through being only against reason. Since you see how despised are all those who commit such ugly deeds, consider yourself very despised and plunge yourself into the profound abyss of contempt owed to one who offends God.

In order to appreciate your nothingness, you remembered the time when you did not exist. Now, in order to recognize your lowliness and vileness, remember when you lived in offense against God. As intimately, deeply, and slowly as you can, consider the miserable state you were in when you were ugly and displeasing in God's eyes and counted as nothing, and as less than nothing. Neither the animals, as ugly as they may be, nor other creatures, as lowly as they may be, have committed any sin against our Lord, nor are they obligated to eternal fire as you were. Hold yourself in contempt and lower yourself utterly to the deepest place that you can. Surely you can believe that, no matter how much you despise yourself, you cannot descend to the abyss of contempt that is merited by one who has offended the infinite good that is God. Not until heaven, when you see how good God is, can you know completely how wicked sin is and what evil the one who commits it deserves. After having felt and imbibed into your soul this contempt for self, raise your eyes to God, considering the infinite goodness that drew you out of a well so deep when it was impossible for you to do it. Consider that supreme goodness that, with such great mercy, drew you forth, without you having any merits, but, on the contrary, very great demerits. Though not everything is sin that man does before God gives grace, man does not and cannot do anything to merit God's pardon or grace. You should know that it was God who "brought you out of darkness into his wonderful light" and changed you from an enemy to a friend, from a slave to a child, from one of no value to one with an existence pleasing to him (cf. Col 1:13). He did not do this because of your past merits or in consideration of services you had rendered, but only through his goodness and through the merits of Jesus Christ our Lord. Count as yours the evil state in which you were, and count hell as the place owed for the sins you had or would have committed, if it were not for God. Whatever else you have, recognize yourself as a debtor to God and his grace. Listen to what our Lord says to his beloved disciples, and through them, to us: "You have not chosen me, but I have chosen you" (John 15:16). Consider what the apostle Saint Paul says: "You are justified freely by the grace of God, through the redemption, that is in Christ Jesus" (Rom 3:24). Establish in your heart that, just as you have received existence from God without attributing to yourself the glory of it, so you have received being that is good from God. The one and the other are for his glory. Carry on your tongue and in your heart what Saint Paul says: "By the grace of God I am what I am" (1 Cor 15:10).

**CHAPTER 66**

Besides what has been said, consider that, when you were nothing, you had no power to move yourself, or to see, hear, or taste, or to understand or will. But when God gave you being, he gave you these faculties and powers. So also, not only is the man in mortal sin deprived of the being that is pleasing in God's eyes, but he is powerless to do works of life pleasing to God. Therefore, if you see someone crippled or maimed, think that thus is the man without grace in his soul. If you see someone blind, deaf, or mute, take him as a mirror in which you look at yourself. When you see any of the infirm (lepers, paralytics, those with body bent over and eyes fixed on the ground, and with all the multitude of infirmities that were presented before Jesus Christ, our true physician), understand that the wicked are just as lost in their spiritual senses as were all these in their corporal senses. Consider that, just as a stone is inclined by its weight to fall downward, so by the corruption of original sin that we bear, we have a most lively inclination to the things of our flesh, our honor, and our advantage. We make an idol of ourselves and perform our works, not out of true love of God but out of self–love. We are very alive to earthly things that interest us and dead toward delight for the things of God. That in us that ought to obey, commands, and what ought to command, obeys. We are so miserable that, beneath our erect human bodies, we carry hidden the appetites of beasts and hearts inclined toward the earth. What shall I say to you, except that in so many defective, ugly, arid, and disordered things that you see, you should notice and recognize the corruption and disorder man has in his senses and works, without the Spirit of God? Do not look at any of these things without entering right away into yourself to consider that, such you would be for your part, if God had not given you salvation.

If you really are healthy, you will recognize that God was the one who opened your senses to the things of God. He subjected your affections to reason; he made bitter what had been sweet to you; he put in you the desire for what before, you found tasteless, and thus he realized new works in you. As Saint Paul says: "It is God who works in us, both to will and to accomplish, according to his good will" (Phil 2:13).

But do not for this reason think that man's free will works nothing in good works, for this would be colossal ignorance and error. Rather, it is said that "God works to will and to accomplish" because he is the principal agent in the soul of the justified person. He gently moves and causes the free will to work and cooperate with him. As Saint Paul says: "We are fellow workers of God" (1 Cor 3:9). He does this "with God inciting him and helping him" that he might freely give his consent to good works. Therefore, man works, for freely and by his own will, he wills what he wills and works what he works. Also, it is in his power not to do it. But God works more principally producing the work and aiding the free will so that it may also produce it. The glory of both is owed to God alone.

Therefore, if you want to be certain in this, do not try to distinguish what goods you have from nature and free will, and what goods are from grace. This question is for the learned. Rather, with your eyes closed, be guided by the holy faith that admonishes us to give glory to God for the one and the other and that "of ourselves, we are not capable even of thinking a good thought" (cf. 2 Cor 3:5). Pay attention to what Saint Paul says, correcting one who attributes some good to himself: "What do you have that you have not received? And if you have received it, why do you glory as if you had not received it?" (1 Cor 4:7). It is as if he had said: If you have the grace of God by which you please him, and if you do very excellent works, do not glory in yourself, but in the one who gave you his grace, who is God. If you glory in using well your free will, and in consenting with it to the good movements of God and his grace, you are not to glory in yourself, but in God. He caused you to consent by gently inciting and moving you and by giving you the same free will with which you freely consent. You may want to glory in the fact that, when you could have resisted the good movement of God's inspiration, you did not resist it. But you ought not to glory in this, for it is not to do something but to refrain from doing it. Even this you also owe to God, who, by helping you to consent to the good, helped you not to resist the good. Any good use of your free will in what touches your salvation is a gift of God that descends from that merciful predestination by which he determined "from eternity" to save you. All your glory must be in God alone, from whom you have all the good that you have. Think that without him, all you have from your own harvest is nothing, plus vanity and iniquity.

In keeping with this, there is a gloss on that text of Saint Paul: "He who thinks he is something, whereas he is nothing, deceives himself" (Gal 6:3). The gloss says that of himself man is only vanity and sin, and if he is anything more, it is through the Lord. In conformity with this, Saint Augustine says:

> You, O Light, opened my eyes and woke me up and illuminated me. I saw that man's life on this earth is temptation, and that no good man can boast before you and that no living man is justified. If there is any good, small or great, it is your gift, and what is ours is nothing but evil. For what then will any man boast? Of evil? But this is not glory but misery. Shall he then glory in good? No, because it does not belong to him. Yours, Lord, is the good; yours is the glory.[124]

Along the same lines, Saint Augustine says:

> Lord our God, I confess to you my poverty. To you is the glory, because yours is all the good that I have done. I confess, according to what you have taught me, that I am nothing but vanity and shadow of death, a dark abyss, "earth void and empty," that, without your blessing, produces no fruit but confusion, sin, and death. If I have had any kind of good, I received it from you. Any good that I may possess, is yours, and I received it from you. If at any time I stood firm, because of you I stood. But when I fell, because of myself I fell, and forever, I would have remained fallen in the mire, if you had not raised me up. Forever, I would have been blind if you had not enlightened me. When I fell, I would never have gotten up if you had not given me your hand, and after you raised me up, always I would have fallen again, if you had not sustained me. Many times I would have been lost if you had not protected me. Thus, Lord, your grace and mercy always went before me, freeing me from all evils, saving me from sins by awakening me to present ones, protecting me from those of the future, and cutting before me the bonds of sins by removing occasions and causes. If you, Lord, had not done this, I would have committed all the sins of the world. For, I know that there is no sin of any type that a man may have committed, that another man may not commit, if the guide, through whom man was made, is not present. But you saw to it that I should not do it, and you commanded me to abstain from it. You filled me with grace so that I might

believe in you, for you, Lord, were directing me to yourself and keeping me for yourself, and you gave me grace and light so that I would not commit adultery and every other sin.[125]

## CHAPTER 67

Consider attentively, daughter, these words of Saint Augustine. You will see how far you ought to be from attributing to yourself any glory, not only for having risen from your sins, but for having sustained yourself so as not to fall again. For, as I told you, if God's hand were withdrawn from you, you would return in that instant to the abyss of nothingness in which you were before. Likewise, if God were to stop protecting you, you would return to the sins from which he drew you, and to others greater. Therefore, be humble and grateful to this Lord, of whom you have such great need in every moment. Recognize that you are dependent upon him, and that all your good depends on his blessed hand. As David says: "In your hands, Lord, are my lots" (Ps 31:16). He uses the word "lots" for God's grace and the eternal predestination that come from the goodness of God and are granted to those to whom they are granted. In the same way that, if he took away the existence that he gave you, you would again be nothing, so, if he took away his grace, you would remain a sinner.

I do not say this to discourage you or to cause you to lose hope at seeing how dependent you are on the hands of God. Rather, it is said so that you may more securely rejoice in the goods God has given you and have confidence that in his mercy he will complete what he has begun in you, insofar as with greater humility, profound reverence, and holy fear, you are prostrate at his feet, trembling and with no reliance on yourself, but trusting in him. This is a good sign that his infinite goodness has not abandoned you, according to what that blessed and most humble Mary sang: "His mercy is from generation to generation on those who fear him" (Luke 1:50).

If the Lord is pleased to give you the knowledge you desire, you will perceive that a heavenly light comes into your soul and a feeling by which, thick darkness having been removed, it knows and perceives that there is no good or being or force in all that has been created, other than that which the blessed and gracious will of God has desired to give and desires to preserve. Then the soul knows how true the canticle is: "The heavens and the earth are full of your glory" (Isa 6:3). In all the creation the soul sees nothing good whose glory is not from God. It understands how truly God said to Moses so that he might tell men, "He who is, has sent me to you" (Exod 3:14). The Lord said in the gospel: "None is good but God alone" (Mark 10:18). All existence and all the good that things possess, whether they be of free will or of grace, have been given by the hand of God, who preserves it. Therefore, the soul recognizes that it is more possible to say that God is in them and works good in them than that they themselves do these things. It is not that they do not work, but that they are secondary causes, moved by God, the principal and universal Maker, from whom they have the power to work. Looking at them, the soul does not find value or support in the things themselves, but in the infinite Being that sustains them. In comparison with him, all these things, however great they may be, appear as a tiny needle in an infinite sea.

This knowledge of God produces in the soul that takes advantage of it, a profound and faithful reverence for the most excellent divine Majesty; it produces in him so great a horror at attributing any good to himself or to another creature that he does not even want to think of it. He considers that, just as the chaste Joseph refused to betray his lord, even though it was solicited by Pharaoh's wife (cf. Gen 39:8–9), so man ought not to exalt himself with the honor that God wants for himself as the husband wants his own wife. According to what is written, "My glory I will not give to another" (Isa 42:8). The man is then so established in this truth that, even if the whole world were to exalt him, he would not exalt himself. But, as a truly just man, he strips himself of the honor that he sees is not his own and gives it to the Lord to whom it belongs. In this light he sees that the higher he is, and the more he has received from God, and the more he owes God, the smaller and lower he is in himself. Whoever truly grows in the other virtues also has to grow in humility, saying to God, "It is fitting that you increase" in me and "that I decrease more every day" in myself (cf. John 3:30).

If with the considerations already mentioned, you still do not find in yourself the fruit of self–contempt that you desire, do not be troubled but call out with persevering prayer to the Lord; he knows how to teach interiorly as well as with external comparisons, how little created things are to be valued, and he is wont to do so. Until this mercy arrives, live patiently and recognize yourself as proud. This is an aspect of humility, just as considering oneself humble is a sign of pride.

# B. Seeing Christ (Chaps. 68–93)

## 1. Prayerful Contemplation of Christ as Spouse (chaps. 68–79)

**CHAPTER 68**

Those who exercise themselves a lot in self–knowledge and deal continually and closely with their own defects often fall into great sadness, distrust, and faint heartedness. Consequently, they must exercise themselves in another knowledge that may cheer and encourage them far more than the first knowledge discouraged them. For this purpose there is no knowledge like that of Jesus Christ our Lord, especially if we consider how he suffered and died for us. This is the joyful news, preached in the New Law to "all the brokenhearted" (cf. Isa 61:1). In it they are given a medicine much more effective for their consolation than their wounds are in causing them sorrow. The crucified Lord cheers those saddened by the knowledge of their own sins, absolves those whom the Law condemns, and makes children of God of those who were slaves of the devil. All those indebted by spiritual debts through their sins and who feel anguish and bitterness of heart when they look upon themselves must seek to know and draw near to him. And it will go well for them as, in another time, it did for those in debt and "oppressed by debts" who joined David and found help in his company (cf. 1 Sam 22:2).

It is customary to advise those who are crossing a river to look upward or at least away from the water, lest they should faint when they see the moving stream. Similarly, anyone who feels discouragement at the sight of his sins should raise his eyes to Jesus Christ on the cross and he will recover strength. Not in vain was it said, "My soul was troubled within me and therefore I remembered you, from the land of Jordan and Mount Hermon, and from the little hill" (cf. Ps 42:7). The mysteries that Christ accomplished in his baptism and passion are enough to calm any tempest of distrust that may arise in the heart. There is no book as effective as the passion of the Son of God for teaching every kind of virtue and how much sin must be abhorred and virtue loved. Yet another reason is that it is the height of ingratitude to forget such an immense work of love as Christ's passion was for us. For these reasons it is helpful after the exercise of self–knowledge to occupy yourself with the knowledge of Jesus Christ our Lord. Saint Bernard teaches this when he says:

> Whoever has any awareness of Christ, knows well how appropriate it is for Christian piety and how necessary and helpful it is for the servant of God and the servant of the Redemption of Christ, to remember attentively for at least an hour a day, the benefits of the passion and redemption of our Lord Jesus Christ, in order to rejoice quietly in awareness of it, and to settle it faithfully in the memory.[126]

Besides this, realize that when God wanted to communicate to human beings the riches of his divinity, he took the incarnation as his means. Thus, in lowliness and poverty, he would be able to conform himself to the small capacity of the poor and lowly, and uniting himself with them, he might raise them up to his own height. So it was that the way God used to communicate his divinity to souls was through his sacred humanity. It is "the door through which anyone who enters will be saved; it is the ladder by which they ascend to heaven" (cf. John 10:9; Gen 28:12). Because God the Father wants to honor the humanity and humility of his only–begotten Son, he gives his friendship only to those who believe in them and enters into familiar communion only with those who meditate attentively on them.

Since there is no reason for you to stop desiring these benefits, make yourself a *servant of this sacred passion*. Through it you were freed from the captivity of your sins and from eternal torments, and you receive the blessings already mentioned. Do not let it be burdensome for you to *think* about that which, because of his great love for you, was not burdensome for him to *suffer*. Be one of those souls to whom the Holy Spirit speaks in the Song of Songs: "Go forth, O Daughters of Zion, and see King Solomon in the garland with which his mother crowned him on the day of his espousals, and in the day of the joy of his heart" (Song 3:11). In no other passage of Sacred Scripture do we read that his mother Bathsheba crowned King Solomon with a garland or crown on the day of his espousals. It was not appropriate for Solomon because, according to history, he was a sinner. Since the scripture cannot err, we must understand the passage to apply to that other true Solomon, namely, Christ. Very rightly is this so, because the name Solomon means peaceable. It was given to the king because he did not wage any wars in his time as his father, David, had in his (cf. Sir 47:15). Thus, God decided that not David, a man of blood, but his peaceable son, should build the solemn Temple in Jerusalem where

God would be adored (cf. 1 Kgs 6). For being peaceable with regard to worldly peace—which sometimes even wicked kings can have in their kingdoms—Solomon received the name that means peaceable. How much more does the name fit Christ, who made spiritual peace between God and human beings! Christ did this at great cost to himself, for the penalty for our sins, which caused enmity between God and us, fell upon him. Thus also he made peace between those two such contrary peoples, the Jews and the Gentiles, "removing the wall of enmity from between them" (Eph 2:14), as Saint Paul says. He refers here to the ceremonies of the Old Law and the idolatry of the Gentiles. The two peoples, having left behind the particular characteristics and rites inherited from their ancestors, might come to a New Law under one faith, one baptism, and one Lord. As children of one and the same Father in heaven, they could then look forward in hope to sharing one and the same inheritance (Eph 4:5–6). He begot them anew through water and the Holy Spirit with greater profit and honor than they had from being engendered the first time by their parents to a birth that was unto misery and dishonor. All these goods come through Jesus Christ. He is the one who makes peace between heaven and earth, peace between one people and another, peace of each person within himself. The last is the most painful war and the most desired peace. The other Solomon could not have made peace in any of these situations because he bore the name only as a figure of the true peacemaker. Likewise the temporal peace of Solomon is the figure and shadow of that spiritual peace that has no end.

If you remember, O spouse of Christ, that which it makes sense never to forget, you will discover that the mother of this true Solomon, who was and is the blessed Virgin Mary, is the one who crowned him with a beautiful garland. She gave him sinless flesh on the day of the incarnation, the day of the union and espousal of the divine Word with his holy humanity and of the Word–made–man with the church. We are that church. From her sacred womb Christ came forth "like the bridegroom from his bridal chamber, and began to run his course like a strong giant" (cf. Ps 19:5), taking to heart the work of our redemption. This was the most difficult thing he could undertake. At the end of his course, on Good Friday, he espoused his church, for which he had labored as Jacob did for Rachel (cf. Gen 29:20), by words that continue present. Then, as Christ was sleeping the sleep of death, the church was drawn from his side, as Eve had been taken from the side of Adam while he slept (cf. Gen 2:21). So excellent and so loving was the work realized that day that Christ, in the gospel, calls it "my day":

"Abraham your father rejoiced that he might see my day; he saw it and was glad" (John 8:56). This happened, as Chrysostom says, when Christ's death was revealed to Abraham, in the figure of his son Isaac, whom God commanded him to sacrifice on Mount Moriah, that is Mount Zion (cf. Gen 22:2). It was then that Abraham saw this painful day and rejoiced. But why did he rejoice? Did he perhaps rejoice at the scourging and sadness and torments of Christ? Certainly, the sadness of Christ was great enough to sadden anyone with compassion, no matter how much joy he might possess. If you do not believe me, let his three beloved disciples speak. It was to them that he said, "My soul is sorrowful even unto death" (Matt 26:38). What did their hearts feel when they heard this word that wounds with the sharp knife of sorrow even those who hear it from afar? So painful were his scourges and torments, the nails and the cross, that anyone who saw them, no matter how hard he might be, would be moved with compassion. I do not know if even the very ones that were tormenting him, upon seeing his meekness in suffering and their own cruelty in wounding him, at times felt pity for the one suffering so much for them (although they did not know that he was suffering for them). If, then, those who abhorred Christ could feel pity at the sight of his torments—unless they were hard as rocks—how are we to say of Abraham, such a great friend of God, that "he rejoiced to see the day" when Christ endured such great suffering?

## CHAPTER 69

But so that you may not wonder at this, listen to something else more marvelous in the words mentioned from the Song of Songs. This garland was placed on him "the day of the joy of his heart." How is this? The day of his extreme sorrows that no tongue can describe, you call the day of his joy, and not a joy that is feigned and exterior, but "the day of the joy of his heart."

O Joy of the angels and river of their delight, on whose face they desire to gaze and through whose overwhelming waves they are overcome at being within you and swimming in your overflowing sweetness! In what did your heart rejoice on the day of your sufferings? In what did you rejoice amid the scourges, the nails, the insults, and death? Do these perhaps not cause you pain? Certainly they do, and more to you than to any other, because your constitution was more delicate. But, because our afflictions cause you greater pain, you choose to suffer your afflictions very willingly, since by those sufferings you remove ours. You are the one who said to your beloved apostles a little before the passion: "Ardently I have desired to eat this Passover with you before I suffer" (Luke 22:15). And you are the one who had said before: "I have come to bring fire upon the earth, and what do I want but that it is kindled? With a baptism, I have to be baptized, and how I live in anguish until it is accomplished" (Luke 12: 49–50). You desire the fire of your love to burn in us so that it sets us aflame, burns us up, and consumes what we are, transforming us into you. You inspire it in us by the favors you did for us in your lifetime, and you cause it to blaze up by the death you endured for us. Who would love you if you had not died of love to give life to those who were dead because they did not love you? Who will be a piece of wood so wet and cold that he does not come forth ardent in loving you unto death when he sees you, a green tree from which anyone lives who eats, burning on the cross and consumed by the torments they were meting out to you and by the love with which you suffered? Who will be so stubborn that he protects himself against the persistent call with which you followed us, from the time you were born of the womb of the Virgin, taken in her arms and laid in the manger, until those same hands and arms received you when they removed you dead from the cross, and you were placed in the holy sepulcher as in another womb? You were aflame so that we would not remain cold; you wept so that we might laugh; you suffered so that we might find rest; you "were baptized" by the shedding of your blood so that we might be washed clean of our iniquities.

You say, Lord: "How I live in anguish until this baptism is accomplished!" Thus you make us understand how burning is your desire for our healing, even though you knew that it would have to cost you your life. The spouse longs for the day of his espousal in order to rejoice. So you long for the day of your passion in order to draw us out from our labors by your sufferings. One hour, Lord, was to you a thousand years for having to die for us. You would hold your life well spent in handing it over for your servants. Since what is desired brings joy when it is attained, there is no reason for wondering that the day of your passion is called "day of your joy," for you desired it. The sorrow of that day was extremely excessive so that in your person may be said: "All you that pass by the way, attend and see if there is any sorrow like to my sorrow" (Lam 1:12). But the love burning in your heart was incomparably greater. If it had been necessary for our good that you suffered a thousand times more than you suffered and were nailed to the cross until the end of the world, you were determined when you mounted it that you would do and suffer all that would be necessary for our healing.

Thus, you loved more than you suffered, and your love could do more than the hatred of the executioners tormenting you. Therefore, your love ended up victorious, and, as a living flame, "great rivers could not extinguish it" (cf. Song 8:7), nor could the many passions that assailed you. For this reason, even though the torments they were meting out to you caused you very real sadness and sorrow, your love was rejoicing at the good that was coming to us from it. So it is called "the day of your gladness of heart." "Abraham saw this day and rejoiced" (cf. John 8:56), not because he lacked compassion for so many sufferings, but he saw that he and the world would be redeemed through them.

Then, in this day, "go forth, daughters of Zion," those who watch for God with faith, "to see the peaceful king" (cf. Zech 9:9), who through his sufferings, goes to make the desired peace. Look at him, since eyes have been given you to look at him. Amid all the marriage finery he wears, look upon the "garland" of thorns he wears on his divine head. Even though Pilate's soldiers, who were Gentiles, plaited it and put it on, it is said that "his mother," the synagogue, puts it on, from whose line Christ descends according to the flesh. For through the accusation of the synagogue and for the motive of pleasing it, Christ was thus tormented.

And if someone says, these are new adornments for a wedding: for a garland, a painful crown; for ornaments for hands and feet, sharp nails that pierce and break; scourges for a belt; his hair matted and reddened with his own blood; his sacred beard plucked; his cheeks red from blows; the soft and fragrant bed usually given to spouses has become a rough cross, set up in a place where malefactors are executed. What does this extreme humiliation have to do with adornments of a wedding? What does being in the company of thieves have to do with being accompanied by friends who rejoice to honor the newly espoused? What fruit, what music, what pleasures do we see here, since the mother and the friends of the espoused eat sorrows and drink tears and "the angels of peace weep bitterly"? (cf. Isa 33:7). There is nothing farther from a wedding than all that appears here. But there is no reason to be astonished at such newness, since the spouse and the mode of espousal are completely new. Christ is a new man, because he is without sin and because he is God and man. He espouses himself to us who are ugly, poor, and full of iniquities. He does this not to leave us in them but to slay our iniquities and to give us his benefits. Consequently, it was fitting according to the divine disposition that he should pay for us. He took our place and likeness so that in the likeness of a debtor, without being one, and by that harsh punishment, without having done anything to deserve it, he might remove our ugliness and give us his beauty and his riches. No spouse can change his bride from bad to good, from hellish to heavenly, from ugly of soul to beautiful. Therefore, men look for brides that are good, beautiful, and rich. The day of the wedding, they come clothed in finery in order to rejoice in the goods that their brides possess and that they have not given to them. But our new spouse finds no soul beautiful or good unless he makes it so. What we are able to give him, our dowry, is the debt we owe for our sins. Because he decided to come down to us, we clothed him as we were, and he clothed us as he is. To destroy our old man in our likeness, he put on us his image of a new and heavenly man. He accomplished this with adornments, which appear to be ugliness and weakness. But they are the highest honor and greatness, since they could undo our many old and resistant sins and bring us to the grace and friendship of the Lord, which is the highest that can be won for us.

This is the mirror in which you should look many times a day in order to beautify what you see to be ugly in your soul. This is "the sign set on high" so that "by whatever serpent you have been bitten, you look here" (cf. Num 21:8) and you receive healing from its wounds. In whatever good comes to you, look here, giving thanks to this Lord through whose sufferings all good come to us, and it will be preserved for you.

## CHAPTER 70

You have already heard that the light your eyes need for seeing is God–made–man and crucified. It remains to tell you how to see him. The only way is through exercise of the devout considerations and interior discourse proper to prayer. But before telling you how to pray, it is helpful to tell you how beneficial the exercise of prayer is, especially for you, who have renounced the world and offered yourself entirely to the Lord. It is fitting for you to have very intimate and familiar communication with him if you desire to enjoy the sweet fruits of your religious state.

By prayer, we understand here, a secret and interior speech with which the soul communicates with God, now by thinking, now by petitioning him, now by giving thanks, now by contemplating, and generally, by all that which comes to pass in one's secret conversation with God. Although each of these has its particular purpose, my intention here is to treat only in general about how important it is that the soul has this special conversation and communication with her God.

If men were not blind, it would have been enough to prove this by telling them to imagine that God permits all who desire to speak with

205

him to enter once a month or once a week, and that he will gladly hear them: he will remedy their ills, grant them gifts, and have friendly conversation with them as between a Father and his children. Suppose that he gave this permission to speak with him each day and many times a day, or even throughout the night and day. Suppose that at any time they were willing and able to converse with the Lord, he would be pleased to do so. Who is there, unless he is a stone, who would not be grateful for such a broad and beneficial permission? Who would not try to use it any time he could, as something very suitable for winning honor through speaking with his Lord and delight in enjoying intimacy with him and benefit in never leaving his presence empty–handed? Then, why is it that the offer of the Most High is not esteemed greatly, since it would be esteemed if a temporal king offered the same? In comparison with the Almighty and what can be drawn from dealing with him, the king is a worm, and what one and all of them can give is a little dust. Why are men not happy to be with God since "his delights are to be with the children of men"? (Prov 8:31). "His conversation has no bitterness" (cf. Wis 8:16), but gladness and joy, nor is his nature mean so as to deny what is asked of him. He is our Father. We would enjoy conversing with him even if no other benefit came to us from it. Moreover, he not only permits us to speak with him, but he pleads, advises, and sometimes commands us to do so. Thus you see how great his goodness is and how much he desires that we converse with him. You will also see how great our wickedness is in not wanting to approach him when he invites and rewards us, though the way we should be approaching him is with pleading and surrendering whatever he asks.

This shows you how little men know about which spiritual necessities are the real ones. For whoever knows them truly, prays truly and asks insistently for remedy. A proverb says: "If you do not know how to pray, go to sea." The many dangers in which sailors find themselves make them invoke our Lord. I do not know why we do not all exercise this office, and with diligence. For we may travel now by land and another time by sea, but we always travel in danger of death. It may be death of the soul, if we should fall into mortal sin, or of body and soul, if we do not rise by repentance for the sin into which we have fallen. If temporal cares and the dust in our eyes were dispelled so that we could care for and see the needs of our hearts, we would walk certainly, crying out to God with our whole being in these and similar words that express our need: "Lead us not into temptation!" (Matt 6:13). "Lord, depart not from me!" (Ps 34:22). All our praying has gone in the direction of our experience, that is, to temporal good or evil. Even this we do not do immediately but only when other means and helps have failed us. We are as people who have placed their ultimate confidence in our Lord, but their first and greater confidence in themselves or in others. Often the Lord gets annoyed with this and says: "Where are your gods in whom you trusted?" (Deut 32:37). Let your allies free you, those that the wind and gusts carry. "See that I alone am and there is no other besides me. I kill and I make return to life; I wound and I heal, and there is none able to deliver from me" (Deut 32:30).

Watch, then, daughter, that these things do not touch you, but that you keep alive the awareness in your soul that real evil for you is not to serve God and real good is to serve him. When you ask for something temporal, let it not be with that urgency and anxiety that usually springs from inordinate love. In great things and in small let your first confidence be our Lord, and after that, the means by which he directs you. Be very grateful for this gift of being permitted to speak and converse with him. Use it very frequently and carefully with regard to good things and bad. By means of such speech and dealings with the Most High, many servants of God have been enriched and helped in their poverty. They understood that God permitted dangers to oppress them so that they would run to him, and they understood that the goods which come to them are given that they may go to him giving thanks.

We read of the Gibeonites (cf. Josh 10:6–7) that, when they were in great danger, surrounded by their enemies, they sent a messenger to Joshua, to whose friendship they had offered themselves, and for which reason they were in danger, and they found favor and remedy by asking for it. The five kings that scripture mentions were conquered in the woodland valley and their cities sacked (cf. Gen 14:1ff.). But because a youth who escaped from the war went to inform the patriarch Abraham of this defeat, the kings and their five cities obtained a remedy by the hand of Abraham, who brought them help. The remedy is obtained through only one messenger who goes to ask the favor from one who can and will give it, rather than through the large number of combatants that may be in the war or in the city. Thus, it is certain that anyone who sends God the messenger of humble and faithful prayer, even though surrounded, destroyed, and placed "in the belly of the whale" (Matt 12:40), will sense the Lord present, he who "is near to all who call upon him in truth" (Ps 145:18).

If they do not know what they have to do, with prayer they find light, since with this confidence King Josaphat said, "When we do not know what to do, we have this remedy, which is to lift our eyes to you" (2 Chr 20:12). Saint James says: "Whoever needs wisdom, let him ask for it from God" (Jas 1:5). By this means Moses and Aaron were instructed by God about what they ought to do with the people. As those who rule others need light in double measure and ready at hand at all times, so they need prayer in double measure. They must be so dexterous in it that they exercise it without difficulty, in order to know the Lord's will about what they must do in particular and in order to attain the strength to fulfill it. Knowledge attained in prayer exceeds that attained through our own reasoning and conjectures, as one who goes to something certain surpasses the one who, as they say, feels his way along. Good resolutions and the effort they cost in prayer are usually incomparably more lively and turn out more true than those made outside prayer. Saint Augustine, who probably experienced this, said, "It is better that doubts be dispelled by prayer than by any other effort."[127] So as not to weary you, and because it would be impossible to tell you in detail the fruits of prayer, I say no more to you than what the highest Word said, namely, that the heavenly Father will give his good Spirit to those who ask him (Luke 11:13). With that Spirit, all good things come.

It should be enough for you that all the saints have used this exercise. Saint Chrysostom says, "Which of the saints did not conquer by praying?"[128] It should be enough and more than enough for us that Jesus Christ, Lord of all, prayed in the night of his tribulation, even to shedding drops of blood (cf. Luke 22:44). He prayed on Mount Tabor (cf. Luke 9:29) in order to attain the splendor of his body. He prayed before raising Lazarus (cf. John 11:41–44). At times he prayed so long that he passed the whole night in prayer. After such a long prayer, Saint Luke says "that he chose among his disciples the number of the twelve apostles" (cf. Luke 6:12–13). By this, says Saint Ambrose,[129] he showed us what we ought to do when we want to begin some endeavor, since in his, Christ first prayed and at such length.

For this reason Saint Dionysius would say that we must start every work with a prayer.[130] Saint Paul warns us to occupy ourselves "insistently in prayer" (Rom 12:12), and the Lord says that "it is fitting to pray always and not to faint" (cf. Luke 18:1), which means, let this work be done with frequency, diligence, and care. Those who want to help themselves by carefully doing works pleasing to God, but do not try to pray, are swimming or fighting with only one hand and are walking with only one foot. The Lord taught us that two things were necessary when he said, "Watch and pray that you enter not into temptation" (Matt 26:41). And he taught the same when he said, "Watch then, praying at all times, that you may be found worthy to escape all these things that must come, and to stand before the Son" of the Virgin (cf. Luke 21:36). Saint Paul unites the two things when he arms the Christian warrior for his spiritual battle against the demon (cf. Eph 6:11–18). Just as a man who eats well will become weak if he lacks the repose of sleep, and even runs the risk of losing his judgment, so it happens with the one who works well but does not pray. Prayer is for the soul what sleep is for the body. There is no estate, however large, that is not exhausted if they spend and do not gain. Nor are there good works that endure without prayer, because with it come the light and the spirit by which are recovered what is lost by occupations, even good ones, of the fervor of charity and interior devotion.

How necessary prayer is appears very clearly in the petitions and fasts with which the prophet Daniel prayed to the Lord to free his people from the captivity in Babylonia (cf. Dan 9:1–19), even though the seventy years the Lord had established as a term to free them were fulfilled. If in something that the Lord has promised to do or to give it is still necessary to beg with diligent prayer, how much more necessary will it be in a thing where we do not have a particular promise? Saint Paul asks the Romans to pray to God for him so that, impediments having been removed, he would be able to visit them (Rom 16:30–32). About this, Origen says: "Even though the Apostle had said a little before: 'I know that when I come to you, my coming will be with the abundance of the blessing of Christ,' nevertheless he knew that prayer is necessary, even for things that he manifestly knew had to happen; he knew that if there were not prayer, without doubt what had been prophesied would not be accomplished."[131] Does it not seem to you that that one was right who said that prayer was the means to obtain what Almighty God had arranged before all ages to give in time? Just as plowing and sowing are the means to harvest wheat, so prayer is the means to obtain spiritual fruits. For this reason we ought not to marvel if we harvest so little, since we sow so little prayer.

Certainly, it follows from a relationship with a good man that we love him and conceive desires for virtue like his. If we are in relationship with God, we could with much greater reason expect these and other benefits from dealing with him, like Moses, who went forth from his conversation with God "full of splendor" (cf. Exod 34:35). The only reason we lack mercy toward the neighbor is that we lack this intimate conversation with God. It is clear that anyone who was prostrate before God during the night, asking pardon and mercy for his sins and necessities, will recognize the words if he should meet another during the day who asks him for what he asked the Lord. He will remember with what great effort and desire of being heard he said them to our Lord, and he will do with his neighbor what he would want God to do with him.

To say in a word what I think about this, I recall what David said: "Blessed be the Lord who has not turned away my prayer nor his mercy" (Ps 66:20). On this, Saint Augustine says, "You can be sure that if God does not remove your prayer, he will not remove his mercy from you." Remember what the Lord said: "The heavenly Father will give the good Spirit to those who ask him" (Luke 11:13). And with this "spirit" we fulfill God's law, as Saint Paul says (cf. Rom 7:25). Thus the mercy of God is near to us and we fulfill his law by means of prayer. Watch how a man will be who lacks these two things because he lacks prayer.

I want to warn you of the error of those who think that, because Saint Paul said "I want the men to pray in every place" (1 Tim 2:8), it is not necessary to pray at length or in a place apart, but that it suffices to mingle prayer with other works done during the day. It is good "to pray in every place," but we ought not to be content with this if we are going to imitate Jesus Christ our Lord and what his saints have said and done in the matter of prayer. You can even be certain that no one will be able to "pray in every place," unless he learned this trade before in a place apart and for a definite space of time.

# 2. Steps for Drawing Near to God (chaps. 71–75)

**CHAPTER 71**

The first step the soul must take in drawing near to God is penance for its sins. To do this well, it helps to disengage oneself from all business and conversation and to be occupied in carefully recalling the sins of one's whole life, making use of some book on confession for this. After having wept sorrowfully over them, it is good to confess them to a spiritual physician, one who has the power and knowledge to give the appropriate remedy for one's infirmity and to make the conscience as peaceful as if the man were to die that day and present himself before the judgment of God. A person may spend a month or two in this exercise, undoing with bitter groans the sins committed with evil pleasures. A good book may help in this, or, as was said before, reflections on one's own death and God's judgment. By thought, one can descend while alive to that deep pool of eternal fire so as not to descend there after death to experience eternal misery.

For this it will also be useful to look at an image of the Crucified or, while imagining him, to think how by one's own sins, one caused the Lord to suffer such torments. Let him look at him well from head to foot, pondering each torment and weeping for each sin. The Lord's pains correspond to our faults, so that he suffered insults in payment for our pride, scourges and sorrows in payment for our pleasures, and so on. Let him think about a son who saw his father scourged and cruelly tormented for something the son, not the father, had done. If he were to hear the voice of the herald saying "whoever does such pays such," the son would feel deep compassion for his father and great sorrow for having done what was going to cost his father so dearly. If he is a true son, he would grieve more in seeing them chastise his father than if they chastised him. It would be very strange if he did not cry out in his great sorrow, confessing that he is the guilty one, and that they should punish him, not his father, who owed nothing. Let us learn from this example to grieve for our sins because God was the one offended and the one punished, and not because of any evil that might come to us for having sinned: "I, Lord, sinned, and you pay for it! My evil actions took you to prison and caused them to denounce you through the streets and put you on the cross!" Let this be the soul's cry, and let its desire be to suffer for God whatever he sends.

Having made this examination of conscience with sorrow and having made the satisfaction that his confessor deems fitting and having received sacramental absolution, the person can be confident of receiving pardon and the consolation of his soul.

## CHAPTER 72

Once the soul has been thus purified from these deadly humors of sins, it should occupy itself in giving thanks for such a great and unmerited gift. Not only has God pardoned him from hell, but he has received him as a son and given him his grace and interior gifts through the merits of the true Son of God, Jesus Christ our Lord. He "died for our sins and rose for our justification" (Rom 4:25), slaying our sins and our old life by his death and raising us to a new life by his resurrection. Job said that "the body of the poor man" whom he had clothed, would, on feeling himself clothed, "cast blessings" on Job, who had done him that kindness. With much greater reason we ought to bless Jesus Christ crucified when our soul feels itself free of evils and consoled by goods, believing that all good comes to us through him. There is no reason why we should be ungrateful for such love and such gifts (cf. Job 31:19–20).

Each time that something goes well for us, we should immediately bless Jesus Christ with special thanksgiving. To do this better and with greater fruit, do what I told you above with regard to thinking about your own sins: find a secluded and empty place, and there look at yourself. With much greater reason you should spend a period of time each day in thinking about the passion of our Lord and giving him thanks for the benefits that have come to us through it, saying from the heart: "I will never forget your justifications, for by them you have given me life" (Ps 119:93).

Use the following method unless something better is offered to you. On *Monday*, think about the prayer of the Lord in the garden, the arrest, and what happened that night in the house of Annas and Caiphas. On *Tuesday*, consider the accusations against him and the processions from one to another judge and the cruel scourging Christ endured bound to the column. On *Wednesday*, see how he was crowned with thorns and mocked, brought out in a scarlet cloak with a reed in his hand so that all the people would see him, and they said: *Ecce Homo* (behold the man). On *Thursday*, we should not neglect the most excellent mystery of how the Son of God, with profound humility, washed the feet of his disciples and afterward gave them his body and blood as food for life. He commanded them and all future priests "to do the same thing in his memory" (Luke 22:19). Be present, then, at that wonderful washing and at that excellent banquet, and hope in God that you will not leave unwashed or dead from hunger. After Thursday, you should consider, on *Friday*, how the Lord was presented before the judge and sentenced to death, how he carried the cross on his shoulders and afterward was crucified on it, with everything else that happened until he commended his spirit into the hands of the Father and died. On *Saturday*, it remains to think of the cruel lancing of his sacred side and how they took him down from the cross and placed him in the arms of his holy Mother, and afterward, in the sepulcher. Accompany his soul to the limbo of the holy fathers and be present at the feasts and in the paradise he grants them. Remember on this day to consider the great afflictions that the Virgin Mary suffered and be for her a faithful companion, helping her to suffer them. Apart from the fact that it is something you owe to her, it will be very beneficial for you. Of *Sunday*, I do not speak, because you already know that the day is for thinking about the resurrection and the glory of those in heaven. In this, you should occupy yourself on this day.

I recommend especially that *on Thursday night* you take as little sleep as possible in order to accompany the Lord. After the trials of the arrest and the long walks to the house of Annas and Caiphas, and after many blows, mockeries, and other evils done to him, he passed the rest of the night in fetters and in a very hard prison. With such treatment from the guards, he did not have time to sleep. Anyone who realized what he suffered there would not stop weeping. It was so great that, as Saint Jerome says, it will not be known until the judgment day.[132] Ask to share in his sufferings and, for him, take each Thursday night as special. He can show you the way to do this. It is a great shame for a Christian not to distinguish that night from other nights. Someone also used to say that sleeping on Thursday night is a great shame for anyone who is able to remain awake. I also think that he should not sleep on Friday night.

## CHAPTER 73

There are two ways to do the exercise of thinking about the events of the life or death of Jesus Christ our Lord. One is to represent the corporal figure of our Lord with the imagination; the other is to think about him without an imaginary representation. Know that the most high and invisible God became visible as a man so that, through the visible, he might place us within where the invisible is. One must not think that it was other than beneficial to see him with the eyes of the body and so to be able to look upon him with the spiritual eyes of faith, as long as the wickedness of the one looking upon him did not impede it. Certainly, all that was corporal in the Lord was specially ordered to have a particular efficacy in helping the devout heart to lift itself to spiritual things. It was no small grace for them to rejoice at such a sight "in which many kings and prophets longed to rejoice and did not attain it" (Luke 10:24). Even those of us who come after, who do not rejoice in this grace so completely, must not fail to take advantage of it insofar as we can. With this intention, our mother, the holy church, very rightly gives us images of the Lord's body, so that awakened through them, we may remember his bodily presence, and so that there may be communicated through the image something of the greatness that would be communicated by his presence. Since an image painted on a piece of wood outside of me brings me benefit, so also does that which is painted on my imagination within me, if I take it as a step by which

213

to move beyond it. For all that is of our Lord, including what touches and represents him, has a marvelous power to lead us to him.

Even though these things may seem lowly, you ought to see them as high because they are means to higher things, and God desires that those that he is going to elevate to greater things should begin by humbling themselves through this lowliness. Those who, immediately after beginning, give themselves to very high thoughts because they seem more pleasing and worthy of their consideration, are certain to fall. Scripture says that "he that is hasty in walking shall stumble; he that is hasty to get rich shall not remain without sin" (Prov 19:2; 28:22). Also it is clear that a house without foundations cannot last long without falling. If later, people like this want to return to thinking about things proportionate to their lowliness, they do not succeed, because they are fond of greater things. Thus, they run a risk, like the bird that leaves the nest before time and is unable to continue its flight or return to the nest. Therefore, it is good to begin at the lowliness of our sins, as has been said, and then to move on to consideration of the sacred humanity of Jesus Christ our Lord, in order to mount to the height of his divinity.

## CHAPTER 74

When you are recollected in your cell during the time you take for this exercise, recite first the general confession, asking the Lord's pardon for your sins, especially those committed since your last confession. Pray some vocal prayers, as was said above when we were dealing with self–knowledge. Afterward, read in some book on the passion about the event on which you want to reflect. The reading will serve for two things. One is that it will show you how that event occurred, so that you may be able to consider it, for you must be very familiar with the life and death of the Lord. The other thing is that it will recollect your heart, so that when you begin to consider, you are not distracted or lukewarm. Even if you do not read at one time all that the book may say about that event, nothing is lost since in other weeks on the same day, it will be possible to finish reading. As I have told you already, the reading should not be such as to wear you out but should awaken the soul's appetite and provide material for reflection and prayer. Books that can be helpful for considering the passion are, among others, the *Meditations* of Saint Augustine in Latin, those of Father Luis de Granada in Spanish, and the Carthusian who writes on all the gospels.[133]

When you have finished the reading, kneel and close your eyes. Beg the Lord to send the light of the Holy Spirit that he may grant you to feel with compassion and love what Christ so lovingly suffered for you. Ask insistently that he will not permit you to be so ungrateful that you do not even dare to think about his passion, which you are obliged to imitate.

Place, then, within your heart the image of the event you want to consider. If this does not go well, realize that you have it there quite near to you. I say this to warn you that you do not have to go by thought to Jerusalem to contemplate the Lord where this thing happened, for this does much harm to the head and dries up devotion. Rather, realize that you have him there present, and place the eyes of your soul on his feet or on the ground near him, and look reverently at what was going on as if you were present, and listen attentively to what the Lord was saying. Above all, with a quiet and simple gaze, contemplate his most sacred heart, so full of love for all that it surpassed all that he suffered exteriorly—although that was ineffable—as the heaven surpasses the earth.

Do not afflict your heart with forced sadness in an effort to wring out a few tears, for this impedes the quiet necessary for this exercise, as the Abbot Isaac used to say. Such efforts usually dry up the heart and make it unfit for the divine visit, which demands peace and quiet. They also destroy bodily health and leave the soul so afraid of the displeasure it experienced that it fears to return again to such a painful exercise.

But if with your quiet thought the Lord gives you tears, compassion, and other devout sentiments, you ought to accept them, as long as the excess with which they overcome you is not so great as to harm your health notably, or to leave you so weak in resisting them that they make you express your feelings with cries and other exterior indications. If you get used to such things, you will eventually do them in public just as in your cell, without being able to resist, and then you will have great notoriety. You are right to flee from this. Therefore, you have to accept these feelings or tears, but without seeking them, lest you lose the thought or *spiritual affection* that caused them. Take care that the thought endures, but, as to the exterior and *sensual* thing, pay no attention. In this way the devout *spiritual* sentiment will last a long time. On the other hand, the sentiment of the sensitive or corporal part does not last, and it does not permit the spiritual sentiment to endure unless it is restrained from following the corporal.

Beginners may take something more from this tender milk than those who have made more progress. These latter try to feel in their spirit the grandeur of the one who suffers and the indignity of the one

215

through whom he suffers, and the great deal that he suffers and the great love with which he suffers. They desire to imitate this love and passion with whatever strength the Lord gives them. If with this he gives them the sentiments already mentioned, let them not reject them but give thanks, but not as for the most important thing. Although I understand that there is a love of God so aflame that, not only does it not bring forth tears, but it even dries and impedes them, I also tell you that there is another tenderness that makes one have these sentiments, already mentioned, in the sensitive part and in the eyes of the body, without this being a culpable thing. Christian doctrine is not a doctrine of stoics that condemns passions that are good. Christ wept and became sad. This ought to be enough for us to believe that these things are good even in perfect men. What great evil have unlettered people done to themselves and to others by taking in hand matters of the spiritual life, making themselves judges of it, and following only their ignorant opinion! I say this about persons who have been deceived, to whom these things have appeared evil.

## CHAPTER 75

It is also helpful to warn you not to work overly hard to fix the image of the Lord deeply in your imagination. This can be dangerous, because sometimes it may seem to the soul that it sees outside it the images that are within. Thus some fall into foolishness and others into pride. Even if it does not come to this, it causes almost irremediable harm to bodily health. Therefore, it is good to make this exercise in such a way that you neither cease completely from representing the image nor do you hold on to it continuously or as something fixed by your interior effort. Instead, little by little and as if without labor, let it be given to you. You can have some devout and well–made images of the events of the passion. Looking at these sometimes may be a relief and may enable you to employ your imagination without them.

Be very careful not only to flee the already–mentioned danger of imagining with labor, but also of *thinking* with effort and mental fatigue. Besides harm to the head, such thinking causes dryness in the soul, which usually causes prayer to be abhorred. Do not think in this way or with such great effort that it seems that you alone, by the strength of your own arms, must accomplish it. This method is more appropriate for studying than for praying. Instead, you must perform your exercise in dependence on the strength of the Lord, who helps you to think. If you are unable to do this without pain in your head or temples, do not proceed forward. Rather, quiet yourself and get rid of this anxiety of heart. Humble yourself before God calmly and simply, asking of him the grace to think as he desires. In no way presume in God's presence to rely on your own reasoning or earnestness, but humble yourself before him with simple affection, as an ignorant child or a poor disciple, who brings a calm attention to learning from his master, as the master helps him. You ought to know that this business is *more of the heart than of the head*, since *love is the purpose of thinking*. By not understanding this and the calm already mentioned, many have wearied many heads, their own and those of others, harming their health and hindering the good things that they could have done. If God grants you this grace of quiet meditation, what you feel during it will endure longer and be more abundant and without affliction. You will find the contrary of all this if you practice in another way.

I have already advised you that your heart must be your dwelling place. Like the diligent bee that makes honey within the hive, you have to enclose yourself, presenting to the Lord what is offered you outside, and asking his light and favor, as Moses did in the physical tabernacle. If the bitterness of some temptation is offered you outside, flee to your heart and close the door after you. Uniting yourself with our Lord, you will leave your enemies outwitted, outmaneuvered, and outside the house. Since the harm they were able to do was by means of thought, if this is closed tight, there is no way by which they can enter.

In any case, to persevere in this exercise and benefit from it, it helps to remain peaceful. I advise you that, if you have strength to kneel in this conversation with God, it is of benefit to do so, since all reverence is owed to the divine Majesty. In this, we have the example of our sovereign Lord and Master. The evangelist recounts that in the Garden of Gethsemane, he prayed to his Father on his knees (Luke 22:41). But if bodily weakness is so great that remaining kneeling, especially in long prayer, hinders peace of soul and leaves it anxious in dedicating itself completely to the Lord, one should take that posture that does not hinder this peacefulness. Prayer does have as fruit *satisfaction* for the penalties we owe. But since the greatest fruit is that drawn through light and the divine will and other gifts of God, one ought to take what is in the middle to arrive at the best, if one cannot carry out everything.

In the same regard, if you are thinking about one thing in prayer, and your soul feels that it is invited elsewhere and that another door of a good thought has been opened to it, you should then leave what you were thinking about and take up what is given to you, presuming that both are good. However, you have to consider that this new thought may be a deception of the demon so that, as you leap from one thing to another like a magpie, he may deprive you of the fruit of prayer. Or it may be the inconstancy of your own heart that, when you do not find what you desire in one thought, you go on to try to find it in another, and another. Consequently, you ought not to leave lightly what you are considering unless you are effectively invited elsewhere with a satisfaction that is wont to remain in the heart when God invites it. This is different from when it places itself there. By asking the Lord for light, by taking account afterward of what fruit you have gathered, and by repeating the experience many times, you can discern what you should do.

In this same regard, if you are reading or praying vocally, and the Lord visits you with some profound sentiment, you should stop what you were doing and enjoy the portion that the Lord is sending you. Once that is finished, you will be able to continue what you were doing before. Since exterior devotion serves to awaken the interior, the former must not be taken as a means to hinder the latter.

I would not speak in such detail if I had not seen people so attached to their own rules and the fulfillment of their own tasks, that, even if there are reasons to think that the Lord wants them interrupted, they do not wish to be. If God wants to lead them by one path, they want to go by another, based on their own prudence. But it is a great truth that there is nothing more contrary to the exercise of prayer than that men think they can rule in it by their own discretion. I have seen many men full of rules for prayer and speaking many secrets about it and yet completely empty of what it is in reality. Relying on their rules and remembering them in the time of prayer, deprives them of that *humility and simplicity of a child* with which they must converse with God, as I have said above. I do not tell you this so that you might suppress reasonable diligence. For our part, we must put this forth, but with *such great liberty* that it does not keep us from depending on the Lord and awaiting his gifts as he wants to give them. Take as quite certain in this matter that the one who benefits more is the one who humbles himself more, perseveres more, and cries out more to the Lord, not the one who knows more rules.

# 3. Meditation on and Imitation of Christ's Passion (chaps. 76–81)

## CHAPTER 76

So that you may profit from the exercise of prayer, I must tell you that the end of meditation on the passion must be to imitate it and to fulfill the law of the Lord. I say this because some take much account of the hours spent in prayer and the sense of sweetness in it, but not of the benefit they derive from it. They think wrongly that one who experiences greater sweetness and spends more hours in prayer is the greater saint. But, in reality, the greatest is the one who, with profound contempt for himself, has the greatest charity. The perfection of the Christian life and the fulfillment of the whole law consist in this. Whoever lives well and prays well has to do it with this end and not content himself with having spent well a period of time in confessing or receiving communion or devout prayer or similar things.

We read that Moses spent forty days and forty nights on Mount Sinai in continuous conversation with the most high God. When afterward he descended to converse with men, he did not narrate visions or revelations or strange secrets, but he bore much light on his face and two tablets of stone in his hands. On one of these were written *the three commandments* that pertain to the honor of God, and, *on the other, the seven* that pertain to the good of the neighbor. This shows us that whoever treats with God with the tongue in prayer must bear light in his understanding for knowing what he ought to do, and the fulfillment of God's will expressed in action, as a law in his hands (cf. Exod 34:28–29). It also shows us that, since he has the office of praying, his life must be that of a person dedicated to prayer. It must be such that in all his dealings, he shows that something of that highest truth and purity with which he has dealt has adhered to him. There are those who spend a period of time weeping over the blows inflicted on the Lord in his passion, and afterward, when they are offered a very small part of the Lord's sufferings, they have so little patience that it is as if they had learned in prayer not to suffer anything. I do not know to whom to compare them, except to those who appear in their dreams to do great things, but upon awaking, do everything in reverse. What can be more foolish, after the patience of the Lord in his sufferings has seemed good to me, than not to desire to be patient in my sufferings? Instead, I say to him: "Lord, carry your cross alone, even though it is very heavy, for I do not want to help you, since I am carrying my own cross, even though it is small." The apostles had compassion and shed tears for the

219

passion of the Lord, but because they fled from imitating him, they were cowards and offended God in this, as bad Christians do. Therefore, you ought not to reflect on the passion with compassion as someone who looks at this affair without running the risk of suffering anything, but as someone who must accompany the Lord in the same suffering. As you look at him, charge your soul to drink his chalice with him, however bitter it might be to you.

Let the first thing in which you are to imitate him, and the principle of greater things, be exterior austerity and mortification of your body, so that you may have some likeness to his divine body, so full of afflictions and torments, the greatest that can be expressed. Look upon him attentively as he tastes gall and vinegar; see how narrow is the bed on which he lies, how stripped he is of clothes, and how clothed he is in torments from head to foot. Charge your soul to flee delicacies for your body in clothing, bed, and food. In this and in everything that you can easily do, afflict your body and make it live on a cross. From your heart, desire the things you cannot suffer. Ask the Lord for strength and weep because, while he is on the cross, you do not deserve to accompany and imitate him. These must be the desires of the Christian who exercises himself in reflecting on the passion, if he wants to imitate it. The Lord came from heaven to earth to converse with men and to teach them the best and most secure path for going there. In being born, he chose poverty, cold, and exile; growing in age, he grew in afflictions, and the end of his life brought the increase of other greater ones. Though these things were so lowly, he honored them so much by joining them to himself that he gave them as marks of honor and signs of security and beauty, in order that they might be desired. If a temporal king, by use of certain apparel, renders it honorable and worthy of imitation by all his vassals, much more will the sovereign King of kings do this, whose worth is incomparably greater than that of anything created, however high it may be. Anyone who does not feel this cannot be a perfect vassal of this Lord, since he does not consider likeness to him to be the supreme honor. "A pleasant thing it is," says Saint Bernard, "to imitate the disgrace of the Crucified; but this is for those who are not ungrateful to the crucified One."[134]

Tell me this. If a king were going along a road on foot and barefoot, weary and perspiring from the roughness of the way, clothed in sackcloth and weeping, as David went, with everything to inspire compassion, what servant of his would there be who, either through shame or love, would not also go on foot and barefoot and like his king as far as possible? (cf. 2 Sam 15:16–17). This the scripture says that the servants and all the people going with King David did. If this king commanded one of the servants with him to ride and be completely rested, it would be a harsh command for the servant. From his heart, he would beg the king not to do him a wrong such that, with his royal majesty so badly treated, his servant would be the reverse. If the king still commanded it, the servant would obey, but with such grief that, with his eyes fixed on the king's sufferings, he would not enjoy in his heart the rest he was taking exteriorly. Considering himself weaker and less honored than the rest, he would hold it as very unfortunate that he does not go conformed to his king. What was lacking in his performance, he would desire in his heart, bearing rest patiently but having the desire for suffering.

In such a way the Crucified leaves the hearts of those who are occupied in looking at him, "if they are grateful," as Saint Bernard said, for such a great favor as God's coming down to journey through this exile in afflictions such as no man ever suffered. When this is the case, no lance remains upright.[135] Within and without, they deeply desire to put the Crucified "as a seal upon the heart and on the arm" (cf. Song 8:6), not only as something that does not distress them or cause them to count themselves less honored, but rather, as Saint James says, "they count it as the highest joy that they are offered diverse trials" (Jas 1:2). Such is the stature of those who are grateful to the Lord that by the knife that is the love of this crucified Lord, they bravely slay the idols of Egypt (Exod 8:26), the honors, riches, and delights that the worldly esteem and love. They offer all these with much love, giving thanks that the Lord has desired to admit them into his company. Burning with love as they see the blood of their Lord shed, they go their way, strong as elephants, searching for all the ways they can find to suffer more. If it fulfills the service of their Lord that they take rest or have riches or honors, they accept through obedience and use them with fear. They have to be consoled whenever they go by horseback, seeing that the one they love more than themselves goes on foot. Such is the loftiness of the Christian life. And in such a way does Christ transform things from the cross that what is bitter and despised, he makes sweet and honorable, and that for which the worldly kill one another, he makes disgusting to taste.

I desire that the thought of the sacred passion may work in you with this efficacy, and that you love it so much that "you may bear in your body his mortification" (2 Cor 4:10). If no one stones, imprisons, or beats you, as they did the Lord and his apostles, "who went rejoicing at suffering for his name" (Acts 5:41), search, as far you can without difficulty, for a way to suffer. Then be very grateful to God when

221

it is offered to you. For if you make good use of what is small, the Lord will give you strength for more, and he will send you more.

I advise you not to count these things as little on the grounds that Saint Paul says that "bodily exercise carries little profit" (1 Tim 4:8). Even if this saying is applied to the things we are talking about, Paul does not want them to be held as little in themselves but as compared with other greater things. There is no doubt that these little things are very useful to lead to greater things, to satisfy for the punishment due in purgatory, to lead to the attainment of greater grace and glory, and to serve the Lord inwardly and outwardly, since in everything we are debtors to him. Regarding all this, the sovereign Master gives light on how we should think. Speaking of greater things, he says that "it is important to do them." Speaking of lesser things, he says that "it is important not to omit them" (cf. Matt 23:23).

## CHAPTER 77

The next thing to draw from meditation on the sacred passion, in order to mount little by little from the low to the high, is to treat the wounds of your passions with the medicine of the passion of the Lord, whom Isaiah calls "a flower from the stem of Jesse" (Isa 11:1). People use flowers as a means of giving health. Through devout consideration, Jesus Christ, crushed on the cross, is placed over our wounds, however dangerous they may be, and he heals them. Saint Augustine experienced this and said:

> When some ugly thought attacks me, I go to the wounds of Christ. When the devil lays traps for me, I flee to the merciful heart of my Lord, and the demon leaves me. If indecent ardor moves my members, it is extinguished when I remind myself of the wounds of my Lord, the Son of God. In all my adversities, I have found no remedy as efficacious as the wounds of Christ. In them I sleep secure, and I rest without fear.[136]

Saint Bernard had the same experience, as do all who, hounded by their passions as the stag is by dogs, go with devout heart "to drink from those" sacred "fountains of the Savior" (cf. Isa 12:3), painful for him but causing joy and refreshment for us.

Those who go there experience the great truth that Moses accomplished figuratively when, by God's command, "he lifted up a metal serpent, placed on a pole" so that "when it was looked upon by those who were bitten by the poisonous serpents," it delivered them from death and "gave them salvation" (cf. Num 21:9). Though this snake

222

appeared to be poisonous, it was not, because it was a metal serpent. Likewise, Jesus Christ our Lord has true flesh "in the likeness of sinful flesh" (Rom 8:3) and subject to pain. But it is far from all sin because it is the flesh of God, formed by the Holy Spirit and guarded by him. Placed high on the cross, dead on it, he frees from death and gives salvation to all those, bitten by temptation, who go to him with faith and love. Since you have such a powerful remedy for healing near at hand, nothing remains except to take very careful account to learn what serpents bite within you. You do this by examining daily and very slowly what inclinations are in the depths of your heart, what passions are alive, into what faults you sometimes fall, and things of this sort. Doing all this, you become so well–practiced and so skillful in knowing your faults that you have them before your eyes and at your fingertips, as they say. You will not arrive at this in little time, or even in much time, unless you are aided by the celestial light by which you may see the roots of your heart. Your heart is so deep that you cannot finish probing it, but God can.

To obtain this knowledge, it will help you a lot to consider the virtues that the Lord exercised in his passion. He has to be a mirror in your soul in place of the one that married women use to be pleasing to their husbands. Look at his meekness, his charity, his unconquerable patience, his profound silence, and your faults will appear, no matter how hidden they may be. Also, it will seem to you that your virtues are faults compared with his, and you will be ashamed of the one and the other. Do not be discouraged, but rather present yourself with them before the Lord, but not without groaning. Act like the child who shows his mother the thorn stuck in his hand and, with his tears, asks her to remove it. The Lord will do the same with you. As he is the mirror revealing our faults, so by his example and his salvation, he is their true remedy. When you see him with such insults as he suffered for love of you, your heart will be enkindled to rid yourself of a liking for honor. His patience will kill your anger. His gall and vinegar will be a remedy against your gluttony. Seeing him "obedient" to his Father "unto the death of the cross" (cf. Phil 2:8) will tame your neck so that you may obey his holy will, even in what is most difficult. The most high God–become–man, Lord of heaven and earth and all in them, obeyed his executioners when they wanted to undress and dress him, when they tied and untied him, when they ordered him to be placed on the cross and extend his arms to be nailed. Seeing this will give you the desire, even with sighs of the heart if you have any feeling, to be obedient, not only to superiors and equals, but even to subjects. It will give you the desire "to subject yourself for God's sake," as Saint Peter says, "to every human creature" (cf. 1 Pet 2:13), even to be mistreated by all. This is the way in which greed will die within you: if you see his pierced hands, giving his blood for the good of men, so that they might fulfill what he commanded when he said to "love one another as I have loved you" (John 13:34). In conclusion, you will verify through experience how true are the words of Saint Paul that "our old man was crucified" (Rom 6:6) with Christ.

If you do not experience this remedy and victory right away as you desire, do not be discouraged, and do not stop what you have started. Recognizing that your hardness and wickedness are greater than you thought, sigh more and beg the Lord with greater humility that his mercy may not permit you to remain infirm, seeing that he, who is God, suffered and died to heal you. Have hope that the one who commands you to call upon him will not be deaf and that he will not be cruel of heart at seeing you infirm and crying out at the door of the hospital of his mercy, that is at his wounds, that one day or another, he will put you in them to cure you.

But I warn you that this matter is not done quickly. Saint Paul said in few words that "those that are Christ's have crucified their flesh with its vices and desires" (Gal 5:24). But those who are not content with having left mortal sin and wish to achieve a perfect victory over themselves, conquering the seven generations of enemies that occupy the promised land (cf. Josh 3:10), find out through experience that what is said in only one word is accomplished in many years. But the sovereign Lord usually provides such people with the hope of perfect salvation, healing them from time to time of some particular infirmity. Thus we read that the captain, Joshua, after having conquered the five kings, said to his men: "Set your feet on the necks of these kings. Fear not, and do not be dismayed. Rather, take courage and be valiant, for, as the Lord has conquered them, so shall he do with all your enemies against whom you fight" (Josh 10:24–25).

You do the same. Determine either to die or to conquer. If you do not emerge victorious over your passions, you will not be able to advance in the exercise of familiar conversation with the Lord. It is not right that that sweetest sleep, which is slept peacefully in his arms, should be given to any but to those who have first struggled and conquered themselves by labors. Neither can they rejoice in being quiet temples of the peaceful Solomon if before they are not worked over with blows of mortification of the passions and the breaking of the will. The smoke that the unmortified passions cause in the soul prevents the vision from being as clear as is suitable for "seeing the King in his beauty" (cf. Isa 33:17), and the passions prevent the purity that the soul needs to be united with God in the relationship of a chaste spouse. This relationship is completely personal, secret, and kept for those to whom the Lord wants to give it, after they have labored many years and with much love, as Jacob did for Rachel (cf. Gen 29:30).

## CHAPTER 78

You have entered the first exterior room of the temple of the true Solomon, the place to consider Christ from the outside. You have sacrificed your irrational passions with the knife of the divine word, an office carried out in the room of the temple that is called *Holy*. If we are to follow along this way, it remains for us to try to enter into the *Sancta Sanctorum* (holy of holies), the most precious place and the goal of the other places. If you ask what this is, I answer that the heart of Jesus Christ our Lord is truly the Holy of Holies. He was not content with suffering outwardly but loved from the heart. In the same way, you ought not to stop at considering and imitating what he suffers outwardly, but you should enter into his heart to gaze on it and imitate it. To make entrance easier and to make more manifest what was in his heart, the Lord permitted that after his death, his sacred heart was opened, although he no longer felt pain. He did this so that men might feel moved to enter through it as through an open door, inviting them to gaze upon the beauties and admirable things that it contains within. But who will tell us with the tongue, since whoever enters there and sees them cannot grasp how great they are, and even what he does understand he cannot say?

Speaking of this figuratively, Saint John says that "the Temple of God was opened, and the Ark of the Covenant was seen in it" (Rev 11:19). In the heart of Christ the Law of God has been observed, and there the manna of celestial bread is kept, and also the precious and complete mercy of God, signified in the golden cover of the ancient ark. All of this is so excellent that it exceeds all that can be thought. David says: "Many marvels you have done, Lord my God," and in your thoughts for my benefit, "there is no one like you" (cf. Ps 40:6). Marvelous is all "that God has done," and more marvelous is what he has suffered. But if you look at "the thoughts" that he had in his heart when he was suffering, practically forgetful of everything else, you will say with a loud cry from your soul, "Lord, there is none like you!" When you see him letting his hand and neck be tied, when you see him suffer blows, thorns, nails, and death, ask him to grant you the gift of telling you why he, who is so strong and powerful, allows himself, without any resistance, to be treated as weak. Saint John will answer you in his name: "He loved us and washed us from our sins in his own blood" (Rev 1:5). Ponder these words, set them firmly in your heart, and pause to think what surpassing and admirable love is burning in his heart that causes him to suffer such outward things. Say within yourself, "What person would there be for whom I, or another like me, would suffer such things, without claiming his own interest, but through pure love of the other person?" You will see that to suffer all that the Lord suffered is not a thing to be sought in another person, because no one would have the strength for it. But to suffer something of what he suffered perhaps would be possible between parents and children, brothers and friends, husband and wife, or people of this type, to whom necessity or relationship or friendship may give strength either to suffer or to die. But this would happen very few times. To suffer for strangers and without one's own interest and without having to, and to die for pure love, is something not seen.

If someone were to die from love, even a slave for a king, how much greater would it be if some of the many beatings and torments that the Lord suffered preceded his death. It would be a great achievement for which the slave would attain pardon, even if he had committed many evils. All would judge that the king should grant him gifts, if it were possible to give them in the other life. For many days, such an exploit would not depart from the mouth of men, and even the king would recount it with great tenderness and pleasure.

Well, let us repeat this case in reverse. Let the king die after having suffered many torments and grave insults for the sake of his slave, from whom he has not received service but serious offenses worthy of a very cruel death. Let the cause of the king's death be the pure love that he had for his slave. This is a thing neither seen nor heard, and of such surpassing love that it would amaze those who heard of it and would give material for preaching the goodness of this king for many days, and even throughout life. This love would be so wonderful, so new, and so lofty that some of weak virtue and little judgment would be scandalized. They would not feel as they should about such a work but would say that it is excessive that the royal majesty, full of every virtue, should give his precious life so that the evil slave, who justly deserves death, might live. Suppose that it were added to the account that the king was so wise and powerful that he could very easily have freed his slave without suffering anything or doing injustice to anyone. In spite of all this, the king wanted to elevate his love so much to let the slave know that he had chosen to suffer so many and so great things never suffered before, because this was better for the slave. It is certain that few eyes would be capable of looking at such a sun overhead, burning with love. If anyone felt the sentiment for this work that he should, it would be a wonder if he did not depart his senses in wonder and fright. If such would be the response of a person who had not received this favor from the king, but only knows it as done for another, what ought we to think would be worked in the heart of the slave for whom the king had died, if he had any judgment at all? Do you not think that such a blow of such a love would wake him up, reduce him to silence, and make him such a captive of love for that king that he would not be able to keep quiet about his praises? Nor could he remember him without tears, nor occupy himself in anything other than in loving and pleasing his king and suffering everything possible for him.

Have you understood this parable that never in the world has been translated into action? Well, know that the heavenly king, Jesus Christ, has done what earthly kings have not done. Saint John says that "he had written on his thigh: King of kings and Lord of lords" (Rev 19:16). Even insofar as he is man and has a human nature, his majesty is so great that it exceeds all created lords and kings. This refers not only to those in this world but also to those in heaven, since he has "a name above every name" (cf. Phil 2:9) and majesty and lordship over all great men and over angels, small and great. Look at this majesty, which has no equal, and lower your eyes to see the lowliness of the slaves for whom he suffers. You will see that, as Saint Paul says (cf. Rom 5:6), we are weak, and sinners, and traitors against God, and his enemies. These titles are so dishonorable and base that they put man in the lowest place and worth in all that is created. This is because there is nothing as low as the evil being, and nothing is evil except the sinner as sinner. Comparing, then, these opposite extremes of such a majestic king and such evil slaves, consider how greatly the Lord loved them. Go to the heart of the Lord. If you have the eyes of an eagle, you will need them there, and even they will not be enough for you to see the radiant and exalted love which that most holy soul has. Because of their great love, the highest angels in heaven are called seraphim, meaning *burning ones*. But Christ's love is of such a degree that if the seraphim had come to Mount Calvary at the time of the Lord's suffering, they would have marveled at his excessive love, in comparison with which their love was tepidity. Christ's most holy soul possesses the greatest majesty and honor that anyone can have in heaven or on earth, for, in the very first instant of his creation, he was united with the person of the Word of

God, so that "the Holy Spirit was poured out upon him without any measure whatever" (John 3:34). Such grace and love were given him that more cannot be imagined, and the soul can hold no more. Thus, with good reason, what was written fits this most holy soul: "The king brought me into the cellar of wine and set in order charity in me" (Song 2:4). Or according to another reading: "He put over me his banner of love" (Song 2:4). Since this soul in being created saw immediately the divine essence and loved it most intensely, "the banner of holy love was placed over it" to show that it was more vanquished by love than any man or angel in heaven or on earth. Because in the war of God's love, whoever is most vanquished is most blessed, most worthy, and most vigorous, this most blessed soul "carries the banner of love." This is so that all in heaven or on earth who desire to love might learn that they must follow this Lord in order to know how to act as disciples toward the master and soldiers toward their captain. He exceeds all in love as he exceeds them in lordship.

Since such a fire of love was placed in the depth of his most sacred soul, it takes little for the flame to break out and burn and scorch the garments of his most sacred body, full of torments that testify to interior love. It is written: "Who can have fire in his bosom without it burning his garments?" (Prov 6:27). When you see them outwardly tying his hands with cruel cords, understand that within he is a prisoner of the bonds of love, as much stronger than physical cords as iron chains are stronger than burlap. It was this love that weakened, vanquished, and captured him, that took him from judge to judge and from the torment of beatings to the torment of the cruel thorns, that placed the cross on him and, at Mount Calvary, placed him on the cross. He stretched out his arms to be crucified as a sign of his heart wide open with love, so far extended that resplendent and powerful rays of love went out to all from the center of his heart. These were going to stop at each one of the men of the past, present, and future, as he offered his life for their good. If the high priest bears the names of the twelve sons of Israel written outwardly on his shoulders and also on his breast (Exod 28:29), much more does our High Priest bear our name on his shoulders as he suffers for men and has them written in his heart. He loves them so truly that, if the first Adam sold us for an apple, and if they sell themselves for very base things, desiring evil through love of evil, this loving Lord values them. He loves them so much that to rescue them from such a miserable captivity, he gave himself as the price for them. This is testimony that he loves them more than they love themselves and more than anyone loves them.

**CHAPTER 79**

Jeremiah says that the heart of man is so wicked "that no one can search it but God" (cf. Jer 17:9–10), and that the more deeply one digs within its wall, the greater abominations are discovered, as was shown figuratively to Ezekiel (cf. Ezek 8:9). If this is so, with how much greater reason will we say that since the heart of Jesus Christ our Lord is better than other hearts are evil, no one will be able to probe it except the Lord himself, whose heart it is. The excessive love of his heart, manifest in his suffering and death for us, is a thing worthy of wonder and should be enough to rob us of our souls and leave us captivated by God. But, if you dig deeper with the light of heaven and search into this reliquary of God, full of ineffable secrets, you will see within it effects of love that will lead us to wonder more than at what happened exteriorly. Remember what happened in the village of Bethsaida while Jesus was healing a deaf man. The gospel says that "the Lord raised his sacred eyes up to heaven, and he groaned" (cf. Mark 7:34), and after this, he cured the sick man. The groan heard outwardly passed in a short time. But it was testimony of another groan, and of profound groans that lasted not a brief while, but for months and years.

In being created and infused into his body in the virginal womb of our Lady, his most holy soul saw the divine essence immediately, as clearly as now, that essence which, because of its majesty, is rightly called heaven. In seeing it, he judged that it was worthy of all honor and service and thus, with the ineffable strength of love that was given to him for loving, he desired to give it. Ordinarily, one who sees God clearly is blessed in body and soul and unable to experience any further pain. But, so that we might be saved by the precious afflictions of this Lord, it was ordained that happiness and joy would remain in the superior part of his soul and not be found in the inferior part or in the body. Thus he renounced the joy that was justly due to him as he accepted and suffered the pains that were due to us.

If that most holy soul, who raised the eyes of his understanding to the divine heaven, had had nothing else to gaze upon, he would not have had any pain, since God is such that only love and joy can come from sight of him. But he already saw also all the offenses that men had committed against God from the beginning of the world and those they would commit until its end. Thus, as profound as was his sorrow at seeing that heaven of the divine Majesty so offended, so great was his desire to see it served. Just as no one is able to fathom the greatness of his desire, no one can fathom the greatness of his sorrow. The Holy Spirit, "who was given to him without measure" (John 3:34) and is symbolized by fire, made him burn with the greatest love in order to love God. The same Holy Spirit, symbolized by a dove, made him sigh bitterly at seeing offended the one whom he loved with unspeakable love.

That you may see how the knife of sorrow that passed through the heart of the Lord, did not wound him in only one part, but was sharp and painful in both parts, recall that the same Lord, "looking up to heaven, sighed and wept over Lazarus" and "over Jerusalem" (John 11:35; Luke 19:41). Saint Ambrose says, "Do not be surprised that he, who wept for one, grieves over all."[137] Seeing God offended and men lost through sin was a two–edged sword that deeply wounded his heart, because of the inestimable love that he had for God and for all men for God's sake. He desired the satisfaction of the divine honor and the remedy for men, even if it should be very much at his own expense. O most blessed Jesus! Seeing your external torments breaks the Christian's heart, but no sight or strength can bear seeing you broken within by sorrows. Three nails, Lord, pierced your hands and feet with grievous pain; it is said that seventy–some thorns penetrated your divine head; your blows and wounds were very many; it is said that your most delicate body received more than five thousand cruel scourges. There were many other pains that came together in your passion, pains so serious that none but you who suffered them could understand them. Therefore, it was said in your person a long time before: "All you that pass by the way, attend, and see if there is any sorrow like mine" (Lam 1:12). With all of this, you, whose love is beyond measure, searched out and discovered new inventions for bearing and feeling within you pains that exceeded in number the nails, the scourges, and the torments that you suffered outwardly. These lasted longer and were sharper in wounding you. Isaiah says, "Every one of us had gotten lost along his way, and the Lord laid upon his Messiah the sins of us all" (Isa 53:6). Such a rigorous sentence of divine justice, your love turned to good. You threw over your shoulders the burden you made of all the sins that men had committed, do commit, and will commit, from the beginning of the world till its ending and without leaving out a single one. You, our Lord and our Lover, did this to pay for them through the sorrows of your heart.

But who can count the number of your pains, since no one can count the number of our sins that caused your pains, but you alone, Lord, who suffered them? You were made for us "a man of sorrows and you tasted by experience our afflictions" (cf. Isa 53:3). One man alone says of himself that "he had more sins than hairs on his head" (cf. Ps 40:13). Beyond this, he even says that God may pardon his other sins that he does not know (cf. Ps 19:13). Well, if one man, David, has so many sins, who will count those of all men, many of whom have committed more and greater sins than David? In what labor you immersed yourself, O "Lamb of God," in order to "take away the sins of the world"! (cf. John 1:29). In your person it is said: "Many calves have surrounded me; fat bulls have encircled me; they opened their mouths over me like a lion that roars and catches its prey" (cf. Ps 22:13–14). But, even in the Garden of Gethsemane, a band of a thousand men of the secular arm, not counting those sent by the priests and Pharisees, came to arrest you. With great cruelty they surrounded and captured you (cf. John 18:3). But to anyone who saw the multitude and greatness of all the sins of the world that encircled your heart, the people who came that night to arrest you would probably appear few in comparison with those who surround your heart. What a frightening sight! How ugly a picture you were bearing in front of you, and one to give such grief, as you were surrounded by our great sins, signified by calves, and our very great sins, signified by bulls! Who will recount, Lord, how ugly are the sins that have taken place in the world? Presented before your ineffable purity and holiness, they would threaten you, and like bulls with open mouth, attack you, demanding that you, Lord, pay the penalty merited by such great wickedness. How rightly it was said before that you "were poured out like water" by external torments and "your heart was melted like wax" (cf. Ps 22:15) by the fire of interior afflictions! Who, Lord, will say that the number of your sufferings can increase since our sins are so innumerable?

## CHAPTER 80

From what has been said, you will see how many and great were the Lord's sufferings and how many and great were our sins that caused them. But, if we probe the innermost depths of the Lord's heart, we find there sorrow for the sins that men have committed and sorrow for those they have never committed. Just as pardon for the first fell upon you, Lord, so did preservation from the others cost you sufferings and death, for grace and divine favors preserving from sin are given to no one without price, but only at the cost of your precious labors. Thus, Lord, all men depend upon you: small and great; past, present, and future; those who have sinned and those who have not; those who have sinned much and those who have sinned little. In themselves, they were "children of wrath" (Eph 2:3), without God's grace, exiled from heaven, and inclined to every sin. If they were to receive pardon and grace, avoid sins and be children of God, and rejoice in God forever in

heaven, you had to pay the price, Lord, paying for the evils and pur-
chasing the goods. Everything is so much at your cost that the pains
come proportionate in number and in magnitude to the great value of
these things. The price for what you purchase has to be made very high
so that thus you may show your love and so that our redemption and
solace may be more firm.

How costly for you, Lord, is the name that Isaiah gave you,
"Father of the world that is to come" (cf. Isa 9:6)! Just as there is no
man according to the generation of the flesh (the "first age") who does
not come from Adam, so there is no one according to the being of
grace who does not come from you. But Adam was a bad "father" and,
for the sake of evil pleasures, he killed himself and his children. But
you, Lord, attained the name of Father at the cost of your sorrowful
groans, by which, like a lioness that roars, you gave life to those killed
by the first father. He drank the poison that the serpent gave him and
became like the father of serpents since he begot sinful children. But
all his children, who in themselves are poisonous serpents, seized hold
of your heart, Lord, and gave you portions of sorrow never before
seen. They did this, not only for the eighteen hours that your sacred
passion lasted, but for thirty–three entire years, from the March
twenty–fifth when you were conceived as man, until the March
twenty–fifth, or eight days after, when you lost your life on the cross.

You called yourself a mother when, speaking with Jerusalem, you
said: "How many times I wanted to place your children under my
wings, like the hen, and you did not want it" (Matt 23:37). To make us
understand the personal love and tenderness of your heart, you compared yourself with the hen that especially loses her calm and is
stricken by what touches her children. Not only are you like her, but
you surpass her and all mothers, as you, Lord, said through Isaiah:
"Can a mother by chance forget the child she bore in her womb? Well,
if she should forget, I will not forget you, because I have you graven on
my hands, and your walls are always before my eyes" (Isa 49:14–16).
Who, Lord, however much he delves within your heart, will be able to
search out the ineffable secrets of love and sorrow that are enclosed
within it? You are not content, Lord, with having a strong love and suffering the afflictions of a father. But, so that no gift be lacking to us and
no labor to you, you desire to be our mother in the tenderness of love
that is wont to cause deep affection. And you desire to be more than our
mother. Of no mother do we read that in order to remember her son
always, she wrote a book in which hard nails are the pen and her own
hands are the paper. Nor do we read that, when the nails were thrust

into her hands and passed through them, blood came forth instead of ink, so that, with grievous pains, she might give testimony to her great interior love that does not permit her to forget what we carry in our hands. If you suffered this on the cross, with your hands and feet nailed, a thing that exceeds all the love of mothers, who will tell of the great love and pain with which you bore all men in the womb of your heart, groaning over their sins with the groans of childbirth? You did this not for an hour or a day but for the whole thirty–three years of your life until, like another Rachel, you died in childbirth on the cross so that Benjamin might be born alive (cf. Gen 35:18). The "serpents" you were carrying within you, Lord, were giving you such bites that they caused you to burst open on the cross. This was so that, at the cost of your pains, the "serpents" would be transformed into simple and meek sheep who, in exchange for your death, would attain a life of grace.

How justly, Lord, if you look at what you suffered for them, you can call men "sons of my pain," as Rachel called her son (cf. Gen 35:18)! The pain that their sins gave you was greater than the delight that they took when they sinned. Your humility and interior affliction were greater than the contempt and pride that they had against the Most High when they offended him by breaking his laws. This was so that in this way, the greater would conquer the lesser and your pains would conquer our sins.

The sins of others grieved you, Lord, more than his own sins ever grieved any man. We read of some that they had such great repentance for having sinned that, unable to contain such great pain within them, they lost their life. What pains did immeasurable love for God and for men work in you, since one spark of that love infused into those other hearts, oppressed them so much that, like gunpowder, it made them explode! We read and know of many who lost their life when they heard very painful news. Tell us, Lord, in your mercy: how did you have strength to suffer that very sad news when you were newly pre-sented with all the sins of all men? You loved them much more than any man loved another or himself. You saw that their evil was greater than any other evil that might come, and you knew that it was greater. Lord, how did you have strength to see your divinity offended and to go on living, since your love is beyond measure? You lived, Lord, when you heard this news, and you lived with its pain for your whole life! But if you had not been given special strength to suffer such pains, they would have worked the death in you that fewer pains worked in others. Therefore, Lord, I am indebted to you not for one death but for many.

Through the pains that you suffered for men as a mother, you can rightly, as we have said, call them "sons of my pain." Since you are also

Father, you call them "sons of my right hand," as Jacob did (cf. Gen 35:18). The greatness of your hand, which is your power, is exercised and manifest in them because you draw them out of sin and place them in grace in this world. In the latter day you shall rank them at your right hand so that they may accompany you in glory, seated with great repose and security, as you are, Lord. You are there at the right hand of the Father, and you count all that you suffered for them to be well spent.

## CHAPTER 81

From consideration of what has been said to you about the mystery of the passion of Jesus Christ our Lord, you will know that you should look at what he suffers outwardly and at the virtues of patience, humility, and other similar ones that he possesses inwardly. I am referring especially to his loving and compassionate heart, from which everything else proceeds. Try to suffer with the Lord in all that he suffers and to imitate him.

But understand that you can have many other helpful considerations about the passion of the Lord. In it you can discover, according to the sufferings of this exile, how precious is blessedness and how great are the torments of hell, how precious is grace and how harmful and horrible is sin. To purchase these goods and free us from these evils, Christ, being who he is, suffered so much. It is a book in which you can read of the immensity of divine goodness and the gentleness of his love; you can also read of the admirable rigor of divine justice that so punished the judge himself for the sins of others.

My desire and plan was to continue with this material and to go on to consider the divinity through the stepping stone of the most holy soul of Jesus Christ our Lord. But because my poor health does not allow it, I will not say more. What I write here is the end of this discourse, except for the recommendation that you persevere in meditation on this sacred passion. For, I have seen persons exercising themselves much in this for years and years without much taste for it. But when they persevered, our Lord paid them what before he had delayed, so that they consider their previous labors well spent in view of their present pay.

I also tell you that there are other exercises of meditation for journeying to the Lord. There is meditation on creatures and on the favors of the Lord, and there is the way of recollection of the heart, which understands the loving that is the end of all thought and of every law. As there are diverse exercises, there are diverse inclinations in people.

It is a very great favor of the Lord to put man in that which will be beneficial to him. Each ought to ask for this with great urgency. By noting his experience and recounting it to someone who knows better, he should try to find the exercise of prayer that is better for him. That is the one he ought to follow.

Also it is helpful to tell you that there are some persons so busy with exterior things that they are unable to give themselves to interior exercises, at least for any space of time. Because of this, they experience discomfort and disgust. If they cannot licitly leave such occupations, they ought to content themselves with the state the Lord gave them and fulfill their obligation diligently and cheerfully. They should make an effort, as far as they are able, to have present our Lord for whose love they do their works.

There are some who are naturally anxious in soul and are without devotion and dry in everything. Even if they spend a lot of time and care in interior exercise, they profit nothing. It is necessary to advise them that, since the Lord does not give them a spirit for long periods of interior prayer, they should content themselves with praying vocally at the stages of the passion. As they go along praying, let them reflect, even though briefly, on that particular event. Let them take some devout image to look at and read devotional books on the passion. Many times, by these steps, they rise to the exercise of interior reflection. If the Lord should will that they not ascend higher, let them thank him for wanting to take them by that path.

Let the scrupulous and the sad know that the Lord is not content with them always going around thinking of the sins they have committed, buried in sadness and depression like a Lazarus in his tomb. They should know it is his will that, after the mortification and penance they have done, by which they have likeness to his passion, they should also take comfort from the hope of pardon by which they are like him in his resurrection. Since they have kissed his sacred feet by weeping for their sins, let them rise to kiss his hands for the benefits received, and let them walk the safe path between fear and hope.

I conclude with this advice. There have been some who through ignorance and pride have been wrong about the way of prayer. Do not take this as an occasion for abandoning it. For the fall of another ought not to separate us from the good but should make us attend to our business with greater caution. Jesus Christ our Lord and his saints have walked by this path as our example. This knowledge ought to strengthen you to follow the same path, so that the few who have strayed may not discourage you. It would be a marvel if there was any good thing that some had not used for ill.

# 4. God's Hearing and Seeing Us in Christ (chaps. 82–87)

**CHAPTER 82**

The great goodness of the Lord has this characteristic: in order that we might keep his commandments and laws, he makes them easy in themselves and easier still in his willingness to pass through them. As we have heard, he has commanded that "we hear and see him, and that we incline our ear to him." All this is very just and easy. Who will not listen to such a teacher? Who will not delight in looking at such a delightful light? Who will not incline his ear to infinite wisdom?

But so that what is easy may be easier still, he decided to pass through this law that he set down for us, and he fulfills it with great diligence. "He hears us, sees us, and inclines his ear to us" lest we say, "I have no one who watches for me and wants to hear my afflictions." It is a great consolation for someone disconsolate to have a person who is ready and willing at any time of the day or night to hear his troubles, and who is always, without missing a moment, looking at his wounds and miseries. He does not say, "I am tired of looking at your misery and your wounds disgust me!" Even if such a person were very hard of heart, we would still desire that he would always hear and see us. For we would believe that, with the trickle of our pains flowing always in his heart, entering there through his ears and eyes as through a canal, he would some day delve deep in his heart and bring forth compassion. However hard he is, he would not be hard as stone, and even that is penetrated by the gentle trickle, even if it ceases for a time. Even if we knew that such a person could give no remedy for our difficulties, his compassion alone would be great consolation. If to such a person we would owe much gratitude, what do we owe to God our Lord? How happy we ought to be at having his ears and eyes fixed on our difficulties, not departing from us for even a short time! He does this, not with hardness of heart, but with profound mercy, and not with mercy of the heart only, but with complete power to remedy our sorrows. Blessed may you be, Lord, forever, for you are not deaf or blind to our troubles, but you always hear and see! You are not cruel, for it is said of you: "Maker of mercies and merciful of heart is the Lord, waiting for us and very merciful" (Ps 103:8). You are not weak since all the evils of the world are weak and small, compared with your infinite power that has neither end nor measure.

We read that in times past God granted the king Hezekiah a marvelous victory over his enemies. Some say that the king did not give to the Lord, who had granted him the victory, the thanks and songs that were owed and customary in the midst of similar favors. Thus God caused him to be so gravely ill that he had no natural remedy (cf. 2 Kgs 19:35). Lest, with a false hope of life he should forget to place his soul in safety, the prophet Isaiah went to him and said by God's command: "The Lord says this: Put your house in order and know that you shall die and not live" (Isa 38:1–3; 2 Kgs 20:1–3). Terrified by these words, the king Hezekiah turned his face to the wall and wept with great weeping, begging the Lord for mercy. He considered how justly he deserved death for not being grateful to the one who had given him life. He saw the sentence of God already given against him: "You shall not live" (cf. Isa 38:10). He found no other superior to the one who had given the sentence to ask that it be revoked. Even had there been such, he had not a worthy case, because what has been given in mercy is justly taken away from one who is ungrateful. He saw himself "in the midst of his days" with the royal generation of David ending with him because he was dying without sons. Besides all this, he was attacked by all the sins of his past life, the fear of which is usually more painful at the last hour. By all these things his heart was broken with sorrow and stirred up like a sea. Wherever he looked, he found many reasons for fear and sadness. But in the midst of such great evils the good king found a remedy. He went to ask for medicine from the one who had wounded him; for safety from the one who had frightened him; for conversion through repentance and hope from the one he had fled in his pride. He asks the judge himself to be his advocate. He finds a way of appealing to God, not as to another higher, but from his justice to his mercy. The reasons he puts forward are his self–accusation; sobs and tears are his rhetoric. He is able to do so much with these weapons in the court of divine mercy that, before the prophet Isaiah, the herald of the death sentence, departed from the king's court, "the Lord said to him: Go back and say to King Hezekiah," captain of my people: "I have heard your prayer and I have seen your tears; I grant you health, and add for you another fifteen years of life; and I will deliver this city from the hand of your enemies" (Isa 38:5–6; 2 Kgs 20:4–6).

Lord, what is this? Do you so quickly place your sword in its sheath and turn anger into mercy? Do a few tears shed, not in the Temple, but in the corner of a bed, by eyes not looking to heaven but at a wall, do they make you so quickly revoke the sentence you had given with the command that the guilty party be notified? What about gathering information by a trial? What about costs? What about the conclusions? What about presenting witnesses for and against? What about the judge being affronted if they revoke the sentence that he gave?

You overlook all these things through your love for us and by concentrating on doing us favors. You say, "I have heard your prayer, and I have seen your tears." You shorten every term for the sake of freeing the guilty one, and no one has desired to receive pardon as much as you desire to give it. You rest more at having pardoned those you want to live than the sinner does at having escaped death. You observe neither laws nor delays. But the law will be that those who have broken all your laws may break their heart with sorrow for the past and propose amendment for the future; they may take the beneficial medicines of the sacraments that you left in your church, or have the intention of taking them. You do not observe delays, since in whatever hour the sinner groans over his sins, you remember them no more (cf. Ezek 18:22). So that sinners would be encouraged to ask your pardon for their errors, you willed to grant this king more favors than he asked of you: fifteen years of life; the liberation of his city; and the sun turning backward ten hours as a sign that, on the third day, the healthy king would go to the Temple; and other secret favors that you did for him. You are kind. You only allowed evils to come to us in order to draw from them greater goods by showing your mercy in our misery, your goodness and pardon in our iniquity, and your power in our weaknesses.

You, then, sinner, whoever may be threatened by that sentence of God, who says, "The soul that sins, that one shall die" (Ezek 18:20), do not be discouraged under the burden of your great sins or under the insupportable weight of God's wrath. Rather, finding encouragement in the mercies of him "who does not desire the death of the sinner, but that he be converted and live" (Ezek 33:11), humble yourself, weeping before the one whom you scorned by sinning. Receive pardon from the hand of that merciful Father, who desires as much to give it to you, and even to do greater favors for you than before, as he did for this king. He raised him up healthy in body and healthy in soul, as he gives thanks saying, "You, Lord, have delivered my soul, that it should not perish, and you cast my sins behind your back" (Isa 38:17).

## CHAPTER 83

You ought not to be troubled that the word spoken to this king, "You shall die and you shall not live," was not fulfilled. You should know that sometimes the Lord commands to be said that which he has determined to be in his high counsel and eternal will. Without fail, that will come to be as it is said. Thus he commanded that King Saul be told that he was going to depose him and choose another better in his place (cf. 1 Sam 15:23). Likewise, he threatened the priest Eli and so fulfilled it. In the same way he threatened King David that he would kill his son from the adultery with Bathsheba (cf. 1 Sam 3:13–14). However much the king pleaded with prayers, fasting, and hair shirt for the life of the child, it was not granted to him, for God had determined that the child would die.

But other times he commands to be said, not what he has determined to do, but what he will do if such a man does not reform. Thus he sent to tell the city of Nineveh that "forty days from now, it would be destroyed" (Jonah 3:4, 10). Afterward, because of their penitence, he revoked the sentence. He had not determined to destroy them, since he did not do it, but he sent Jonah to tell them what their sins deserved and what would come for them if they did not reform.

Externally, it appears that there is a change from saying "it will be destroyed" and then not destroying it. But in the supreme will of God, it is not so, because he never decided definitely to destroy it. As Saint Augustine says, "God changes the sentence, but he does not change his counsel."[138] Here he willed not to destroy the city because of the penitence that he had willed to incite through fear of the threat. This is what he says through Jeremiah:

> Suddenly, I will speak against nations and kingdoms that I am going to destroy and uproot. But if that nation repents of its evil, I also will repent of the evil that I was planning to do to them. And suddenly, I will speak of nations and kingdoms that I will build and plant. But if they should do evil in my sight, not heeding my voice, I also will repent of the good that I said I would do for them. (Jer 18:7–10)

It follows from this that we do not know when God is sending us his ultimate determination and when he is only sending a threat. Therefore, we ought not to despair or stop asking him in his mercy to revoke the sentence he has given against us, as he did with the king and the city of Nineveh, and they obtained what they asked. Even though David did not obtain what he asked, he did not for this reason sin in asking God to revoke the sentence given, because it was not clear to him whether it was a determination or a threat. Likewise, if God should promise to do some favor, we must not be careless in serving him, saying, "I have as guarantee the word of God that deceives no one." The Lord says that if we depart from doing what he wills, he will repent of the good that he promised us. It is not that repentance takes place in God, for there can be no change in him. But it means that, just as one who repents changes in order to undo what he had done, so God will undo the sentence of punishment that he had given against man, if he does penance. And God will undo the good that he had promised if a man separates himself from him.

## CHAPTER 84

We return then to our subject. It seems rather clear how well God accomplishes this law, "hear and see," for as soon as he "heard" the king's prayer and "saw" his tears, he consoled him and others as well. As David says, "The eyes of the Lord are upon the just, and his ears respond to their requests to deliver their souls from death and to keep them in time of famine" (Ps 33:18–19). I imagine that this word pleases you, but that the condition with it makes you afraid. It is a blessing to have the eyes and ears of the Lord upon us, but you probably say: "What shall I do, since it says 'upon the just' and I am a sinner?"

So it is, and you should recognize it as true. If there had been sinless men, who would be so more rightly than the holy apostles of Jesus Christ our Lord? Since they were closest to him in bodily conversation, they were also closest in holiness, without anyone equaling them, except the blessed Mother of God, who equals and exceeds them and angels. Though Saint Paul says, in his own person and in that of the apostles, that they received "the first fruits of the Spirit," he means that they received greater grace and gifts than others. But with all this, the Lord taught them to pray the prayer of the Our Father, in which we say, "Forgive us our debts and faults" (cf. Matt 6:9, 12). Since this is our daily prayer, it is clear that we are admonished that we have faults, and that we commit some each day. For this reason Saint John said, "If we say that we have no sin, we deceive ourselves, and the truth is not in us" (1 John 1:8). All men have sinned, except the God–man and his true Mother. For whom, then, are these words spoken: "The eyes of the Lord are upon the just, and his ears respond to their requests"?

My answer is that God is not at fault, nor does he act by words alone. We see that as he spoke, so he fulfilled what he said with King Hezekiah and with innumerable others whom he has looked upon and heard. But know that one is *just* who is not in mortal sin but in grace and is a friend of God. There are many such, even though they have venial sins, because of which no one can say truly that he is without sin.

That you might give thanks to the Lord for the grace and justice given through his merits to those prepared for them, you need to know that the just have two kinds of goods: one by nature and the other by grace. This is despite Pelagius, who said that man is just through the good works he does by his own nature, without the necessity of grace and virtue infused by God. His error is condemned by the Catholic Church, which commands us to believe that by nature we are sinners through original sin and through other sins we have committed by our own will. True justice does not consist in morally good works that we do by our own nature. Therefore, Saint Paul says that "no one is just" (cf. Rom 3:10), meaning "in himself." In this way all are sinners "in themselves." Justice must be given to us; we do not have it by our own work. Having it is thus a privilege proper to Christ alone, who is truly just, not through another but through himself, and in his works and death is true justice. If true justice consisted in works from our own nature, or if through such works we merited that justice be given to us, "Jesus Christ would have died in vain" (Gal 2:21), as Saint Paul says, for we would have been able to attain justice without the death with which Christ won it for us. The same apostle says that "Christ has become our justice" (cf. 1 Cor 1:30). He says this because the merit of our justice is in Christ's works and death. This merit is communicated to us by faith, and by the love that is its life, and by the sacraments of the church, as we stated above. Thus we are incorporated into Jesus Christ. The Holy Spirit is given to us, and his grace infused into our souls makes us adopted children of God and pleasing to him. We also receive virtues and gifts so that we are able to act in accord with the elevated being of the grace given to us. Through all this we become truly just in God's eyes with a particular justice that dwells in us and is in us, different from that by which Christ is just.

From this it follows that the good works we performed before were lowly and imperfect; true justice did not lie in them, nor were they sufficient to merit it as if it were of our own invention. But the good works that we do now in the state of grace are of such high value that they are truly just works and merit an increase of our own justice, as Saint John says: "Let the one who is just become more just" (Rev 22:11). They are works worthy of attaining to the kingdom of God, according to what Saint Paul said, that a "crown of justice" is kept for the just one (2 Tim 4:8).

This ineffable gift we owe to Jesus Christ our Lord. But this is not all. Just as by divine arrangement no one attains grace and justice except through the merits of this Lord, so no one who possesses them can preserve or increase them without being joined to this Lord, as a living member to its head, as a branch to the vine, as a building to its foundation. In winning for them grace and justice, he won for them the right to merit God's kingdom, as was said above, and also to attain by prayer whatever they ask for fittingly. But if they are going to enjoy this and use it well, they must not be like a people cut off that becomes a party or a head unto itself. Neither can they be like a man who stands on his own feet and can walk without the help of anyone. Rather, they must be joined to this blessed head so that it preserves grace for them, and from it comes spiritual virtue that may precede, accompany, and follow the good works that they do. Without that head, such good works will not be able to be meritorious, as the Council of Trent says.

In this way the prayers of such a just man will be worthy of the ears of God and worthy of attaining what is asked. "Solomon asked God" (cf. 2 Chr 6:21) that whoever prayed in the temple that he had made upon the earth, God would hear from heaven and would grant whatever he asked. Jesus Christ our Lord, as man, is the true and most excellent temple of God. In him, as Saint Paul says, the fullness of the divinity dwells corporeally (Col 2:9). Paul means that the divinity does not dwell in Christ solely through the life of grace, as it does in the saints, both men and angels, but in another way of greater weight and value, namely, through personal union. Through this union, the sacred humanity is raised to possess the dignity in the being and person of the Word of God, a divine Person. This is the temple of which David said: "God heard my voice from his holy temple" (Ps 18:7). Whoever cries out in prayer in this temple, moved by his Holy Spirit, joined to him as a living member who asks help through the merits of his head, Jesus Christ, such a one will justly be heard by God, as was David and all the just who have been heard. But prayer made outside this temple, no matter by whom it is made, is hoarse and profane. It is unworthy of the ears of God because, not being inspired by Jesus Christ, it does not bear the royal seal by which it may be recognized and considered just and so attain what it asks. In order that Christ in heaven may attend to our petitions as our advocate, it is necessary that we on earth should be his living members, moved to pray through him. His mercy is so great that many times he causes the petitions of his dead members to be heard, that is, those who have the faith of the church but are not in charity. But here we are speaking of those who have dignity and merit, created in Christ, to attain what they ask. Our mother, the holy church, knowing the need we have of Christ in our prayers, is accustomed to say at the end of those addressed to the heavenly Father: Grant this to us "through Jesus Christ our Lord." She learned this from her Spouse and Teacher who said: "Anything you ask the Father in my name, he will give it to you" (John 16:23).

Let thanks be given to your name, Lord, for through it we are heard. You are not content as our Mediator to merit for us the grace that we receive through you or to be our head, which teaches and moves us through your Spirit to pray as is fitting. But you also desire to be our high priest in heaven, so that, representing to your Father the sacred humanity that you possess and the passion that you accepted, you attain the effect that we ask upon earth by invoking your name.

So, as the holy gospel says, "The Lord being baptized, the heavens were opened to him" (Matt 3:16). Although many have entered after him, they are open to no one except through him. Thus, we can say that the heart of his eternal Father, which is open to receive our prayers, is open to Christ. He is the ear of the Father, and through him we have the grace and favors by which we are heard. Without him no one would be heard, just as no one would be just without him. In any case, because of the Lord's great love for us, he took our evils as his own and paid for them with his life and death. With the same love he loves us now when he is in heaven, and, if one of his little ones is naked or clothed, full or hungry, he says that he himself is such (cf. Matt 25:40, 45). Thus, when we pray, he prays in us, as Saint Augustine says.[139] He also says that when God hears us, it is Christ that he hears. This is because of Christ's ineffable union with his own, signified by the name of spouse with his bride and head with his own body. He loved it so much that, though ordinarily we see that one puts up his arm to receive a blow in order to shield his head, this blessed Lord, being the head, put himself before the blow of divine justice and died on the cross to give life to his body, which we are. Having brought us new life through penance and the sacraments, he indulges, maintains, and defends us as something so much his own that he is not content with calling us servants, friends, brothers and sisters, or children, but, in order to better show his love, he bestows on us his own name. Because of this ineffable union of Christ, the head, with his body, the church, he and we are called one Christ. Saint Paul explains this most delightful mystery, full of all consolation, saying that "the heavenly Father made us pleasing in his beloved Son," and that "we were nourished in good works in Christ Jesus" (Eph 1:6; 2:10). To those of Corinth he said, "You are in Jesus Christ" (cf. 1 Cor 1:30). This way of speaking using the word *in* allows us to understand the union of Christ and his church. In this way the Lord speaks through Saint John:

"Whoever is in me and I am in him, this one bears much fruit; for without me you can do nothing" (John 15:5).

Thanks to you, Lord, for your love and goodness, by which you gave us life through your death. And thanks be to you because in your life, you guard ours and have us with you in this exile, and that, if we persevere in your service, you will take us with you and will treat us with affection in heaven, where you are, in accord with what you said: "Where I am, my servant will be" (John 12:26).

## CHAPTER 85

From what has been said, you probably see the great need all men have of the favor of Jesus Christ in order that their prayers may be heard as pleasing before God's throne. But such is not the case for Christ, for he has no need that anyone should speak for him. It is he and only he whose voice is heard for himself. As Saint Paul says, "He is able by himself to approach his Father and to intercede for us" (Heb 7:25). He also says that Christ, "in the days of the mortal life that he lived, offering prayers to the Father with a loud cry and tears, was heard for his reverence" (Heb 5:7). Christ asked his Father to save him from death, not allowing him to remain in it but raising him to immortal life. As he prayed, so it was done. He also "offered prayers and tears" to his Father for us many times. Because these came from a heart full of love, they are called "a loud cry."

Christ always possessed equally the love that made him cry out, whether he was walking along a path or weeping. But with what great love did he hang on the cross! Looking at the exterior and at the type of action, we see that offering his most sacred body on the cross for us was a greater cry than offering prayers, just as going to suffer and suffering death are greater than thinking or talking about them. Remember what God said to Cain: "The voice of your brother's blood cries to me from the earth" (Gen 4:10). Remember also what Saint Paul said to the Christians: "You have arrived at a shedding of blood that speaks better than that of Abel" (cf. Heb 12:24). This is because Abel's blood cried out to the divine justice for vengeance against Cain who shed it, while Christ's blood, poured out upon the earth, cried out to the divine mercy, begging pardon. Abel's blood asks for wrath; Christ's blood asks for gentleness. The first work is one of anger; Christ's work is reconciliation. The blood of Abel asks for vengeance against Cain alone; that of Christ seeks pardon for all the wicked that have been and will be, provided that they want to receive it with the necessary preparation. This includes even those who were shedding his blood. Abel's blood could benefit no one, because he did not have the power to pay for the sins of others, but Christ's blood washed the heavens and the earth and the sea, as the church sings: "he drew forth from the depths" of limbo "those who were prisoners," as the prophet Zechariah says (cf. Zech 9:11). The cry of Christ's blood asking for mercy is truly loud, and it made inaudible the voices of the sins of the world that were demanding vengeance against those who had committed them. Consider, daughter, if only one sin of Cain was raising such cries demanding vengeance, what shouting and what cries and uproar will all the sins of all men make, demanding vengeance in the ears of God's justice? But, however much they cry out, the blood of Christ cries out incomparably louder, begging pardon in the ears of divine mercy; it makes the voices of our sins inaudible, and they remain so low that God becomes deaf to them. Incomparably more pleasing to him was the voice of Christ, and his passion and death asking for pardon, than all the displeasing sins of the world demanding vengeance.

What do you think that silence of Christ meant and his becoming "like a deaf man who did not hear, and as a dumb man who opens not his mouth" in the time when he was accused (Ps 38:14)? Certainly, the sins of those whose mouths accused Christ cried out, full of lies, against the one who owed them nothing. He, though able justly to respond, kept a silence that was well–used in return for their boldness. Therefore, though in justice it might be done, they cannot accuse the rest of the world of sins. But let them be mute, for they accused Christ without cause. Though able to respond, he became deaf. It is just, then, that divine justice, to which Christ offered himself for us, became deaf, even though we have done things that demand vengeance. Rejoice, spouse of Christ, and let all sinners rejoice when their sins weigh on their hearts, if they desire to take the remedies that are in the Catholic Church. For God is deaf to our sins with regard to punishing them and holds his ears very attentive for granting us favors. Do not be afraid of accusers or outcries, even if you have given reason, since Christ was accused and, with his silence, silences the cries of our sins.

It was prophesied that "he would have to be silent as the lamb is silent before the shearer" (Isa 53:7), but the more he was silent and suffered before men, the louder the cries he was giving forth before the divine justice, paying for us. And these cries "were heard," as Saint Paul says, "because of his reverence" (Heb 5:7). He means that through the great humility and "reverence" with which, as man, he humbled himself to the Father "even to death, death on a cross" (Phil 2:8), reverencing that most excellent divine majesty, losing his life for

245

its honor, he was heard by the Father, about whom it is written: "He had regard for the prayer of the humble, and did not despise their petition" (Ps 102:18). Well, then, who is as humble as the blessed Lord, who says, "Learn of me, because I am meek and humble of heart" (Matt 11:29)? For this he was heard, according to what was prophesied in his person: "The Lord did not take away his face from me, and when I cried to him, he heard me" (cf. Ps 22:24). The same Lord says in the gospel: "I give you thanks, Father, that you always hear me" (John 11:41–42).

The Father hears Christ praying for you. Since it cost him so dearly to attain the grace by which you may be just and heard by God, try to gain that grace if you do not have it. And having obtained it, exercise it in offering prayers to God, since "his ears are attentive to such prayers." Thus we ought to hear the Lord with the prophet Samuel, saying, "Speak, Lord, for your servant hears" (1 Sam 3:10). In the same way the Lord says to us, "Speak, servant, for your Lord hears." As we said, to hear God does not mean merely to receive the sound of his words but to believe them, delight in them, and put them into practice. So the ears of the Lord are attentive through Christ to our prayers, not only to hear what we say—for in this way he also hears blasphemies said about him that displease him—but the Lord hears our prayers to fulfill them. To see how true it is that the Lord hears the groans we present to him, hear what the same Lord says through Isaiah: "Before they call, I will hear them" (Isa 65:24).

Blessed be your silence, Lord, by which you were silent inwardly and outwardly on the day of your passion. Outwardly, you did not curse or respond; inwardly, you did not contradict but accepted with great patience the blows and shouts and sufferings of your passion. Since you spoke thus in the ears of God, we may be heard even before we speak! This is not strange, for when we were nothing, you made us, and, before we knew how to ask, you maintained us in our mother's womb and outside it. Before we learned to know what you had fulfilled for us, you gave us the adoption of sons and the grace of the Holy Spirit in holy baptism. Before sins had thrown us down, you guarded us. When we fell through our own fault, you raised us up and sought us without our seeking you. And what is more, before we had been born, you had already died for us and made us fit for your heaven. In this, it is not so much that you have taken such care of someone, but that, before he had cared for you, you have cared for him. It is not so much that, seeing what we needed, you give it many times, without waiting for us to tire ourselves asking for it, but that you tired yourself so much in asking for it and gaining it for us.

What shall we give you, O most blessed Jesus, for this silence with which you were silent before those who wished and did you evil? And what shall we give you for those cries, so loud and so full of love, that you gave for us before your Father? In your infinite goodness, please grant us the favor of being as silent as the dead are with regard to offending you and when we suffer cheerfully whatever you will for us. Would that we were so alive to proclaim your praises that neither ourselves, whom you redeemed, nor the heavens, nor the earth, nor under the earth, with all that is in it, would ever cease singing your praises with all our strength and with great joy and serving you with the most fervent love.

You are not content, Lord, with having ears ready for our prayers, to hear us with attentive haste; but as one who very truly loves another and takes pleasure in hearing him speak or sing, so you, Lord, speak to the soul redeemed by your blood: "Show me your face; let your voice sound in my ears; for your voice is sweet, and your face is very lovely" (Song 2:14). What is this you say, O Lord? Do you desire to hear us, and is our voice sweet to you? How does our face appear beautiful to you, since it has been made ugly by the many sins that you have seen us commit, and we are now ashamed to raise it to you? Truly, either we merit much in your presence, or you love us much. But do not allow, Lord, do not allow that from your good treatment we draw forth pride, since that by which we please you and appear good to you is the grace that you gave us. Besides this, you give gifts and rewards to your own more plentifully than they deserve. Glory be to you then, Lord, from whom and in whom is all our good. To us and upon us, let there be shame for our wickedness and unworthiness. You are our joy; you are our glory in which we glory, not in vain, but with much reason and truth. For it is a great honor to be loved by you, so loved that you handed yourself over to the torments of a cross for us. Through that cross, all goods come to us.

## CHAPTER 86

You have heard of the speed with which God "hears" the prayers of the just. It remains for you to hear of the great love with which he regards them in order to fulfill in everything the "hearing" and "seeing" that he commands of us. "The eyes of the Lord," says David, "are upon the just," to deliver them from death, "but the countenance of the Lord is against the wicked, to cut off remembrance of them from the earth" (Ps 34:16–17). From this it appears that the Lord puts his eyes upon the just as the shepherd does upon his sheep, so that he will not lose them. Also he puts his eyes on the wicked, so that they do not go off without the punishment that their sins deserve. There are two things here for us. One is how much good we have in the body and soul that God made. The other is what we ourselves made, which is sin. If we had not added evil over the good that we have from God, there would have been nothing within us that the Lord would have looked at with angry eyes, but only with eyes of love. For any cause naturally loves its effect. We have made ugly and destroyed what the beautiful God had well constructed. But even our evil does not impede the surpassing goodness by which he desires to save the good that he created and to destroy the evil that we committed. The corporal sun diffuses itself liberally and goes about inviting whoever might want to receive it and gives its light to all who put no impediment. And if they do put an impediment, it is as if the sun insists that they remove it. If some hole or crack is found, however small, light enters through it and fills the house with light. If all this is so, what are we to say of the supreme divine Goodness that with such yearning and strength of love goes about surrounding its creatures, in order to give itself to them and fill them with color, with life, and with divine splendors? What occasions it seeks to do us good! To many, for a small service, it has given favors that are not small! How many prayers there are for those who are separated from him that they might be converted! How many embraces to those who come to him! What searching for the lost! What guidance to the right path for those who wander! What pardon of sins without putting them before one's face! What joy in giving salvation to men, making them understand that he desired more to pardon than the sinner desired to be saved and pardoned!

Therefore, he says to sinners: "Why do you want to die? Know that I do not want the death of the sinner but that he be converted and live. Turn to me and you will live" (Ezek 33:11; 18:32). Our death is separation from God; therefore, our life is turning back to him. To this God invites us, not placing his eyes of wrath principally on his handiwork, which we are, but against the sins that we have committed. God wishes to destroy these as long as we do not impede him. We impede him when we love our sins, giving them life by our love for them which, when they are loved, kill us. Such is the desire that the highest Good has of destroying our evil so that his handiwork is not destroyed. Therefore, whenever man desires it, and as many times as he so desires, and for as many evils as he might have done, if he does penance and asks the Lord to pardon him, he is ready to receive us. He pardons what we deserve, heals what sickens us, straightens what we have twisted, and gives us grace to abhor what before we used to love. In such a way does he destroy our wickedness and take it away from us that David says, "As far as the east is from the west so far has God removed our sins from us" (Ps 103:12).

Thus it is that the beginning and the first "look" of his eyes is not against the man he has created but against the sin that we committed. If man's look is to destroy, it is because he did not let God execute his wrath against the sins that he wanted to destroy. Instead, man desired to preserve and give life to that which was killing him and displeasing God. Justly, then, his death should live and his life should forever die, since he refused to open the door to the one who, through love and with love, desired and was able to kill his death and give him life.

But someone will say: "What remedy is there so that God may not look at my sins to punish me but at his handiwork to save it? Saint Augustine responds with brevity and truth: "You look at them."[140] He means: "Recognize them and do penance and God will not look at them. But if you put them behind your back, God has to put them before his face." David used to beg the Lord on account of his sins, saying, "Have mercy on me, Lord, according to your great mercy," and he also said, "Turn away your face from my sins" (Ps 51:3, 11). But, let us see, what did he plead to arrive at such a great favor? Certainly, it was not services he had rendered. For well he knew that, if a servant serves his lord diligently for many years, and afterward betrays him in a way worthy of death, the lord would not look at the fact that he had served him but at the betrayal he committed and that he was obligated not to commit. Therefore, by paying what he owed before, he could not pay for what he owes now. Nor did David offer sacrifices, because he knew well that "with burnt animals, God is not delighted" (Ps 51:18–19). But this one, who neither in past service nor in present merits found remedy, found it in "the heart contrite and humbled," and asks to be pardoned, saying, "For I know my iniquity and my sin is before my eyes always" (Ps 51:5). Wonderful power did God give to this "looking at" and sighing over our sins, since after them follows God's "looking at them" to undo them. When we turn our eyes with sorrow to what we have done wickedly, he turns his own to save and console the one he made.

## CHAPTER 87

Someone will ask: "From where do we get such strength to look and to weep so that it draws God to look at us and pardon us?"

Certainly, it does not come from oneself. The thief, knowing that he has done evil in stealing, does not merit to be pardoned from the gallows, even if he weeps more and more. But pardon comes from another look, one very friendly and so strong that it is cause and font of all our good. Of this sight, David says: "God our Protector, look! Look on the face of your Christ" (Ps 84:10). Twice he begs God to look so that we may understand with what affection we have to look at this face and how very important it is to do so. Just as God looking at us causes all our goods, so God looking at his Christ brings to us the sight of God. Do not think, my daughter, that the graceful and lovely rays from God's eyes descend directly from him to us when he receives us in his grace, or that, when we are in it, they descend to us as something separate from Christ. If you think this, you are blind. But know that the rays are directed to Christ, and from there to us through him and in him. The Lord will not give any speech or sight of love to any person in the entire world, if he should see him separated from Christ. But through Christ he looks at all those who desire to look and to weep, however evil they may be, in order to pardon them. In Christ, he looks on such to preserve them and to increase the good received. The beloved being, Christ, is the reason for our having been received in grace. If Jesus Christ were to depart from among us, no one would be beloved or pleasing before the eyes of God, as was said above. Be aware then, daughter, of the need you always have of Christ and be deeply grateful. For the good you have did not come from you, but through Christ, and in him you must be preserved and increased by God.

This was prefigured in the beginning of the world when the just Abel, pastor of flocks, offered to God a sacrifice from his herd. The sacrifice was accepted, as scripture says: "The Lord looked on Abel and his offerings" (Gen 4:4). This looking on him means that Abel was pleasing to him, and therefore his offerings were pleasing. As a sign of invisible gratitude, God sent visible fire that burned the sacrifice. This prefigures our just and sovereign shepherd, who says of himself, "I am the good shepherd" (John 10:11). He is also priest, and consequently, as Saint Paul says, "he has to offer gifts and sacrifices to God" (Heb 5:1). But what will he offer that is worthy? Certainly not brute animals, much less sinful men, for these are more likely to provoke God's anger than to attain mercy. Not without reason did God command in the Old Law that the animal that was going to be offered should be male not female, neither too young nor too old, and not lame or blind (cf. Deut 15:19–21). The reason for these and many other conditions was to make it understood that what had to be offered to take away sins could not be something sinful (cf. Lev 22:19ff.). Since no one and nothing was without sin, this High Priest had nothing to offer for the sins of the world except himself, thus making the priest a victim. Being "pure," he offered himself to purify the unclean (cf. Heb 9:13–14); being "just," he offered himself to justify sinners (cf. 1 Pet 3:18); being pleasing and beloved, he offered himself so that the unloved and displeasing might be received into grace. This sacrifice was worthy for himself as for those for whom he offered it, for it is all the same thing. Therefore, those of us who had been separated from God "like lost sheep" (1 Pet 2:25), were brought back, washed, "sanctified," and made worthy of being offered to God (cf. 1 Cor 6:11). It is not that we would have had anything worthy of our own invention that would have pleased God. But sprinkled with the blood of this Shepherd, and adorned in the beauty of the grace and justice given by God, and incorporated in him, we are washed from our sins, looked upon by God, and pleasing to him as a sacrifice offered by this High Priest and Shepherd. Thus Saint Peter says, "Christ died once for us, so that he might offer us to God, having been put to death in the flesh, but alive in the spirit" (1 Pet 4:18).

We will see then how our Abel [Christ] offers to God an offering from his flock, and God looks upon this flock because he first looked upon his dearly beloved Son. Just as before, "visible fire came upon the sacrifice" (1 Kgs 18:38), so also it came here in the form of tongues on the day of Pentecost (cf. Acts 2:3). This happened after Christ ascended "into the heaven, so that he might appear before the face of God for us" (Heb 9:24). Through this, we may understand that, from God's eyes looking "at the face of his Christ," a face that Esther says "is full of graces" (Esth 15:17), the fire of the Holy Spirit went forth and enkindled the gifts that this great Shepherd and High Priest offered to his Father. These were his present and future disciples.

God promised Noah that, after it had rained a great deal, he "would look at his bow" that he put in the clouds "as a sign of friendship" with men (cf. Gen 9:16), so as not to destroy the earth by water. Much more, looking at his Son placed on the cross, with his arms extended like a bow, God removes from his rigorous bow the arrows that he was already going to hurl. Instead of punishments, he gives embraces. He is more conquered by the brave bow that is Christ to do mercy, than moved by our sins to punish.

Although we had strayed and turned our backs to the light, which is God, not wanting to look on him but to live in the darkness of our sins, we are carried by this Shepherd on his shoulders. While he is carrying us, the Lord looks upon us and thus makes us look at him. He has such special care for us that he does not take his eyes from us even for a moment, lest we get lost. From where do you think that loving word came that God says to the sinner who repents of his sin, if not from that loving gaze with which God looked upon Jesus Christ? "I will give you understanding and I will instruct you in the way you have to go, and I will fix my eyes upon you" (Ps 32:8). He is the wisdom that shows us the true path by which we walk without stumbling. He is the true Shepherd, through whom, insofar as he is man, we are looked upon, and who, insofar as he is God, looks upon us, removing dangers from ahead in which he sees that we would fall. He holds us firm in the dangers that come to us and frees us from those into which we have fallen through our own fault. He cares for that which fulfills us even though we become careless. He remembers our advantage even when we forget about his service. He watches over us when we are asleep. He keeps us with him when we would like to separate ourselves. He calls us when we flee and embraces us when we come back. He is the last to break friendship and the first to plead with us, even when he is offended. In everything and through everything he maintains a regard for us that is so vigilant and loving that he orders all to our advantage. What shall we say to such favors except to give thanks to that true Shepherd? So that his sheep might not wander far from the eyes of God, he offered his face to such great dishonors. This was so that when the Father saw the Son so afflicted and blameless, he would look at the guilty with eyes of mercy, and that we might carry in our heart and in our mouth the words "Look, Lord, on the face of your Christ," proving by experience that "God hears us," and "sees us," and "inclines his ear to us," more than we to him (Ps 84:10).

# 5. Our Justification and Redemption in Christ (chaps. 88–93)

**CHAPTER 88**

Such are the weeds that our enemy has sown among believers that they draw perverse understandings from the words of divine scripture that speak of the most precious mystery of Jesus Christ our Lord and from the good that we possess in him and through him. Concerning these, I must warn you, so that you do not run into danger.

In calling Christ "our justice" (1 Cor 1:30), or saying that we are made pleasing "in him" (cf. Eph 1:6), or other similar words, do not think that those who are in grace do not possess their own justice within themselves, distinct from that by which Jesus Christ our Lord is just, by which they may be just and pleasing to God. Believing such would be a very serious error, born from failure to recognize the love that Jesus Christ our Lord has for those who are in the state of grace. To such love his loving heart would not consent that he, being just and full of goods, should say to his justified ones: "Be content that I possess these goods and consider them in me as yours, even though in yourselves you remain unjust, naked, and poor." No head would say such a thing to his living members, and no spouse would say it to his bride, if he loved her greatly. The heavenly Spouse was given as an example to husbands so that they would love and treat their brides as he does. "Husbands," says Saint Paul, "love your wives, as Christ loved his church, and delivered himself up for her, to sanctify her, cleansing her with baptism and the word of life" (Eph 5:25–26). Well, then, if he sanctifies, washes, and cleanses her with his own blood, which gives power to the sacraments to cleanse by the grace they give, how can she who has been cleansed and washed with such an efficacious thing remain unjust or impure?

This is the kind of cleansing that God had promised to give in the time of his Messiah, when he said, "I will pour upon you clean water, and you shall be cleansed from all your filthiness" (Ezek 36:25). The Lord testified at the supper on Holy Thursday that his eleven disciples "were clean," but not as he wished, for they were not "all clean" (cf. John 13:10). This is because venial sins are caused in the soul by some inordinate affections that are like dust clinging to the feet. They are removed by the sacraments and by the good dispositions of the one receiving them. Just as the feet of the body are washed with physical water, so the Lord did then, washing them outwardly and inwardly and leaving them cleansed of all sin, as Saint John witnesses, saying, "The blood of Christ cleanses us from all sin" (1 John 1:7). Long before his blood had been shed, the prophet Micah called it the sea in which all our sins are drowned. He said, "God will cast all our sins into the depth of the sea" (Mic 7:19). Well, if these, and many other passages of scripture, testify that man is pardoned and cleansed of all sin, who will dare to say that a man is never cleansed of it?

To say that sin remains in man as sin and that, through love of Jesus Christ our Lord, man is only freed from the punishment due to such sin, does not suffice to verify the scriptures and is not fitting to the honor of Jesus Christ. The punishment owed for sin, as well as the injustice and ugliness caused by it, may be less evil for man than the guilt of the same sin. But it cannot be said that Christ "saves his people from their sins" (Matt 1:21) if his taking them away by his merit means only that the sins are not counted for punishment. It cannot be said unless he takes away the guilt by giving his grace and obtains cleansing so that man can abhor sin and keep God's law. If one looks well at the divine scripture, it must be seen that, when the pardon of sin is given, given with it are "newness of life and a clean heart, as a new creature" (Rom 6:4), as David asked (Ps 51:12), according to what had been prophesied: "I will give you a new heart, and I will put a new spirit within you; I will take away your heart of stone and give you a heart of flesh. I will put my spirit in the midst of you, and I will make you walk in my commandments, and keep and do my judgments" (Ezek 11:19–20). God promises this to those to whom he first said that "he would cleanse them from all their impurities." Later he says, "I will save you from all of them" (Ezek 36:29). He said this to show clearly that "saving from sins" is not only removing punishment for them but giving interior purity and a heart and grace and spirit that suffice to make one keep God's commandments. Saint John says that the Lord says: "I am at the door and I knock. If anyone opens to me, I will come in to him, and eat with him, and he with me" (Rev 3:20). In God's name Isaiah invites "the hungry to come and eat and the thirsty to drink" (cf. Isa 55:1). Through Saint Paul the Lord says, "Go out from the midst of evil ones and touch not any unclean thing; and I will receive you and be a Father to you, and you shall be my sons and daughters" (2 Cor 6:17–18). In these and in many other passages it seems clear that the goods given along with justification are more and better than merely not imputing sin by punishment. There are given grace, purity of heart, virtues, and the Holy Spirit of the Lord. Thus, one may keep the law and, through life as a son and full of good works, rejoice in God forever. Because Christ won these goods for us, along with pardon of punishment, he is proclaimed at full voice as *Savior of sinners.*" This is more for the first than for the second. For he frees us from guilt and makes us abhor sin; he obtains for us participation in God for the present and the right to possess him forever in heaven. In this he frees us from greater evil and obtains for us goods of greater value than delivering us from any penalty whatsoever.

## CHAPTER 89

It can happen that the blindness of some becomes very great. They think that the favor of Jesus Christ suffices for those in whom sin remains and that he takes punishment from them. They also think that because they are incorporated into Jesus Christ, who is very much loved by the Father, they are also loved, pleasing, and cleansed, even though sin remains in them. They even think that it honors Jesus Christ to perceive his Father's love for him so highly that it vanquishes the horror that he has for those in whom sin remains.

But honor such as this is completely contrary to his true honor and to the truth of the divine scripture. It is certainly no honor for a judge to refrain from punishing evildoers or to treat them well because they are companions of his son. This would demonstrate that the son is not a perfect lover of goodness, since he loves evil servants. It also shows that the father does not love justice, since he tolerates and loves those he ought to punish impartially. Those who desire to be servants pleasing to Jesus Christ our Lord are not to commit the evil of mortal sin. Christ is the head who influences his living members by the influence of his spirit and grace so that they live a life separated from sin and like his own. It would be a frightening monstrosity in the natural order to have under the head of a man or brute animal members living in opposition to it. The same is true in the spiritual order when the head is pure, just, and virtuous. The branches are fresh and laden with fruit when they are living in the vine. Through this comparison Christ wanted us to understand that such are his own who by grace are incorporated into him (cf. John 15:5). They are like him, having their own goods that they receive from him and through him. Thus is fulfilled what Saint Paul says: "Those who are to be saved, God ordained that they should be conformable to the image of his Son" (Rom 8:29). Well, how can there be likeness between a head, which always kept the commandments of his Father, and members who, however much pardoned and justified, are forever breaking and shattering the first and ninth commandments of God? There is no participation of good with evil (cf. 2 Cor 6:14) or of Christ with one who breaks the Father's commandments. For he preached, "Not everyone who cries out to me, Lord, Lord, shall enter into the kingdom of heaven, but he who does the will of my Father" (Matt 7:21).

It is so far from the truth that the favor of Christ means that those who break the commandments are in the grace of the Father or of Christ, that the same Lord says, "If you keep my commandments, you shall abide in my love; as I also have kept my Father's commandments and do abide in his love" (John 15:10). Who will hope that, having broken his commandments, he may be loved by the Father out of consideration for Jesus Christ, who remains in the love of the Father and keeps his commandments? The slave will only be loved in the way of the Son. He will keep in his grace and love only the one who keeps his commandments, as he clearly said in the words already mentioned. Lest anyone be deceived, he first said, "Abide in me and I in you." And then he said, "Abide in my love." To show what he meant by abiding in him and in his love, he said, "If you abide in me, and my words abide in you, you shall ask whatever you will, and it shall be done to you" (John 15:4–9). This means that the one who breaks his words should not imagine that he abides in his love or is incorporated into his body as a living member. For the sentence of the divine scripture is fixed: "Abhorrent to God is the wicked man and his wickedness alike" (Wis 14:9). To make clear how his own are not abhorrent but are loved in themselves, the Lord said to his disciples, "Now I do not tell you that I will ask the Father for you; for the Father himself loves you because you have loved me, and have believed that I came forth from him" (John 16:26–27). It is as if he said:

A short time ago I said to you: "I will ask the Father, and he will give you another Paraclete" (John 14:16). But do not think that I have to pray for you as one asks his friend to give something to others toward whom he is ill–disposed. What he gives them is solely because he loves much the one who asks while the others remain unloved and displeasing as before. In this matter, it is not so. Having loved and created you, your Father loves you very much and is pleased with you. As people loved with your own proper love and having your own grace and justice, you have the license to enter before his throne and to ask him in my name for what you need. I pray for you as for a beloved people to whom the Father grants favors because I ask them and because I ask them for you.

Those whom Jesus Christ our Lord has incorporated into himself are his living members. When they did not possess grace, he obtained it for them so that they might please the Father. Having obtained grace, they perform works that are valuable for meriting eternal life as a "just" reward of their services and as an inheritance "owed" to sons and daughters. If it seems disproportionate to human lowliness to do something that has equality of merit with the majesty and eternity of the celestial kingdom, do not consider man alone in this, but honored and accompanied by the heavenly grace infused into his soul and "made a partaker of the divine nature," as Saint Peter says (2 Pet 1:4). Consider him as a living member of Jesus Christ our Lord, incorporated into him and living and working through the spiritual influence coming from him and participating in his merits. These things are so elevated that they equal the things that are awaited and are sufficient so that those who live thus may affirm that they fulfill God's law. They also fulfill what Saint Paul asks of the Colossians and Thessalonians when he tells them that "they should live worthily of God" (Col 1:10). He would not have asked them for such a high thing had he not understood that, with the favors already mentioned, they would be able to fulfill it, and that it was more the work of God not theirs. The same apostle gives thanks to God for making them "worthy of the lot of the saints in light" (Col 1:12). What this "lot" is, Jeremiah declares saying, "My portion is the Lord, and therefore will I wait for him" (Lam 3:24). David says of God, "You are my portion forever" (Ps 73:26). Worthy of this "portion" is the one who fulfills the law of God by the good works already mentioned, and whoever is found faithful in the trials that God sends him, as is written: "The Lord tried them and found them worthy of himself" (Wis 3:5). For the one and for the other, it is written that "God will pay the wages of the labors of his holy ones" (Wis 10:17).

## CHAPTER 90

Let no one be afraid to attribute the highest spiritual honor and the greatest spiritual riches and perfect freedom from sins to those whom the heavenly Father justifies through the merits of Jesus Christ our Lord. Let no one think that their being such damages the honor of the same Lord. Since everything they possess comes through him, not only does their valor not diminish his honor, but it even manifests and enlarges it. It is clear that the more just and beautiful they are, the more manifest is the great value of the merits of the one who so well obtained them for those who neither possessed nor merited them. Scripture says, "If the crib is full, the strength of the ox is manifest" (Prov 14:4), and this is right, because by his work, he filled it with sustenance. Saint Paul says to some whom he had helped by his teaching and labors that "they are his honor and crown before the Lord" (cf. 1 Thess 2:19). Well, then, how much more shall they be honor and crown to Jesus Christ our Lord who through him are brought to the honor of sons and daughters and to riches! In fact, it will be all the more so inasmuch as the riches are greater.

The Lord is not like some who have little concern or pleasure with the honor or virtue of their servants, lest their own honor be damaged. Neither is he like vain women who avoid being accompanied by beautiful servants, lest they dim their own beauty. Certainly, as Saint Paul says, Jesus Christ our Lord has "charity which surpasses all our understanding" (Eph 3:19) to hold our good as his own. So that we would possess many benefits, he lost his most precious life on the cross. He is the natural son of God, and through him we are adopted sons and daughters. Being the unique Son, he took us for brothers, giving us his God as God and his Father as Father, as he said, "I ascend to my Father and to your Father, to my God and your God" (John 20:17). Speaking of the same Lord, Saint John says, "We saw his glory as the glory of an only–begotten Son" (cf. John 1:14); he also says that "he is full of grace and truth." Thus, the glory and spiritual riches of adopted sons must be as that of sons of a Father who is God.

If "grace and truth came through Jesus Christ" (John 1:17), as Saint John says, it was not so that it might remain in him alone, but that it might be drawn from him to us and that we might receive from his fullness in such abundance that Saint Paul calls what we have at present "an unspeakable gift" (cf. 2 Cor 9:15). That we might know the riches of the inheritance that we hope to enjoy in his company, Saint Paul entreats God "that he might give us a spirit of wisdom and of revelation" (cf. Eph 1:17), because such knowledge is much greater than our reason can achieve.

Glory and grace be to you, Lord, forever, because you have so honored and enriched us with present gifts and have consoled us with the hope of being heirs of God together with you, and because you had such love for us that it moved you, more than Job, not "to eat your portion of bread alone but that the orphan should eat from it" (cf. Job 31:17). Just as the love of the Father in you was not sterile, but full of many goods, so you, Lord, desiring to make us your companions in this, asked the Father "that the love with which you loved me may be in them" (John 17:26). "Rejoicing, I will rejoice in the Lord, and my soul will rejoice in God; for he has clothed me with the garments of salvation and has covered me with the robe of justice, as a bridegroom bedecked with a crown, and as a bride adorned with her finery" (Isa 61:10). Such a confession of the goods that come to us through Jesus Christ, together with others similar in the divine scripture, certainly gives honor to Jesus Christ. It gives more honor than saying that neither the power of his blood nor of his grace nor of the sacraments nor of the infusion of his Spirit into a man nor his incorporation into Christ is enough to take away man's sin but only causes him not to be condemned because of it. What is this but to think ill of God the Father, who promised to send with his Son a complete remedy against sin, and promised that, in his time, "sin would have an end" (Dan 9:24)? If, after the coming of his Son, sin remains even in the one who participates in the Son, does God not fulfill what he promised? How can the word be fulfilled that says: "I will pour upon you clean water, and you shall be cleansed from all your filthiness" (Ezek 36:25), if, in fact, I am not purified, but a clean mantle is thrown around me, and I am told that the justice and purity of Jesus Christ our Lord are imputed as mine? This means that it is better to cover my stain than to remove it. By the very fact of saying this, one denies that Jesus Christ our Lord is the Messiah promised in the Law. He must then await another messiah who not only frees from the condemnation of sin but frees from sin itself. For it is clear that the one who would be able to free from both things would be a greater savior than the one who is able to free from only one. To such cliffs as these, blind pride ascends in the one who receives it.

## CHAPTER 91

Divine scripture says that "Christ was made for us wisdom, justice, sanctification, and redemption" (1 Cor 1:30). No one should take this to mean that the just do not have within themselves their own justice. If we "are just" because Christ is just, and not through any justice we may have, it will also be said that there is no "wisdom" in us by which we may be wise or "sanctification" or "redemption." Saint John says that "the unction of the Holy Spirit, which teaches all things, abides in the just" (1 John 2:20, 27). Saint Paul says, "You are washed; you are sanctified" (1 Cor 6:11). Saint Peter says, "You are redeemed from your vain conversation" (cf. 1 Pet 1:18). Well, then, as Christ "was not redeemed," because he had no sin, it follows that this "redemption" must reside in us, and by it we are called "redeemed," in spite of the fact that scripture says that "Christ was made for us redemption." Because in this, as in the other three words, what is meant is that these things are given us through his merits.

The apostle says that "Christ is our life" (cf. Col 3:4), but it does not follow from this that the just do not live, since the Lord says: "the one who eats me, the same lives by me" (John 6:58). Anyone would be devoid of human reason who, on hearing it said that God is the beauty of the rose, or the strength of the lion, or things of this kind, denied that these creatures have beauty or strength distinct from that of God. The scripture says, "God is your life and the length of your days" (Deut 30:20). This way of speaking means that God is the efficient cause of these things and the one that gives them to us.

Occasion must not be taken for the same error from the act that scripture says that "we are made the very justice of God" (2 Cor 5:21), and that the Father "has made us pleasing in his beloved Son" (Eph 1:6), and things of this sort. This manner of speaking, as was said above, explains the mystery of Christ as the head and the just as his living members, joined intimately to him so that the good they have received may be preserved and grow. If these sayings were understood to say that the just did not possess these goods within themselves, but because Jesus Christ possesses them, what response could be given to Saint Paul, who says that "the just are justified through the redemption which is in Jesus Christ" (Rom 3:24)? Since there was no "captivity" in him, there was no "redemption." Therefore, it has to reside in the justified, even though won by the Lord.

The same apostle says, "Who shall separate us from the love of God, which is in Jesus Christ?" (Rom 8:35). But it does not follow from this that it is not within us, and very deeply within, since he says in another place that "the love of God is poured forth in our hearts by the Holy Spirit, who is given to us" (Rom 5:5). He speaks similarly when he says, even of natural goods, that "in God, we live and move and are" (Acts 17:28). But no one will say that we do not have being, life, and operations distinct from those of God.

Scripture speaks thus to show that we do not have this good from ourselves, and we are unable to preserve it within ourselves. Sometimes it says that such goods are not ours and we do not work them, exactly as the Lord says to his disciples, "You have not chosen me, but I have chosen you" (John 15:16). Yet in another place he says, "It is not you that speak, but the Spirit of your Father speaks in you" (Matt 10:20). Lest anyone understand this to mean that the man himself was not acting freely, he says elsewhere that the man does such a good but he does not mention that God does it. "I will give you a new heart" (Ezek 36:26), says God in Ezekiel, and he says to men in the same prophet: "Make for yourselves a new heart" (Ezek 18:31). Saint Paul says that "it is not of him that wills nor is it of him that runs" (cf. Rom 9:16), but in another place he says, "I desire the good, and I run, and not as for an uncertain thing" (cf. Rom 7:15–21). Thus he speaks in many other places, implying that the good that they have, they have from God, and that God and man concur in the good work (1 Cor 9:26), but that the glory of the one and the other is owed to God, since all good comes from him. In the same way our Lord said, "My doctrine is not mine but his that sent me" (John 7:16). So he could say, "My works and my justice are not mine but his that sent me." Anyone who would interpret this to mean that the Lord did not possess wisdom, doctrine, and other goods within himself would clearly be deceiving himself seriously. "My doctrine is not mine" means "I do not have it of myself but from my Father." Therefore, it must not be drawn from similar words that the just do not have "within themselves their own justice," but rather, that they do not have it "from themselves."

Thus, what the Council of Trent says agrees with what the Lord says. The council says that justice is ours because through it, placed within ourselves, we are justified; the Lord says here and elsewhere that "the word which you heard is not mine" (John 14:24). Even though it abides in us, we do not have it from ourselves but as given from God's hand. For this reason it is said to be the justice "of God."

## CHAPTER 92

Knowing a truth and knowing how to use it properly are two very different things. The first without the second is not only useless but even causes harm. As Saint Paul says, "The one who thinks that he knows something has not known as he ought to know" (1 Cor 8:2). He says this because some Christians knew that what had been sacrificed to idols could be eaten just as what had not been sacrificed. But they used that knowledge badly, because they ate in front of those who were scandalized to see it eaten.

I have told you this so that you are not content with knowing the truth that those who are in the grace of the Lord are just and pleasing with their own grace and justice, and that the value of their good works is so high that it merits for them an increase of grace and glory. Try to put this truth in its place, for there are people who make poor use of it either by excess or defect. The first run the risk of pride and the second of laziness and cowardice. Many have seen that, by the grace of God, they are in a short time freed from great evils in which they had long been, and yet are not free in many years from the dangers that their good works present to them. Remember what David says: "The wicked put a trap along his way" and also "They put it on the road itself" (cf. Ps 140:6). Not only do our enemies seek "to draw us from the right path" by inciting us to do evil, but they also place the trap "in the very road" (cf. Ps 142:3) of good works, inciting us not to use the good as we ought, so that the Sage's words may be verified in us: "I have seen another evil under the sun: riches gathered to the hurt of their owner" (Eccl 5:12). It would be better for one who misuses a thing not to have it at all.

Such people see their good works and hear people say how much they merit by them. Then their head becomes giddy with vanity and haughty complacency. They do not look at the many faults in their works, and they do not regard them as God's favor—which they are—and they do not try to advance. They are like people of mean and mediocre heart who are satisfied with very little. It is right, as Saint Bernard says, that "we should not be careless in looking at the things we have from God, but we should be careful to attain the great deal which is lacking to us."[141] Some are so blind with ignorant pride that, even though their tongue says something else, their heart feels it very true that, because of their merits, God is obliged through pure justice to give them what they ask and hope for. They do not see that their merits are God's grace. If he denies them something, they complain within their hearts and hold themselves as offended that, since they have served so well, he does not do them justice when he denies them something.

Do not let this evil pride move you, for at times God has to complain of it in Isaiah, saying, "They ask of me judgments of justice and desire to approach God and say: why have we fasted and you have not seen it, and humbled our souls, and you have not approved it" (Isa 58:2–3). That such a dangerous poison may not enter your soul with other poisons that follow upon it, you ought to adopt the excellent teaching that Jesus Christ our Lord said in Saint Luke:

> Which of you having a servant who plows or feeds cattle, would say to him when he comes in from the field: "Go now and rest," and would not rather say to him, "prepare my supper, gird yourself and serve me till I have eaten and drunk, and afterward you shall eat and drink?" Does he by chance thank that servant for doing the things that he commanded him? I think not. So you also, when you have done everything that has been commanded you, say: We are unprofitable servants; what we were obliged to do, we have done. (Luke 17:7–10)

From such words, you ought to gather how advantageous a sentiment it is for a Christian to consider himself as God's slave. He should do what the slave does, but not with the heart of a slave that is full of fear and not love. Of this, Saint Paul says: "You have not received the spirit of bondage again in fear; but you have received the spirit of the adoption of sons, by which we cry," saying to God: "Father, Father" (cf. Rom 8:15). As Saint Augustine says, "The difference in brief of the Old Law from the gospel is the fear that there is in love."[142]

Leave aside, then, the "spirit of bondage," because it does not belong to "sons of God," and leave behind the "spirit of fear," because even though fear of God is God's gift and therefore is not evil, nonetheless fear is imperfect when it is directed to punishment. Understand by *servant* a man who considers himself subject to God by obligations stronger and more just than those of the slave of any other man, however high his price. From this perspective, everything within or outside of him that works for good, everything he does as a loyal slave for God's glory and pleasure, as well as all that he gains, he gives to his Lord. Likewise, there is no slack or neglect in his service today just because he has served many years in the past. He does not consider himself without obligation to perform one service because he has done another. As the holy gospel says, he possesses continually a "hunger and thirst for justice" (cf. Matt 5:6). He considers all that he has done as little in view of the greatness of what he has received and of what the Lord deserves from anyone who serves him. Thus he fulfills what Saint Paul says: "Forgetting the things that are past, he stretches forth to serve again in the future" (cf. Phil 3:13). He also understands that what he does, however much, does not profit God; neither is God obligated to thank the doer as though he regards the works as born from our own natural strength. In fact, the one who works is unable to pay even what he owes. Therefore, the holy gospel says, "When you have done all the things that were commanded you, say: we are unprofitable servants; we did what we had to do" (Luke 17:10). I say that the works do not profit God but those who perform them, who gain eternal life, as will be said in the next chapter.

Having understood the name of slave in this way, you will see that it is a name connoting humility, obedience, diligence, and love. The Virgin Mary possessed such sentiments when, taught by the Holy Spirit, she responded, "Behold the handmaid of the Lord; be it done to me according to your word" (Luke 1:38). She confesses her own lowliness; she offers her service and love freely, without attributing to herself any other honor or interest than being considered as serving as a slave in whatever the Lord might command for his glory. She felt all of this in calling herself by the name of servant. Saint Paul boasts of the same name and calls himself by it when he says: "Paul, a servant of Jesus Christ" (Rom 1:1). Finally, all who serve God, whether great or lowly, have to feel this about themselves if they desire that their service does not change into ruin for them.

Profit, then, from this truth, and you will find an effective remedy against the dangers that usually arise from good works, not because of their nature, but through the imperfection of the one who does them. Get used to saying many times with heart and lips:

I am God's slave because he is God and because of the thousands of benefits that I have received from his hand. No matter how much I do for him, I will pay back neither the least measure of what he has given me in becoming man, nor the least of the torments he suffered for me, nor any sin which he has pardoned me, nor any other from which he has freed me, nor any good intention that he has given me to serve him, nor one day of heaven, which I hope to obtain.

As Jacob said, "I am too small for any of God's mercies" (Gen 32:11). The Lord says that those who do "all that is commanded" must humble themselves and say: "we are unprofitable servants; we did what we had to do." How much more ought I to humble myself since I fall into such great failings through ignorance, weakness, or malice? I am a slave, and a poor one at that, for I do not serve God as I can and ought. If my merits were the measure, there would have been days when I would have been sent to hell for the sins I committed, and for many others into which I could justly have been permitted to fall.

Let this, then, be your sentiment concerning yourself, and let this be the position in which you place yourself since this is what you merit on your part. Let your care be to serve the Lord as well as you can, without casting a glance at your service, and without imagining that God owes you thanks "or that you can respond" to what you owe him, "even one for a thousand," as Job says (cf. Job 9:3). If you hear talk of how much your good works merit, do not let your heart be consoled but say: "It is your favor, Lord. Let thanks be given to you that you give such value to our unworthy service." Thus you may always remain in your place as a negligent and unworthy servant.

## CHAPTER 93

Now that your soul has been reassured about the above–mentioned dangers by the knowledge of the Lord's teaching, you can rejoice safely at the greatness and worth the Lord bestows on those who belong to him. You can bless him for infusing his grace into those who by nature are slaves, thus making them adopted sons of God, "and if sons, heirs also" (Rom 8:17). It is right that those received as God's sons should live and work in conformity with the condition of their Father. For this, the Lord gives them the Holy Spirit, together with many virtues and gifts with which they can serve him, fulfill his word, and please him. Those whose services, however great in themselves, did not rise up to eternal life, have already drunk from the water of grace, which is so powerful that "it has become a fountain within them springing up into eternal life" (John 4:14). It is a fountain of such value that their good works, however small, "ascend to eternal life," and even merit it, for the reasons already mentioned.

Look at what proceeds from you by looking at yourself within yourself; then look at yourself in God and in his grace. Considered in yourself, you are a great sum of debts, and however much you might do, not only will you not be able to merit eternal life, but you will not even pay what you owe. But in God and his grace, the very service you are obligated to render is received as merit for eternal life. Though the Lord is not obligated either to thank you or to pay for what you have done, he ordains things so creatively that the good works of those who belong to him may be rewarded by possession of him in heaven. Though he acts in this way, God owes nothing to *anyone* because of who he is, yet he owes *himself*, whose arrangement is very just and ought to be accomplished in its entirety. Glorify God, then, for these favors. Understand that if God had not been a merciful Father to Saint Paul, giving him a life full of good merits, he would not have dared to say when he was already near to death that "the just judge had laid up for him a crown of justice" (cf. 2 Tim 4:6–8). God crowned him through justice, but he first gave him the merits of grace. Thus, everything redounds to the glory of God, whether he is just in rewarding the good done or is merciful in giving us the good we have done. No one can deny this unless he desires to deprive God of his honor.

Put yourself, then, in your proper place, and consider yourself worthy of hell and of all evils and unworthy of the smallest goods. Do not be discouraged at such lowliness. Rather, trample underfoot all cowardice, and hope in God's mercy that placed you on the road and will strengthen you along it so that you may take it forward, until in eternal life you lay hold of the fruit of the good works that you have done here by his grace.

# C. SEEING THE NEIGHBOR IN CHRIST (CHAPS. 94–96)

**CHAPTER 94**

You have already heard with what eyes you must look at yourself and at Christ. To complete consideration of the words of the prophet who tells you to "see," it remains to consider with what eyes you must look at your neighbor. This is to be done so that you may be enlightened from every side and that "no darkness may overtake you" (cf. John 12:35).

For this purpose you need to observe that those who look well at their neighbors look at them with eyes that pass through the self and through Christ. I mean that human beings experience afflictions in their bodies, and sorrows, ignorance, or weakness in their souls. It is clear that when people feel pain from heat, cold, or sickness, they do not want to be rejected and spurned because of their weakness but to be endured, tended, and shown mercy. From what takes place within themselves, both with regard to feeling afflictions and desiring the remedy for them, people learn through experience what the neighbor feels, being of the same weak nature. With the same compassion with which they look at themselves and desire to be relieved, let them look at, tend, and suffer with the neighbor. Thus they will fulfill what the scripture says: "From yourself, understand the things that pertain to your neighbor" (Sir 31:18). Otherwise, what could be more abominable than to desire mercy in your own mistakes and vengeance against others; to desire that others put up with your faults with great patience (since to you your failings seem small) while being unwilling to put up with anyone else, as you make the tiny speck in the other person into a huge beam? Those who want everyone to watch out for and console them (cf. Luke 6:41) while they are unkind and careless about others do not deserve to be called men, for they do not look at others with human eyes, which ought to be merciful eyes. Scripture says, "To have a weight and a weight and a measure and a measure is an abomination before the Lord" (Prov 20:10). This indicates that those who have a large measure for receiving and a small one for giving are displeasing in God's eyes. Their punishment will be that, since they do not measure out to the neighbor with the mercy they desire to be measured to them, God will measure out to them with the same harsh and stingy measure that they use when measuring the neighbor. For it is written: "By the measure with which you measure, you will be measured," and, "judgment without mercy will be done to the one that has not done mercy" (cf. Matt 7:2).

Therefore, daughter, whatever you see in your neighbor, consider how you would feel in the same situation and how you would want others to feel toward you if the same thing should happen to you. With those eyes that pass through yourself, have compassion on your neighbor and give whatever remedy you can. Then God will measure to you with the same merciful measure with which you measure, according to his word: "Blessed are the merciful, for they shall obtain mercy" (Matt 5:7). In this way you will have drawn knowledge of your neighbor from your knowledge of yourself, and you will be merciful with everyone.

## CHAPTER 95

Now consider how you must draw love of neighbor from knowledge of Christ. Reflect on the great mercy by which the Son of God became man for love of men, and with what great care he sought their good throughout his life. Consider the excess of love and sorrow with which he offered his life on the cross for them. Just as looking at yourself, you saw your neighbor with human eyes, so looking at Christ you will see your neighbor with Christian eyes, which is to say, with the eyes of Christ. If Christ dwells in you, you will experience things as he did (cf. Phil 2:5). You will see how very right it is that you are obligated to endure and love your neighbor. Christ loved and esteemed them as the head loves his own body, as the husband loves his wife, as brothers and sisters love one another, as a loving father loves his children. Beg the Lord that he open your eyes to see the flaming fire of love that burned in his heart when he mounted the cross for the good of all: little and great; good and bad; past, present, and to come; including even those who crucified him. Consider that his love has not grown cold. To the contrary, if the first death had not been sufficient as a remedy for us, with what love would he die now as he died then! In his body he offered himself once to the Father on the cross for our healing; by his will he continually offers himself with the same love. Tell me, then, how can anyone be cruel with those with whom Christ was so merciful? How can anyone find a way to wish evil to those for whom God desires every blessing and salvation? It is not possible to speak or write of the profound love engendered in the heart of the Christian who looks at the neighbor, not according to exterior things like wealth or descent or the like, but as beloved members of Christ's body, intimately united with him by every kind of relationship and friendship. The proverb says, "Whoever loves Beltran, loves his dog."[143] How much do you think the lover of Christ will love his neighbors who are Christ's mystical body? Also, the same Lord has said, with his own lips, that he receives the good or evil done to the neighbor as done to himself (cf. Matt 25:40, 45). Profound consideration of these words leads the good Christian to treat the neighbor with deep reverence, tender love, and gentle meekness. He becomes patient with others, watchful and careful not to offend or harm them but, instead, to help and cheer them. It seems to such a Christian that he is dealing with Christ himself, whom he sees in his neighbors. He holds them in his heart and considers himself their slave, more obligated to serve and benefit them than if they had purchased him with a great sum of money. Considering how dearly Christ paid for man on the cross when he purchased him at the cost of his precious blood, what can a Christian do but give himself totally to Christ's service and desire that ways be offered for showing gratitude and love? So he hears from the mouth of God: "If you love me, feed my sheep" (cf. John 21:17); "Whoever receives one of these little ones, receives me" (cf. Mark 9:37); "Whoever does works of mercy to one of these, does them to me" (Matt 25:40). The Christian takes it as a special grace to have near such a wonderful way of showing and exercising love for Jesus Christ. For such a person, the affliction borne for the sake of the neighbor seems little and the years of service seem short (cf. Gen 29:20) because of his great love for Christ, and for others through him and in him. Therefore, the Christian continually bears in his heart that which Christ, in his love, commanded so strictly when he said: "This is my commandment, that you love one another as I have loved you" (John 15:12).

## CHAPTER 96

Add to this another consideration on how to look at your neighbor. From one point of view it is very true that the Lord does not seek or desire return for his favors. But from another point of view he gives nothing from which he does not want return, though not for himself, since he is fully rich and unable to grow in wealth. What he gives, he gives through pure love. But the return he desires is for the neighbors who need to be esteemed, loved, and helped. It is as if a man had lent another a lot of money and had done him many other favors. Then he said to him: "Of all this that I have done for you, I do not need your pay. But the entire claim I have against you, I cede and transfer to the person of so and so, who is in need, or is my relative or servant. Pay him what you owe, and with that, I consider myself paid."

In this way let the Christian enter into reckoning with God. Let him consider what he has received, as much in the sufferings and death that the Son of God passed through for him as in the particular mercies that he has given after having created him: not punishing him for his sins; not destroying him for his weaknesses; waiting for and pardoning him as many times as he has asked pardon; giving him good things instead of evil; and other innumerable favors that cannot be counted. Let the Christian consider that this loving engagement of God with him has to be a model and rule for his dealings with his neighbors. God has worked such favors in him to make him understand that, even if the neighbor does not merit in himself to be tolerated, loved, or helped, God wills the good the other does not merit, to be granted in exchange for what is owed to God. Let the Christian recognize himself as obligated and a slave of others. Let him look at God, who owes nothing to anyone, looking at our neighbors. Let the title by which the one in need begs for help be this: "Do this for me, since God has done it for you."

Let a man fear very much being cruel or unloving toward someone in need, lest God be such with him by taking away the goods he had given and punishing him as being ungrateful for the pardon of past wrongs. He did this with that wicked servant who had received from his lord remission of ten thousand talents and then was cruel toward his neighbor, throwing him in prison because he owed him a hundred pence, without giving him freedom or respite. We do not read that that lord whose servant had defrauded his estate of "ten thousand talents," became angry with him, but that he treated him with such great mercy that, when his slave asked for time, he gave him freedom and pardon of the debt. The lord becomes angry at the servant's cruelty toward his neighbor and admonishes him severely: "Wicked servant, I pardoned you all that you owed me, because you asked me. Was it not right, then, that you should have had mercy on your neighbor, as I had mercy on you?" (cf. Matt 18:32–33). In his anger "he handed him over to the torturers until he should pay all the debt, which had been pardoned him." God does not punish sins once they are pardoned, but he does punish the ingratitude of the one pardoned, an ingratitude that is greater insofar as the pardon was of more and greater sins. Even if we could believe that such a servant loved his lord, what is written would apply to him: "Anyone who closes his ear to the cry of the poor, will himself cry out and not be heard" (Prov 21:13).

Understand then, my daughter, that the sight of yourself and the sight of Christ and the sight of the many goods you have received from his hand rightly engender in your heart esteem and love for your neighbor that nothing can remove from you. Suppose that your flesh says to you: "What do I owe to him that I should do him good?" "How shall I love him when he has done evil to me?" Respond that perhaps you would listen to these objections if your neighbor were the cause of your love. But since the cause is Christ, who receives the good done to the neighbor and the pardon given to the neighbor as if they were given to him, what place can there be for hindering love and good works toward the being of the neighbor, whoever he is? What room is there for doing the evil that I would like to do, since I am not reckoning with him, but with Christ? In this way there will burn within your heart charity of such a kind that "the many waters" of evil works that may be done to us "will not be able to quench it" (cf. Song 8:7). Instead, charity will go forth victorious and rise above as a living flame, and you will deal with your neighbors without stumbling or losing your virtue because they lose theirs. Thus says David, "Much peace they have, Lord, who love your law, and they have no stumbling block" (Ps 119:165). Such is the law of charity by which the whole law is summed up and fulfilled. As Saint Paul says, "Whoever loves the neighbor has fulfilled the law" (Rom 13:8).

This esteem for the neighbor, by which we honor him as an adopted son of God and a brother of Jesus Christ our Lord, and this love we hold for him as belonging to Christ is what Saint Paul recommends to the Philippians, and to us in them, saying: "In humility, consider each other as better; do not consider your own interest, but that which serves others; let this mind be in you, in the example of Jesus Christ, who having the form of God, humiliated himself to take the form of a servant" (Phil 2:3–7), a thing he did to benefit us. These two things, humility and love of neighbor, the Lord taught and entrusted to us in that wonderful act that he performed near to his death when he washed the feet of his disciples. This office is so lowly that it shows humility, and, being done for the benefit of the neighbor, it shows charity. We, his lowly servants and disciples, must learn these two things from him, since the Lord and Master performed this office.

Strengthened, then, by this example and by what has already been said, weigh neighbors with the weight of the fact that they are adopted sons of God and that Jesus Christ gave himself for them on the cross. Hold as precious and honor the one whom God has so greatly honored. As his beloved spouse, love those who are joined with him as members with their head. In this way your love will be well founded and strong. Love that does not arise from these sources is very weak and presently becomes weary and dries up. Like a house built upon shifting sand, it collapses to the ground in any combat and occasion that presents itself.

# PART FOUR

◆

# "Forget Your People!"

(CHAPS. 97–99)

# CHAPTER 97

The next sentence says, "Forget your people and your father's house" (Gen 12:1). To clarify these words, note that all human beings are divided into one of two groups or kinds of cities, the one good and the other evil. These cities do not differ because of diversity of places, for the citizens of one and the other live together and even within the same house. They are distinguished, rather, by the diversity of their affections. This is what Saint Augustine says:

> Two loves built two cities. The love of self to the point of despising God built the *earthly* city; the love of God to the point of despising oneself built the *heavenly* city. The first exalts itself; the second does not exalt itself but God. The first desires to be honored by men; the second holds it as an honor to have a pure conscience in God's eyes. The first raises its head high in its own honor; the second says to God: "You are my glory and the one who lifts up my head" (Ps 3:4). The first is desirous of commanding and dominating; in the second, they serve each other in charity, with the greater doing good for their charges and the latter obeying those in charge. The first attributes its strength to its own forces and glories in them; the second says: "I will love you, Lord, my strength" (Ps 18:2). The wise men in the first city seek created goods, or if "they did know the Creator, they did not honor him as such, but became vain in their thoughts, saying: we are wise, and they became fools" (Rom 1:21–22). In the second city, the only wisdom is the true service of God and hope for the reward of honoring the same God in the company of the saints and angels, "so that God may be all in all" (1 Cor 15:28).[144]

All sinners are citizens of the first city, while all of the just are citizens of the second. Since all descendants of Adam, except the Son of God and his blessed Mother, are sinners, even from conception, we are all, naturally speaking, citizens of that city out of which Christ draws us by his grace in order to make us citizens of his city. The wicked city is not a collection of streets and squares but a coming together of human beings who love and trust themselves. It is called by different names that show its wickedness.

It is called Egypt, which means darkness or distress. Inhabitants of this city either do not have the light of the knowledge of God through lack of faith, or they have faith, but as Christians who live badly, their faith is dead through lack of that charity that is its life. For this reason Saint John says that "the one who does not love God, does not know God, for God is Love" (1 John 4:8). He means that such a one does not possess the loving knowledge needed for salvation. Living in this way (some in the darkness of infidelity and others in the darkness of their sins), they do not possess joy but rather constraint and sadness. For, as Tobit says, "What joy can I have since I do not see the light of heaven?" (Tob 5:12).

The earthly city is also called Babylonia, which means confusion (cf. Gen 11:9). This name was given when the proud wanted to build a tower reaching to heaven to defend them from God's wrath if he should ever destroy the world again by water. Also, they wanted to build such a building to win a name for themselves in the world. But the Lord hindered their foolishness by confusing their language so that they did not understand one another. From this arose quarrels, with each one thinking that the other was mocking him. A person would say one thing, and another would answer with the contrary. Thus, the result of pride was "confusion," quarreling, and division. Very properly does this name fit the city of the wicked, for they desire to sin and not be punished; they want to flee the chastisements of God by avoiding offending him, but if they were able, by force or by cunning, to sin and not be punished, they would try it. They are proud, and their whole purpose is to have their name known upon the earth. If they can, they make towers of their vain works, and if they cannot, they make them in their thoughts. Such as these, God destroys just when they are at the height of their enjoyment. This is in accord with what is written: "God resists the proud" (Jas 4:6). Unwilling to live in unity of language, "giving obedience to God" (cf. Jas 4:7), they are punished by not being able to understand themselves, God, one another, or any created thing. Lacking God's wisdom, they understand nothing for their good as they ought to do. How many things go on in the hearts of the wicked that drive them mad and leave them unable to help themselves! At one time they want one thing and at another time something else, even the very opposite of the first thing. Now they do something, and then they undo it; they weep when they should rejoice and rejoice when they should weep; now they are at the point of despair and then they vainly exalt themselves. They seek something with great diligence, and after having attained it, they regret having sought it, or they do not find in it what they expected. They desire one thing but do another, since they are ruled, not by reason, but by passion.

For this reason everything is the opposite of what it should be. Being a *rational animal* with a soul, the human being has to live according to reason. But these people live according to their appetites. They live the bodily life proper to beasts but not the life of reason proper to human beings. Therefore, since God is spirit and must be served, not by a bestial life, but by a spiritual life, these people do not serve him, as said above, because their life is contrary to his law. Also, since the unity of Christians is born of unity within oneself and with God, these citizens, separated from God, are unable to have good and lasting peace with one another. Instead, their conversations, works, and meetings lead to quarrels, with each one living according to his desires and without concern for pleasing the other person. They are sensitive to affront and injury to themselves but make no attempt to bear with each other. These people do not use themselves or creatures for the end for which they have been created, but rather they desire themselves and all other things for themselves, thus making themselves the ultimate end of everything. Consequently, with good reason, they are called Babylonia, since everything goes contrary to the Creator.

Citizens of the earthly city are also called Chaldeans. At times, they are named Sodom, or Edom, or one of a thousand other names that represent the wickedness of this people. All the names taken together cannot adequately show its malice.

This is the people called the *world*. The word does not refer here to the world created by God, which is good, created by the one who is the supreme Good. It is used for those who have no other feeling and no other love than for what is visible. Saint John calls this the "pride of life, the concupiscence of the flesh, and the concupiscence of the eyes" (1 John 2:16–17). Whoever loves this shall perish, "but whoever does the will of God, shall abide forever," as the same Saint John says. Saint Paul says, "Anyone who does not have the Spirit of Christ, does not belong to him" (Rom 8:9) and, consequently, will belong to the world. Saint James says that "friendship with this world is enmity with God" (Jas 4:4).

## CHAPTER 98

You have heard enough reasons for spurning this people, and you can see how much God wants you to leave it to save yourself. For this is the spiritual Egypt from which God commanded Israel to depart in a hurry in order to journey, even though with labors, toward the land of promise. It is the people from which God commanded Abraham to go out when he said to him, "Go forth out of your country and from your kindred, and out of your father's house; go to the land that I will show you" (Gen 12:1). He fulfilled this with simple obedience "without knowing where he was going" (Heb 11:8), as Saint Paul says. From this same people God commanded Lot to go out, so he would not suffer the punishments that God wanted to send. He commanded Lot to save himself "on the mountain" (cf. Gen 19:17), which means the height of faith and a good life. Finally, God refers to this people when he speaks to those who want to belong to him:

> Do not keep company with unbelievers. For what company can evil have with good or light with darkness? What concord can there be between Christ and Belial or between the faithful and the unbeliever? What agreement can there be between the temple of God and idols? You are the temple of the living God. As God says, "I will dwell in them and I will walk among them, and I will be their God, and they shall be my people." For this reason go out from among them, and separate yourself, says the Lord, and do not touch anything of theirs, and I will receive you and be to you a Father, and you shall be my sons and daughters, says the Lord Almighty. (2 Cor 6:14–18)

When you hear such promises, you should strive to become a stranger to this wicked people for the good promised you and for the evil you avoid. It is not safe to be under the roof of a house that is certain to fall and to take down all who might be in it, and we would give no little thanks to whoever warns us to flee from it. Well, know for certain (and this I warn you as coming from God) that the day will come in which the vision that Saint John saw concerning this evil people will be fulfilled spiritually. He said: "I saw another angel that descended from heaven; he had great power and held the earth illuminated by his splendor. And he cried out with a strong voice, and said: Fallen, fallen is Babylon the great, and is become the habitation of demons and the house of every unclean spirit and of every unclean and horrible bird" (Rev 18:1–2). And further on, he said, "An angel took a great stone, like a millstone, and cast it into the sea, saying: With such violence as this the great city of Babylon will be thrown into the sea, and she will never more be found" (Rev 18:21). Those who desire to be saved should not be careless. They should not think that, though they keep company with the wicked, their scourges will not include them. The same Saint John said that he heard another voice from heaven saying, "Go out from her, my people, and do not be participants in her crimes, and do not receive from her plagues, for her sins have reached unto heaven and the Lord has remembered her iniquities" (Rev 18:4–5).

Even if it is very advantageous for a good person to flee even physically the company of evil (and in fact it is almost necessary for one beginning in goodness if he does not want to be lost), yet this going out from the midst of Babylonia that God commands here is understood, as Saint Augustine says, as "going out with the heart from among the evil, loving what they despise and despising what they love."[145] If we consider what is corporal in one and the same city or house, Jerusalem and Babylonia are next to each other insofar as the body. But if we consider hearts, they are very far apart. In Jerusalem we recognize the city of God; in Babylonia, the city of the wicked.

Forget your people, then, and go forth to the people of Christ, knowing that you cannot begin a new life if you do not go forth with sorrow from the old. Recall what Saint Paul says: "Jesus, in order to sanctify his people by his blood, suffered outside the gate of Jerusalem. Since this is so, let us go forth to him outside the camp, imitating him in his reproach" (Heb 13:12–13). Saint Paul says this to warn us that "Christ suffered outside the city." He means that if we want to follow Christ, we must go forth from this city, that is, from the assembly of those who love themselves wrongly. Christ could well have cured the blind man within Bethsaida (cf. Mark 8:23), but he chose to lead him out of it and give him sight. Thus he taught us to take leave of ordinary life and to follow the narrow way along which Truth itself says that few walk (cf. Matt 7:14).

Let no one deceive you. Christ does not want those he loves to serve him and the world, and through his blessed mouth he promised that "no one can serve two masters" (Matt 6:24). Since he said that he and his disciples and his kingdom were not of this world (cf. John 8:23), it is not right that you should be of this world, if only so that you might not end up as the disobedient Absalom ended: "hung by his hair from a holm oak, he was lanced through with three lances by the hand of Joab" (2 Sam 18:9, 14). He hung there and lost his life. So it will happen with the man who disobeys the heavenly Lord and displeases him by a wicked life: his thoughts and affections are like hairs that keep him hanging from this world. His whole purpose is to be magnified upon the earth, and that things will go well with him in what is visible. But what good can come to him since the tree from which he hangs is a holm oak that produces fruit for pigs? This world does not satisfy, and it only yields fruit for men who are beasts. The demon, called "the prince of this world" (John 12:31) because he rules and commands the wicked, pierces such beastly men with the three lances (already mentioned): "pride of life, concupiscence of the flesh, and concupiscence of the eyes" (1 John 2:16). He treats his own in such a way that he does not even fill them with the food of pigs. Rather, like another Adonibezec, he keeps them with their toes and fingers cut off lest they do some good, placed under the table to eat, not from a full plate, but from the bits that are left over (cf. Judg 1:6–7). He keeps them hungry now, and afterward he will take them with him to eternal hunger and torments. He can give nothing else. Such is his treatment. If the worldly really thought about this, it would be enough to make them go forth from the company of the demon and the world and draw near to God, as the prodigal son did. When he saw himself in such a lowly job and realized that he could not even fill himself with the food of pigs, he took hold of his senses and counsel and saw how different it was to be in the house of his father from being in the house of the world. He left the evil that he had and went to his father, begging him for mercy, and he found it (cf. Luke 15:16ff.).

You do the same, and if you want the Lord to receive you, leave your people. If you want him to remember you, "forget your people." If you want him to love you, do not love yourself in a disorderly fashion. If you want him to care for you, do not confide yourself to your own care. If you want to please him, do not look at yourself or take pleasure in how you look. If you want to please him, do not fear to displease the entire universe for his sake. If you want to find him, do not hesitate to leave father and mother, brothers and sisters and house, and even your own life for his sake. It is not because it is fitting that you despise these things but because it is fitting to look with such truth and with all your love at Christ that you do not turn by a hair from pleasing him to pleasing any creature, however beloved it may be, not even if it is yourself. Saint Paul preaches that "those who have wives should have them as if they did not have them; those who buy, as if they did not possess; and those who sell, as if they did not sell; and those who weep, as though they did not weep; and those who rejoice, as if they did not rejoice" (1 Cor 7:29–31). He adds the reason, saying, "because the form of this world is passing quickly." I say the same to you, my daughter, first because the world is quickly passing, and second, because you already are not your own. Thus, you have parents, brothers and sisters, relatives, house and people, as though you did not have them. This does not mean that you are not to reverence, love, and obey them, for grace does not destroy the order of nature, and even in heaven itself one must have a child's reverence for father and mother. Rather, it means that these things are not to occupy your heart and interfere with your love for God. Love them in Christ and not in themselves. Christ did not give them to you to be a hindrance to what you must always do, which is to serve him. Saint Jerome tells of a young woman who was so mortified in affection for her family that she did not even want to see her own sister, a young unmarried woman, but contented herself with loving her for God.[146] Believe me that, just as one cannot write on a parchment if it is not well cleaned and removed from the flesh, so the soul is not ready for God to write his particular favors on her until the affections that spring from the flesh are quite dead.

We read that in times past they put the Ark of God on a cart so that two milk cows could draw it while their calves remained shut up in a certain place. Even though the cows "were groaning" for their calves, they never left their way or turned back or to the side, "neither to the right hand nor to the left," as the scripture says (cf. 1 Sam 6:10–12). Instead, by the will of God that they were doing, they bore the Ark to the land of Israel, the place where God dwelt. Those who have had the cross of Jesus Christ our Lord placed upon their shoulders (that is the Ark where he is and must truly be found) must not leave or delay their journey because of these natural affections of love for parents, children, houses, and other similar things. Neither must they rejoice frivolously over the prosperity of their relatives nor be troubled by their adversities. The first of these is to depart from the path to the right hand and the second to the left. Rather, they must follow his way fervently, entrusting to the Lord the guidance of the one and the other. They must be as dead to these things as if they had nothing to do with them. Or, at least, they must not let themselves be conquered by sadness or joy over what touches their relatives, even if they experience some feeling. This is what it means that the cows did not stop bearing the Ark of God, even though they bellowed for their offspring.

When parents see that their children desire to serve God well in a way that they do not like, they must consider what God wants. Even though they groan with love for their children, let them conquer themselves with the love of God and offer their children to him. They will then be like Abraham, who was willing to slay his only son through obedience to God, without caring what his feelings desired (cf. Gen 22:9–10). The natural sorrow that is experienced in these moments should be borne patiently. It will not go without reward, for the Lord ordained such love, and when it is conquered for love of him, it is equivalent to suffering martyrdom.

Forget your people, daughter, and be like another Melchizedek, of whom it is told that he had not "father or mother or any lineage"

(Heb 7:3). In him, as Saint Bernard says, an example is given to God's servants. They must hold their people and their relatives in such forgetfulness that they may be in their hearts as Melchizedek was in this world, having nothing in their hearts that might captivate them and slow down the rapid journey by which they journey to God.[147]

## CHAPTER 99

I would not want vanity to blind you, as it has blinded many who presume upon their carnal lineage. Therefore, I want to tell you what Saint Jerome says to a young woman:

> I do not want you to look at those young women who belong to the world and not to Christ. Forgetting the purpose they began, they rejoice in their delights and delight in their vanities and glory in the body and in their family origin. If they considered themselves daughters of God, they would never, after their divine birth, consider nobility of body to be anything. If they realized that God is their Father, they would not love nobility of the flesh. In the beginning of the world, God made a man and a woman from whom descended the throng of the human race. Why do you glory in the nobility of your lineage? Ambitious greed, not equality of nature, produces nobility of line. There can be no difference between those engendered by the second birth. Through it, rich and poor, free and slave, have the lineage without which they do not become children of God. The lineage of earthly flesh is darkened by the splendor of heavenly honor and completely disappears. Those who before were unequal in worldly honors are clothed equally with the nobility of celestial and divine honor. There is no room for vanity about lineage, and no one made beautiful by divine birth is without lineage. The only place for vanity about lineage is in the thoughts of those who do not hold heavenly things more important than human things. And if they do consider them, with what vanity they act in considering themselves greater than others because of little things and equal to them in greater things. They esteem others as men placed on the earth beneath them, and they believe that they are their equals in the things of heaven. But you, whoever you are, young woman belonging to Christ and not to this age, flee all the glory of the present life so that you can obtain that which is promised in the age to come.[148]

From what Saint Jerome says, you can see how fitting it is to forget your people and your father's house, realizing that what you have from your parents according to the flesh is being conceived in sin, full of many miseries, and born in God's wrath because of the first sin of Adam that we inherit through our conception. Our parents gave us a body so humbly engendered that we avoid thinking or speaking about it. The soul infused into the body is stained by original sin, even though God created the soul without it. The body is full of a thousand necessities, subject to infirmities and death, and it is proper to do penance in suffering it. If one layer of skin that covers were removed, the most beautiful bodies would be terrible to behold. If you look at a body from outside, it is white, but if you consider what it encloses within, you would probably say that it is a vile heap of waste covered with snow. Would to God that the worst thing about the body were that it is full of pain and shame. But this is the least problem. It is the greatest enemy we have and the greatest traitor ever seen; it walks about seeking death, eternal death, for the one who gives it food and all that it needs. A body, to have a little pleasure, considers it nothing to anger God and hurl the soul into hell. A body is lazy as a jackass and more spiteful than a mule. If you think not, try leaving it without a bridle, so that it goes where it wants, and be a little careless in guarding yourself from it, and then you will see what you have.

O Vanity, deceiving those who presume on their lineage! God creates all souls and they are not inherited, and the flesh that is inherited is a thing for shame and fear. Let such as these hear what God said to Isaiah: "Cry out!" "What shall I cry out?" Isaiah asked. The Lord responded: "All flesh is grass and all its glory is like the flower of the field" (Isa 40:6). The Lord commands his prophets to cry out, but they are deaf to his cries and do not hear them. They desire more to glory in the baseness of their flesh than in the exaltation granted by the Holy Spirit.

Spouse of Christ, do not be blind or ungrateful. God does not esteem you because of your lineage but because you are a Christian. He does not esteem you because you were born in a canopied room but because you were born again in holy baptism. The first birth is with dishonor; the second, with honor. The first is to lowly station; the second, to nobility. The first is in sin; the second is in justification for sins. The first is "of the flesh that kills"; the second is "of the spirit that gives life" (cf. John 6:64). Through the first birth we are children of men; through the second, we are children of God. Through the first, even though we are heirs of the estate of our parents, we are heirs also insofar as we are sinners and full of many labors. But through the second birth we become brothers and sisters of Christ and, together with him, heirs of heaven. At present we receive the Holy Spirit and we expect to see God "face to face" (cf. 1 Cor 13:12). Well, what do you think God will say to one who places greater value on being born of men as a miserable sinner than on being reborn of God to be just and afterward blessed? Such as these are like a son born of a king and a very ugly slave. The son prized being the slave girl's son and boasted of it and neither considered nor remembered being the king's son.

"Forget your people," then, that you may belong to God's people. The people that is yours is evil, and for this reason he says "forget your people." Of yourself, you are nothing but a very lowly sinner. But if you shake yourself free from what is yours, the Lord has to receive you in what is his, in its nobility, its justification, and its love. But as long as you cling to yourself, you will not receive him. Christ desires that you despoil yourself, for he wants to bestow gifts on you as he is able. Of yourself, what do you have but debts? "Forget your people." This means that though you are a sinner, you estrange yourself from your past sins and live no more according to the world. "Forget your people" by placing no value on your lineage. "Forget your people" by casting disturbance from your heart and realizing that you are in a desert alone with God. "Forget your people," for there are so many and such sufficient reasons for doing so.

# PART FIVE

# "Forget Your Father's House!"

### (CHAPS. 100–102)

## CHAPTER 100

The next sentence is "Forget your father's house." This father is the devil, for according to Saint John, "Anyone who commits sin proceeds from the devil, for the devil sinned from the beginning" (1 John 3:8). This is not to say that the devil created or begot the wicked, but that they imitate his works. According to the holy gospel, the person who imitates another's works is said to be his child (cf. John 8:39–41). This accursed father lives in the world, which is to say in the wicked. It is written in the book of Job: "He sleeps in the shadow, in the hollow part of a reed, and in moist places" (cf. Job 40:16). "Shadow" refers to riches. These do not give the rest that they promise but prick the heart with worries as with thorns. Whoever possesses them experiences that they are not really riches, but only their shadow. In fact, they are really poverty, and there is nothing less than what their name claims. The "reed" is the glory of this world. The more it appears great from the outside, the emptier it is within. Even what appears outwardly is so changeable that it is rightly called a reed in that it sways with every wind. "Moist places" are those souls made lax through the carnal delights that they pursue without restraint. These are the opposite of the souls spoken of in the holy gospel: "When an unclean spirit is gone out of a man" in whom he was dwelling, "he walks through dry places seeking rest and finds none" (cf. Matt 12:43). In those souls who live apart from carnal desires, the devil cannot find a place to lodge. Rather, his dwelling place is in the midst of avarice, ambition, and sensual pleasures. For this reason he is called "the prince of this world" (John 12:31). He is leader and lord of the world, not because he created it, but because the wicked, although they belong to God, who created them, decide to belong to the devil by imitating him. They conform themselves to his will, and thus they will also justly be conformed to him in the punishment of hell when, on the last day, Christ will address them severely: "Depart from me, you cursed, into everlasting fire which was prepared for the devil and his angels" (Matt 25:41).

If we reflect carefully on this "house of the devil," we find that it is the evil self–will of the wicked. There the devil sits like a king on his throne, and from there he gives orders to everyone. Therefore, "to forget your father's house" is nothing other than to forget and forsake one's own will in which, at some time, we have given lodging to this evil father; it is to embrace the divine will with all one's heart, saying, "Not my will, Lord, but yours be done" (Luke 22:42). This is one of the most profitable warnings we can receive. In forsaking our own will, we will also forsake the sins that spring from it like branches from a root. Saint Paul means this when, listing the multitude of sins to be committed in the last days, he puts first that "they shall love themselves" (cf. 2 Tim 3:2). As the gloss says, this suggests that the disordered love of self is the root and the source of all sins. Once this is forsaken, the person remains subject to God, and, from this subjection, all good comes to him.

Again, the cause of our experiences of disgust, depression, and distress is nothing but our desire to see our own will accomplished. If it is not accomplished, we suffer pain. But if all this is forsaken, what can trouble us? Depression does not arise from trouble that comes to us, but from our desire that it not come. Not only are the pains of this world removed, but also those of the other world. Saint Bernard says, "Let self–will cease and there will be no more hell."[149]

But just as it is most beneficial to deny our own will, so it is the most difficult thing to do. Even if we work hard at it, we will not be successful unless the same Lord who commanded that the stone be removed from the sepulcher of Lazarus (cf. John 11:39) removes the hardness that crushes those underneath it, and unless he kills this mighty Goliath, who can be vanquished by no one except by the invincible One. Yet, even though we are unable to free our neck from these chains, we must not cease trying, in accord with the strength the Lord gives us. From our heart, we must call on him. We should also consider the evils that come upon us through following our own will and the benefits that come from not following it. Reflect also on the sublime example of Christ, who said of himself, "I came down from heaven, not to do my own will, but the will of him that sent me" (John 6:38). He did not do this only in matters of little importance, as some do, but also in matters of great dishonor, which, as they say, reach to the very soul. Such was the passion that Christ suffered for us. But in that he conformed himself to the Father's will and cast aside the will of his flesh to avoid suffering. By so doing, he gave us an example that we must love nothing so much that we would not cast it aside at God's command, and that nothing is so painful that we would not embrace it for him.

**CHAPTER 101**

We cannot rise to things that are high unless we begin with things that are low. Therefore, I advise you to get used to self–denial in smaller things so that you may ascend to the height of self–denial in greater things. The purpose is not to remain in smaller things but to pass through them to what is greater. Do not do, think, or say anything that is directed by your own desire or will. Whenever you become aware of being drawn to anything like this, be determined not to do it. Things must not take you captive, but you, with Christian freedom, must take them captive. Before you eat, you must mortify your gluttonous appetite and order the food in obedience to God, who commands that you eat in order to sustain your life. Before you engage in household matters, you must mortify greed, and afterward, engage in the work because God commands it for your own necessities and those of your neighbors. Through these examples you will understand that, in all things, you have to get rid of the property of your own will and do them because God or your superiors command them.

Recall that this is the way the elders of the desert trained their disciples, taking from them what they wanted and making them do what they did not want, so that, in all and from all, they would have their will denied. They had firm hope that one who proved himself well in these matters would arrive at perfection, and they thought ill of the other, reasoning that anyone who failed in small things would fail in greater ones. Therefore, make yourself lowly and "subject to every creature," as Saint Peter says (1 Pet 2:13), so that anyone at all may be able to pass you by, to trample you underfoot, and to contradict your will, as if you were a little bit of mud. Love and thank whoever helps you more in this, because he helps you to conquer your enemies, your own opinion, and your own will.

Count your mother as your abbess and obey her with profound humility and without tiring.[150] Do not be like those women who take the veil of chastity and then get out of hand, casting away obedience to their parents and superiors, and not obeying them even when they are living at home. Some go out of the house without permission. They have the reputation of serving God, but, in fact, nothing is more contrary to his service than what they are doing. Christ obeyed his Father in life and in death. He also obeyed his most holy Mother and Saint Joseph, as Saint Luke tells us (Luke 2:51). Let no one think that, without obedience, he can please one who was such a friend of obedience that, so as not to lose it, he lost his life on the cross. Do not be frightened that I recommend obedience to you so much. The greatest

287

danger of your state is that you are not enclosed. Not to provide for flight from your own will and subjection to that of another is to add danger to danger, and it will be bad for you. Your safety is in not wanting liberty.

To accomplish this, do not be content with obeying your parents, but do the same with the elders who are in your house. If you want to be completely obedient, also obey those who are younger, as long as this does not disturb the order of the house. If you have to command others in external things, consider yourself subject to them in what is internal. To do this with greater vigor, remember when the sovereign "Master and Lord" knelt down, as if he were subject or less, to wash the feet of those who loved him well, including the one who used his washed feet to go to deliver to death the one who had washed them with such great humility and love. Remember this passage many times, and bear in your soul that word which he said then: "If I, being Lord and Master, have washed your feet, how much more ought you to wash each others' feet?" (cf. John 13:5, 14).

Love those under you who may be in your house as though you were their father or mother. Work for them as if you were their slave. Bear patiently the sorrow of their conditions, the insolence of their words, and even injurious deeds. Do not be humble with those outside the house and proud with those inside. Exercise virtue with those who are nearer at hand, and practice within your house so that you know how to converse outside it.

Remember that holy woman taught by God, Saint Catherine of Siena. (I want you to read her life, not so that you desire her revelations, but so that you imitate her virtues.) Even though her parents hindered her in the path she took to serve God, she did not upset or leave them. They put her out of the cell where she performed her holy exercises and put her instead to serve in the kitchen. But because she humbled herself and obeyed, she found God in the kitchen as well as, or even better than, in her cell. Do not be overwhelmed if, at the time when you desire to pray, your parents or prelates command you to do something else. Rather, offering your desire to the Lord, do what your superiors command with great humility and calm, having confidence that when you obey those over you, you are obeying God. This is what he commands in the fourth commandment.

This does not excuse you from humbly requesting your parents to give you a place apart and some free time for your spiritual exercises. Having first asked the Lord, have confidence in your parents' goodness. At one time they might grant it, and at another time they might not. But all will be for your advantage if you dare to take it obediently and calmly as from the hand of God. Your parents will give an account to the Lord, and not just any account, for what they ask of you. You do not have to consider this, but it is fitting that they consider it. For, as Saint Ambrose says, "It is a favor of our Lord, and a very profitable one, to have a son or daughter who desires to serve the Lord in virginity, with contempt for the world and a particular call to a spiritual life."[151]

## CHAPTER 102

If you have paid attention to what I have just said, you will see that I have recommended two things. One is that you should not hold on to your own will. The other is that you should follow the will of God.

To clarify these two elements, I must tell you that it is not the vice of self–will to desire and ask specific things of God such as that he "deliver you from some spiritual ill" in which you run great risk, or that he grant you some virtue that you particularly need. Such prayer is a means, and a very good one, for doing the will of God, who commands us to depart from evil and do good. If you think about it, asking for a particular thing because of your particular need helps you to pray with greater efficacy and deeper groaning, and these are reasons for God to grant easily what is asked. Perhaps he will not grant it because of the tepidity with which the petition is usually made when something is asked in general. This teaching conforms to divine scripture, where the Lord teaches us in the Our Father to ask for things in particular. David did the same when particular necessities presented themselves to him, and the saints used to do the same when asking for themselves or for others.

We can do likewise, asking for temporal things, as we read of the blind man (and many others) who asked sight from the Lord (Mark 10:51). Temporal things are less precious, love of them is more risky, and contempt for them may be praiseworthy. Therefore, one has less liberty with the temporal than with the spiritual for allowing the heart to desire and ask for something. However, this does not mean that the petition for something temporal ceases to be good, as long as the request is made without too much anxiety and in a way that pleases the Lord.

You will probably ask me how you recognize the fulfillment of the Lord's will, in which our good lies. I answer that where there is a commandment and word of God or of his church, you have no further need to inquire but can take it for certain that such is the Lord's will. When these are not present, you must take what your superior commands as the same, as long as it is clear that the command is not against the law of God, the church, or natural reason. Saint Paul says that "the Christian must obey, not only to avoid punishment, but because of the obligation of conscience" (Rom 13:5). How much more will this be true in Christian superiors, of whom we must think that God helps them to command what is just! If all this is lacking, take as God's will the counsel given you by anyone from whom you ought to take it. Do not think that because of this you have no need of asking for the light of the Holy Spirit to ascertain how to please the Lord. Because our needs are so many and so particular, without this master, another does not suffice. "And the king will desire your beauty."

# PART SIX

# "The King Will Desire Your Beauty!"

## (CHAPS. 103–13)

## CHAPTER 103

It is amazing that there is in the creature a beauty that can attract the blessed eyes of God and be desired by him. A blessed thing it is for the soul to be enamored by the beauty of God. But there is nothing strange that one who is ugly should love one that is beautiful; nor is there any wonder that the creature loves the Creator, for so it ought to do, and besides, it receives thereby an eternal reward. But that God loves and delights in his creature calls for wonder and thanksgiving and gives reason for ineffable glory and joy. It is a great honor to be imprisoned for Jesus Christ, and Saint Paul calls himself by this most honorable title, "a prisoner of Jesus Christ" (cf. Eph 3:1), when his body is bound by chains of iron and his soul by chains of love. But what will it be for a man to hold God prisoner by love? If it is great wealth not to possess one's heart because it has been given to God, what will it be to possess God's heart as our own? For God gives his heart to those to whom he gives his love, and after giving his heart, he gives all that he is. Without doubt we belong entirely to the one to whom we give our heart. Many and great are the blessings that the infinite and divine Goodness gives to human beings, but compared with the gift of his heart, the others deserve little attention. Job says, "Lord, what is man that you should magnify him, and set your heart upon him?" (cf. Job 7:17). This passage implies that when God gives his heart, he gives himself. There is as great a difference between his giving his heart through love and his giving other things as there is between God and creatures. If we owe him thanks for his other gifts, it is because he gives them to us with love. If we must rejoice in the gifts, we should rejoice much more in having found grace and love before the most sublime eyes of God. This is our true dignity, and we can indeed glory in it. We cannot glory in our love for him, for cursed is anyone who accounts himself great and glories in his works; but we can glory that so high a King, whom the angels adore, desires in his goodness to love lowly creatures such as we are.

Consider then, daughter, if it is right "to hear and to see and to incline your ear" to God, given that the reward is that "God will desire your beauty." Indeed, even if these words of command were full of difficulty, they would become easy to fulfill in the light of such promises.

How much more is this so, seeing that what he asks of us is very small and we have the favor of his grace!

But you will probably say: How does the soul possess beauty since, of itself, it is sinful, and concerning sinners it is written that "their face is blackened more than coal" (Lam 4:8)? If our Lord searched for physical beauty, it would not be surprising that he would find it, for he is beautiful and he created all things beautiful, so that they might be some tiny trace of his ineffable beauty. Compared with his beauty, all other is mere deformity. We know that David, speaking of the spouse of this great king, says that "all her beauty lies within" (Ps 45:14), that is, in the soul. He is very right about this because the beauty of the body amounts to very little and can be found in one whose soul is very ugly. What good is it to be ugly in what is of greater value and beautiful in what is less? What good is the beauty men can see if within where God sees there is ugliness? An angel on the outside; a devil on the inside!

Not only does physical beauty not help one to be loved by God, but for the most part, it becomes the occasion of being unloved by God's love. Just as spiritual beauty imparts sound judgment and wisdom, so physical beauty often takes them away. No small war is waged between chastity, humility, and recollection on the one side, and physical beauty on the other. It would have been better for many women to have had very ugly faces, and thus be less sought after, than to have great beauty with great vanity, and thus to be overcome. For no small evil God says to such a soul, "You have lost your wisdom in your beauty" (Ezek 28:17). In another place, he says, "You have made your beauty to be abominable" (Ezek 16:25). He says these things because when bad habits are joined with corporal beauty, the beauty becomes abominable and is converted into real ugliness.

I see clearly that if those who look on beautiful things and those who are beautiful were pure in seeking God alone in his creatures, the more beautiful the creatures, the more clearly they would see them as a mirror of God's beauty. But where in our time is there anyone who does not have to fear the scripture that says that "creatures have been turned into a trap and a snare for the feet of the unwise" (Wis 14:11) who use them to offend God? They stop at creatures that were created so that we might serve God through them and ascend to him as by a ladder. Among such unwise people was Augustine for a while, and for this he afterward wept and said, "I was going along, Lord, made ugly through the beautiful creatures which you created."[152] Where is the purity of the beautiful woman who, the more beautiful she is in body, the more she guards her soul? Naturally, when we are clean, we are more careful not to get dirty than when we are not clean. Many persons do the opposite and, being ugly, they would not sin so much. They use the very cleanness as an occasion of getting dirty. Of these, scripture says, "A golden ring in a swine's snout is a woman who is fair and foolish" (Prov 11:22). Very little glory would the swine take in the gold in his snout and, however shiny it is, he would not hesitate to soil it by putting it into the filthy mire. So is the foolish woman who, without the slightest revulsion, uses her beauty for a thousand frivolities and indecencies of body and soul.

Well, then, if physical beauty does not help to keep the soul's beauty, but rather hinders it, what do you think happens in the souls of those who look upon that beauty? It would be good if such people did not have eyes to see, or feet to walk, or hands to groom themselves, or the desire to see and be seen. From one or other of these things, the resolute desire for sensual delight tends to arise, and they receive as many mortal blows to the soul as the wicked desires that they keep. And who can count these? What will these wretched men and these miserable women say when the women, who are so beautiful in appearance and so ugly in fact, lack the bodily beauty for which they have labored so much, and their bodies become as corrupt in the tomb as were their souls within their beautiful bodies? What will they say when they are thus presented, stripped of all good, before the eyes of that One whom they were unconcerned about pleasing? Let them be ashamed of their secret sins. They will then find by experience that the day threatened by God has come, and "he destroyed the names of the idols from the earth" (Zech 13:2). The vain and beautiful woman is an idol who wants to counterfeit the true God by painting herself as God did not paint her. She desires that the hearts of men be wrongly occupied with her. For this, she does all that she can, and what she cannot do, she desires to do. God will destroy these women of repute. They will then know that it is useless to be spoken of by men if they are erased from the book of God.

Concerning this kind of beauty, I warn you, friend of Christ, not even to call it to mind. Even vain women go about without much care in places where they are unseen by anyone, keeping their beauty for times when many people see them or when some high prince sees them. How much more should the spouse of Christ proceed in this way? She is awaiting the day when she will be seen by all the angels and by the Lord of men and angels. Then shall the tearful face appear more beautiful than the smiling face, and the lowly garb better than the costly, and virtue better than physical beauty.

But do not think that it is enough to preserve your own heart free from this vanity. You also have to be careful and very careful not to cause the heart of anyone who sees you to be diverted from God by the tiniest bit. Young women of this world desire, in their vanity, to appear fair to men. But the virgin who belongs to Christ should fear and flee nothing so much as the desire to look good. There can be no greater foolishness than to desire what is a danger for you and for the other. Remember what Saint Jerome says to a young woman: "Watch out that you give no occasion to anyone of evil desire, for your spouse is jealous. It is worse to be an adulteress against Christ than against one's husband." In another place he says:

> Recall that I have told you that you have become the sacrifice of God. The sacrifice gives sanctification to other things, and whoever partakes worthily in it, will be a participant in the sanctification. Well then, act so that through you, as through a divine sacrifice, other women with whom you live may be sanctified. May anyone who touches your life by seeing or hearing you feel within the power of sanctification! Desiring to look at you, may such a person be made worthy of becoming a sacrifice![153]

## CHAPTER 104

From all this you will see that such a great honor as being a spouse of Christ does not just keep going by itself without care. To the contrary, since it is the highest title that can be named, possessing it fittingly demands greater care than anything else. Do not think that you can live without care because you do not have an earthly man as husband, but realize that you are obligated to see more and more how much greater your spouse is and how many more things he demands of you. With a husband here, a wife is able to fulfill her role as long as she does not have great faults. But this is not so with the heavenly Spouse, whom you must love with all your heart and strength. Even a word or a brief time of idleness will have its penalty. This should not seem overly severe to you, because the same thing happens even here in this world where, the higher the station of the husband, the better the wife is obligated to be. Consider, if you can, the one you have taken as spouse. Or to put it better, consider the one who took you as his spouse. You will see that even if what he commanded is small, by the fact of his commanding it, there is no small commandment or small sin, as Saint Jerome says.

So that you will not hold this dignity unworthily and that the honor might not become dishonor, I want to place before you an example in which you may see yourself and from whom you might draw something. It was a young woman named Asela about whom Saint Jerome speaks:

> Nothing was more cheerful than her gravity or graver than her cheerfulness. Nothing was sweeter than her sadness or sadder than her sweetness. Her pale face was a mark of abstinence but did not show hypocrisy. Her word was silent and her silence spoke. Her walking was neither very slow nor very hurried. Her dress was constantly of the same style. Her purity was without affectation, her dress without curiosity, her adornment without adornment. Through nothing but the goodness of her life, she merited that in the city of Rome, where there is so much pomp and where being humble is taken for wretchedness, the good would speak well of her and the wicked would not dare to murmur against her.[154]

This is the model that you must consider for external things. For those within, there is none but Jesus Christ placed on the cross. To him you must conform yourself all the more because you have the name of the greater union of marriage with him.

## CHAPTER 105

Do not falter before the great sanctity that your title demands, and do not fear your state more than you rejoice in it. Hearing its great demands, do not waver but exert yourself the more. The burdens of marriage and its maintenance do not fall principally on the wife's shoulders, but she does her part by taking good care of what the husband earns, and by working as much as she can in her weakness. So do not think that the Lord took you as spouse in order to leave on your shoulders the labors of maintaining your soul, for you are not equal to that. Neither does he desire that you have the honor for being what you ought to be. May it please him that you learn to give him your heart and to respond to the inspirations that he will send, and that you do not profane by tepidity or pride or negligence or indiscreet fervor the pure water that will rain upon your soul! For the rest, your soul must repose in confidence, not in yourself, but in your spouse, who knows how, desires, and is well able to support you as long as you do not leave his house by your own will. Even in the things that I told you above that you have to do, do not hope in yourself alone, but ask the Lord to help you so that in everything you may know him as your loving father and spouse.

The state of virginity that you possess must not be taken on lightly because of some fleeting devotion or because of not finding a man to marry but as something of great importance. There has to be much advice and experience and preparation to serve Christ. One has to have entrusted himself to God with the whole heart for days and years, so as not to guard negligently what has been taken up lightly. But when virginity is assumed rightly and for the right reason, the person should be very happy, because it is a state of incorruption and fecundity. The blessed Virgin Mary, in her excellent and most pure virginity, is called Virgin of virgins, and she is the protector of virgins. She gave forth fruit without losing the flower of her purity. So virgins who are truly virgins bring forth fruit within their souls and possess integrity in their bodies. Christ, the heavenly Spouse, is not like earthly spouses, who deprive their brides of beauty and integrity, but he is the guardian of beauty and lover of purity. Saint Agnes says: "For him alone I keep my faith; to him alone I entrust myself with all devotion; loving him, I am chaste; touching him, I am pure; receiving him, I am a virgin. Children are not lacking to this wedding in which birth is painless and the fruitfulness of every day is increased."[155] Saint Agnes speaks as one experiencing the sweetness of the heavenly marriage. Confusion is the lot of the woman who is called a spouse of Christ but does not enjoy her Spouse's qualities and sweetness any more than a stranger would.

How many sorrows, how many cares and anxieties virginity avoids! Some of these necessarily come with marriage according to the flesh, while others usually arise from the husband's poor character. But the children of virginity are joy, charity, peace, and other similar things that Saint Paul enumerates (Gal 5:22). The spouse is good, peaceable, rich, wise, handsome, and, as the bride says in the Song of Songs, "he is completely desirable" (Song 5:16). Do you not think that the king does a great favor for the one whom he takes, not only as a slave or a servant, but as a bride? Does it not seem to you a good exchange to have birth without pain instead of birth with pain, to have children of rest, who bring with them gifts, pleasure, and honor, rather than children of care? Speaking to the mother of a young woman, Saint Jerome says: "I do not know why you consider it bad that your daughter refused to be the wife of a gentleman in order to be the bride of the king. Thus she made you the mother–in–law of Christ."[156]

Nothing remains, then, my daughter, except that you be happy with the vocation that the Lord in his goodness gave to you and that you take care to be what you ought to be. Fear your own weakness as much as you trust in the Lord, who will complete in you what he has begun. Thus, neither vain joy at the favor granted nor fear at your great debt will cast you down. Travel between fear and hope until fear is taken away by the perfect love of heaven, and hope is taken away when we possess present what we have awaiting here in its absence, and without fear of losing it.

## CHAPTER 106

We have strayed far from the question we were asking: From where does beauty come to the soul so that God desires it? The reason for the digression was that we did not think that this king would have such desire for physical beauty. Now let us return to our topic.

You should be aware that four things are required to make a thing completely beautiful. The first is the *fullness* of all that pertains to it. If something is lacking, it cannot be called beautiful, for example, the body lacks a hand or foot or something similar. The second requirement is *proportion* of one member with another, and, if it is an image of another thing, it has to be drawn out very much according to the model. The third is that it must have *purity of color*. The fourth is that it must be of *sufficient grandeur*. Littleness, even if well proportioned, is not an attribute of what is completely beautiful.

If we consider the sinful soul, we will not find in it even one of these qualities. There is not *fullness* because one cannot be called beautiful when faith, charity, and the gifts of the Holy Spirit (things one ought to have) are lacking. The sinful soul does not have *proportion* within itself because its senses do not obey reason and its reason does not obey God. Even more, since the soul was created in God's image, it was right that, to preserve its beauty, it would be like its model in virtues as it is in its natural being. Well, then, since God is good and the soul evil, since God is pure and it is impure, since God is meek and it is angry, and the same in other things, how can there be beauty in an image so out of conformity with its model? Then the third thing, a spiritual *light* of grace and knowledge enlivening the beauty of the soul as colors do to the body, is also lacking, for the sinful soul is walking in darkness and is "made blacker than coal," as Jeremiah says weeping (Lam 4:8). Even less does the sinful soul have the fourth quality, *grandeur*, since there is nothing smaller or meaner than being a sinner, who is nothing, and less than nothing. Therefore, since it lacks all the qualities to make it beautiful, without doubt, it will be ugly. Since all souls created in bodies that come from Adam are ordinarily sinners, it follows that all are ugly.

## CHAPTER 107

It is so difficult, or better, impossible for creatures to remove the ugliness of sin by their own strength that even all creatures together are unable to make an ugly soul beautiful. The Lord indicates this through Jeremiah, saying, "If you wash yourself with lye and with much soap, you are still stained before me" (Jer 2:22). He means that, to remove this stain, neither the "lye" of prophetic reprimands, nor the severe chastisements of the Old Law, nor even God's gentle attractions and promises are of benefit. Men were stained in the midst of punishments and consolations, threats and promises. "By the works of the Old Law, no one was justified in the eyes of God" (cf. Rom 3:20), as Saint Paul says. Therefore, there could no be beauty that God would desire because there was not justification, which is the cause of beauty.

If in the Law and sacrifices given by God, beauty could not be granted, it is clear that even less was it given in the natural law that did not have as many remedies against sin as the Law of scripture had. The beauty, then, in the souls of many who were just in terms of the natural law, as well as in terms of scripture, reached them through the shedding of the blood of the precious Lamb, Jesus Christ our Lord. As Saint John says, he "was slain from the beginning of the world" (cf. Rev 13:8). Even though he was slain on the cross "in the last days of the world," which the apostles call the time of Christ's coming, he is said to be slain "from the beginning of the world," because it was then that his death began to work pardon and grace in those that had them, receiving it as in trust to pay it afterward on the cross. God ordained that, just as a father was the head and source of sin and death for all those who came from him in the ordinary way, so there would be one through whom all those who desired would be freed from the evil in which the other had placed us, and even from the evils that we ourselves add. Saint Paul says, "Just as through the disobedience of one man, many were made sinners, so through the obedience of another man, many will be made just" (Rom 5:19). The "obedience" of Jesus Christ to his Father, obedience "to death, even to the death of the cross" (cf. Phil 2:8), does not only justify when it is imitated but also by bestowing true justice. So also the evil that Adam did to us was not only that he was an example of sin but that he made us sinners when he sinned. Saint Peter said that "there is no other name under heaven by which we can be saved, except in that of Jesus Christ" (Acts 4:12). As we have said, this applies not only to the time from which God became incarnate but from the beginning of the world, for those who were in

God's grace were so through the merits of that Lord, through faith and penance.

Even though by circumcision a child was given grace by which he was just and original sin pardoned, circumcision did not give grace. That was kept for the sacraments of the new law (cf. Gal 5:6). But circumcision was a statement of the faith then possessed that the Messiah was to come. If afterward, when grown, he lost grace through some mortal sin, he offered some animal as God commanded (cf. Lev 7:37), whose blood was shed in the Temple, not to justify, since it had no power for that, but so that the sinner might profess the faith he had in the Lord who was to come. By this faith and by the interior penitence for his sins that God inspired in him, he was made a participant in the precious blood of Christ, which was to be shed for the pardon of sins.

Not only in the Law of scripture was there a remedy for sin through faith and interior penance, as we have said, but it was also in the law of nature, even though it did not require such explicit faith in our Lord. Also there were exterior protestations of that faith inspired by the Lord, "who desires that all" be saved (1 Tim 2:4), so that even though there are diverse peoples and diverse exterior rites, the Savior might be one, "a mediator between God and men, the man Christ Jesus," as Saint Paul says (1 Tim 2:5).

## CHAPTER 108

Consider how ugly sin is and how necessary it is to flee the stain that it causes. Once received into the soul, it could not be washed away even with all the shedding of blood that God commanded to be offered in his temple. Neither was all human strength enough to do it. If the beautiful Word of God had not come to beautify us, the ugliness of sin would have endured forever. But when the Lamb without stain came, he had the power, knowledge, and will to wash away our stains. He destroyed our ugliness and gave us his beauty.

See how right it is that the Son of God, rather than the Father or the Holy Spirit, agreed to make our ugly souls beautiful by his blood. Consider that, as eternity is attributed to the Father, and Love is attributed to the Holy Spirit, so beauty is attributed to the Son of God insofar as he is God. For he is perfection without any defect and the "image of the Father" (cf. Heb 1:3), as Saint Paul says. Engendered by way of the understanding, the Son is completely like his Father, who gave him the same essence as he possesses. For this reason "whoever sees him, sees the Father," as the holy gospel says (John 14:9). Well, then, through such equal *proportion* of the Son with the Father, beauty is rightly attributed to him, since the image is drawn from its own model. *Light* is not lacking to him since he is called the Word, which is a thing engendered by and in the understanding. Saint John says, "He was the true light" (John 1:9). *Grandeur* is not lacking to him since he possesses infinite immensity.

Therefore, it was fitting that this beautiful one, through whom we were made when we did not exist, should come to make amends for us after we were lost. Clothing himself in flesh, he took the likeness of our ugliness and gave to our souls the loveliness of his beauty. Although our being punished or soothed could not take away our stain, the beautiful one being punished was of such value that, when the bitter lye of his passion fell upon his shoulders, the mild soap of his whiteness fell upon us. God says to the sinner, "Though you wash yourself with lye and cleansing herbs, you will not be clean" (Jer 2:22). But, explaining that he was to send a remedy for this stain, he says in another place, "If your sins be as scarlet, they shall be made white as snow; if they be crimson red like blood, they shall be white as white wool" (Isa 1:18).

David believed this when he said: "You shall sprinkle me with hyssop and I shall be clean; you shall wash me and I shall be made whiter than snow" (Ps 51:9). Hyssop is an herb, small and rather hot, that has the property of cleansing the lungs by which we breathe. They joined this herb with a branch of cedar and attached the herb to the stick with a scarlet cord, twice dyed. Joined together, they called this hyssop. Moistened by blood and water or, at other times, by water and ashes, they sprinkled the leper with it, or one who had touched something dead, and by that sprinkling, they were considered cleansed. David knew very well that neither the herb, nor the cedar, nor the blood of birds or animals, nor the water, nor the ashes could purify the soul, although they could represent purification. Therefore, he does not ask God to take the hyssop in hand and sprinkle him with it, but he speaks through the humanity and humility of Jesus Christ our Lord, who is called an herb because he was born from the earth of the blessed Virgin Mary, and because he was born without the work of a man, as the flower of the field is born without being plowed or sown. Therefore, scripture says, "I am a flower of the field" (Song 2:1). This herb is called small because of the lowliness that he assumed in this world, to the point of saying, "I am a worm and no man; the reproach of men and the outcast of the people" (Ps 22:7). This humiliated flesh is the remedy against our pride, so insane that it cannot be cured other than by this great humility. For it is not right that the worm exalt itself, seeing that the king of majesty is cast down.

Do not forget that the hyssop is hot because Christ, by the fire of love burning in his heart, desired to come down to cleanse us. He helped us understand that he who is exalted, abases himself. Since this is so, how right is it that one who has so much reason for lowering himself, should exalt himself? If God is humble, man must be the same. This medicinal flesh was joined to a branch of cedar when it was placed on the cross and fixed by thin woolen thread, twice dyed. Hard nails, thick and long, fastened his hands and feet to the cross, but they would have been almost useless to hold him if the thread of burning love had not attached him to the cross, and if he had not desired to hand over his life to kill our death. Consequently, it was not the nails that held him, but love. This love is doubled like scarlet that has been twice dyed, because to satisfy the honor of the Father, who was offended by sins, and by love for sinners who were lost, he suffered what he suffered.

## CHAPTER 109

The clothing that the High Priest of the law wore had to be twice–dyed scarlet cloth because the holy humanity of Christ, which is his vestment, had to be dyed in blood, shed for love of God and neighbor.

His flesh placed on the cross is the veil that God commanded Moses to make of "violet and purple and scarlet twice dyed" and of closely woven white linen, embroidered by the needle and wrought with beautiful variety (cf. Exod 26:31). His holy humanity is tinged with blood like "purple"; it is burned with fire, signified by the "scarlet cloth," as we have said; it is white as linen with chastity and innocence; and it is "closely woven" because it was not slack or loose but tightly woven under all virtuous discipline and with much labor. That it has the color of the heavens is well signified by the "violet," because it is formed by the supernatural work of the Holy Spirit, and for this reason is called heavenly. It has many other lovely qualities and virtues formed by the very subtle knowledge of the wisdom of God. He commands that this covering hang on four pillars that support it. This means that Christ was placed on the four arms of the cross, and the four Gospels place him and preach him revealed before the world.

The royal prophet David was enlightened in knowing the mysteries of Christ that were to come. Thus, when he saw himself deformed by that ugly sin by which he took the sheep and killed the shepherd, he feared the wrath of the Omnipotent, with which he was threatened by the mouth of the prophet Nathan (2 Sam 12:10). He begs God to beautify his ugliness, not with material hyssop, for as the same David says to God: "You will not be delighted with the sacrifice of animals."

But he asks to be sprinkled by the blood of Jesus Christ, who was bound to the cross by cords and bonds of love. David is confessing that even though his ugliness is great and impossible for him to remove, "he shall be made whiter than snow" (cf. Ps 51:9) by the blood that falls from the cross.

O beautiful blood of the beautiful Christ! Even though you are redder than rubies, you have the power to make us whiter than milk! Who could watch with what violence you were poured out by the executioners and with what love you were shed by the Lord himself! Lord, you willingly extended your arms and feet and let your arms and ankles be covered with blood to remedy the evil laxity of our desires and works! Your enemies exercised great power against you, but your love exercised far greater power, so that your love, not your enemies, overcame you. David calls Christ "beautiful above all the sons of men" (Ps 45:3). But he who is beautiful beyond men and angels desired to hide his beauty and to be clothed in the exterior of his body in the likeness of the ugliness of our souls. This was so that our ugliness would be absorbed in the abyss of his beauty, just as a tiny piece of hay is absorbed in a great fire. Thus he would bestow on us his beautiful image by making us like him.

## CHAPTER 110

We have already mentioned the conditions required for one to be beautiful. If we consider them, we find that they are all present in a most excellent manner in the divine Word. But he concealed and hid them all, so that, hidden in him, they might be manifest in us.

The Word of God is completely whole, perfect and full, for he lacks nothing and can lack nothing, and he removes any deficiency from everything. But look at him, so rich in the bosom of the Father, made man in the womb. See him in the arms of his Mother and through all the course of his life and death. Consider how many times in his life he was lacking food and drink. In Bethlehem he did not have a bed to lie on or a place to stay, so the Virgin placed him in a manger. Consider how many times he lacked anything to alleviate cold or heat and had nothing but what was given to him. If in life "he had nowhere to lay his head" (Matt 8:20), as he puts it, what will you say about his extreme poverty in death? There he even less had a place to lay his head. Either he had to recline on the cross and suffer extreme pain from the thorns that pierced him more, or he had to lower his head and move about, and this caused great pain. O Sacred Head, of which the bride says, "It is as the finest gold" (Song 5:11), because it is the head of God! How great the cost by which you pay what we have done against your love, by reposing in creatures, loving them and wanting to be loved by them, making a bed of repose in what we should have passed by along the way toward rest in you! Saint Paul declares the cause for Christ's deficiency and poverty, saying, "You know well, brothers, the grace that our Lord Jesus Christ earned for us, that, being rich, he became poor for our sakes, that through his poverty, we might be rich" (2 Cor 8:9). You see here completely concealed the first condition of beauty, which is to be complete in every way. So much is lacking on the earth to him who in heaven is abundance itself.

If you contemplate the second quality of the beautiful Word of God, that he is the most perfect image of the Father, equal to him and proportionate with him, you will find that, no less than with the first quality, he conceals it upon the earth. Tell me. What is the Father other than strength, knowledge, honor, beauty, goodness, joy, and other similar goods, which all together constitute infinite good? Then place aside this admirable model, glorious in itself and adored by the angels. Recall that event (that ought to pass and pass through to the innermost part of our souls) when the beautiful image of the Father, Jesus Christ our Lord, was brought forth from his meeting with Pilate. He was cruelly beaten, clothed in a purple garment, with a crown that was an object of ridicule by those who saw him and of searing pain in the one who wore it. His hands were tied with a reed in them; his eyes were full of tears and of blood that flowed from his head. His cheeks were pallid, discolored, and covered with blood, defiled by the spittle aimed at his face. In this sorrow and dishonor he was brought forth to be seen by all the people, with the words "Behold the Man" (John 19:5). This was done so that his shame might be increased at being seen by them, and that they might have compassion on him when they saw him thus and might cease tormenting one that they saw suffering so greatly. But, oh, with what evil eyes they looked upon the pains of the one who was suffering more for the perdition of these men than for his own sorrows! Instead of extinguishing the fire of their furious loathing with the water of his dishonors, it burned them more and more, as a fire of tar burns in water. They did not listen to the word Pilate spoke to them: "Behold the Man." They did not want to look upon him there, but they said that they wanted to see him on the cross.

Listen, soul redeemed by the sufferings of Christ, and let us all listen to this word—"Look at this man" or "Behold the Man"—so that we may not be far from the redemption of Jesus Christ, not knowing how to look upon his sufferings and be grateful for them. When people bring something out to show it, usually they make it attractive so that those who see it will love it. When they decide to bring something that they want feared, they surround it with weapons and with as many things as they can to make those who see it tremble. When they want to bring out some image in order to make people weep, they clothe it in mourning and put on it everything that might incite to sadness. Well, tell me what Pilate's intent was in bringing Christ forth to be seen by the people? Certainly, it was not to make them love or fear him. Therefore, he did not make him beautiful; nor did he surround him with weapons and warriors. He brought him forth in order to placate the cruel hearts of his Jewish enemies at the sight of the redeemer, not through love, because Pilate knew well that they deeply despised him. But he desired to placate them by the power of his torments and at the personal cost to his delicate body. Pilate adorned Christ with the great adornment of many awful torments to arouse compassion in the hearts of those who saw him, however great the evil they wished him. So it is to be believed that he brought him forth as beaten and humiliated as possible. He looked Christ over in his disfigurement much as they look over a bride in her adornment. Pilate did this to placate the wrath of those who hated Christ, because he had not been able to placate them by other means that he had tried. Then, tell me. If the manner of Christ's coming forth was enough to extinguish the fire of loathing in the hearts of those who despised him, why would the sight of him and his coming forth not enkindle the fire of love in the hearts of anyone who knows him as God and confesses him as Redeemer?

A long time before this happened, the prophet Isaiah had seen this event, and, contemplating the Lord, he said these words:

> He has no loveliness or beauty. We looked at him, and his appearance did not attract us. We wished him despised and the most abject of men, a man of sorrows who is acquainted with infirmity. His countenance was as hidden and despised, whereupon we esteemed him not. Surely he bore our infirmities and suffered our sorrows, and we esteemed him as a leper and one struck by God and afflicted. (Isa 53:2–4)

If you consider these words of Isaiah one by one, you will see how hidden was Christ's beauty on the day when he suffered to make us beautiful. Speaking to Christ, the bride in the Canticle says: "Behold, you are beautiful and fair, my Beloved" (Song 1:15). But in this passage Isaiah says that "he has no loveliness or beauty" and that the One on whose face the angels gaze and desire to keep looking (1 Pet 1:12) has no "appearance to attract us." The One who, by the Father's command, was "adored by all the angels" (Heb 1:6) when he entered "into this world," now, when he is departing from the world, is despised by the most despicable men.

David says that Christ "is exalted over all the works of God's hands" (Ps 8:7). But Isaiah says that "he is the most abject of all men." If he was being compared with good men, the scorn would not be as great. But what will you say when he is compared with Barabbas, a murderer, agitator, and thief, who appears better to them than Christ, the giver of life and the one who makes peace between the Father and the world? What will you say when Christ is so far from taking what is not his that David says that "he paid for what he did not take"? (Ps 69:5).

Christ had no reason for bearing sorrow, for its cause is the sin that abounded in the world. But here Isaiah calls him "a man of sorrows," meaning full of sorrows. Even though he did not know evil delights by experience, he is a man who knows very severe sufferings from experience, and in such abundance that he would say by the mouth of David: "My soul is very full of pain" (Ps 88: 4).

Christ is called light because, by his admirable words and deeds, he cheered the world and drew it out of darkness. But Isaiah says that this light "had his countenance as hidden." If he is only seen by the eyes of the body, I do not know who could recognize him by his face, because of the way it had been treated. There is little to marvel at in this. The ever blessed Virgin (who on that day was the most pitiable of women) had brought him forth and wrapped him in swaddling clothes; she gazed on his face as on a shining mirror. But with all this, I think that, if she was present at this event of such great sorrow, she looked and looked again with great attention at the tears of those eyes and the sorrow of his heart, to see if he was her most blessed Son, who had been of such different aspect and manner when she had known him before.

If those who were looking at him believed that all this was happening to the Lord, not because he owed it, but because he loved us who did owe it, it would be a relief to Christ in his pain. But what shall we say to Isaiah's statement that they took him "as wounded by God and afflicted"? They thought that God afflicted him thus for his own sins, and that he merited that and much more. Therefore, they demanded that he be placed on the cross. They diverted their eyes from seeing him outwardly because they were disgusted with him as with a leper, and they turned from him in their hearts because they held him to be evil and worthy of what he was suffering and much more. It was a thing to look at and weep over. But they looked at him and spat on him. If they did not look at him, they were disgusted with him as with something extremely ugly. What they were saying about him were insults that hurt as did the sufferings. In all, they were saying that he merited nothing but that they should put him on the cross.

## CHAPTER 111

Who will not marvel and praise God for his infinite knowledge? In such an extraordinary way he decided to redeem the lost world by drawing the greatest goods from the greatest iniquities that men committed. What worse thing has been done or will be done in the world than to dishonor, torment, and crucify the Son of God? But from what else did such great benefit come to the world than from this blessed passion?

When he was adorning this Spouse with the finery of great sorrows, Pilate thought that he was adorning him only for the eyes of that people, but he adorned him to be seen by the entire world. Though Pilate did not know it, he was serving what God had promised so long before when he said: "All men will see the salvation of God" (Luke 3:6). Jesus Christ is this salvation, the one to whom the Father said: "I hold it a little thing that you raise up the tribes of Jacob to serve me, and that you convert to me the survivors of Israel. I gave you as a light of the Gentiles, so that you might be my salvation to the farthest part of the earth" (Isa 49:6). Jesus Christ preached in person, only "to the sheep of the house of Israel that had been lost" (Matt 15:24). But afterward, his holy apostles began to preach among the same people of Israel. They did not convert all of the Jews but only some of them who, in the passage from Isaiah, are called "the remnant." But "the salvation from the Father," which is Jesus Christ, did not stop among the Jewish people but went forth when it was preached by the apostles in the world. The preaching of the name of Christ is now increasing in more distant lands so that he may be the light, not only of the Jews who believed in him when he preached to them in his own person, but also of the Gentiles, who were in the blindness of idolatry very far from God.

Then is fulfilled what the holy man Simeon said in his swan song before his death: "Now you dismiss your servant, O Lord, in peace according to your promise. Because my eyes have seen your salvation, which you prepared before the face of all peoples, a light to the revelation of the Gentiles, and glory for your people Israel" (cf. Luke 2:29–32). Let us consider that Christ was placed by Pilate's own hand to be seen by the people in his own house, and afterward in the height of the cross on Mount Calvary. It is clear that there were a great number of people that had come to the Passover of every state and lineage, both native born and foreigners, but it was not then that Christ was placed "before the face of all peoples, to be seen by them," as Simeon says in his canticle. Therefore, Christ is placed "before all the nations and is seen by them" when he is preached in the world by the apostles and their successors. Of them, David says, "Their sound has gone forth into all the earth and their words unto the ends of the world" (Ps 19:5). Thus preached, Christ is "light," then and now, "for the Gentiles" who desire to believe in him. He is also "the glory of the Jews" who also desire to believe in him, as Saint Paul notes when he says: "From them, Christ comes, according to the flesh, he who is over all things, God blessed for all ages" (Rom 9:5).

Let us consider, then, another way in which God ordained things differently than Pilate was thinking. Pilate thought that he was only placing Christ before the face of the people there when he said, "Look at this man." And when the people did not want Christ released but demanded his crucifixion, Pilate thought that Christ would be seen no more by anyone. But because the Father saw that it was not right that so few and such wicked eyes should look upon such a spectacle as that of his only–begotten Son, "the image of his beauty," and that he should not be presented before such hard hearts, he arranged to grant the Son another and greater voice that would sound in the world through many very holy heralds who would say, "Look at this man." The voice of Pilate by which Christ was sentenced to death was only one, and it was puny, wicked, and fearful. Moreover, Pilate did not merit being the herald of this word, "Look at this man." Therefore, God commanded others to be heralds, men so fearless that they did not fear, nor do they fear, to die rather than to leave out a single point of the preaching and confession of the truth and the glory of Christ. Pilate was unclean, for he was an infidel and a sinner. But concerning the heralds of this word, "Behold the Man," Isaiah had prophesied: "How beautiful upon the mountains are the feet of those who preach good news of peace and riches and who say 'your God shall reign, O Zion'" (Isa 52:7). The "God of Zion" is Jesus Christ, and in his person David says, "I am appointed king by the hand of God over Zion, his holy mountain, preaching his commandment" (Ps 2:6–7). This king "who preaches the commandment of the Father," that is to say, the word of the holy gospel, began to reign in Zion when he was received as the king of Israel in the Temple on Mount Zion on Palm Sunday. To show that this kingdom had to be of spiritual things, it is said in David that "he was appointed king over Mount Zion," which is the mountain where the Temple was, in which divine worship was offered to God. Afterward, when this same Lord sent the Holy Spirit on those who belonged to him, and he was preached publicly in the midst of Jerusalem and in the ears of the priests and Pharisees, then his kingdom was growing. When "about three thousand men" were converted by the first sermon of Saint Peter (Acts 2:41), his kingdom was growing. When more people were converted, "the apostles were preaching to Zion: your God shall reign," as someone says. Even though this Lord is known to few, yet his kingdom always keeps growing until, at the end of the world, he reigns over all men, rewarding the good with mercy and punishing the wicked with a rod of iron (cf. Ps 2:9), that is, with rigorous justice. This is the voice of the preachers of Christ who say, "Your God shall reign."

Since sin reigns in the heart of an impure man, Christ does not reign. It is not right that anyone who does not allow Christ to reign in his heart should preach Christ's reign to others. Therefore, Isaiah says, "Beautiful are the feet of those who preach peace." By "the feet" is understood the desires of the soul, which have to be "beautiful." For this reason Christ does not want the feet of the preachers to be covered above with shoes, because God makes public their beauty as an example to many. But let the one who has clean feet take care and not think that he has them clean except by the grace of the one who, on Holy Thursday, washed the feet of his disciples with material water, and washes the souls of all those washed with his blessed blood.

It was not right that such a pure king as Christ should have been announced by a mouth as unclean as Pilate's. Nor was it right that, for a spectacle in which so many and such great marvels were to be seen (as was Christ when he came forth to be seen by that people), there should be only one herald, who would make so little sound. Pilate planned that there would not be any memory of Christ or anyone who would have compassion on him, but God ordained that, in place of the few who spat on him, there were, are, and will be many who adore him with reverence. Instead of those who were disgusted at the sight of him and did not want to look at him, there are many more who return to look on that most blessed face as in a shining mirror, even as Christ is placed on the cross. Instead of those who thought that he was suffering what he deserved, there are many who confess that he did no evil that he should suffer, but rather that they sinned, and he suffered out of love for them. If the cruelty of those men was so great that they had no compassion on him but demanded that he should die on the cross,

God wills that there be many who desire to die for Christ, and these say with their whole heart:

> Wounds you have, Friend,
> And they cause you pain!
> I would suffer them for you!

Let Pilate not think that he adorned Christ to no purpose, even though he was unable to move those who were there to compassion for him. Many remember these sufferings of Christ with such great compassion for him that they are beaten, and crowned, and "crucified" in heart "with him," as says Saint Paul about himself and many others (cf. Gal 2:19).

## CHAPTER 112

It is entirely fitting, my daughter, that these very just motives and lively examples move you to the point where, having left behind all tepidity, you fix in your heart with profound love the one who, for your sake and with great suffering, was fixed upon the cross. Do not be one of those who heard that voice in vain, but rather be one for whom hearing it was the cause of his salvation. Do not be one of those who did not know how to esteem the one who was present, but be one of whom Isaiah speaks: "We desired to see him" (Isa 53:2). Many prophets and kings have longed to see the face and hear the voice of Christ our Lord (cf. Luke 10:24).

Look then, O daughter, at Christ, this man who is announced by his unworthy herald. Look at this man so that you may hear his words, because he is the Teacher whom the Father gave us. Look at this man so that you might imitate his life, because there is no other path of salvation except him. Look at this man so that you might have compassion on him because he was such that seeing him was enough to move to compassion even those who wished him harm. Look at this man so that you might weep because we by our sins put him where he is. Look at this man so that you may love him, for he has suffered so much for us. Look at this man so that you may become beautiful, for in him you will find all the colors of beauty that you desire: bright red from the blows they had recently given him; blue for those they gave him the night before; yellow from the abstinence of his whole life and from the afflictions of the past night; white from their spitting in his face; black from the blows with which they bruised his sacred face. His cheeks were swollen and colored with as many colors as the executioners could paint on them, according to what is prophesied by Isaiah: "I have given my cheeks to those who plucked them and my body to those who wounded it" (Isa 50:6). What shades of color, what clean water, what a pure white, what a bright red you will find here to make yourself beautiful, if you do not leave them by your negligence! Look at this man, my daughter, for whoever does not look at him shall not escape death. "As Moses lifted up the serpent on a staff in the desert," so that the wounded who looked upon it might live, and anyone who did not look upon it might die, so whoever does not look with faith at Christ hanging on the wood of the cross, shall die forever (cf. Num 21:9; John 3:14–15).

I told you above that we have to pray to the Father, saying, "Look, O Lord, on the face of your Christ" (Ps 84:10). So also the eternal Father commands us saying: "Look, O man, upon the face of your Christ. If you want me to look at his face in order to pardon you through him, then you look at his face in order to ask pardon through him." In the face of Christ, our mediator, the Father's gaze and ours come together. The rays of our faith and love and the rays of God's pardon and grace come to rest on his face.

Christ is called the Christ of the Father because the Father engendered him and gave him what he has; he is called our Christ because he offered himself for us, imparting to us all his merits. "Behold," then, "the face of your Christ," believing in him, trusting in him, loving him, and all others for his sake. "Behold the face of your Christ," thinking about him and comparing your life with his, so that in him, as in a mirror, you may see your faults and how far you are from him. Thus, recognizing the faults that spoil your beauty, you may use the blood and tears streaming down his beautiful face to wash away your blemishes and become beautiful.

Just as the Jews averted their eyes from Christ when they saw him mistreated, so Christ turns his eyes from the wicked soul, seeing it full of leprosy. But after it has been made beautiful by the grace he won through his sufferings, he places his eyes upon it and says: "How beautiful you are, my friend, how beautiful you are. Your eyes are doves' eyes, besides what is hid within" (Song 4:1). Twice he uses the word *beautiful* because she has to be beautiful and just in body and in soul: inwardly by desires, and outwardly by deeds. Because what is within is more important than that which is outward, he says "besides what is hid within." Because, as Saint Augustine says, the soul's beauty consists in loving God, he says "your eyes are doves' eyes." This refers to the simple and loving intention that looks only to what pleases God without any mixture of self–interest.[157]

Look, then, at Christ, so that Christ may look at you. Just as you must not think that he has done anything to merit taking upon himself an image without beauty, do not think that you have merited the beauty he has given you. Through grace and not by obligation, he clothed himself in our deformity; through grace and not by obligation, he clothed us in beauty. To those who think that their beauty comes from within themselves, God says through Ezekiel: "You were perfect through my beauty which I had put upon you; but trusting in your beauty, you played the harlot in your name, and you have prostituted yourself with every passerby, to be his" (Ezek 16:14–15).

God says this because when a soul attributes to itself the beauty of justice that God gave her, it is like "playing the harlot with herself," for she desires to rejoice over herself, in herself, and not in God, her true Spouse, from whom her beautiful being comes to her. She desires to be glorified in her own name (which is "to play the harlot in her name"), rather than to glory in God, who has given her all she has. Therefore, rightly does God take from her the beauty that he had bestowed on her since she wants to exalt herself with it. Since this vain and evil pleasure taken in oneself is pride, the beginning of all evil, therefore he says: "You have prostituted yourself with every passerby." For pride, vainly relying on the self as support, is carried off by every wind and made captive by any sin that passes by. This is completely reasonable, because pride does not want to be humbled by taking God as its support.

Therefore, behold this man in himself, and behold him within you. Behold him in himself so that you may see who you are; behold him in yourself in order to see who he is. The insults and sorrows you see in him are yours, for you merited them; the good within you belongs to him, for it was given to you without any merit on your part.

## CHAPTER 113

If you know how to profit from what has been said, you will employ all your attention in looking with spiritual eyes at this Lord, and you will find this seeing more advantageous than seeing him only with the eyes of flesh and blood. To the eyes of flesh Christ appeared deformed, but to those of faith, he appeared very beautiful. To the eyes of the body, Isaiah says, "his face was as though hidden" (cf. Isa 64:7). But to the eyes of faith, nothing is hidden. They are like the eyes of a lynx that can see, as it were, through walls. The eyes of faith pass through exterior appearances and enter into the interior. There they find divine strength under the appearance of human weakness, and under the appearance of deformity and disdain, they find beauty with honor. Speaking in the person of those who see only with the eyes of the body, Isaiah said, "We saw him and he had no beauty" (cf. Isa 53:2). But you, daughter, take up the light of faith and look more deeply within, and see how this one, who comes forth in the likeness of a sinner, is just and justifies sinners; he who dies is innocent as a lamb; he whose face is discolored is very beautiful in himself, and looks as he does, so that he might make the deformed beautiful. The more the spouse suffers and abases himself for the bride, the more she ought to exalt him. The more he comes, wounded and covered with sweat and blood for love of her, the more beautiful he appears as she looks upon the love with which he bore his afflictions for her. Clearly, if we see why Christ took upon himself this deformity, he will appear more beautiful, even while he is the more deformed.

Tell me. If the first condition of beauty was hidden when, though he was rich in all things, he abased himself to the point of lacking many things, what other reason did he have than that no good should be lacking to us? If he became unlike the image of his beautiful Father, it was only because the Father decided not to bestow beauty on us unless his Son took on our deformity. If the third condition of beauty, light or color, was hidden when that sacred face was darkened and drained of color, and those shining eyes were dulled as he was dying and then dead, what other reason was there except to give light and living color to our darkness? He prefigured this when from his saliva and the earth, signifying his divinity and his humanity, he made a paste, signifying his passion. Through his lowliness the blind man, representing the human race, received his sight. If the fourth condition of beauty, which is to be great, was hidden when he became man and the lowest of men, why did he do this, if not to be conformed to the lowly and to make his greatness theirs? This is in accord with what was prefigured in the great Elisha, who, in order to raise the young boy who was small, contracted himself and made himself the boy's size and thus gave him life (cf. 2 Kgs 4:34).

If, as Saint Augustine says, when we love God, we become beautiful, it is clear that in the work of greater love, we are more beautiful.[158] Where did Jesus Christ demonstrate his great love for his Father more clearly than in his suffering for his Father's honor? As he said, "That the world may know that I love the Father, arise, let us go hence" (John 14:31). But where was he going? Clearly, it was to suffer. So, the greater the work, the more beautiful it is, for the good is beautiful and evil is ugly. From this, we see clearly that inasmuch as Christ suffered more, it was a greater work. Therefore, the more lowly and deformed he became, the more beautiful he is to the eyes of anyone who knows that he suffered voluntarily for the honor of the Father and for our benefit. These are the eyes with which you must look at this man so that he may always appear beautiful to you, which he is. Also let Pilate (there in hell where he is) know that Christians look at Christ with the eyes given by God, and the more deformed Pilate tried to make him, the more beautiful Christ appears to them.

Now hear how Saint Augustine expresses all this:

Let us love Christ. But if we find anything deformed in him, let us not love him (even though he found many deformities in us and yet loved us). But if we find anything ugly in him, let us not love him. For, it is said of him when he was clothed in flesh, "we saw him and he had no beauty." But if you consider his mercy in becoming man, he will also seem beautiful to you. For what Isaiah said, "we saw him and he had no beauty," he said in the person of the Jews. Why did they see him without beauty? The answer is that they did not look at him with understanding. But to those who understand "the Word made man," Christ appears a great beauty. So said one of the friends of the Bridegroom: "I glory in nothing but in the cross of Jesus Christ our Lord" (Gal 6:14). Does it seem a little thing to you, St. Paul, not to be ashamed of the dishonors of Christ, but even to honor them? Why did Christ not have beauty? It was because "Christ crucified is a stumbling block for the Jews and foolishness for the Gentiles" (1 Cor 1:23). But why did Christ have beauty on the cross? The answer is that the things of God which appear foolishness are more full of wisdom than all human wisdom, and the things of God that appear weak, are stronger than the greatest human strength (cf. 1 Cor 1:25). Since this is so, let Christ, your Spouse, appear beautiful to you, since God is beautiful, and Christ is the Word of the Father. He was beautiful also in the womb of his mother where, without losing his Divinity, he took on humanity. The Word was beautiful when he was born an infant because even though he was an infant without speech when he nursed at the breast and was carried in his mother's arms, the heavens spoke his praises and the angels sang them. The star brought the Wise Kings who adored him in the manger where he was placed like food for gentle and quiet animals (cf. Lk 2:1–20; Mt 2:1–12). Beautiful is Christ in heaven and on earth; beautiful in the womb of his mother and in her arms; beautiful in his miracles and in his scourges; beautiful in inviting us to life and in despising death; beautiful in giving forth his soul when he died and in taking it up again in his resurrection; beautiful on the cross, in the sepulcher, in heaven and in the understanding. The highest and truest beauty is justice, and you will not see anyone beautiful if you do not find him just. And since Christ is completely just, he is also completely beautiful.[159]

It is certain that if you looked upon Christ with these eyes, he would not seem deformed to you, as he did to those carnal men who despised him in his passion. Rather, he will seem to you as he did to the holy apostles, who beheld him on Mount Tabor with "his face resplendent like the sun and his clothing white as snow" (Matt 17:2), so white that, as Saint Mark says, "no fuller on earth would be able to make them so white" (Mark 9:2). This refers to us, who are called the clothing of Christ because we surround him and are clothed in the faith, love, and praise we have for him. We are so whitened by him that no one on earth would be able to impart to us the beauty of grace and justice that he gave us (cf. Isa 49:18; Eph 2:10). Let Christ appear to you like the sun, and the souls redeemed by him, white as snow. I am speaking of those souls who confess and abhor with sorrow their own deformity and beg to be made beautiful and washed in the bath of the Savior's blood. They come out of this bath so beautiful, just, and rich with grace and with the gifts they receive through Christ, that they are able to enamor the very eyes of God. Thus, to him may be sung with great truth and joy these words: "The king will desire your beauty" (Ps 45:12).

# NOTES

## INTRODUCTION

1. Some authorities, following Luís de Granada, give 1500 as the year of Avila's birth. The date 1499 is based on the records of the Inquisition. For fuller discussion of this and other biographical information, see *OC* I, 15–22.

2. "Nowadays we know too well that the stream of history flows on relentlessly and there is never a barrier across it." Steven Runciman applies this principle to the fall of Constantinople in 1453, but it applies with equal validity to just about any turning point in history. It certainly applies to the situation of the church in Spain and in Europe during the sixteenth century, that "best of times and worst of times," which was in the making long before it dawned and had such tremendous effects long after it passed. See Steven Runciman, *The Fall of Constantinople: 1453* (Cambridge: Univ. of Cambridge Press, 1965), xi.

3. Hubert Jedin, "Catholic Reformation or Counter–Reformation?" in *The Counter–Reformation*, edited by David M. Luebke, 21–45 (London: Blackwell, 1999).

4. *OC* I, 5–14.

5. Fray Luís de Granada, *Vida del padre maestro Juan de Avila y las partes que ha de tener un predicador del evangelio* (Madrid: Edibesa, 2000).

6. Avila is the surname of John of Avila, not his place of origin.

7. Granada, *Vida*, 32.

8. For a critical presentation of information on the early life of John of Avila, see the biographical introduction in *OC* I, 15–22.

9. For further discussion of attitudes toward Jewish converts and the expulsion of unconverted Jews, see Tarsicio de Azcona, *Isabel la Católica: Estudio crítico de su vida y su reinado* (Madrid: BAC, 1964), 367–77, 639–53. In English, William Thomas Walsh treats the topic critically in his biography *Isabella of Spain: The Last Crusader,* first published in 1930 and later reprinted (Rockford, IL: TAN Books, 1987), 342–71. See also Henry Kamen, *The Spanish Inquisition: A Historical Revision* (New Haven, CT: Yale Univ. Press, 1998), 8–27.

10. Kamen, *Inquisition*, 28.

11. *OC* I, 40–41.

12. Perhaps the best expression of the Master's position on the question of the entrance of men of Jewish ancestry into the Jesuits is a letter of

317

two of his disciples, written under Father Avila's influence. Upon hearing that their acceptance into the Society was delayed because of the Jewish ancestry of one of them, they wrote to the Jesuit provincial, voicing their dismay at hearing that an attitude so contrary to the gospel of Christ as racial discrimination existed within the Society where they thought that only the spirit of Christ reigned (*OC* I, 140–43).

13. M. B. Murphy, "University of Salamanca," *New Catholic Encyclopedia* 12, 610–12; *Britannica, Micropaedia* 10, 347. Vitoria was at Salamanca after Avila's school days, but his presence shows the university's continued interest in questions arising from the discovery of the New World. During his twenty years at Salamanca (1526–46), Vitoria opened each school year with a lecture on world problems, especially those arising from the discovery. Notes from twelve of these lectures were published and, on the basis of these, Vitoria is considered the founder of international law. It is interesting to note that one of the questions under discussion was the rights of the native Indians in the New World. Meanwhile, at home, Spain was dealing with problems of discrimination against Christians on the basis of race.

14. Jaime Contreras, "Alcalá: la Universidad que formó a San Juan de Avila," *ACI* (Madrid: CEE, 2000), 941–56.

15. The text of the dedicatory prologue to the Polyglot Bible is found in John Olin, *Catholic Reform from Cardinal Ximenes to the Council of Trent, 1495–1563* (New York: Fordham Univ. Press, 1990), 61–64.

16. José Luís Abellán, *El Erasmismo español* (Madrid: Espasa–Calpe, S.A, 1982), 36. For a general treatment of the thought of Erasmus, see Richard G. Villoslada, "Erasme," *Dictionnaire de spiritualité ascétique et mystique: doctrine et histoire*, vol. 4, part 1 (Paris: Beauchesne, 1960), cols. 925–36.

17. *OC [1970]*, vol. 5, letters 5 and 225.

18. In the prologue of *AF*, Avila mentions that his only other published work was a summary of the Ten Commandments meant to be sung. The use of song as a means of learning catechism was a method used by Father Contreras and adopted by the Master. See *OC* II, 753–57.

19. We owe to Father Granada the account of Father Avila's return to the pulpit of the Church of the Savior in Seville, an event transformed into a festival by disciples of the Master. Father Granada also tells of Father Avila's later assessment of his days in prison (Granada, *Vida*, 118).

20. *OC [1970]*, vol. 5, letter 58.

21. *OC [1970]*, vol. 5, letters 5 and 25.

22. Sebastián de Escabias, SJ, *Casos notables de la ciudad de Córdoba (1618?)* (Madrid: Sociedad de Bibliófilos Españoles, 1940), 7.

23. John C. Olin, *The Catholic Reformation: Savonarola to Ignatius Loyola* (New York: Fordham Univ. Press, 1992), 198–208.

24. *OC* I, 156–57.

25. Though certainly Master Avila's failing health was a factor in his decision not to enter the Jesuits, he was also displeased by their concern

over purity of blood, which Avila considered contrary to the gospel. See *OC* I, 150–53.

26. Father Nadal, SJ, reports these words of Avila in a letter to Ignatius dated March 15, 1554. See *OC* I, 150.

27. Granada, *Vida*, 12–13.

28. Ibid., 61.

29. *OC* I, 258ff.

30. *OC* I, 266ff.

31. *Tratado sobre el sacerdocio*, *OC* I, 907–46.

32. *Tratado del amor de Dios*, *OC* I, 949.

33. *OC* II, 10–13.

34. *OC* I, 169.

35. *OC* I, 172–73.

36. *OC* I, 174–77.

37. *OC* I, 178–85.

38. This testimony was given during the process of beatification held at Jaén (*OC* I, 186). Such handwritten notes would have been invaluable for the insight they would have given into the intellectual development of John of Avila.

39. *OC* I, 192–93.

40. *OC* I, 186–93.

41. The material in this section is based on an unpublished manuscript of Francisco Martín Hernández, in which he compares the two editions of the *AF* with regard to their doctrinal content. A detailed discussion of the question is found in *OC* I, 382–404.

42. Jerome, *Letter* 22. This letter contains Jerome's vision of his judgment, where he is called a follower of Cicero rather than of Christ.

43. Granada, *Vida*, 146.

## *AUDI, FILIA:* LISTEN, O DAUGHTER

44. Sancha Carrillo had given up a life at court to live a consecrated life in the house of her parents under the direction of Master Avila. At her request, he began writing the *AF.*

45. In this case we give the numbering found in the Vulgate, which was the one used by Avila, and follow it by the numbering found in contemporary versions. In subsequent references we will use the numbering of the psalms found in contemporary versions. Translations of biblical texts will be made directly from the Spanish text as given by Avila who, at times, seems to quote from memory and, at times, to adapt the scriptural text to his context. Since Avila translated from the Latin Vulgate, our translations of biblical passages into English will be based on the English translation of the Vulgate found in the Rheims–Douay–Challoner version.

46. The 1556 edition of *AF* was put on the Index in 1559. Avila had intended to revise his work in light of the decrees of the Council of Trent

on justification, but it was published without his permission and without the modifications he intended.

**PART ONE**

47. Psalm 45 is a wedding song. The idea of the soul's drawing Christ to love her is to be understood as the bride's preparation for the wedding so that the king will desire her beauty and, as it were, "fall in love" with her. Part Six of *AF* will echo and complete this introductory allusion to an underlying theme of the entire work.

48. Bernard of Clairvaux, *Sermon 3 on Christmas Day*; PL 183, 22. Translations of the fathers are made from the text given by Avila.

49. Augustine, *City of God*, 1, 5; PL 41, 154.

50. Augustine, *Sermon*, 4, 2; PL 38, 815.

51. Avila, as most others of his day, considered Paul to be the author of Hebrews.

52. John Chrysostom, *Homilies on Matthew*, 40f.; PG 57, 444.

53. The saying that Avila attributes to Jerome is found almost exactly in Gregory the Great, *Letter*, 122; PL 77, 1054.

54. Ibid.

55. Augustine, *On the Psalms*, 46, 7; 125, 6; PL 36, 519.

56. Augustine, *Sermon*, 293, 2; PL 39, 2302.

57. Jerome, *Letter*, 100, 5; PL 22, 817.

58. Jerome, *Life of Hilarion*, 5; PL 23, 32.

59. Jerome, *Letter*, 22, 11; PL 400–401.

60. Ibid., 79, 507; PL 22, 731.

61. Ibid., 22, 7; PL 22, 398.

62. Ibid., 125, 11–12; PL 22, 1078–79.

63. Ibid., 15; PL 22, 1080–01.

64. Ibid., 117, 6; PL 22, 957.

65. Gregory the Great reports this quotation of Augustine (see *Letter*, 60; PL 77, 997).

66. Bernard, *Homily on the Virgin Mother*, 3, 9; PL 183, 75.

67. Cf. Jerome, *Letter*, 22, 5; PL 22, 397.

68. Ibid., 108, 13; 130, 8; PL 22, 877, 1114.

69. Ibid., 22, 16; PL 22, 403, 411.

70. Augustine, *Sermon*, 137; PL 38, 759.

71. Cf. Jerome, *Letter*, 43, 39; PL 478–79.

72. Augustine, *The Good of Widowhood*, 22, 27; PL 40, 448.

73. Ambrose, *Exposition of the Gospel of Luke*, 1, 2, 1; PL 15, 1633.

74. Gregory the Great, *Exposition of the Book of Job*, 1, 6; PL 75, 733.

75. Augustine, *Confessions*, 1, 9, 2; PL 32, 763.

76. Augustine, *City of God*, 1, 14; PL 41, 422.

77. Ibid.

78. Augustine, *Sermon*, 99; PL 38, 598.

79. Basil the Great, *Homily on Ps. 37:1*; MG 30, 82.

80. Jerome, *Letter*, 22, 7; PL 22, 398.
81. Augustine, *On the Psalms*, 90, 9; PL 37, 1168.
82. Augustine, *Deeds of Pelagius*, 30, 55; PL 44, 351.
83. Augustine, *On the Psalms*, 36, 4; PL 36, 366.
84. Bernard, *Sermon 2 on the Feast of All Saints*, 3; PL 183, 462.
85. Psalms 120–34 are called Songs of Ascent and were used by pilgrims to the Temple in Jerusalem. The Levites sang one psalm on each step as they ascended nearer to the divine Presence. Avila uses this figure to speak of the person putting his foot on the first step toward perfect union with God and praying in the words of the first two verses of the first of the Songs of Ascent, Psalm 120:1–2. For the fifteen steps, see the description of the ideal temple in Ezekiel 40:20–22, 28–31; cf. Josephus, *The Jewish Wars*, V, 5. See also the apocryphal Gospel of the Nativity of Mary in Ante–Nicene Fathers VIII, 6: "And when the circle of three years had rolled round, and the time of her weaning was fulfilled, they brought the virgin to the temple of the Lord with offerings. Now there were round the temple, according to the fifteen Psalms of Degrees, fifteen steps going up; for, on account of the temple having been built on a mountain, the altar of burnt–offering, which stood outside, could not be reached except by steps. On one of these, then, her parents placed the little girl, the Blessed Virgin Mary....The virgin of the Lord went up all the steps, one after the other, without the help of any one leading her or lifting her."
86. Athanasius, *Life of Antony*, 20, 47; PL 73, 146.
87. Augustine, *Sermon*, 158, 2; PL 38, 865.
88. Augustine, *Correction and Grace*, 9, 24; PL 44, 930.
89. Bernard, *Letter to the Brothers of Monte Dei*, 1, 1; PL 184, 315, 382.
90. Augustine, *On the Psalms*, 34; PL 30, 310.
91. Athanasius, *Life of Antony*, 13; PL 73, 134.
92. Ibid., 9; PL 73, 132.
93. Augustine, *Soliloquies*, 1, 2; PL 32, 885.
94. Gregory, *Letter*, 1, 1; PL 76, 1078.
95. The Spanish *credulitas* as used here does not have the negative connotation of the English word *credulity*; it designates something weaker than faith but not false faith.
96. Jerome, *Letter*, 76, 2; PL 22, 689.
97. Bernard, *On the Canticle of Canticles*, 15, 16; PL 183, 847.
98. Jerome, *Letter*, 22, 7; PL 22, 398.
99. Augustine, *Sermon*, 37, 20, 30; PL 38, 235.
100. Augustine, *City of God*, 1, 22, 5; PL 41, 756–57.
101. The reference is to Richard of Saint Victor, *De Trinitate*, 1.1.2.

**PART TWO**
102. Jerome, *Letter* 15, 2; PL 22, 355.
103. Athanasius, *On the Incarnation*, 57; PG 25, 195–98.

104. "On Distinguishing True from False Revelations," in *Jean Gerson: Early Works*, trans. Brian Patrick McGuire, Classics of Western Spirituality (New York: Paulist Press, 1998), 336–37. Gerson (1363–1429) lived at the time of the Great Schism, when there were various claimants to the papacy.

105. Avila is here referring to the *alumbrados* or "enlightened ones," who considered themselves so completely abandoned to God that they had arrived at a state of perfection in which they could not commit sin, even if they acted against the commandments. See Marcelino Melendez Pelayo, *Historia de los heterodoxos españoles* (Madrid: BAC, 1987), 2:145–49.

106. Augustine, *On the Psalms* 14, 4; PL 37, 1540.

107. Augustine, *Confessions*, 1, 10, 35; PL 32, 803.

108. Bonaventure, *The Garden of Paradise* 7.

109. Augustine, *Deeds of Pelagius*, 30, 55; PL 44, 351.

110. Gregory the Great, *Moralia*, 1, 34; PL 76, 750.

111. Gregory the Great, *Dialogue*, IV, 1, 1; PL 77, 156.

112. Bernard, *Treatise on the Degrees of Pride*, 10–20; PL 182, 958–72.

113. John Gerson, *On the Distinction of True from False Visions*, Opera (Paris, 1606), 1:580–81.

114. Augustine, *On Christian Doctrine*, Prologue 6, 7; PL 34, 17–18.

115. John Climacus, *Ladder of Paradise*, 23; PG 88, 970. Jerome, *Letter*, 100, 1; PL 22, 814.

116. Augustine, *Christian Doctrine*, Prologue, 6; PL 34, 17.

## PART THREE

117. Athanasius, *Life of Antony*, n. 693; PG 26, 975.

118. Council of Trent, Session 4, *On the Reception of the Sacred Books*.

119. Bernard, *Song of Songs*, Sermon 35, 1; PL 183, 192.

120. Augustine, *Sermon on the Fourth Weekday*, 5, 7; PL 40, 690.

121. Gregory the Great, *Homiliae in Evangelia*, 17, 4; PL 76, 1103.

122. Jerome, *Letter*, 24; PL 22, 1216.

123. Augustine, *On the Psalms*, 33; PL 36, 320.

124. Augustine, *Sermon*, 99, 6; PL 38, 598.

125. Augustine, *Confessions*, 1, 10, 34; PL 32, 801.

126. Bernard, *Letter to the Brothers of Monte Dei*, 1, 1; PL 184, 327. (This work, which circulated under Bernard's name, was actually written by his friend, William of Saint–Thierry.)

127. Augustine, *Letter*, 147, 1; PL 33, 597.

128. John Chrysostom, *Homilies on Matthew*, 57, 4; PG 58, 563.

129. Ambrose, *Exposition of the Gospel of Luke*, 1, 5, 43; PL 1732–33.

130. Pseudo–Dionysius, *On the Divine Names*, 3, 1; PG 3, 679.

131. Origen, *Commentary on the Epistle to the Romans*, 1, 10, 15; PG 14, 1276.

132. Jerome, *Commentary on Isaiah*, 1, 14, 53; PL 24, 524ff.

133. The *Meditations* ascribed to Augustine are actually by John of Fécamp. The work by Luís de Granada (d. 1586) is probably his *Guide for*

*Sinners.* The Carthusian, Ludolph of Saxony (d. 1378), wrote a popular *Life of Jesus.*

134. Bernard, *Sermon, 25,* on the Canticle of Canticles; PL 183, 902.

135. The idiom "no lance remains upright" means that the enemy has been completely defeated and is unable to return to the battle. See *Audi, filia,* ed. A. Granado Bellido (Madrid: San Pablo, 1997), 387 n. 55.

136. Augustine, *On the Psalms,* 68, 6ff.; PL 36, 846f.

137. Ambrose, *On Penance,* 1, 2, 7; PL 16, 532.

138. Augustine, *Sermon,* 22, 6; PL 38, 152.

139. Augustine, *On the Psalms,* 85, 1; PL 39, 1685.

140. Ibid., 50, 14; PL 36, 595.

141. Bernard, *On Consideration,* 1.2; PL 182, 750.

142. Augustine, *On the Psalms,* 77,7; PL 36, 986.

143. This would be like the saying "Love me; love my dog."

## PART FOUR

144. Augustine, *City of God,* 1, 14; PL 41, 436.

145. Augustine, *On the Psalms,* 64, 2; PL 36, 774.

146. Jerome, *Letter,* 24, 4; PL 22, 428.

147. Pseudo–Bernard, *Mirror for Monks,* 2; PL 184, 1178.

148. Jerome, *Letter,* 148, 21; PL 22, 1213.

## PART FIVE

149. Bernard, *Sermon,* 3, in Easter Time, 3; PL 183, 290.

150. Sancha Carrillo, for whom *AF* was first written, was living a consecrated life in her parents' house. Thus, Avila tells her that her mother is like an abbess to her.

151. Ambrose, *On Virgins,* 7, 32; PL 16, 208f.

## PART SIX

152. Augustine, *Confessions,* 1, 1; PL 32, 676.

153. Jerome, *Letter,* 22, 16; PL 30, 181.

154. Ibid. 24, 5; PL 22, 428.

155. Saint Agnes, in Ambrose, *On Virgins,* 1, 1; PL 16, 201.

156. Jerome, *Letter,* 22, 20; PL 22, 407.

157. Augustine, *On the Psalms,* 54, 8; PL 36, 634.

158. Ibid., 103, 4; PL 37, 1338.

159. Augustine, *Sermon,* 44, 1ff.; PL 38, 258.

# SELECTED BIBLIOGRAPHY

The following works have been especially useful in preparing this volume. The critical editions of Father Avila's works provide abundant bibliographical material for works in Spanish: editions of the Master's works; translations into other languages; and a multitude of books and articles on various aspects of the life, ministry, and writings of John of Avila. Unfortunately, there is little available in English on John of Avila and his works, but a few historical studies of his times are included for the help they afford in placing this sixteenth–century saint into his context.

Abellán, José Luís. *El Erasmismo español.* Madrid: Espasa–Calpe, S.A., 1982.

Avila, Juan de. *Audi, filia.* Edited by A. Granado Bellido. Madrid: San Pablo, 1997.

Avila, Juan de. The *Audi filia, or A Rich Cabinet Full of Spiritual Jewels.* Translated by Toby Matthews, 1620. English Recusant Literature 1558–1640, vol. 49. Menston: Scolar Press, 1970.

Avila, San Juan de. *Obras Completas: Nueva edición crítica.* Vols. 1–2. Edited by L. Sala Balust and Francisco Martín Hernández. Madrid: BAC, 2000–2001.

Avila, San Juan de. *Obras Completas.* Vols. 1–6. Edited by L. Sala Balust and Francisco Martín Hernández. Madrid: BAC, 1970.

Azcona, Tarsicio de. *Isabel la Católica: Estudio crítico de su vida y su reinado.* Madrid: BAC, 1964.

Contreras, Jaime. "Alcalá: La Universidad que formó a San Juan de Avila." *ACI.* Madrid: CEE, 2000.

Esquerda Bifet, Juan. *Diccionario de San Juan de Avila.* Burgos: Monte Carmelo, 1999.

———. ed. *Escritos sacerdotales.* Madrid: BAC, 2000.

———. *Introducción a la doctrina de San Juan de Avila.* Madrid: BAC, 2000.

Evenett, H. Outram. "Counter–Reformation Spirituality." In Luebke, *The Counter–Reformation*, 48–63.

García Oro, José. "Los projectos educativos del Maestro Avila en el contexto escolar español del siglo XVI." *ACI*, 195–226.

# SELECTED BIBLIOGRAPHY

Granada, Fray Luís de. *Vida del Padre Maestro Juan de Avila*. Madrid: Edibesa, 2000.

"Hacia el doctorado de San Juan de Avila." In *Toletana: Cuestiones de Teologia e Historia*. Salamanca: Instituto teológico San Ildefonso, 2004.

Huerga, Alvaro, "El Magisterio de San Juan de Avila," *ACI* , 509–52.

Jedin, Hubert. "Catholic Reformation or Counter–Reformation?" In Luebke, *The Counter–Reformation*, 21–45.

Jedin, Hubert, *A History of the Council of Trent*. Translated by Dom Ernest Graf, OSB. 2 vols. St. Louis: B. Herder Book Co., 1957, 1961.

Kamen, Henry. *The Spanish Inquisition: A Historical Revision*. New Haven, CT: Yale Univ. Press, 1998.

Luebke, David M., ed. *The Counter–Reformation: The Essential Readings*. Oxford: Blackwell Publishers, 1999.

*El Maestro Avila: Actas del Congreso Internacional*. Madrid: Conferencia Episcopal Española, 2000.

Muñoz, Luís. *Vida y virtudes del venerable varón el P. Maestro Juan de Avila*. *Vidas del Padre Maestro Juan de Avila*. Edited by L. Sala Balust. Barcelona: Flors, 1964.

Oddi, Longaro Degli, SJ. *Life of Blessed Master John of Avila: Secular Priest Called the Apostle of Andalusía*. London: Burns and Oates, 1898.

Olin, John C. *Catholic Reform from Cardinal Ximenes to the Council of Trent, 1495– 1563*. New York: Fordham Univ. Press, 1990.

———. *The Catholic Reformation: Savonarola to Ignatius Loyola*. New York: Fordham Univ. Press, 1992.

O'Malley, John W., SJ. "Was Ignatius Loyola a Church Reformer? How to Look at Early Modern Catholicism." In Luebke, *The Counter–Reformation*, 66–82.

Procesos de beatificación de Juan de Avila, 1623–1625. *Archivio Segreto Vaticano*. Arch. Congr. SS Rituum–Processus, 630.

Rabil, Albert, Jr. *Erasmus and the New Testament: The Mind of a Christian Humanist*. San Antonio: Trinity Univ. Press, 1972.

Roa, P. Martin de. *Vida y maravillosas virtudes de Doña Sancha Carrillo*. Seville, 1615. Reprint, Madrid: Apostolado de la Prensa, 1930.

Runciman, Steven. *The Fall of Constantinople: 1453*. 1965. Reprint, Cambridge: Cambridge Univ. Press, 1998.

# INDEX

disciples, 10–11, 14–15, 16;
education, 6–8; family, 4–6;
health, 15, 16, 19;
imprisonment, 11, 12–13, 21;
Jewish background, 5; letters,
16, 17–18; life, 1–16; Master
of Sacred Theology, 13;
memorials and treatises,
18–19; ordination and
ministry, 2–3, 10–15; patron of
diocesan priests, 16; poverty,
5, 11; as preacher, 13–14;
sermons, 16, 17; treatises,
18–21; writings, 16–21; *see also*
specific headings, e.g.: *Audi,
filia* (John of Avila); Faith
John of God, 13, 18
John of Ribera, 18
Juan de Brocar, 22, 35
Juan de Villarás, 18, 21, 24
Justification, doctrine of, 22, 23, 24,
25–26, 29, 252–65

*Life and Virtues of Master John of
Avila* (Muñoz), 4
Lineage, 6, 280–82
*Listen, O Daughter* (John of Avila).
*See Audi, filia* (John of Avila)
Luís de Puertocarrero, Count of
Palma, 22
Luís of Granada, 3, 4, 7, 10, 12,
17, 18, 25, 214
Luke, St., 208, 287
Luther, Martin, 26, 28, 148, 149,
155
Lutherans, 23, 109, 151

Magdalen, St., 138–39, 140
Mark, St., 187, 316
Mary, 189, 201, 263; chastity, 70;
humility, 189; virginity, 57,
298
Mohammed, 124, 132
Molina, Alonso, 23
Muñoz, Luís, 4, 14

Neighbor, love of, 37, 265–70

Origen, 176, 209

Passion, 9, 181–202, 212–13,
219–36
Paul, St., 25, 77, 80, 107, 108, 121,
122, 129, 148, 166, 180, 191,
195, 196, 222, 224, 244, 245,
250, 253, 254, 255, 257–58,
259, 260, 262, 263, 275, 298,
309; Abraham, 136; apostles,
240; baptism, 140; charity,
192; chastity, 51, 65; Christ as
mediator, 301; Christ as
spouse, 253; compassion of
confessor, 101; "crown of
justice," 241; divinity of
Christ, 242; end times, 151;
faith, 27, 41, 103, 112, 120,
124, 126, 135, 136, 138; gifts
of God, 82, 100; giving thanks
to God, 97; God as Light,
113; grace, 194; honor of God,
47, 64; hope, 104, 105, 110;
Jews, 155; John of Avila
and, 12–13, 20; justification of
the law, 88; keeping
commandments, 158, 159;
knowledge of truth, 261; love,
140; love of neighbor, 270;
love of truth, 152; obedience,
276, 290, 300; pardon of sins,
26; patience, 91–92; peace, 74,
123, 201; pleasures of the
flesh, 50; poverty of Christ,
305; prayer, 182, 208, 209,
210; "pride, 150, 165;
"prisoner of Jesus Christ,"
293; sin, 86, 132, 227, 286,
300; temptation, 101; thanks to
God, 89; union of Christ and
church, 243; vainglory, 44;
wisdom, 145, 147, 167
Paul III, Pope, 15

# Other Volumes in This Series

# Other Volumes in This Series

# Other Volumes in This Series

# Other Volumes in This Series

**Safed Spirituality** • RULES OF MYSTICAL PIETY, THE BEGINNING OF
WISDOM
**Shakers, The** • TWO CENTURIES OF SPIRITUAL REFLECTION
**Sharafuddin Maneri** • THE HUNDRED LETTERS
**Sor Juana Inés de la Cruz** •
**Spirituality of the German Awakening, The** •
**Symeon the New Theologian** • THE DISCOURSES
**Talmud, The** • SELECTED WRITINGS
**Teresa of Avila** • THE INTERIOR CASTLE
**Theatine Spirituality** • SELECTED WRITINGS
**'Umar Ibn al-Fāriḍ** • SUFI VERSE, SAINTLY LIFE
**Valentin Weigel** • SELECTED SPIRITUAL WRITINGS
**Vincent de Paul and Louise de Marillac** • RULES, CONFERENCES, AND
WRITINGS
**Walter Hilton** • THE SCALE OF PERFECTION
**William Law** • A SERIOUS CALL TO A DEVOUT AND HOLY LIFE, THE SPIRIT
OF LOVE
**Zohar** • THE BOOK OF ENLIGHTENMENT

The Classics of Western Spirituality is a ground-breaking collection of the
original writings of more than 100 universally acknowledged teachers
within the Catholic, Protestant, Eastern Orthodox, Jewish, Islamic, and
Native American Indian traditions.

To order any title, or to request a complete catalog, contact Paulist Press
at 800-218-1903 or visit us on the Web at www.paulistpress.com